SOCIAL SURVEY DIVISION/OFFICE OF POPULATION CENSUSES AND SURVEYS

SOCIAL SCIENCE BRANCH/DEPARTMENT OF EMPLOYMENT

WOMEN AND EMPLOYMENT
A LIFETIME
PERSPECTIVE

he report of the 1980 DE/OPCS Women and Employment Survey

Jean Martin

Ceridwen Roberts

LONDON/HER MAJESTY'S STATIONERY OFFICE

ISBN 0 11 691090 9

Authors' note

The survey on which this report is based was undertaken jointly by Jean Martin of the Office of Population Censuses and Surveys and Ceridwen Roberts of the Department of Employment. The researchers worked under the guidance of a Steering Group chaired by Peter Brannen which included representatives of both Departments.

Large scale surveys are not possible without the researchers being able to call upon the contributions of specialist skills of many people. Staff in various branches of OPCS and DE together with members of the Steering Group and colleagues in both Departments provided valuable technical back-up and support, theoretical and practical advice and helpful criticism when called upon throughout the study.

In particular, within OPCS, we wish to thank the interviewers who have demonstrated that it is possible to collect reliable work history data, and Hazel Green and David Elliot for their technical contributions to the analysis. At all stages, the advice of members of the Steering Group proved invaluable; in particular the contributions at the design stage of Janet Lewis, Marion Rout and Barbara Thomas. Sylvia Shimmin acted as consultant to the project and made an important contribution to both the design of the survey and the framework of the report. In addition, at the analysis stage, Shirley Dex and Heather Joshi enthusiastically provided helpful comments and advice. Peter Brannen, Francis Butler and Jean Todd were sources of advice, support and critical comment throughout the project, and Barbara Ballard helped with the final stages of publication.

In thanking all those who helped us to carry out and write up this survey we include of course the women and men who took part in the survey. Whilst many people collaborated in the study, the analysis of the survey data and the interpretation of the findings presented in this book are the responsibility of the authors, and the views expressed are their own and do not necessarily reflect those of the sponsoring Departments.

Jean Martin

Ceridwen Roberts

Contents

List of Tables

List of Figures

Notes on the tables

Percentages have been rounded to the nearest whole number and as a result may add to between 99 and 101. The total is still shown as 100. Percentages of less than one per cent are shown as 0; cells with no cases are indicated by – .

Base numbers are given in italics. Where a base number is less than 30 statistics have not been given.

The varying positions of percentage signs and bases in the tables denote the presentation of different types of information. Where the percentage sign is at the head of a column and a total of 100 is shown the whole distribution adds to 100% (±1). When the total of 100 is not shown footnotes indicate the reason percentages do not add to 100, or cumulative percentages are shown. A percentage sign and base at the side of an individual figure signifies that this proportion of the people had the attribute being discussed and that the complimentary proportion (not shown on the table) did not. In the more complex tables both the side and column headings define the group under discussion, indicating the proportion of the group who have a particular attribute.

Details of significance tests are not given in the report, but they have been carried out where appropriate. Differences referred to in the text are significant at the .05 level unless otherwise indicated.

Chapter 1 Introduction

The background to the survey

The last twenty years have seen an explosion of interest in, and writings about, women. Central to much of this has been a concern with the relationship between home and work and the way in which women's position in society in general, and in the labour market in particular, is influenced by and influences their reproductive role and their role in the domestic division of labour, that is in household and family care tasks. Though explanations of changes in knowledge are complex, this growth of interest was both linked to, and a product of, the major economic, social and political changes in women's position in society which had been occurring in Britain at the same time. The general elements of these changes are well known; they include the increasing proportion of women in employment such that by 1979, 61% of women of working age had a job compared with 54% in 1971 (OPCS, 1982a, Table 5.2); pressure for greater equality for women, leading to legislative action (Snell *et al*, 1981); the changing nature of the family as the rising divorce rates of the 1970s led to an increasing proportion of one parent families, usually headed by a woman (Popay *et al*, 1983); and the emergence of the women's movement concerned to develop strategies to promote radical change in the position of women and men (Wandor, 1973). Women were accordingly the centre of much political, social and intellectual attention from a range of different perspectives.

The employment changes were quite marked. Throughout the sixties and seventies there had been a significant rise in the level of economic activity among women. Most of the rise was accounted for by increasing proportions of women returning to work after having children, and having an increasingly shorter period of time out of the labour market. Most of these women returned to work part time. In fact almost all the growth in employment from the 1950s onwards can be attributed to the increase in part time work.[1] For example, over a million and a half part time jobs were created between the mid 60s and the end of the 1970s. These jobs were predominantly filled by married women (Robertson and Briggs, 1979). Indeed, by 1979, 18% of all employees worked part time and of these, 94% were women (OPCS, 1982b, Table 4.7).

During the 1970s important legislation affecting women's rights and opportunities at work was introduced. The decade began with the passing of the Equal Pay Act which came into effect fully at the end of 1975 at the same time as the Sex Discrimination Act. In addition the maternity provisions of the Employment Protection Act 1975 gave statutory maternity pay and job reinstatement rights to those women who met certain qualifying conditions. Legislation reflects changes in, as well as shapes, social behaviour and attitudes. It is not surprising therefore that, although the demand for equal pay for the same work was a long established one, (first passed as a TUC resolution in 1888), it was not until the mid 1960s, when women were returning to work in increasing numbers, that the pressure for legislative intervention was strong enough to lead to political action (Snell *et al*, 1981). Once the political momentum for legislative intervention had built up, the issue of equal pay was very rapidly linked to the wider issue of equality of opportunity for women.[2] As soon as it was agreed that sex discrimination both existed and was unacceptable, the argument for legislation to combat it was rapidly acceded to and legislation against sex discrimination more generally was seen as an essential complement to the Equal Pay Act. To a certain extent also events in the USA were influential here as legislation against sex discrimination had been enacted there in 1965.

There are limits to the powers of legislation, however. As the 1974 White Paper *Equality for Women* pointed out 'the causes of continued inequality are complex and rooted deeply in tradition, custom and prejudice' (Home Office, 1974). Much research activity in the late 1960s and throughout the 1970s was concerned to examine the reasons for women's disadvantaged position and to identify the structural barriers to equality of opportunity. Some research, particularly that done specifically to provide background for the discussions about legislative change, was essentially descriptive and statistical (DE Manpower Papers Nos 9–12, 1974, 1975) aiming to establish the position of women in employment. Other studies were more analytical and attempted to explain the reasons for inequality between the sexes in terms of the economic and social institutions of society (Barker and Allen, 1976a and 1976b). In addition, outside the boundaries of formal research, there developed a large volume of writing about women devoted to critiques of the position of women in society. These included accounts, often experientially or biographically based, of the consequences to both women and men of the current arrangement of their roles and the sharp demarcation between paid work outside the home and unpaid work within it (Greer 1971; Comer 1972). In practice these approaches were not totally distinct; the critiques and analytical studies often used research findings and statistics, while much of the research about women was undertaken because of, or informed by, a concern with the consequences of women's current position. Common to almost all the writings on women was the recognition that women's position in employment and in the labour market more generally could not be understood without reference to their domestic roles and the unpaid work women undertake at home. All were contributing to our knowledge of women's position in the labour market, although many studies were very small scale and could only point to areas which needed further investigation.

It was against this background of economic, political and intellectual change that a programme of research on women in the labour market was initiated in the Department of Employment in the late seventies comprising a number of diverse studies. Individual projects were set up to investigate issues generated either by the workings of the Equal Pay and Sex Discrimination Acts or the maternity provisions of the Employment Protection Act or by more general developments arising from women's increased participation in the labour force.[3] The largest single project and, in a sense, the cornerstone of the whole programme was a national survey of women of working age which is reported here.

Reasons for the survey

Information about women's labour market activity is available from government surveys and official statistics, the range of which has increased over recent years. By 1979 it was possible to use either the General Household Survey (GHS) or the Labour Force Survey (LFS), in addition to the Census of Population, to get data on economic activity rates of women with different demographic characteristics such as age, marital status, number and ages of children and so on. From these or other sources, such as the Census of Employment or New Earnings Survey (NES), the jobs women do, industries they work in and pay they receive could be identified and any changes over time monitored (Buxton and MacKay, 1977; Hakim, 1982). However, none of these sources focus on women directly or cover all the issues which are germane to understanding why and when women take paid work, with what consequences, and how this relates to the wider issue of their role in the family.

In addition, official statistics and surveys have increasingly been criticized for using definitions and classifications that are inappropriate for women (Oakley, 1979, Hunt, 1980). Questions are asked and categories devised, it is argued, which reflect men's position and experiences and may not adequately describe and measure women's experiences. Particular examples of this are found in the area of economic activity. Not only is the official definition and measure of unemployment criticized for its limited applicability to women (Dex, 1978), but general measures of current economic activity are held to undercount the full extent of women's employment or indeed economic contribution (Hunt, 1980). Women who regularly do casual or seasonal work or who are homeworkers or part time workers either in very small establishments or working a few hours a week are, it is claimed, often missed out of official statistics, whilst there is no official measure of

the extent and nature of the economic contribution of unpaid domestic work done at home.[4] Moreover all the standard surveys and official statistics are carried out on a cross-sectional basis collecting information about the current situation or very recent past of the respondent. This cannot reflect women's lifetime employment, which is known to be more extensive than cross-sectional data suggests.

Surveys are well established as a tool in social research in general, and government information seeking in particular, for obtaining data on specific topics or groups within the population (Marsh, 1982). Several previous surveys on aspects of women's employment provide valuable sources of data on women's employment situation and attitudes to work and employers' practices towards and attitudes to women workers. Chief of these, perhaps, was Audrey Hunt's survey conducted in 1965 for the Ministry of Labour (Hunt, 1968; see also Thomas, 1944, and Hunt, 1975). By 1979 however, Hunt's study was fourteen years old and there had been, as we have indicated, considerable changes in both the behaviour and attitudes of women in the intervening years, as well as equal opportunity legislation.

By the end of the 1970s not only had the rate of increase in the number of women in the labour force slowed down (Department of Employment 1983), but the rate of unemployment amongst women was rising and had begun to cause concern.[5] Registered female unemployment had been much lower than male unemployment in the early 1970s (1.2% compared with 4.2% in 1971) but had increased proportionately faster than male unemployment over the 1970s, until it reached 5.2% in 1980, though this was still lower than the unemployment rate for men (7.8%) (*Employment Gazette*, 1984). Part of the increase of registered unemployed women was accounted for by the greater propensity of women to register rather than an increase in unemployment as such, reflecting both the phasing out of the 'married women's option' and the increasing proportion of young single women, who were more likely to register, amongst the unemployed.

It was well known that the registered unemployment figures undercounted the extent of unemployment amongst women and survey data, chiefly from the General Household and Labour Force Surveys, was used increasingly to provide information about the unregistered unemployed women. However, little work had been done to explore whether the category 'unregistered unemployed', generated from survey statistics, adequately encompassed women without jobs who were looking for work. Moreover in the absence of a single measure of unemployment for women it was impossible to ask women about the experience of being unemployed and so get some sense of the problems unemployment produced. A further reason for this survey therefore grew out of both the interest in establishing the extent and nature of unemployment amongst women and the need to get a representative sample of all unemployed women.

2

However, in order to understand women's employment and unemployment properly it is necessary to have the detail of women's moves in and out of the labour market and the proportion of their potential working life they spend in the labour market so that the consequences of having or not having a paid job can be better understood. Moreover, as Hunt showed in 1965, only in a special survey can women's work histories be collected, and measures of the extent of women's work experience generated.[6] Therefore, it was felt that a new survey was needed to establish the current position of women in employment in order to identify what the effects of the changes in the 1970s had been, to show what having or not having a paid job meant for women in the 1980s, and to generate data about women's lifetime employment.[7]

The objectives and scope of the research

In contrast to the earlier survey conducted in 1965, 'at a time of full employment when the problem of increasing the labour force was urgent' (Hunt, 1968), the scenario in 1980 was very different. The economy in Britain as in most western industrial societies had moved into a deep recession with both reduced economic and employment growth. Unemployment was rising rapidly and was forecast to continue rising (OECD 1982). Unemployment provided both an initial impetus to the study and to a certain extent influenced its focus. If the survey was both to establish the extent of current unemployment amongst women and to understand what unemployment meant for women it needed to compare unemployed women both with those women who were employed and with those who were economically inactive; it also needed to establish how important a paid job was for women and how much of their lives they spent in employment. The overall focus or objective of the survey was therefore to establish the place of employment in women's lives.

As the emphasis was on employment, it was clear that we were chiefly concerned with the paid work women do rather than the unpaid work they do at home and elsewhere. That is not to say we took no account at all of domestic work; women's employment cannot be understood without reference to their roles as wives and mothers and the work this involves, but we did not aim to collect detailed information on this area.[8] A survey with such a broad focus inevitably has a large number of detailed aims, but most can be subsumed under two broad goals: firstly to establish what factors determine whether or not women work and to identify the degree to which domestic factors or more broadly the sexual division of labour shapes women's lifetime labour market involvement; secondly to examine women as workers, and to collect full information about the work they do, their pay and conditions of employment, as well as the way they behave in the labour market when they leave jobs or look for work. The study also set out to determine the importance of work to women and their job priorities.

Underlying both these related goals was the assumption that the situation of women is different from that of men. Indeed the first issue would never arise with men because it would generally be assumed that all men work from the time they leave full time education until retirement unless they are unemployed or suffer from ill health. Much research also starts from the assumption that paid work is of central importance in men's lives, but is not as important in women's lives. These assumptions reflect the widespread view in our society that women have a choice about employment, at least at certain stages of their lives, in a way that men do not. It is legitimate for, and indeed expected that, women will be primarily concerned with rearing children during part of their lives. As a consequence they are likely either to withdraw from the labour market or to combine domestic responsibilities with part time paid work. It is also assumed by many people, and embodied in the state's social security and tax systems, that married women will be financially dependent on their husbands, who are seen as the primary breadwinners; as a consequence it is seen as less important for women to work than for men (Land, 1976). One aim of the survey therefore was to test the validity of these assumptions. The survey was thus designed to answer questions, many of which are hardly, if ever, asked about men (Oakley, 1981).

An important and innovative feature of the survey was the collection of detailed work histories covering the whole of our female respondents' working lives since leaving full time education. By finding out the proportions of women who had worked at past stages of their lives it was intended to build up a picture of women's lifetime economic activity and show how this was changing over time. It was hoped that this would enable us to test how typical the two phase work or bimodal profile, demonstrated by cross-sectional analysis, is for all women (Hakim, 1979). Lifetime movement in and out of employment would also illustrate very clearly the impact of domestic responsibilities on women's employment.

To explore domestic responsibilities in some detail and their effects the study set out to compare the roles adopted by wives and husbands with respect to both paid and unpaid work. Crucially the issue here was to establish whether husbands were primary wage earners and wives secondary wage earners in a family in terms of the hours they worked and the contribution they made to family income. Linked to this was the share both took in child care and household work. Domestic work and responsibilities are not restricted to child rearing and looking after the home. Some women may also have extra responsibilities caring for elderly or sick dependants; others may face additional problems such as bringing up children single handed. The study aimed to identify the extent of this extra work amongst women and to see whether it affected women's employment in any way.

In focussing on women as workers the research set out not only to describe the jobs women do and hours they work, and so identify variation amongst women workers, but also to explain some of the variation. Several factors appeared likely to be important. Amongst these were women's position in the life cycle; their employment status, that is whether they were full or part time workers; whether they were working only with women, that is the importance of occupational segregation in women's employment; and whether they worked in unionized or non-unionized establishments. In addition, women's own educational and occupational level was likely to affect their job opportunities and attitudes to their job.

Finally, it was also thought to be very important for the research to describe women's attitudes to working and not working, and to establish what the consequences of working or not working were as a context in which to place any discussion of the meaning of unemployment. We knew, for example, that not all non-working women were unemployed. Amongst this very heterogeneous group some women would be happily withdrawn from the labour market either temporarily or permanently, while others would be actively seeking work and perhaps experiencing stress and hardship as a consequence of not finding it. It was also likely that working women were similarly heterogeneous, some being much more fully committed to market or paid work than others. Various means are available for looking at the consequences of working or not working. As well as studying women's attitudes to working or not, their financial situation and levels of stress, we intended to examine the occupational effects of absence from the labour market and the consequences of return to full or part time employment and collect data so that it would be possible to measure the effect on life time earnings of employment breaks and part time work.

The method of enquiry
In this section we give a very brief account of the methodology used for this survey. A full description of the methods used and their development is given in the technical report of the survey (Martin and Roberts, 1984), which also contains copies of the survey documents and additional tables. It was decided that the survey should cover a nationally representative sample of women in Great Britain. All women of working age, that is 16–59, were included, irrespective of their current work status. Women not in employment for whatever reason (for example, full time education, unemployment, domestic commitments or ill health) were of as much interest as those currently working. Their inclusion was necessary to give a complete picture of women's past and current labour market activity and their future plans.

Although the survey focused on women, a small sample of the husbands of married women was also included in order to examine the attitudes of husbands to women's employment in general and their attitudes to their own wives' employment in particular, as well as their views about the domestic division of labour between themselves and their wives. We also intended to compare the attitudes of husbands and wives with each other. This sample is not, however, a representative sample of men in general.

Many of the issues or themes the survey was intended to include could each be a topic for a survey in its own right. Some compromises were therefore inevitable in the extent of their coverage when included in a single survey of this kind. The range of topics included was not however the only constraint which limited our range and depth of questioning. Data collection was based on a single interview with respondents carried out by the interviewers employed by OPCS. In order to ensure a good response rate we did not wish these interviews to last longer than about an hour on average. Altogether 5,588 women and 799 husbands were interviewed.

In addition the survey aimed to collect several different types of information each of which in turn had its limitations. For example, it was intended to collect retrospective work histories from all women, but this meant that the oldest women might have working lives of up to 45 years. Both problems of memory and the amount of information that could be covered affected the level of detail of questions that could be asked in the work histories. There was also interest in the influence on employment behaviour of women's attitudes and intentions; these could be investigated at the time of the interview but we could not study their effect on future behaviour. Conversely, although it is possible to study employment behaviour in the past, women's reporting of subjective influences on their actions at that time is likely to be defective because of both recall difficulties and distortion by subsequent events. We therefore asked mainly about current attitudes and intentions, although some questions were included about reasons for past behaviour.

Although asking factual questions about the present might seem to pose few problems, there were occasions when we were limited by informants' knowledge; for example, some married women did not know the details of their husbands' earnings. There were other questions about working conditions where informants could not answer on their own account, for example, whether they were in a pension scheme or would get sick pay.

The size and scope of the survey affected the final form in which questions were asked. The questionnaire aimed as far as possible to have relatively few open questions. Instead, respondents could choose their answer to most questions from a list of possible answers generated through pilot work. In particular, the collection of the work history information was carefully structured so that all work histories were in a similar form.

Development of the survey methodology
A survey of this size and scope required considerable development and pilot work. This took place in three

broad stages. Firstly, unstructured depth interviews were conducted by OPCS with working and non-working women, with and without children, to elicit their descriptions of their jobs, both currently and in the past, their reasons for working and not working and their views about work in general. In addition a commercial research organisation was commissioned to undertake in-depth interviews with a sample of women who were not working and might broadly be defined as unemployed (Schlackman, 1979). Information from these interviews provided a basis for the structured approach used in the main survey.

Secondly, a semi-structured interview schedule was drawn up and a pilot study conducted to test the questions and the order of topics. After this the questionnaire was revised to produce a more structured final questionnaire. The third stage was a small dress rehearsal test of the final questionnaire on the basis of which minor adjustments were made and the processing arrangements developed and tested.

Sample design

The survey required a representative sample of women of working age (ie aged 16–59) in Great Britain, irrespective of whether or not they were employed. Since no list of such women exists they had to be identified from a sample of the general population. A sample of 10,000 addresses was therefore selected from the electoral register in England and Wales and Scotland in three stages. At the first stage a random sample of 120 local authority districts were selected with probability proportionate to the size of the electorate. The districts had been stratified by region, whether they were metropolitan or non-metropolitan, and the proportion of the population in socio-economic groups 1–5 or 13 (that is, employers, managers, professional and intermediate non-manual workers). At the second stage four wards were selected from each of the 120 districts, with probability proportionate to size of the electorate. At the final stage around 21 addresses was selected from the electoral register for each of the 480 wards so that each address had an equal chance of selection.

Table 1.1   Response of sampled addresses and of women approached for interview

	No.	%	
Set sample of addresses	9,944	100	
Ineligible addresses (empty, demolished, business premises, institutions etc)	526	5	
Addresses containing domestic households	9,418	95	
			%
Total households at selected addresses	9,587		100
No woman aged 16–59 in household	3,536		37
Non-contact of household	220		2
Refusal to give household composition	125		1
Total households with at least one woman aged 16–59	5,706		60
			%
Total women aged 16–59 identified	6,734		100
Non-contact	176		3
Refusal	970		14
Interviewed	5,588		83

The interviewer sift and response to the survey

Interviewers visited the selected addresses and attempted to contact a responsible adult who could provide sufficient information about the household to establish whether there were any women aged 16–59 who would be eligible for the survey. Table 1.1 shows that the original sample of 9,944 addresses contained 9,587 private households, (some containing more than one household), and that 60% of households contained at least one women aged 16–59.

Altogether 6,734 women in the eligible age range were identified by the interviewers. At 2% of addresses insufficient information was obtained to determine whether there was a women eligible for the survey. Table 1.1 shows that the response rate among women eligible for the survey was 83%; interviews were achieved with 5,588 women. For the 17% who were not interviewed we have information about their age and work status from the sift stage allowing us to examine non-response bias. This is described in the technical report of the survey (Martin and Roberts, 1984b).

Although women were our main focus of interest, as we have indicated earlier, the research design included a small sample of the husbands of married women who had been interviewed for the survey. At every fourth address selected for the survey the husband of any married women with whom an interview had been obtained was approached for interview. Table 1.2 shows that 984 husbands were approached and interviews were obtained with 799 (81%).

Table 1.2   Response of husbands approached for interview

	No.	%
Total husbands approached for interview	984	100
Non-contact	98	10
Refused interview	87	9
Interviewed	799	81

The structure of the report

This report describes the main results on the range of topics covered in the survey. The amount of data collected during the interview was very considerable and the results presented here are by no means an exhaustive analysis of all the data that was obtained. While it is important to remember they relate to the situation in 1980 when the fieldwork was undertaken, we do not expect our main findings to be materially affected by social and economic change over the intervening period though we return to this issue in more detail in the concluding chapter.

It was clear from the beginning of the survey that a data set of this kind justified extensive analysis in particular areas of study if the data were to be fully utilised. The Department of Employment accordingly commissioned special analyses to be carried out for some topics. Dr Shirley Dex was commissioned to undertake secondary analysis of the work histories. She has examined the range of employment profiles women have, and by linking data from the work histories with data from other sources she has looked at the interplay of supply and demand in shaping women's economic participation. In addition she has developed occupational and industrial profiles and analysed women's attitudes to working (Dex 1984a and 1984b). Heather Joshi was also sponsored by the Department of Employment to undertake secondary analysis (Joshi, 1984). She has carried out regression analysis of the determinants of women's paid work activity. Both secondary analyses have been carried out in close consultation with the research team working on the main analysis, and where appropriate findings from these projects are incorporated in or referred to in this report. The survey data have also been deposited at the SSRC Data Archive at the University of Essex and are available to the research community for further analysis. Two projects are already underway.[9]

Another research project of a different kind was carried out immediately after the main survey. This was a qualitative follow-up study of unemployed women identified on the main survey conducted by A Cragg and T Dawson. The aim of this study was to follow women up six months later to supplement the information collected during the structured main interviews with an approach which allowed women to describe their situations and experiences in their own words, in order to further our understanding of the consequences of unemployment for women (Cragg and Dawson, 1984). Where relevant material from this study is also referred to in this report.

Plan of the report
As the survey had discrete research questions to answer as well as an overall theme the results are presented in fairly self contained chapters which can be read on their own. Initially we concentrate on the current situation at the time of the interview establishing the extent of current economic activity on a range of definitions in Chapter 2 and discussing all aspects of the employment of working women in Chapters 3–6. Women's jobs are described in Chapter 3 and the issue of the extent and nature of occupational segregation first raised. Chapter 4 details the hours women work and examines variations in the pattern of working. This chapter also considers working women's childcare arrangements as they are closely linked to working hours. Chapter 5 covers women's pay, conditions of employment, training and promotion opportunities and shows how this varies for different groups of women and in relation to the degree of occupational segregation. The chapter finishes with an account of unionisation. Chapter 6 deals solely with working women's attitudes to working in general and their jobs in particular and discusses variations in women's job satisfaction.

In Chapter 7 we focus on non-working women, discuss the extent to which they are unemployed or economically inactive and show how different categories of non-working women vary by demographic characteristics and work attitudes and intentions. Chapter 8 looks at women's domestic responsibilities and their role *vis-à-*

vis their husbands. In this chapter we consider also the extra problems of women who either care for children alone or have additional caring roles. Chapters 9 and 10 are the two chapters which analyse the work history data. Chapter 9 deals with movements in and out of employment and between full and part time work over women's lives and relates these to women's domestic circumstances. Chapter 10 focusses on the jobs women have had, identifying not only the extent and direction of occupational mobility over women's working lives, but also the numbers of job changes they make and the reasons for these, and the times of their lives when women are particularly prone to job changes.

Chapter 11 continues this theme by looking at how women find jobs. A particular issue is whether women who are job changing, but staying in the labour market are different from unemployed women or women returning to work after a domestic break in their job search behaviour and the priorities they accord to different aspects of jobs. The final data chapter deals with more general attitudinal results, covering the extent to which women and husbands think women should or should not work and under what circumstances, as well as general views about women working and about the equal opportunities legislation. The concluding chapter draws these findings together, assesses their implications and attempts to show what the place of employment is in women's lives in the 1980s.

Notes
[1] For a useful overview of women's labour force participation see Hakim, (1979); the annual reports of the Equal Opportunities Commission provide useful summary statistics.
[2] As Snell *et al* (1981) show, considerable evidence was examined by two Parliamentary Select Committees considering the two anti-discrimination bills, and they argued that a case for legislation had been made.
[3] Among the projects were studies on the operation and effects of the Maternity Provisions of the Employment Protection Act 1975 (Daniel, 1980 and 1981a); a review of the implications of microelectronic technology on women's employment (Arnold *et al*, 1982); two projects on payment systems, one focussing on informal or non-job-evaluated payment structures (Craig *et al*, 1984), the second on job evaluation (White and Gobedian, 1984); a study of female redundancy and unemployment (Martin and Wallace, 1984); and several projects linked to the national survey. One of these was a follow-up study of unemployed women (Cragg and Dawson, 1984). Two other projects were additional analyses of the national survey (Joshi, 1984; Dex, 1984a and 1984b).
[4] The exact nature of the economic contribution of domestic labour has aroused considerable theoretical debate, not all of which is easily accessible to the non-academic. A clear presentation of the argument for taking a broader view of economic activity and according value to non-market or family work is found in Nissel (1980).
[5] An early instance of concern voiced at national level, in July 1977, is the request of the Advisory Committee on Women's Employment (a committee with representatives of both sides of industry, political parties and other interest groups set up to advise Ministers on all aspects of women's employment) for a paper on the issue of female unemployment.
[6] Hunt did not collect full work histories in her study but rather asked women to summarize their work pattern to date and then to give more details of the preceding ten years. More detailed histories, though with a training emphasis, were collected on the National Training Survey conducted in 1975 and subsequently analysed by Greenhalgh and Stewart (1982) and Elias and Main (1982).
[7] We rejected the view, held by some feminist researchers, that survey techniques are inherently anti-women and should not be used to examine issues related to women (Graham, 1983). Firstly, the

argument that survey researchers' categories reflect dominant assumptions and modes of thought and so fail to reflect the social reality of the world of the researched, and the meaning that their actions have for the actors could apply to any non-dominant group and is not specific to women. Taken to its logical conclusion it would mean that virtually no social inquiry occurred. Secondly, in order to make generalizable statements about all women, essential if we were to discuss the position of women as such, we needed to have a statistically valid representative sample of our research population; survey methodology is the only research tool for dealing with large numbers of research subjects.

8 Recognition of domestic activities as 'work', however, illustrates the problems of terminology any discussion of women's work can generate. Colloquially women may refer to their activities at home as their 'work', or even their 'job' because being a busy housewife or mother is an identifiable role with an associated set of tasks which have to be done. Moreover this ties in with the increasingly heard argument that the economic contribution of unpaid work should be recognised. However 'going (out) to work', 'having a job' or 'working' is generally associated with employment or market work. Accordingly in our survey we use everyday language which describes as 'working' women who have jobs whilst women who have no current regular job in which they are employed and are not self-employed are described as 'not working'.

9 These are a programme of research comprising five linked projects funded by the Equal Opportunity Commission and based at the Institute of Employment Research at the University of Warwick, and a separate programme at the Department of Sociology, University of Surrey.

Chapter 2 Working and non-working women: definitions and levels of current economic activity

Introduction

One of the aims of the survey was to describe the extent of economic activity for women in 1980, that is how many women of working age were in paid work or looking for a job. This chapter describes the situation at the time the survey was carried out, while Chapter 9 looks more comprehensively at women's lifetime economic activity. The chapter starts by applying the definitions of paid work used in major surveys and for official statistics to the data from this survey. One issue of considerable interest is, in fact, the appropriateness for women of the commonly used definitions of paid work. We therefore examine the effect of changing the definitions of some categories on measuring the levels of women's economic activity. In addition we show how economic activity varies among different groups of women at different life stages, and compare the demographic characteristics of working and non-working women. Lastly the chapter looks particularly at part time workers and contrasts their demographic characteristics with those of full time workers.

Current levels of women's economic activity

The main categories of economic activity used in surveys and official statistics were developed to describe men's economic activity. They have been applied to women subsequently without a full consideration of whether they are equally applicable to women. For this survey it was decided both to use the standard definition of paid work and to ask additional questions to determine whether the use of the standard definition distorts estimates of the extent of economic activity for women, a possibility we noted in Chapter 1.

To investigate women's current employment status we felt it was necessary to distinguish between women working in a paid job at the time of the interview, and therefore in employment, from those not working in a paid job and so not employed. This became our major categorisation in the questionnaire. In the interview women who were not full time students were defined as 'working' or 'not working' according to whether or not they had a paid job. These terms were used rather than 'employed' and 'not employed' because they reflect common usage and so were easily used and understood by our informants; also they avoid any confusions between being 'employed' as opposed to 'self-employed'. In the analysis we have divided the sample into 'working' and 'not working' women, with a third category for the small number of full time students, and use these terms throughout the report.

We were aware that some women who do not have a current paid job and therefore would be classified as 'not working' do have regular or occasional paid work. Whilst it was important to identify this kind of work in order to describe as accurately as possible the full extent of women's economic activity, in the interview we did not define these women as 'working' for two reasons. Firstly, pilot work confirmed that we could not meaningfully ask them the full range of questions that we asked of women who had a paid job. Secondly, and possibly more importantly, the vast majority of such women (90%) did not think of themselves as 'working' – their work was too irregular or insignificant in its effects on their lives. Although these women have therefore been defined as 'not working', the extent and kind of paid work they undertook will be described later in this chapter and also in Chapter 3 in the discussion of subsidiary occupations.

Working women

Women were defined as 'working' if they said either that they had a paid job at the time of the interview or that they had a job from which they were temporarily absent because of sickness, holidays or because they were on maternity leave but intended to return to their job. Those who were receiving maternity pay but did not expect to return to their job were not included as working women because, clearly, they would not think of themselves as currently having a paid job. Those full time students who also had jobs were excluded from the main 'working' category because their main full time activity was being a student.

Working women were further divided into full time and part time workers. Women's own definitions of whether they were full or part time workers were used rather than the standard definition based on whether or not a person works more than thirty hours a week (excluding meal breaks and overtime). This was done because women who work less than the normal working week for their particular job generally consider themselves to be part time and are treated as such by their employers.

However, as all working women were asked for details of the number of hours they usually worked each week we could compare self-definitions of full and part time with the application of the standard definition. We discovered that 3% of working women classed themselves as part time workers but would be classified as full time on the standard definition. Of the 5% of women who classified themselves as full time but were working less than thirty-one hours per week over half were teachers, for whom an exception to the standard definition is made on most surveys.

Figure 2.1 Women of working age grouped by economic activity

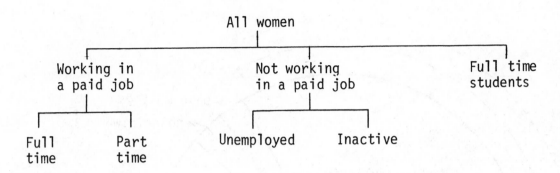

Non-working women

Women were defined as 'not working' if they neither had a paid job nor were full time students at the time of the interview. They were further sub-divided into the 'unemployed' and the 'economically inactive' on the basis of the definition described below. Whether the usual definition of unemployment can be meaningfully applied to women is a complex topic and will be discussed in more detail in Chapter 7 which deals with alternative definitions of unemployment. However, for the purposes of this chapter we define as 'unemployed' any woman who said she was not working in a paid job because she was:

i) waiting to take up a job already obtained
ii) looking for work
iii) prevented from looking for work by temporary sickness or injury

Again, following this definition, women who were 'unemployed' together with all working women were here classed as 'economically active'. All other women who were neither working nor unemployed nor full time students were defined as 'economically inactive', regardless of whether or not they did small amounts of regular or occasional paid work. Figure 2.1 illustrates the main groups and sub-groups of women in the survey according to their economic activity.

We applied the above definitions to identify the proportions of women in each of the main groups. This is shown in Table 2.1. The majority of women, 60%, were working in a paid job at the time of the interview, 34% full time and 26% part time. A further 5% were classified as 'unemployed', making a total of 65% who were economically active on this definition. Of

Table 2.1 Current economic activity

	%
Working full time	34
Working part time	26
Total working	**60**
'Unemployed'	5
Total economically active	**65**
Economically inactive	30
Full time students	5
	100
Base	*5,588*

the remaining 35% of women 5% were full time students and 30% were economically inactive.

Subsidiary economic activity

All 'non-working' women were asked whether they did any paid work on a regular or occasional basis. This was done in order to identify any subsidiary work wherever possible, both to describe the full extent of women's economic activity and to see which women did this type of work and what sort of work was undertaken. Surveys such as the General Household Survey and the Labour Force Survey understate this kind of work because many women do not think of it as 'work' and do not mention it (OPCS, 1982a; 1982b). We cited examples of the most likely kinds of work – childminder, mail order agent, outworker and seasonal worker, in order to encourage respondents to mention any such work. Overall 13% of non-working women said they did such work (9% of the 'unemployed' and 14% of the economically inactive). If these women were to be defined as working, on the grounds that they were doing some paid work, the proportion of working women in our sample would rise to 65% from the 60% based on the standard definition. If the women doing this work were to be counted as economically active, then 69% of our sample would be classed as economically active compared with 65% on the standard definition. This is a smaller increase than might at first sight be expected because the unemployed have already been included as economically active and therefore only the inactive women doing this kind of work make an additional contribution.

Among the full time students 38% either had a job or did paid work of some kind. Students have not been classed as economically active, but if those doing some work were included along with the non-working women who had some paid work the total economic activity rate of women in the survey would rise to 71%. The proportions of women in the different categories of economic activity according to the standard definitions and using the broader criteria discussed above can be seen in Figure 2.2. Figure 2.3 is an extension of Figure 2.1, with the sub-groups of non-working women and students further divided according to whether or not they were doing any paid work. The proportion of

Figure 2.2 Proportion of women classed as economically active according to standard and broader definitions

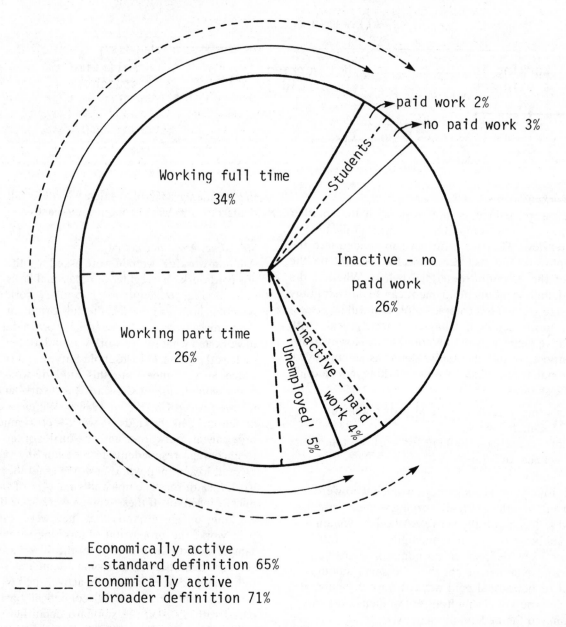

paid work 2%

no paid work 3%

Working full time 34%

Students

Inactive - no paid work 26%

Working part time 26%

Inactive - paid work 4%

'Unemployed' 5%

———— Economically active
– standard definition 65%

– – – – Economically active
– broader definition 71%

Figure 2.3 Proportion of women in different economic activity groups

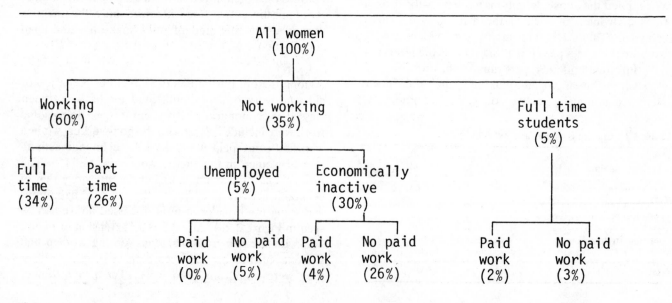

All women
(100%)

Working
(60%)

Not working
(35%)

Full time students
(5%)

Full time
(34%)

Part time
(26%)

Unemployed
(5%)

Economically inactive
(30%)

Paid work
(0%)

No paid work
(5%)

Paid work
(4%)

No paid work
(26%)

Paid work
(2%)

No paid work
(3%)

women in each of the resulting sub-groups is also shown.

The factors affecting women's levels of economic activity

There is a considerable amount of information about rates of economic activity among women both overall and for women in different age and marital status groups, both at present and going back over more than a hundred years, enabling changes over time in different groups of women to be studied and comparisons made with men's economic activity rates. Thus using sources like the Census and more recently the General Household Survey it has been possible to identify considerable change over the last 50 to 60 years in both the level and pattern of women's economic activity (Hakim, 1979).

Whilst overall men's rates have remained consistently high, declining only in the youngest and oldest age groups, a reflection of the increasing length of full time education and the growing tendency for men to retire at earlier ages, women's rates have changed substantially. There has been both an overall rise in levels of women's economic activity and the emergence of a bimodal or two phase work profile (*ibid*). These changes are related and are chiefly accounted for by the dramatic increase in the labour force participation of married women who have in growing numbers returned to the labour market after a period of domestic absence and who have done so after increasingly short absences from the labour market; a feature of most Western industrial societies over the last thirty years (OECD, 1979, 1980).

Women's economic activity rates, unlike men's, vary considerably among different groups of women reflecting the relationship between economic activity and the stages most women pass through in the course of their lives. Thus, women's activity rates vary by age, marital status, and the number and ages of any children; these variables are of course interrelated and taken together tell us something about the stage in their lives women have reached. We now go on to look at the relationship between economic activity and each of these factors, first separately and then in combination.[1] However, to facilitate the comparisons we exclude full time students. Most students are young, single and childless and consequently their inclusion would lower the activity rates of young single and childless women generally, making it difficult to see how they compare with those of other women. We therefore start by presenting the overall activity rates without full time students in Table 2.2. Since students comprise 5% of all women their exclusion raises all the other proportions slightly. Thus 63% of women were working, 35% full time and 28% part time, 6% were unemployed and 31% were economically inactive.

Economic activity and age

As Table 2.3 shows, women of different ages in the sample had different levels of economic activity. Clearly this is because a woman's age is a good indicator of life stage, in particular of whether or not she is likely to have children and the ages of the children which, as we shall see, are much more closely associated with economic activity than her age per se. Accordingly we interpret the changes shown in Table 2.3 and illustrated in Figure 2.4 in terms of life stages. Economic activity was at its highest among women in their teens, as few had yet had children. Thereafter the rates fall as increasing proportions of women leave the labour force when they start having children. The mid to late twenties is the peak childbearing age which is reflected in the low rate of economic activity for this group. Thereafter activity rates rise as women in their thirties and forties return to work as their children get older. Apart from women in their teens, those in their forties had the highest activity rates of all women (78%) although they were more likely to be working part time than full time. Activity rates declined slowly among women in their early fifties (73%) and declined to 58% among women in their late

Table 2.2 Current economic activity of all women except full time students

	%
Working full time	35
Working part time	28
Total working	**63**
'Unemployed'	6
Total economically active	**69**
Economically inactive	31
	100
Base	5,295

Table 2.3 Current economic activity by age: all women except full time students

Economic activity	Age									All women except full time students
	16–19	20–24	25–29	30–34	35–39	40–44	45–49	50–54	55–59	
	%	%	%	%	%	%	%	%	%	%
Working full time	73	56	31	23	30	33	35	33	25	35
Working part time	1	9	18	33	37	41	38	34	28	28
Total working	**74**	**65**	**49**	**56**	**67**	**74**	**73**	**67**	**53**	**63**
'Unemployed'	14	7	5	5	4	4	5	6	5	6
Total economically active	**88**	**72**	**54**	**61**	**71**	**78**	**78**	**73**	**58**	**69**
Economically inactive	12	28	46	39	29	22	22	27	42	31
	100	**100**	**100**	**100**	**100**	**100**	**100**	**100**	**100**	**100**
Base	346	565	683	762	643	584	554	566	592	5,295

Figure 2.4 Current economic activity by age: all women except full time students

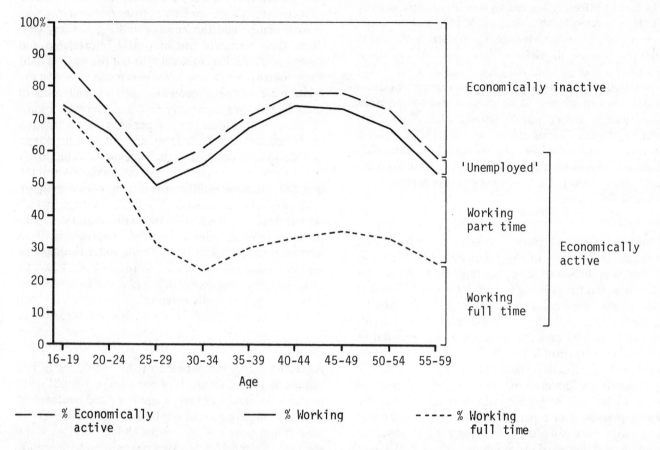

Legend:
— — % Economically active — % Working ----- % Working full time

fifties. In her separate analysis of these data Joshi confirms that much of this pattern is explicable by other factors which change over the life cycle, notably family formation. However, when these factors are taken into account, age is still associated with the decline in participation over the last phase of the cycle, particularly for married women. This association, Joshi argues, is a combination of the effect of getting older and of belonging to an earlier generation which was less accustomed to participating in paid work particularly when married (Joshi, 1984.)

Economic activity and marital status
In the survey we identified a small number of women who were cohabiting as opposed to being legally married; we have included this group with the married

women for most purposes since there were too few (2%) for separate analysis. Similarly we have generally combined the widowed, divorced and separated, as each is a fairly small group and most of the differences in their rates of economic activity are explained by differences in age between the groups.

Table 2.4 shows the economic activity of women in the survey by their marital status. The rates for married women and for the widowed, divorced and separated are fairly similar and significantly different from those for single women. It can therefore be argued that it is somewhat misleading to analyse economic activity for all non-married women together as is sometimes done (Popay *et al*, 1983); they are not a homogeneous group and the changes in the relative proportions of single to

Table 2.4 Current economic activity by marital status: all women except full time students

Economic activity	Marital status				All women except full time students
	Married/ cohabiting	Widowed/ divorced/ separated	Single	All non-married women	
	%	%	%	%	%
Working full time	27	40	79	64	35
Working part time	33	23	3	11	28
Total working	**60**	**63**	**82**	**75**	**63**
'Unemployed'	5	7	10	9	6
Total economically active	**65**	**70**	**92**	**84**	**69**
Economically inactive	35	30	8	16	31
	100	**100**	**100**	**100**	**100**
Base	*4,060*	*469*	*766*	*1,235*	*5,295*

widowed, divorced and separated women that have occurred over time affect time series comparisons of economic activity rates for these women. There is however also a practical objection to showing separate figures for single women which has affected the way some analyses have been carried out in this survey, namely that there are too few single women in the older age groups or with children for simple tabulations to show the interrelationships between marital status, age and number or ages of children.

Economic activity and children

In our society at present, women bear the greater part of the responsibility for the care of young children. Whatever the reason for this, whether it is because women want or are expected to do this or because alternative facilities for childcare are limited, in practice the majority of women are directly responsible for most of the care of their children until they start school and thereafter outside school hours and during the holidays until the children become old enough to look after themselves. This means that the presence of dependent children and, in particular, young children has a major effect on the economic activity of many women.

We show in Table 2.5 the economic activity of women respondents with different numbers of children under 16 compared with women with no child under 16. Women with dependent children were significantly less likely to be economically active than those with no dependent children, and there is some decline in economic activity with each additional dependent child. In all groups women with children under 16 who were working were more likely to be working part time than full time.

Looking just at the number of children under 16 a woman has takes no account of their ages, although the more children under 16 a mother has the younger the youngest is likely to be. However, women with only one dependent child may have just started their family or have other children who are now aged 16 or over, in which case the one dependent child is likely to be a teenager. Obviously women in these two situations are likely to be very different in terms of economic activity, because pre-school children are much more demanding in terms of the care they require.

Table 2.6 shows that looking at women's economic activity in relation to the age of their youngest child accounts for more variation in economic activity than does the number of children under 16. In this table we have also shown separately the activity rates for women with children who are all 16 or over compared with those for childless women. From this it can be seen that the highest activity rates were those of childless women (93%), followed by those of women whose youngest child was aged 11–15 (81%).

Since the number of children under 16 a woman has and the age of the youngest are related, we show in Table 2.7 their combined effect on economic activity. Interestingly, there was little difference in levels of economic activity between women with one and two children under 16 once the age of the youngest is taken into account; this is also confirmed by Joshi. Nor was there any significant difference in economic activity among any women with a youngest child under 5 until there were at least four children under 16, which is relatively uncommon. These results demonstrate that the age of the youngest child has a greater effect on economic

Table 2.5 Current economic activity by number of children under 16: all women except full time students

Economic activity	Number of children under 16						All women except full time students
	1	2	3	4 or more	All women with children under 16	No children under 16	
	%	%	%	%	%	%	%
Working full time	21	14	12	11	17	54	35
Working part time	35	38	32	25	35	20	28
Total working	**56**	**52**	**44**	**36**	**52**	**74**	**63**
'Unemployed'	5	3	4	6	4	7	6
Total economically active	**61**	**55**	**48**	**42**	**56**	**81**	**69**
Economically inactive	39	45	52	58	44	19	31
	100	**100**	**100**	**100**	**100**	**100**	**100**
Base	*1,096*	*1,065*	*358*	*97*	*2,616*	*2,679*	*5,295*

Table 2.6 Current economic activity by age of youngest child: all women except full time students

Economic activity	Childless women	Age of youngest child				16 or over	All women except full time students
		0–4	5–10	11–15	All ages 0–15		
	%	%	%	%	%	%	%
Working full time	78	7	16	31	17	32	35
Working part time	6	20	48	45	35	34	28
Total working	**84**	**27**	**64**	**76**	**52**	**66**	**63**
'Unemployed'	9	4	4	5	4	5	6
Total economically active	**93**	**31**	**68**	**81**	**56**	**71**	**69**
Economically inactive	7	69	32	19	44	29	31
	100	**100**	**100**	**100**	**100**	**100**	**100**
Base	*1,301*	*1,038*	*868*	*710*	*2,616*	*1,378*	*5,295*

Table 2.7 Current economic activity by number of children under 16 and age of youngest child: all women with children under 16 except full time students

Economic activity	Number of children under 16											
	1 child aged			2 children youngest aged			3 children youngest aged			4 children youngest aged		
	0–4	5–10	11–15	0–4	5–10	11–15	0–4	5–10	11–15	0–4	5–10	11–15
	%	%	%	%	%	%	%	%		%	%	
Working full time	11	16	32	4	17	28	5	15		8	14	
Working part time	16	49	44	23	49	48	22	43		10	41	
Total working	**27**	**65**	**76**	**27**	**66**	**76**	**27**	**58**		**18**	**55**	
'Unemployed'	5	5	4	3	3	7	2	6		4	9	
Total economically active	**32**	**70**	**80**	**30**	**69**	**83**	**29**	**64**		**22**	**64**	
Economically inactive	68	30	20	70	31	17	71	36		78	36	
	100	**100**	**100**	**100**	**100**	**100**	**100**	**100**		**100**	**100**	
Base	*388*	*230*	*478*	*435*	*429*	*201*	*165*	*165*	*28**	*50*	*44*	*3**

*Base too small to show percentages

activity than the number of children under 16, with the exception of the small group of women with more than three children; therefore in most subsequent analyses we shall take into account only the age of the youngest and not the total number of children under 16. Other forms of analysis confirm that the main effect of dependent children is captured by the age of the youngest (Joshi, 1984).

Labour market participation and life stages

It is clear from the preceding discussion that any consideration of the independent effects of age, marital status, presence of children and age of youngest child must take into account the interrelationships between these factors. This can be done for any measure of economic activity, but we decided to look at the proportion of women working, since much of the survey is based on the distinction between working and non-working women. Taking each of the three variables of interest in turn we have standardised for the other two. This means we have calculated, for example, the proportion of women in each age group who would be expected to be working if each age group were identical in terms of marital status and the presence of children and age of youngest child as the sample as a whole. A detailed account of the procedures used is given in the technical report (Martin and Roberts, 1984).

From Table 2.8 we can see that there is no difference between the standardised proportions of married and non-married women working. This means that the large difference between the unstandardised proportions for the two groups is entirely due to their different age distribution and the presence of children and age of the youngest child. Once these differences are allowed for, married women were just as likely to be working as non-married women. However as we shall show later in the chapter among working women married women are more likely than non-married women to be working part time.

Table 2.9 shows the standardised proportion of women working by the age of the youngest child. There are still large differences between the three groups of women with children under 16, revealing that these variations were not accounted for by differences between the women in age or marital status. However, the difference between women with a youngest child aged 11–15 and those whose children were all over 16 has disappeared, showing that the variation was due to differences in age between the two groups. As would be expected, childless women still had a much greater likelihood of working than any of the women with children.[2]

It is clear from Table 2.10 that when the proportions of women working in different age groups are standardised for marital status and the presence of children and age of youngest child, the differences between the

Table 2.8 Estimated proportions of women working by marital status, standardised for age and age of youngest child, compared with unstandardised proportions

Marital status	Estimated standardised proportion of women working*	Unstandardised proportion of women working	Base
Married	63%	60%	4,060
Not married	63%	75%	1,235

Table 2.9 Estimated proportions of women working by age of youngest child, standardised for age and marital status, compared with unstandardised proportions

Age of youngest child	Estimated standardised proportion of women working*	Unstandardised proportion of women working	Base
0–4	24%	27%	1,038
5–10	57%	65%	868
11–15	73%	76%	710
16 or over	74%	65%	1,378
Childless	83%	83%	1,301

Table 2.10 Estimated proportions of women working by age, standardised for age of youngest child and marital status, compared with unstandardised proportions

Age	Estimated standardised proportion of women working*	Unstandardised proportion of women working	Base
16–29	65%	60%	1,594
30–39	71%	61%	1,405
40–49	67%	74%	1,138
50–59	50%	60%	1,158

*For details of method of estimation see technical report (Martin and Roberts 1984)

Table 2.11 Current economic activity by life cycle stage: all women except full time students

Economic activity	Life cycle stage								All women except full time students
	Childless women aged:		Women with youngest child aged:			Women with all children aged 16 and over, aged:			
	Under 30	30 or over	0–4	5–10	11–15	Under 50	50 or over		
	%	%	%	%	%	%	%		%
Working full time	82	67	7	16	31	40	27		35
Working part time	3	12	20	48	45	37	32		28
Total working	**85**	**79**	**27**	**64**	**76**	**77**	**59**		**63**
'Unemployed'	11	6	4	4	5	5	5		6
Total economically active	**96**	**85**	**31**	**68**	**81**	**82**	**64**		**69**
Economically inactive	4	15	69	32	19	18	36		31
	100	**100**	**100**	**100**	**100**	**100**	**100**		**100**
Base	*887*	*414*	*1,038*	*868*	*710*	*468*	*910*		*5,295*

three younger age groups diminish. In fact, much of the difference between the two youngest age groups would not be apparent if we looked at the proportion of economically active women rather than the proportion working; it is the higher rate of unemployment in the youngest age group which accounts for much of the difference. There is, however, a significant fall in the proportion of women working between women in their forties and those in their fifties. This could be either a genuine age effect, with women stopping work early, as retirement age approaches, or a generational effect, since the older women were less likely to be working at younger ages than women currently at those ages (see Chapter 9).

Analysis of the relative importance of the three variables on women's working shows, as would be expected from the above results, that the presence of children and the age of the youngest child are by far the most important determinants of whether or not women work. Age has some effect, in that women in their fifties are less likely than younger women to work, and marital status has no significant effect at all.

The results presented above are a reflection of the way women's labour market activity varies at different stages of their lives. In order to take account of this in later analyses we categorised women according to what seem to be major life stages in respect of their relationship with employment.[3] The categories are shown in Table 2.11 with the proportions of working women in each category. Childless women have been divided into those under 30 and those aged 30 or over because most of the former group can be expected to have children at some time in the future whereas many of the latter are more likely to remain childless; as we shall show, these groups of women differ in many important respects.

Demographic characteristics of working and non-working women

The preceding section has described how economic activity varies among different groups of women at different stages of their lives. Another way of looking at the same basic information is to compare the characteristics of women in different economic activity categories; this will need to be taken into account in intepreting later analyses. We show therefore in Tables 2.12–2.15 the same data on which several of the preceding tables have been based, but percentaged differently so that, for example, the age distributions of working and non-working women can be compared, as opposed to looking at the proportions of working and non-working women in different age groups.

The age distribution of working women was fairly even except at the extremes; the economically inactive women were more concentrated in the younger age groups and among those nearing retirement age. As one would expect, most of the economically inactive women had children: 61% of this group had a child under eleven compared with only a quarter of the working women. The majority of women in all groups (except the full time students) were married, but there were proportionately fewer married women or women with children among the full time workers and the 'unemployed'. Like the economically inactive women, the majority of part time workers were married and had children under 16, although their youngest child was in most cases five or over. Part time working women tended to be older than inactive women, reflecting the fact that their children were older; there were fewer women under 30 among the part time workers than among any other group.

Full and part time workers

Although the preceding section looked briefly at the demographic characteristics of full and part time workers compared with those of other women, the main focus of the discussion so far has been on whether women participate in the labour market at all rather than the extent to which they participate. However, a survey of this kind enables us to look more closely at part time work, in particular at the patterns of part time work and the situations of part time workers. It is important to do this because part time work is a major feature of women's employment, and growth in part time employment in recent years is the main determinant of the current level of women's employment (Robertson and Briggs, 1979). Over the period 1971–81 for example part time work increased from about 15% to about 20% of total employment as the number of part time employees grew by about one million, almost all of whom were married women, while the numbers of full time workers declined (*Employment Gazettes*).

Table 2.12   Age distribution by economic activity: all women

Age	Working full time	Working part time	Total working	'Unemployed'	Economically inactive	Full time student	All women
	%	%	%	%	%	%	%
16–19	14	0	7	16	2	78	10
20–24	17	3	11	14	10	14	11
25–29	11	8	10	12	19	3	12
30–34	9	17	13	13	18	1	14
35–39	10	16	13	9	11	2	12
40–44	10	16	13	7	8	1	10
45–49	10	16	12	9	7	1	10
50–54	10	13	11	11	9	0	10
55–59	8	11	9	10	15	–	11
	100	**100**	**100**	**100**	**100**	**100**	**100**
Base	*1,877*	*1,477*	*3,354*	*301*	*1,641*	*293*	*5,588*

Table 2.13   Marital status by economic activity: all women

Marital status	Working full time	Working part time	Total working	'Unemployed'	Economically inactive	Full time student	All women
	%	%	%	%	%	%	%
Married	56	90	71	60	86	5	71
Cohabiting	2	1	2	2	1	1	2
Total married	**58**	**91**	**73**	**62**	**87**	**6**	**73**
Widowed	3	3	3	4	3	0	3
Divorced	5	3	3	4	4	1	4
Separated	2	1	2	3	2	0	2
Total ever married	**68**	**98**	**81**	**73**	**96**	**8**	**82**
Single	32	2	19	27	4	92	18
	100	**100**	**100**	**100**	**100**	**100**	**100**
Base	*1,877*	*1,477*	*3,354*	*301*	*1,641*	*293*	*5,588*

Table 2.14   Number of children under 16 by economic activity: all women

Number of children under 16	Working full time	Working part time	Total working	'Unemployed'	Economically inactive	Full time student	All women
	%	%	%	%	%	%	%
None	**77**	**37**	**59**	**64**	**31**	**95**	**53**
One	12	26	18	18	26	3	20
Two	8	28	17	12	29	1	19
Three	2	8	5	5	11	1	6
Four or more	1	2	1	2	3	0	2
All women with children under 16	**23**	**63**	**41**	**31**	**69**	**5**	**47**
	100	**100**	**100**	**100**	**100**	**100**	**·100**
Base	*1,877*	*1,477*	*3,354*	*301*	*1,641*	*293*	*5,588*

Table 2.15   Age of youngest child by economic activity: all women

Age of youngest child	Working full time	Working part time	Total working	'Unemployed'	Economically inactive	Full time student	All women
	%	%	%	%	%	%	%
Childless	54	5	32	39	6	94	28
0–2	2	7	4	8	33	1	13
3–4	2	7	4	5	11	0	6
5–10	7	28	17	12	17	3	15
11–15	12	21	16	11	8	1	13
16 or over	23	32	27	25	25	1	25
	100	**100**	**100**	**100**	**100**	**100**	**100**
Base	*1,877*	*1,477*	*3,354*	*301*	*1,641*	*293*	*5,588*

We saw earlier in the chapter that 35% of all women in the survey excluding students were, on their own definition, working full time and 28% were working part time. If we focus on working women, then 44% were working part time. Clearly then, part time working is a very important form of economic activity for women, and we shall be looking at why women work part time and how part time work fits into the whole of their working lives in subsequent chapters.

There was considerable variation in the number of hours usually worked each week by women who defined themselves as part time workers; some worked over thirty hours a week while others worked only a few hours. In this section we have divided part time workers into two groups according to whether they worked more or less than sixteen hours per week. This division was chosen because people working sixteen hours or more (with the appropriate length of service qualification) are covered by most employment protection legislation, whereas those working fewer hours are less likely to have protection in law.

Earlier in the chapter we looked at the proportions of full and part time workers among different groups of women. However, it is difficult to compare full and part time workers because the figures shown so far are based on all women and are therefore affected by the proportions of non-working women in each group. We have therefore repercentaged the results to show the relative proportions of full and part time workers among working women as opposed to all women. These proportions are shown by women's age, marital status and presence of children and age of youngest child in Tables 2.16–2.18 with those working part time divided on the basis of their hours of work as described above.

The proportion of part time workers increased with age among the younger age groups, reaching a peak among women in their early thirties who were most likely to be caring for young children; a quarter of this age group of working women were working under 16 hours a week. After that, the proportion of women working part time decreased slowly with age, showing little change once they reached their mid forties. Table 2.18 shows a

Table 2.16 Proportions of full and part time workers by age: working women

	Age									All working women
	16–19	20–24	25–29	30–34	35–39	40–44	45–49	50–54	55–59	
	%	%	%	%	%	%	%	%	%	%
Full time	98	87	64	41	45	45	48	49	47	56
Part time	2	13	36	59	55	55	52	51	53	44
16 hrs or more	1	6	21	34	33	39	36	36	36	28
Under 16 hrs	1	7	15	25	22	16	16	15	17	16
	100	100	100	100	100	100	100	100	100	100
Base	258	366	335	430	430	435	407	377	316	3,354

Table 2.17 Proportions of full and part time workers by marital status: working women

	Marital status				All working women
	Married	Widowed/ divorced/ separated	Single	All non- married	
	%	%	%	%	%
Full time	45	63	96	86	56
Part time	55	37	4	14	44
16 hrs or more	35	24	3	9	28
Under 16 hrs	20	13	1	5	16
	100	100	100	100	100
Base	2,435	293	626	919	3,354

Table 2.18 Proportions of full and part time workers by age of youngest child: working women

	Childless women	Age of youngest child					All working women
		0–4	5–10	11–15	All ages 0–15	16 or over	
	%	%	%	%	%	%	%
Full time	93	26	25	42	32	48	56
Part time	7	74	75	58	68	52	44
16 hrs or more	5	35	43	41	40	38	28
Under 16 hrs	2	39	32	17	28	14	16
	100	100	100	100	100	100	100
Base	1,086	276	553	538	1,367	901	3,354

strong association between the presence of children and part time working, but it is interesting to note that similar proportions of women with a youngest child under five and with a youngest child aged 5–10 worked part time; however the former group were more likely to be working under 16 hours a week. The rate of part time working among women with a youngest child aged 11–15 was not very much higher than among those whose children were all 16 or over.

As we pointed out earlier in the chapter, the three variables shown in these tables are interrelated; this makes it impossible to see their independent effects on part time working without allowing for these relationships. We used the same technique of standardisation as before to show the independent effects of marital status, presence of children and age of youngest child, and respondents' age on whether women work full or part time. To simplify the analysis no subdivision of part time workers according to their hours was made.

Table 2.19 shows that if married and non-married women were of the same age and were equally likely to have some children and to have a youngest child of a similar age, then it would be expected that 47% of married women and 29% of non-married women would be working part time. The fact that the difference between the non-married and married women has diminished means that part of the difference between the unstandardised proportions was due to married women being older on average than non-married women and being more likely to have children. However, since the standardised proportions are still significantly different we can conclude that there is a real difference in the extent of part time working according to a woman's marital status, with married women being more likely to work part time.

When we standardise for age and marital status, the figures in Table 2.20 show that part time working was equally high for women with a youngest child under 5 or aged 5–10. The proportion drops sharply among women with a youngest child aged 11–15 and drops again when all children are 16 or over. As expected childless women were least likely to work part time, but the standardised figure (14%) is higher than the unstandardised figure (7%), reflecting the fact that part of the reason that childless women were less likely to work part time is that they were younger and more likely to be single than women with children.

The standardised figures for part time working by age (Table 2.21) are very different from the unstandardised figures, showing that the difference between the two younger age groups was due to differences in marital status and the presence and age of children rather than age itself. Conversely, there was a rise in part time working between women in their thirties and fifties which was concealed by the fall in part time working as children get older. As with the fall in the overall proportion of women working in this age group, these results do not show whether women change from full to part time working as they get older or whether this is a generational effect because the older women were more likely to have worked part time at younger ages than women currently of those ages.

From the analyses we can see that, as with overall labour force participation, the presence of children and the age of the youngest child are the major determinants of whether women work full or part time. There was no difference between married and non-married women in whether they worked at all or not. Married women are more likely than non-married women to work part time. Joshi's analysis explored these issues in greater detail and concluded that after other factors had been taken into consideration marital status made little important difference to the chances of a woman being either economically active or at work. The higher incidence of part time work among the married remains when allowance for a number of other variables including children has been made. This association between part time work and being married may well be accounted for by different financial circumstances and domestic commitments or other factors correlated with marriage, which were not separately identified and measured in the survey, but are reflected in the presence of a spouse (Joshi, 1984).

Table 2.19 Estimated proportions of women working part time by marital status, standardised for age and age of youngest child, compared with unstandardised proportions

Marital status	Estimated standardised proportion of women working part time*	Unstandardised proportion of women working part time	Base
Married	47%	55%	2,435
Not married	29%	14%	919

Table 2.20 Estimated proportions of women working part time by age of youngest child, standardised for age and marital status, compared with unstandardised proportions

Age of youngest child	Estimated standardised proportion of women working part time*	Unstandardised proportion of women working part time	Base
0–4	70%	74%	276
5–10	70%	75%	553
11–15	50%	58%	538
16 or over	42%	52%	901
Childless	14%	7%	1,086

Table 2.21 Estimated proportions of women working part time by age, standardised for marital status and age of youngest child, compared with unstandardised proportions

Age	Estimated standardised proportion of women working part time*	Unstandardised proportion of women working part time	Base
16–29	37%	18%	959
30–39	41%	57%	860
40–49	47%	54%	842
50–59	53%	52%	693

*For details of method of estimation see technical report (Martin and Roberts 1984)

18

Summary and conclusions

While cross-sectional data does not adequately depict the extent of women's lifetime employment it does provide a necessary starting point for a study of the place of employment in women's lives. In this chapter we have shown the extent of employment amongst women of working age at the time of our interview in 1980. We have discussed the demographic characteristics of working and non-working women and have identified the main factors which are likely to affect whether women take a paid job or not and whether they work full or part time.

Overall 60% of women in our survey were employed; 34% full time and 26% part time. The 40% of women who were not working in a paid job can be divided into those who, with the employed, constitute the economically active, namely the unemployed (5% of all women of working age), full time students (5%), and the economically inactive, that is women who were not working for domestic reasons (30%). Whilst we used the usual definition of paid work in this chapter, we also looked at the implications of broadening or altering this. We found that some women, who would normally be described by both standard criteria and themselves as not working, in fact undertook paid work on a regular or occasional basis. If they were to be included in a broader definition the economic activity rate of women of working age would rise to 69%.

Total activity rates and whether women are working full or part time vary by a woman's age, marital status and the number and ages of her children but these factors are highly interrelated, and some have more important effects than others. Age is particularly likely to reflect other life cycle factors and so, apart from the oldest women, showed little independent effect on activity rates. The age of the youngest child accounted for more variation in economic activity than the number of children under 16 a woman had (with the exception of the few women who had more than three children). Accordingly, in most analyses, we classified women by the age of their youngest child. Having a child under five had the greatest effect on the likelihood of a woman working; significantly more women worked with a child aged 5–10 than with a child under 5. The effect of having children on women's labour market participation diminished as the children grew older un-til the time when the youngest child was 11 or more, at which point there was little difference in the economic activity of mothers with children 11–15 or 16 plus. However there is a long term effect to having children; women who had children were significantly less likely to work than childless women, holding other factors constant.

Marital status was shown to have no effect on whether women work or not once their age, whether they had children, and the age of the youngest child was taken into account. These three main factors were combined to create a life cycle variable reflecting major life stages for women. Women's labour market activity varied markedly at different stages of their lives with the highest proportion of working women being found among childless women under 30 and the lowest proportion among women with a youngest child under 5.

Whilst marital status had no effect on whether a woman works or not it was an important determinant of whether a woman worked full or part time; married women, with or without children were significantly more likely to work part time than non-married women with or without children, when other factors were held constant. In fact marital status had a more important effect on working part time than a woman's own age though the presence of children and age of the youngest child were the major determinants of whether women work full or part time.

Overall then, it is clear from these cross-sectional results that not working in a paid job is associated overwhelmingly with the most intense period of childbearing and rearing. Domestic responsibilities go wider than childrearing however, and married women, regardless of whether they have dependent children or not, are more likely to work part time than non-married women.

Notes

[1] In her complementary analysis Joshi (1984) combines a number of socio-economic variables with these demographic characteristics to explain variations in participation, variously measured.

[2] In the model fitted by Joshi (1984) the long term effect on participation is attributed to the loss of earning potential due to an interrupted work history rather than the fact of childbearing *per se*.

[3] A similar life cycle measure was used by Alan Marsh in his study of women and shiftwork (Marsh, 1979) and by Jean Martin (Martin, 1978).

Chapter 3 Women workers in the occupational structure

Introduction

It is often argued that most women workers are concentrated in a few occupations and industries which are characterised by low levels of skill, low pay, no training or promotion prospects, few fringe benefits and insecurity of employment and as such can be considered secondary workers in the labour market.[1] In this and the next two chapters we consider the evidence from the survey in relation to this argument. In this chapter we examine the extent to which women are concentrated in particular occupations and industries in the occupational structure and segregated from men in employment. Standard occupational classifications, however, have their limitations when applied to women's occupations; we begin the chapter by discussing these limitations and then introduce the classification system devised for the survey. Having described the occupational distribution of women in the survey, we subsequently consider the extent to which they are segregated from men at their place of work and compare this with the level of segregation experienced by the small sample of husbands. Finally, we explore the reasons why some women and men in the study think of their work as 'women's work' or 'men's work'.

Classifying women's occupations and industries

A number of different schemes are available for classifying occupations. They vary both in terms of level of detail, ie the number of categories to which occupations can be assigned, and the principles underlying the choice of particular categories. The majority of government surveys covering employment and the labour force use the OPCS Classification of Occupations, which was developed primarily for use on the Census. This classification system is revised for each Census and in 1980, when this survey was carried out, the 1970 version was still in general use.

According to the 1970 classification, occupations are assigned to one of 253 occupational unit groups (OPCS, 1970). These can be aggregated to form 18 occupational orders, or used in conjunction with information about an individual's employment status to classify the occupation to a socio-economic group (SEG) or to one of the Registrar General's social classes (ibid).

The OPCS occupational classification system was originally devised at a time when the large majority of employees were men working in manufacturing industries. Though there have been revisions, the level of discrimination between jobs in the service sector (where many women's jobs are located) in no way matches the fine distinctions originally drawn for the manufacturing sector. The resulting distributions of women's occupations classified at the level of occupational order, SEG, or social class show that the majority of women's jobs fall into a small number of categories. It may, of course, be argued that women are not in fact to be found in as great a variety of occupations as men and that the classifications accurately reflect the concentration of women into a relatively small number of occupations compared with men. Alternatively, the schema may be rightly criticised for failing to discriminate adequately between the jobs women do in terms of both the level and range of skill the jobs cover.[2] In addition the small number of categories is partly a reflection of the fact that many of the categories in which women's occupations are concentrated encompass a wider range of jobs than is the case in typically male job categories. This problem applies both at the most detailed level and at the aggregate level (for example to SEG or social class) resulting in the classification of the majority of women to only two or three categories, which severely limits the usefulness of these classifications.

To deal with some of these problems it was decided that for this survey we would modify one of the main classifications, social class, to discriminate more finely among women's jobs, by subdividing the categories into which a large proportion of women's jobs fall.[3] The categories of the new classification, which we have called occupational groups, can be recombined to form the original social classes as this is useful for comparative purposes. We chose social class as opposed to SEG as the basis of the classification because social class is intended to be an ordinal classification and because it has relatively few codes which contain only a small number of women's occupations. SEG has several codes into which few occupations fall and is frequently condensed into a smaller number of categories, called social groups, making it very similar to social class for analysis purposes, though strictly speaking it is not ordinal.

In choosing to base our classification on social class we recognised that we were retaining some of the inadequacies of the classification of occupations with regard to women's occupations. We did not change the assignment of any occupation to a particular social class, even when this resulted in apparent anomalies. For example, all nursing occupations are assigned to Social Class II, so that it includes nursing auxiliaries as well as graduate nurses and other nurses with high levels of professional training. Our occupational groups classification is shown in Figure 3.1. We have distinguished in Social Class II two main groups of sub-professionals where relatively high proportions of women are found, namely teaching and nursing, medical and social occupations. Social Class III non-manual has been divided into clerical and sales occupations. Amongst semi-skilled jobs, Social Class IV, we separated women doing factory work from those working in domestic type occupations, whilst our other semi-skilled occupations category covers a diversity of semi-skilled jobs.

This is the main occupational classification used on this survey but other classifications, such as occupational orders and SEG, have also been used occasionally when results from this survey have been compared with data from other sources.

Figure 3.1 Women's Occupational Groups

Social
class

I   1. *Professional occupations*   *mangt*
        Barrister, solicitor, chartered and certified accountant, university teacher, doctor, dentist, physicist, chemist, pharmacist, dispensing optician, qualified engineer, architect, town planner, civil servant (Assistant Secretary level and above).

II   2. *Teachers*
        Primary and secondary school teacher, teachers in further and higher education (not universities), head teacher, nursery teacher, vocational and industrial trainer.

II   3. *Nursing, medical and social occupations*
        SRN, SEN, nursing auxiliary, midwife, health visitor, children's nurse, matron/superintendent, dental nurse, dietician, radiographer, physiotherapist, chiropodist, dispenser, medical technician, houseparent, welfare occupations (including social workers), occupational therapist.

II   4. *Other intermediate non-manual occupations*
        Civil Servants (Executive Officer to Senior Principal level and equivalent in central and local government), computer programmer, systems analyst, O & M analyst, librarian, surveyor, personnel officer, manager, self-employed farmer, shopkeeper, publican, hotelier, buyer, company secretary, author, writer, journalist, artist, designer, window-dresser, entertainer, musician, actress.

III 5. *Clerical occupations*
        Typist, secretary, shorthand writer, clerk, receptionist, personal assistant, cashier (not retail), telephonist, receptionist, office machine operator, computer operator, punch card operator, data processor, draughtswoman, tracer, market research interviewer, debt collector.

III 6. *Shop assistant and related sales occupations*
        People selling goods in wholesale or retail establishments, cashier in retail shop, check-out and cash and wrap operator, petrol pump attendant, sales representative, demonstrator, theatre/cinema usherette, programme seller, insurance agent.

III 7. *Skilled occupations*
        Hairdresser, manicurist, beautician, make-up artist, cook, domestic and institution housekeeper, nursery nurse, travel stewardess, ambulance women, van driver and deliveries, baker, weaver, knitter, mender, darner, tailoress and dressmaker (whole garment), clothing cutter, milliner, upholsterer, bookbinder, precision instrument maker and repairer, instrument assemblers, laboratory assistant, driving instructor, policewoman.

IV   8. *Semi-skilled factory work*
        Assembler, packer, labeller, grader, sorter, inspector, machinist, machine operator, people wrapping, filling or sealing containers, spinner, doubler, twister, winder, reeler.

IV   9. *Semi-skilled domestic work*
        Waitress, barmaid, canteen assistant, childminder, playground or playgroup supervisor, nanny, au pair, home help, care attendant, ward orderly, housemaid, domestic worker.

IV 10. *Other semi-skilled occupations*
        Agricultural worker, groom, kennel maid, shelf-filler, bus conductress, ticket collector, postwoman, mail sorter, laundress, dry cleaner, presser, mail order and catalogue agent, market and street trader, collecting saleswoman, traffic warden, telephone operator.

V   11. *Unskilled occupation*
        Cleaner, charwoman, kitchen hand, labourer, messenger.

Figure 3.2 Industry Groups

MANUFACTURING INDUSTRIES

1. *Food, drink and tobacco processing*
   Processing or manufacture of all food, drink and tobacco products.
   not production of the raw materials
   not retail or wholesale distribution.

2. *Textiles, clothing, footwear, leather goods*
   Manufacture of all textiles (eg wool, rope, carpet, synthetic fibres), clothing, footwear, leather goods, fur.
   not retail or wholesale distribution
   not upholstery and bedding.

3. *Engineering, metal goods, metal manufacture*
   Mechanical, instrument, electrical, shipbuilding and marine engineering, manufacture of vehicles and all types of metal goods (excluding toys), metal manufacture (from raw materials).
   not civil engineering.

4. *Other manufacturing industries*
   Manufacture and processing of coal and petroleum products (include oil refining), manufacture of chemicals (eg paint, soap, fertilisers), plastics, pharmaceuticals, rubber, bricks, pottery, cement, glass (and goods made of these materials), timber, furniture and other wooden goods, upholstery and bedding, paper, printing and publishing, toys, games, sports equipment, musical instruments.

SERVICE INDUSTRIES

5. *Distributive trades*
   Wholesale and retail distribution of all goods (all shops including sub-post offices), pre-packing of food when no processing involved.
   not road haulage and transport
   not filling stations, main post offices, cafes, pubs etc, dry cleaners.

6. *Professional and scientific services*
   Accountancy, schools (including nursery schools), other educational establishments (in-

cluding school meals service and educational administration), legal services, hospitals and other medical, dental research and development services, day nurseries and creches, local authority health and social services (eg social workers, people working in L.A. homes and centres for handicapped), religious organisations.

7. *Insurance, public and local government administration*
   Insurance, banking and other financial institutions, estate agents, property companies, advertising, market research, typing, duplication, copying services, employment agencies (not government), computer services and other business services, office cleaning, security firms (not transport), management consultants, Civil Service, armed forces, police, fire service, other local government services not included elsewhere.
   not hospitals, schools, building and civil engineering establishments, training services.

8. *Other services*
   Construction and civil engineering, gas, electricity, water, road haulage, transport, postal services and telecommunications, packing and despatch of goods (without processing or distribution), travel agents, school crossings, hotels, pubs, restaurants, entertainment and sports services, personal services (eg hairdressing, private domestic service, child-minding, home helps), laundries, dry cleaners, filling stations, shoe-repairers, motor repairers, welfare and charitable services, old people's homes, playgroups, museums, art galleries, trade unions, employers' organisations.

PRIMARY INDUSTRIES

9. *Agriculture, forestry, fishing, mining, quarrying*
   Farming, horticulture, mining and quarrying of coal, stone, slate, extraction of chalk, sand gravel, gas, oil.

We classified the industries in which women worked according to the 1968 Standard Industrial Classification which was in general use at the time of our survey (CSO, 1968). This has 207 categories at the most detailed level of coding which can be aggregated into 25 main categories. A number of these categories contain very few women and so we have condensed the original 25 categories into 9 groups of industries for use on this survey. These groups are shown in Figure 3.2.

The occupations and industries of the main job of the working women

We look first at the occupations of the working women in the survey classified into the 18 occupational orders of the OPCS classification (Table 3.1). Full and part time workers are shown separately as they tend to have rather different occupations. By way of comparison, the corresponding distribution of male occupations based on results from the 1980 General Household Sur-

Table 3.1 Occupational order for jobs of full and part time working women, and working men (1980 GHS)

Occupational order	Full time	Part time	All working women	Working men (1980 GHS)
	%	%	%	%
Managerial general	–	0	–	1
Professionals supporting management	2	0	1	6
Professionals in health, education and welfare	16	10	13	5
Literary, artistic and sports	1	1	1	1
Professionals in engineering and science	1	0	1	5
Other managerial	5	1	4	12
Clerical	41	22	33	6
Selling	6	13	9	4
Security	0	0	0	2
Catering, cleaning and hairdressing	10	41	23	3
Farming and fishing	1	2	1	2
Material processing (excluding metal)	1	1	1	3
Making and repairing (excluding metal)	6	4	5	6
Metal processing, making, repairing	3	1	2	20
Painting, assembling, packing	6	3	5	5
Construction and mining	0	–	0	6
Transport	1	1	1	11
Miscellaneous	0	0	0	1
	100	**100**	**100**	**100**
Base	*1,877*	*1,477*	*3,354*	*8,024*

vey is shown (OPCS, 1982a). The concentration of the women into a relatively small number of occupations can be seen clearly. The three occupational orders with the highest proportions account for 69% of all women's jobs whereas four occupations have less than 1% of women each. In contrast, the three orders with the highest proportions of men account for only 43% of men's jobs and no occupation has less than 1% of men.

Turning next to our own classification, Table 3.2 shows the way in which jobs falling into Social Classes II, III non-manual and IV have been subdivided, although there are still 30% of women in the clerical category. It is highly likely that the jobs in this category are in fact fairly heterogeneous and that if we had had more information they could have been further subdivided. The original version of our new classification had a separate category for childcare occupations but relatively few women (2%) fell into this category and so it was incorporated into the semi-skilled domestic category.

Hunt's survey in 1965 classified women's occupations by socio-economic group (SEG). We therefore look next at the distribution of women's occupations by socio-economic group and compare our results with the 1965 distributions to see how women's occupations have changed over fifteen years (Table 3.3). Overall, it

is striking how little has changed though the most significant difference, which is well established from other sources, is the decline in manual relative to non-manual occupations among women.

Lastly in this section, we look at the industries in which the women in the sample worked. Table 3.4 gives the distributions for the working women, showing full and part time workers separately, and also shows a distribution for male occupations from the 1980 GHS, and the 1965 distribution for women from Hunt's survey. In 1980, women were more likely than men to work in service industries and proportionately more women worked in service industries than they did fifteen years ago. This reflects the rise in economic activity among married women over this period which was mainly due to the increase in women working in service industries, particularly in part time jobs, though there was also some decline in women working in manufacturing industries.

It can be misleading, however, to distinguish between women working in manufacturing and service industries in this way because women working in manufacturing industries are not necessarily working in manufacturing occupations (Arnold *et al* 1982). Table 3.5 relates women's occupations to the industries in which they work. Although using our classification not all

Table 3.2 Occupational group and social class of full and part time working women

Occupational group	Social class	Full time		Part time		All working women	
		%		%		%	
Professional	I	1		1		1	
Teaching	} II	8	} 24	3	} 12	6	} 19
Nursing, medical and social		7		6		7	
Other intermediate non-manual		9		3		6	
Clerical	} III non-manual	39	} 45	20	} 32	30	} 39
Sales		6		12		9	
Skilled manual	III manual	8		6		7	
Semi-skilled factory	} IV	13	} 20	7	} 32	10	} 25
Semi-skilled domestic		4		20		11	
Other semi-skilled		3		5		4	
Unskilled	V	2		17		9	
		100		**100**		**100**	
Base		*1,877*		*1,477*		*3,354*	

Table 3.3 Socio-economic group of full and part time working women (compared with Hunt's 1965 survey)

Socio-economic group	Full time %	Part time %	All working women %	Working women 1965 (Hunt) %
Employers and managers	8	2	5	5
Professional workers	1	1	1	0
Intermediate non-manual *Nursing Medical Teachers*	20	11	16	8
Junior non-manual	42	34	39	36
Personal service	6	20	12	15
Supervisors – manual	1	1	1	1
Skilled manual	5	3	4	7
Semi-skilled manual	13	8	11	16
Unskilled manual	2	17	9	8
Own account non-professional	1	2	1	3
Farmers – employers and managers	0	0	0	0
Farmers – own account	0	0	0	0
Agricultural workers	1	1	1	1
	100	**100**	**100**	**100**
Base	1,877	1,477	3,354	3,892

(Handwritten roman numerals I–V appear in left margin; handwritten note "Nursing Medical Teachers" beside Intermediate non-manual.)

Table 3.4 Industry group of full and part time working women, working women in 1965 and working men (1980 GHS)

Industry group	Full time %	Part time %	All working women %	Working women 1965 (Hunt) %	Working men 1980 (GHS) %
Manufacturing industries					
Food, drink and tobacco processing	4	3	3	4	3
Textiles, clothing and footwear	6	4	5	10	2
Engineering and metal manufacture	10	5	8	11	20
Other manufacturing industries	7	3	5	6	9
Total manufacturing	**27**	**15**	**21**	**31**	**34**
Service industries					
Distribution	14	18	16	18	10
Professional and scientific services	25	30	28	17	9
Insurance, banking and public administration	16	8	12	7	10
Other services	17	26	21	25	31
Total service	**72**	**82**	**77**	**67**	**60**
Primary industries					
Agriculture, forestry, fishing, mining, quarrying	1	3	2	2	6
	100	**100**	**100**	**100**	**100**
Base	1,877	1,477	3,354	3,892	8,024

Table 3.5 Occupation by industry of working women

Occupational group	Food, drink, tobacco %	Textiles, clothing, footwear %	Engineering and metal manufacture %	Other manufacturing %	Distribution %	Professional and scientific services %	Insurance, banking and public administration %	Other services %	Primary industries %	All working women %
Professional	–	–	–	1	1	2	0	0	–	1
Teaching	–	–	–	–	–	22	0	0	–	6
Nursing, medical and social	–	–	0	–	–	23	1	2	–	7
Other intermediate non-manual	2	2	3	8	13	1	8	6	19	6
Clerical	26	14	43	36	22	19	73	27	21	30
Sales	3	–	0	1	49	0	1	2	–	9
Skilled manual	8	21	7	19	3	5	2	10	–	7
Semi-skilled factory	50	55	41	30	3	0	0	2	6	10
Semi-skilled domestic	2	1	2	1	1	14	2	33	2	11
Other semi-skilled	–	5	1	1	5	2	1	6	52	4
Unskilled	9	2	3	3	3	12	12	12	–	9
	100	**100**	**100**	**100**	**100**	**100**	**100**	**100**	**100**	**100**
Base	113	173	262	176	543	901	416	701	62	3,354*

Includes 7 cases whose industry was not known

24

occupations can be clearly categorised as service or manufacturing it is clear that many women in manufacturing industries were in service occupations, particularly in clerical work. Only in two industrial groups, textiles, clothing and footwear and food, drink and tobacco manufacture, both dominated by female employees, were over half the women clearly engaged in production jobs.

From Tables 3.1–3.4, one can see that both the occupation and industry distribution of part time workers differed from those of full time workers. Tables 3.6 and 3.7 show the proportions of the part time workers in the sample in each occupational and industry group. From these it is clear that, overall, there were proportionally more part time workers among manual than non-manual occupations and among the lower level occupations in each group. Part time workers were also generally more likely to be found in service than in manufacturing industries. The exception is the insurance, banking and public administration category which also had a lower proportion of part time workers than the other service sector categories.

We have already shown that women's occupations and the industries in which they work are interrelated, and we wanted to take account of this in looking at the proportion of part time workers. However, because of insufficient numbers, we could not look at the proportion of part time workers in all the combinations of occupation and industry groups and so we compared the proportions in the four combinations of non-manual and manual occupations and service and manufacturing industries (Table 3.8). This shows that proportionally more part time workers were found in manual occupations in service industries than might be expected from consideration of the separate effects of being in a manual rather than a non-manual occupation and in a service rather than a manufacturing industry. The growth over the 1970s of part time employment in service industries in both the private and public sector, but particularly the latter, is well known from other sources. However, whilst we have shown women's industrial distribution here we rarely use this variable in subsequent analyses in this or later chapters as we found it had little explanatory value compared with occupation.

Table 3.6 Proportion of part time workers in different occupational groups

Occupational group	% of part time workers	Base
Non-manual		
Professional		26*
Teaching	22%	196
Nursing, medical and social	43%	223
Other intermediate non-manual	19%	204
Clerical	29%	1,028
Sales	60%	290
Total non-manual	**34%**	1,967
Manual		
Skilled manual	39%	239
Semi-skilled factory	30%	352
Semi-skilled domestic	80%	371
Other semi-skilled	53%	129
Unskilled	85%	295
Total manual	**59%**	1,386
All working women	**44%**	3,354

*Base too small to show percentage

Table 3.7 Proportion of part time workers in different industry groups

Industry group	% of part time workers	Base
Manufacturing		
Food, drink and tobacco	35%	113
Textiles, clothing and footwear	34%	173
Engineering and metal manufacture	25%	262
Other manufacturing	27%	176
Total manufacturing	**29%**	724
Services		
Distribution	50%	543
Professional and scientific services	48%	901
Insurance, banking and public administration	30%	416
Other services	56%	701
Total services	**48%**	2,561
Primary industries	65%	62
All working women	**44%**	3,354*

*Includes 7 cases whose industry was not known

Table 3.8 Proportion of part time workers in non-manual and manual occupations, and manufacturing and service industries*

Occupation	Industry	% of part time workers	Base
Non-manual	Manufacturing	21%	267
Non-manual	Service	35%	1,671
Manual	Manufacturing	34%	456
Manual	Service	70%	890

*Women working in primary industries have been excluded

Occupational concentration and segregation

In general, studies of men and women's jobs both in Britain and more generally in industrial societies show that men and women are concentrated in different occupations (Hakim, 1979; OECD, 1980). In Britain about a quarter of all occupations have a higher proportion of women workers than the labour force as a whole, whilst three quarters of all occupations have a higher proportion of men workers than the labour force as a whole (Hakim, 1979). Within occupational categories too, women and men are often found disproportionately at different levels, with men doing the more skilled, responsible and better paid work. Thus there is both horizontal and vertical separation between men and women at work, and this has changed very little over the last eighty years (Hakim, 1981).

The political response to concern about inequality resulted in the Equal Pay and the Sex Discrimination Acts which came into force at the end of 1975. Legislation on equal pay, though it did noticeably decrease the differential between men and women's earnings, can have only a limited effect on women's earnings when men and women work in very different occupations (Snell *et al*, 1981). As the 1974 White Paper *Equality for Women* explicitly, and the Sex Discrimination Act implicitly recognised, one key to improving the relative position of women *vis-à-vis* men at work was to tackle the processes whereby horizontal and vertical concentration occurred and were maintained through recruitment to jobs and access to training and promotion opportunities (Home Office, 1974).

In the 1970s, research interests focused on explanations of 'inequality' and 'discrimination' by looking at the structure of opportunity for women. Research suggested that the labour market, whilst highly segmented, can be seen as comprising two main sectors: a primary sector of well rewarded, skilled and secure jobs, in which men predominate, and a secondary sector of lower paid less skilled and less secure jobs in which, in the UK, women are disproportionately found (Bosanquet and Doeringer, 1973). Occupational concentration, as Hakim amongst others has pointed out, is central to this description of the labour market and to the study of how men and women are treated in employment (Hakim, 1979).

There are two main ways in which occupational concentration has been studied in Britain; firstly on the basis of aggregate data on the proportions of men and women in different occupational categories derived from the national census and labour force surveys, and secondly by looking at concentration at the company or establishment level. These approaches measure different things and studies of establishments show higher levels of concentration than national data, reflecting, for example, the incidence of establishments with no or very few women or men in the country as a whole. Hakim in her study discusses this at the overall level of the occupational group. She therefore is able to show that in 1971, whilst men and women were highly segregated in terms of the relative proportion of men and women in different occupations, total segregation in terms of an occupation being completely one sex was rare; no women worked in women only occupations, though 14% of men worked in occupational groups where only men were found (ibid).

By contrast, Hunt in her 1973 survey looked at segregation at the level of establishment and found that 18% of establishments did not employ men and women on the same work and the incidence of total segregation was particularly marked in managerial or supervisory and skilled manual jobs (Hunt, 1975). A similar study of establishments conducted in 1979 confirmed the picture that total segregation was more marked at this more local level (or finer unit of analysis); of the sample of jobs studied in the survey of establishments, 45% had no women in them and 21% had no men, making a sizeable majority of the jobs studied single sex (EOC, 1981 and McIntosh, 1980).

There are considerable methodological problems in collecting data on occupational segregation from establishments through an employer interview and sample of jobs approach, yet the situation at the company or establishment level is particularly important for two reasons. Firstly, under the Equal Pay Act in operation in 1980, men and women's pay and conditions of employment could only be compared if both men and women were doing the same or broadly similar work or work rated as equivalent on a Job Evaluation Scheme in the same establishment or company.[4] Secondly, the immediate situation at the workplace is likely to have more effect on women's attitudes to their jobs and their own position as women workers than the general situation, as well as on employers' attitudes to the women workers they employ.

Accordingly, we have looked at occupational segregation at the establishment level in a totally new way using data based on the perspective of the women workers themselves.[5] We focused on the situation at women's place of work and asked our respondents whether there were 'any men doing the same sort of work' as them at their place of work or only women. From their answers we derived an absolute measure of occupational segregation, separating our respondents into two groups; those women who work with men doing the same sort of work as them and those who do not, whom we describe as working in 'women only' jobs. Thus we are not measuring degrees of segregation or whether women are working disproportionately with women in the sense that women are over represented in comparison with their share of the labour force. Our measure is clearer cut than this and consequently it is a strong measure allowing us to identify the extent of total job segregation working women experience at work. Analysis at this level also enables us to compare women working full time with those working part time which other studies rarely, if ever, do.[6] Later in the chapter we use the measure to consider how many of the husbands we interviewed also experience total job segregation at work.

The extent of occupational segregation

Overall just over half the working women in our sample (57%) said that only women did the same sort of work as them at their workplace, whereas 34% said that both men and women did their sort of work as Table 3.9 shows. For 9% of working women, comparisons were not possible because there was no one else doing the

Table 3.9 Proportions of full and part time workers who work in jobs where only women or both men and women do the same sort of work as themselves

Whether women only or both men and women do the same sort of work as informant	Full time		Part time		All working women	
	%	%	%	%	%	%
Informant works at home	3		6		4	
Informant works alone	1	6	4	13	2	9
Informant is the only person doing that work	2		3		3	
Only women do the work	54	58	61	70	57	63
Men and women do the work	40	42	26	30	34	37
		100	**100**	**100**	**100**	**100** **100**
Base	1,877	1,765	1,477	1.282	3,354	3,047

26

same work as themselves at their place of work: either they worked alone at home or elsewhere, or they were the only person doing their type of work. In the rest of this section, we look only at the women who could compare themselves to others doing the same type of work at their workplace. Of these women, 63% worked only with other women (58% and 70% of full and part time workers respectively) and 37% worked where both men and women did the same kind of work as themselves.

The proportion of women working where only women did the same work as themselves differed among women in different occupational groups and between full and part time workers within each occupation (Table 3.10). Occupational segregation at the work-place level was lowest among the high level occupations, which fall in Social Classes I and II, and also among women in other semi-skilled occupations. It was highest, as might be expected, in the semi-skilled domestic category where 78% of women doing mainly catering or child caring types of jobs worked only with women. In all manual occupations segregation occur-

red for 70% or more of women. In all groups with the exception of 'other semi-skilled' women working part time were more likely to experience job segregation than women working full time, though this is likely to reflect the different types of jobs done by full and part time workers in the same occupational group.

Because our classification concentrates on the extent of occupational segregation we also show for comparison (in Table 3.11), the extent of workplace segregation using the standard occupational orders. This does not differ significantly overall, though it shows a wider range of occupational segregation in manufacturing occupations than our combined measures. We also looked at occupational segregation at the workplace level by the industry in which women worked (Table 3.12). There was a marked overall difference between manufacturing and service industries in so far as 72% of women in manufacturing worked only with other women compared with 61% in services. What is of note is that whilst full time workers in the service industries were markedly less likely overall to experience job segregation than women working full time in manufactur-

Table 3.10 Proportions of full and part time working women in different occupational groups who work at a place where only women do the same work

Occupational group	Full time		Part time		All women working with others	
	% in 'women only' jobs	Base	% in 'women only' jobs	Base	% in 'women only' jobs	Base
Professional		17*		6*		23*
Teaching	24%	148	32%	38	25%	186
Nursing, medical and social	42%	120	46%	90	44%	210
Other intermediate non-manual	42%	131		22*	42%	153
Clerical	64%	691	80%	241	68%	932
Sales	54%	111	67%	168	62%	279
Skilled manual	66%	136	77%	78	70%	214
Semi-skilled factory	76%	245	78%	93	73%	338
Semi-skilled domestic	70%	64	79%	261	78%	325
Other semi-skilled	50%	58	40%	52	45%	110
Unskilled	59%	44	77%	232	74%	276
All women working with others	**58**%	1,765	**70**%	1,282	**63**%	3,047

Base too small to show percentages

Table 3.11 Proportions of full and part time working women in different occupational orders who work at a place where only women do the same work

Occupational order	Full time		Part time		All women working with others	
	% in 'women only' jobs	Base	% in 'women only' jobs	Base	% in 'women only' jobs	Base
Managerial general		–				–
Professionals supporting management	36%	33		3*	36%	36
Professionals in health, education and welfare	32%	284	41%	37	35%	421
Literary, artistic and sport		9*		7*		16*
Professionals in engineering and science		13*		4*		17*
Other managerial	54%	68		11*	56%	79
Clerical	62%	727	78%	255	66%	982
Selling	53%	116	64%	180	60%	296
Security		10*		3*		13*
Catering, cleaning and hairdressing	71%	163	78%	539	77%	702
Farming and fishing		11*		15*		26*
Material processing (excluding metal)		26*		19*	57%	45
Making and repairing (excluding metal)	82%	109	87%	39	83%	148
Metal processing, making and repairing	60%	52		19*	58%	71
Painting, assembling and packing	79%	119	70%	40	77%	159
Construction and mining		1*		–		1*
Transport		19*		8*		27*
Miscellaneous		3†		2*		5†
All women working with others	**58**%	1,765†	**70**%	1,282†	**63**%	3,047†

Base too small to show percentages
†Includes 3 cases whose occupational order was not known

Table 3.12 Proportions of full and part time working women in different industry groups who work at a place where only women do the same work

Industry group	Full time		Part time		All women working with others	
	% in 'women only' jobs	Base	% in 'women only' jobs	Base	% in 'women only' jobs	Base
Food and drink and tobacco	57%	70	68%	38	61%	108
Textiles, clothing and footwear	82%	111	82%	44	82%	155
Engineering and metal manufacture	71%	191	72%	60	71%	251
Other manufacturing	70%	122	72%	39	70%	161
Total manufacturing	71%	494	73%	181	72%	675
Distribution	63%	245	65%	254	64%	499
Professional and scientific services	51%	450	71%	408	61%	858
Insurance, banking and public administration	42%	281	68%	110	50%	391
Other services	56%	276	73%	305	65%	581
Total services	53%	1,252	70%	1,077	61%	2,329
Primary industries		14*		22*	47%	36
All women working with others	**58**%	1,765†	**70**%	1,282†	**63**%	3,047†

*Base too small to show percentages
†Includes 7 cases whose industry was not known

ing, this variation between industries did not hold for part time workers; occupational segregation was equally high for both manufacturing (73%) and service industries (70%).

These results highlight the very different position of full time workers in the service industries as compared with other groups. We have already shown in Table 3.5 that women in higher level occupations were more likely to be working in service industries. Taking these results together suggests that full time women workers in higher level occupations, particularly in service industries, differ considerably from other working women. In Chapter 5 we examine whether this difference persists when we take account of women's pay and conditions of employment and we consider to what extent full time women workers in the higher level occupations constitute a primary sector workforce.

We also asked women whether their immediate supervisor was male or female since this might reflect the likelihood of promotion and affect their specific attitudes to their job and to men and women working together in the same job. Of the women who had an immediate supervisor, 43% had a woman supervisor and 55% had a man; 2% had both a man and a woman. Female supervisors were more common among part time workers (49%) than among full time workers (39%). This is probably a reflection of the higher degree of occupational segregation among part time workers; they are more likely to be working in situations where all those involved in the type of work, including the supervisors, are women. To test this explanation we compared the proportions of women with female supervisors among women who worked only

with other women and those who worked with men and women for full and part time workers separately (Table 3.13). Women who worked in 'women only' jobs were more likely to have female supervisors and this largely, but not entirely, accounted for the difference in this respect between full and part time workers.

So far in this section we have looked at the women in our sample. We did, however, ask similar questions of the small sample of husbands who were interviewed. Although these in no way constitute a representative sample of all working men, we thought it would be interesting to contrast their answers with those of the women. Of the husbands, 94% were working in situations where there were other people doing the same sort of work as themselves. Of these, 81% worked only with other men in their type of work whereas the comparable figure for women was 63%. Thus the husbands were much more likely to be working in 'men only' jobs than the women in 'women only' jobs. The overwhelming majority of husbands (98%) had male supervisors. Even among those who worked with women as well as men, the proportion with male supervisors was still high; 95% compared with 99% for those who worked in 'men only' work. So for the vast majority of husbands we interviewed their world of work was male dominated, giving them little, if any, direct evidence that women workers were similar to or equal with them.

Women's work, men's work?
The analysis so far has shown the factual situation at their place of work reported by the women who were interviewed. The situation at one establishment, however, may be very different from that at another. For example, some women in our sample may have

Table 3.13 Proportions of full and part time employees with female supervisors by whether only women or men and women do the same sort of work

Whether women only or men and women do the same sort of work	Full time		Part time		All employees	
	% with female supervisor	Base	% with female supervisor	Base	% with female supervisor	Base
Works only with women	47%	1,007	56%	884	51%	1,891
Works with men and women	28%	725	35%	372	30%	1,097
All women working with others in the same sort of work	**38**%	1,732	**48**%	1,256	**44**%	2,988

reported that they worked only with other women yet know that in other establishments men and women were working together doing the same type of work. This wider knowledge might well affect how they think about their work. For example, women teachers who teach only with other women at their particular school may well not think of teaching as women's work because they know men also teach. In order to find out whether occupational segregation at their workplace was reflected in women's own definition of the relationship between gender and jobs, we asked our informants whether they thought of their own work as 'mainly women's work', 'mainly men's work' or 'work that either men or women do', and we show how their answers related to our measure of occupational segregation.

Overall, 40% of all working women who worked with others doing the same sort of work said they thought of their work as women's work; 1% thought of it as men's work and the remaining 59% thought of their work as work either men or women do. Part time workers were more likely to think of their work as women's work (47%) than full time workers (34%). Whether this was because of the actual work they did or because they did it part time is difficult to assess, particularly as some types of work are only available part time. Table 3.14 shows the relationship of the women's views to our measure of workplace occupational segregation. These results show very large differences in the proportions of women who thought of their work as women's work

between those who worked only with other women (54%) and those who worked with men as well (15%). Whilst this finding is not unexpected, it is very marked and shows that women's attitudes mirror their reality of experiencing job segregation at work.

This becomes even clearer when we look at the attitudes of women in different occupational groups in Table 3.15. There were significant differences both between occupational groups and within them in the proportion of women who thought of their work as mainly women's work. Only a very small proportion of teachers and women in the other intermediate non-manual groups thought like this (15% and 14% respectively) whereas 55% of semi-skilled domestic workers and 53% of unskilled women saw their work as mainly women's work. These overall proportions, however, hide big differences within occupational groups. In teaching 38% of women working only with women thought of their work as women's work compared with 7% of those women who taught with men. Amongst unskilled women 61% of those working only with women felt they did women's work whilst 31% of those working with men felt this. It is, of course, likely that women working only with other women are doing different work from those who work with men, even within the same broad occupational group.

We went on to explore why women who defined their work as 'women's work' did so. We asked our informants whether they thought men could do the same

Table 3.14 Proportions of full and part time working women who think of their work as mainly women's work by whether only women or both men and women do the same sort of work

Whether women only or men and women do the same sort of work	Full time		Part time		All working women	
	% who think of their work as women's work	Base	% who think of their work as women's work	Base	% who think of their work as women's work	Base
Works only with women	50%	1,020	59%	900	54%	1,920
Works with men and women	12%	745	20%	382	15%	1,127
All women working with others in the same sort of work	34%	1,765	47%	1,282	40%	3,047

Table 3.15 Proportions of women in different occupational groups who think of their work as women's work by whether they work with women only or with men and women

Occupational group	Works only with women		Works with men and women		All who work with others in same work	
	% who think of their work as women's work	Base	% who think of their work as women's work	Base	% who think of their work as women's work	Base
Professional		4*		19*		23*
Teaching	38%	47	7%	139	15%	186
Nursing, medical and social	58%	92	22%	118	38%	210
Other intermediate non-manual	31%	65	2%	88	14%	153
Clerical	51%	634	14%	298	39%	932
Sales	56%	173	17%	106	41%	279
Skilled manual	45%	150	3%	64	32%	214
Semi-skilled factory	58%	248	22%	90	46%	338
Semi-skilled domestic	66%	252	19%	73	55%	325
Other semi-skilled	48%	50	15%	60	30%	110
Unskilled	61%	204	31%	72	53%	276
All women working with others in the same sort of work	54%	1,920	15%	1,127	40%	3,047

*Base too small to show percentages

sort of work as themselves and, if so, whether they thought men would be prepared to do their sort of work. Although only 17% of these women thought men would not be able to do their sort of work, 56% thought men would not be prepared to do it. The other 27% thought that men both could and would be prepared to do their kind of work. These proportions did not vary significantly between full and part time workers, but differed according to whether the women worked only with other women or with both men and women, as Table 3.16 shows.

Although overall, women who thought of their work as women's work were more likely to think that men would not be prepared to do the work, rather than that men could not do it, answers varied between women in different occupational groups. Women in the higher level occupations where there tended to be less occupational segregation were more likely to think that men could and would be prepared to do their type of work, whereas women in the lower level non-manual jobs (clerical and sales), and in most of the manual occupational groups, were likely to think that men would not be prepared to do their sort of work.

We followed these questions by asking all the women who thought of their work as 'women's work' their reasons for this view. Table 3.17 shows the distributions of different reasons analysed by the women's answers to the two preceding questions. By far the most common response, given by over half the women, was simply to re-assert that their type of work is generally considered to be 'women's work'; a concept which it is difficult to unpack but which probably covers aspects of all the other reasons. Some women, however, gave answers reflecting their views on whether men could or would be prepared to do the work. Lack of appropriate technical or personal skills was often mentioned by those women who thought that men could not do the work; those who thought men would not be prepared to do it mentioned low pay and the boredom of the work as well as lack of appropriate personal skills.

Again, our small sample of husbands were asked similar questions about their own jobs. Altogether 60% said that they thought of their work as 'men's work' (compared with 40% of women who thought of their work as 'women's work'). Like the women's, the husband's views were strongly related to whether or not they worked with women in their type of work; only 19% of those who worked with women thought of their work as 'men's work' compared with 70% of those who worked only with other men. Of the men who thought of their work as 'men's work', 47% thought that women would not be able to do their sort of work and 22% said that, although women could do the work, they would not be prepared to do it. These figures are very different from the corresponding figures for women who were much less likely to believe that men could not do their type of work.

To find out what lay behind these views men who thought of their work as 'men's work' were asked for their reasons; we related these to their views about whether women could or would be prepared to do their sort of work (Table 3.18). The two most common reasons, that the work was too heavy or that the physical working conditions were too unpleasant, were given both by men who thought that women could not do the work and by men who thought that women would not be prepared to do the work. Men who thought that women both could and would be prepared to do the work were also likely to think that the work was too

Table 3.16 Of the women who think of their work as women's work the proportions who think that men could or would do the work by whether they work with women only or with men and women

Whether men could or would be prepared to do the same work	Work only with women and think of their work as women's work	Work with men and women and think of their work as women's work	All who work with others in same work and think of their work as women's work
	%	%	%
Men could not do the work			
Men would not be prepared to do the work	18	8	17
Men could and would do the work	61	29	56
	21	63	27
	100	**100**	**100**
Base	*1,039*	*166*	*1,205*

Table 3.17 Reasons why women think of their work as women's work, by whether they think men could or would do the work

Reasons why women think of their work as women's work	Men could not do the informant's job	Men would not do the informant's job	Men could and would do the informant's job	All women who think of their work as women's work
	%	%	%	%
The work is generally considered 'women's work'	57	48	56	51
The pay is too low	8	20	16	17
Men don't have the right personal skills	19	14	11	14
The work is too boring	7	14	6	11
Men don't do this kind of work	5	8	10	8
Men don't have the right technical skills	21	4	6	8
Men would be embarrassed/considered effeminate	5	6	7	6
Other reasons	2	9	7	8
Don't know	1	1	1	1
Base	*216*	*741*	*359*	*1,316**

Excludes 14 women whose views are not known
Percentages do not add to 100 because some informants gave more than one reason

Table 3.18 Reasons why husbands think of their work as men's work by whether they think women could or would be prepared to do the work: interviewed husbands who think of their work as men's work

Reasons why husbands think of their work as men's work	Women could not do the husband's work	Women would not do the husband's work	Women could and would do the husband's work	All husbands who think of their work as men's work
	%	%	%	%
The work is too heavy	82	63	29	62
The physical conditions are too unpleasant	25	51	16	29
Women lack the necessary personal skills	9	11	20	13
Women don't do/aren't trained for this kind of work	3	6	27	11
Women would be unacceptable or embarrassed	6	6	11	7
Women lack the necessary technical skills	5	7	4	5
The job is incompatible with domestic responsibilities	2	2	7	4
Base	*185*	*86*	*115*	*386**

* Excludes 4 women whose views are not known
Percentages do not add to 100 because some informants gave more than one reason

heavy for many women, but gave reasons which reflected custom rather than any real objection to women doing the work. For example, some of the skilled manual workers commented on the fact that women do not do apprenticeships and therefore are not eligible for their type of work.

As we have shown, occupational segregation between men and women exists to a marked degree both in terms of the jobs they do and their views about what is men's and women's work and why this is so. There is, moreover, a close correspondence between the reality of the experience men and women face at their place of work and their attitudes to what type of work men or women could or would be able to undertake. Thus their experiences and views reflect the segregated nature of the labour market. More crucially, women's apparent acceptance of their different position in the labour market from men is shown by the explanation they offer for why men do not do their type of work. They emphasise the low wages or the boring nature of the work that they themselves undertake. Implicit in this perhaps is an acceptance that men are first and foremost workers and primary breadwinners and have to secure as good pay and employment conditions as possible while their own situation is rather different. We look at this in more detail in Chapter 6 where we examine women's attitudes to working and their jobs, and in Chapter 8 where we focus on how husbands and wives share unpaid work in the home.

Subsidiary occupations

Finally in this chapter we look at working women's second jobs and the paid work done by non-working women and full time students. We were interested in this for several reasons. For the working women we wanted to know whether the pressures of being, in most cases, both a paid worker and a housewife would mean that few women have a second paid job. For all women we were interested in the significance of subsidiary work in terms of hours and earnings, and for non-working women we looked at whether the type of subsidiary work they were doing was likely to be related to the type of work available if they returned to work.

Among the working women 11% were doing another job or paid work (8% of the full time and 15% of the part time workers). As we mentioned in Chapter 2, 13% of non-working women and 38% of full time students were also engaged in some form of paid work. Although we asked for details of all second jobs or subsidiary work only 8% of the women doing second jobs were doing more than one type and the numbers were too few for any further analysis. The remainder of this section looks only at the first subsidiary job mentioned.

Table 3.19 shows the occupational categories of the subsidiary jobs or work undertaken by the different groups of women. The most striking feature of these results is that among all groups, except the students,

Table 3.19 Occupations and proportions in service industries of subsidiary work of full and part time working women, non-working women and full time students

Subsidiary occupation	Working women			Non-working women	Full-time students
	Full time	Part time	All		
	%	%	%	%	%
Professional	–	0	0	1	–
Teaching	10	2	5	3	1
Nursing, medical and social	1	1	1	0	1
Other intermediate non-manual	2	2	2	2	1
Clerical	6	8	7	6	4
Sales	1	3	3	2	48
Skilled manual	4	5	4	5	5
Semi-skilled factory	0	1	1	2	1
Semi-skilled domestic	13	12	12	10	32
Other semi-skilled	60	61	60	63	3
Unskilled	3	5	5	6	4
	100	100	100	100	100
Percentage in service industries	96%	95%	95%	90%	96%
Base	*153*	*242*	*395*	*273*	*123*

over 60% of the jobs fell in the 'other semi-skilled' category. Further examination of these occupations revealed that most of them were mail order agents. The only other occupational category with more than 10% of subsidiary occupations among the working and non-working women was semi-skilled domestic occupations, which includes childcare occupations such as child-minding and babysitting.

The jobs done by the full time students were very different from those done by the other two groups. Over half of the students had jobs in the sales category; these were mainly girls still at school who worked as shop assistants on Saturdays. A large number of the students's jobs also came into the semi-skilled domestic category. Some of these students were working as bar-maids or waitresses. We also looked at the industrial category in which the subsidiary jobs fell; over 90% of the jobs in all groups were in service industries, the majority in distributive trades, which is scarcely surprising in view of the high proportion of mail order agents and shop assistants among the students.

When we compared the occupational categories of the working women's subsidiary and main jobs we found little correspondence. Even if we ignore mail order work, which is unlikely to be related to women's main jobs, the majority of women were doing different second jobs or work from their main job. Among those non-working women who were not engaged in mail order work there was no evidence that the paid work they were doing would help provide a way back into the labour market in terms of their being able to get a job doing similar types of work. There might, however, have been some psychological benefit from keeping on the edges of the labour market which we could not determine. Looking at the descriptions of the work done by these women, it was apparent that almost all the work could be carried out at home or done from home and most of these women were limited to this sort of work by the presence of young children. In contrast, the students had no such constraints and were, therefore, more likely to go out to a separate place of work.

That subsidiary occupations played a relatively minor part in the lives of most of these women is reflected in the average weekly hours of work and earnings in these jobs. Many of the women (one third) worked too little and too irregularly to be able to estimate their hours and earnings, but among those who could, most women, with the exception of the students, worked less than five hours and earned less than £6 a week from this

kind of work. Table 3.20 shows the average weekly hours and earnings for the different groups of women. The students differ from the other groups in working longer hours and earning more; many were working a complete Saturday or several evenings a week. For the majority (63%) of working women (73% of full time and 57% of part time), earnings from subsidiary jobs accounted for less than 10% of total net earnings from all jobs, although, as might be expected such earnings were a higher proportion for part than full time workers. In fact 24% of part time workers with subsidiary jobs obtained more than 30% of their total net earnings from their second jobs; for 7%, second jobs contributed more than 50% of total net earnings. These figures suggest that it is very much a minority of part time workers who do two part time jobs of equal importance.

The results presented in this section suggest that subsidiary work, in the form of any job or paid work done in addition to their main job by the working women and any paid work done by non-working women and students, is of limited importance both in terms of the number of women who do such work and the hours of work and earnings involved. It is of greater importance to students than other women; a higher proportion do such work and they work longer hours and earn more than any other groups of women. How vital the financial contribution of earnings from this sort of work is for the non-working women was not assessed, nor were any psychological benefits this work might have for these women.

Summary and conclusions

However women's occupations are currently classified (and we considered a variety of classifications including our own in this chapter), the nature of their occupational distribution, the extent of occupational concentration and the degree of occupational segregation at the workplace is crucial to any understanding of women's position in the labour market. The industrial and occupational distribution of working women in our sample showed that women are concentrated predominantly in a few occupations mostly in the service sector. This distribution has remained relatively stable over the last 15 years. Women working in part time jobs are more likely to be in the service sector and in low level jobs; in fact 70% of women working in manual service jobs in our sample were working part time.

Occupational segregation at the level of the work place, as measured by the proportion of women working only

Table 3.20 Average weekly hours and earnings from subsidiary occupations of full and part time working women, non-working women and full time students

	Working women			Non-working women	Full-time students
	Full time	Part time	All		
Average hours worked per week by those able to estimate	4.4 hrs	5.3 hrs	5.0 hrs	5.0 hrs	8.7 hrs
Base	*88*	*148*	*236*	*142*	*107*
Average earnings per week of those able to estimate	£5.20	£5.70	£5.50	£4.10	£9.80
Base	*133*	*205*	*338*	*227*	*104*

with women doing the same kind of work as themselves, was quite high overall: of women working with others doing the same job 63% worked only with other women. In general women in higher level occupations were less likely to be in women only jobs; for example, teaching had the lowest proportion of women who said they worked only with women. Women were much more likely to work only with other women if they worked part time; this was true of all occupational groups and in all industries. Interestingly, however, full time workers in manufacturing industries were as likely as part time workers in either manufacturing or service industries to work only with women. In contrast full time women workers in the service sector had noticeably lower levels of occupational segregation. As might be expected women who worked in women only jobs were more likely to have female supervisors.

Women who worked only with women were more likely to think of their work as 'women's work' and accordingly women working part time were more likely than women working full time to think of their work in this way. Women working in high level occupations were least likely to think of their work as 'women's work' and there was little difference by whether they worked full or part time. Whether a woman worked with men or not appeared to influence her view of whether a man could and/or would do her job. There was a clear realisation, however, that if men were not doing these jobs it was likely to be because they were not prepared to do them, usually because the work was women's work or had too low pay.

We compared the women's view of the segregated world of work with those of their husbands who were interviewed. Husbands were markedly more segregated from women than their wives were from men at work, as 81% worked only with other men and almost all (98%) had male supervisors. More men thought of their work as 'men's work' and a much higher proportion of men said women could not do the work rather than would not be prepared to do it. All this shows that the husband's world of work is more peopled by men than their wives' world of work is peopled by women and it is likely that this experience shapes men's attitudes towards women's abilities as workers too.

The degree of occupational concentration and segregation which we have shown to exist in men and women's main worlds of work is heightened in those jobs which women take as subsidiary or second jobs. Overwhelmingly these jobs or types of paid work, most of which were quite small in terms of either the hours women worked at them or money they earned doing them, were in jobs such as selling or the semi-skilled domestic category which included waitressing, bar work and babysitting.

Notes

[1] The most well known application of dual labour market theory to the position of women workers was an article by Barron and Norris (1976). This approach was criticised in general and specifically for women workers by Beechey, (1978). Subsequently early accounts of dual or segmented labour markets have been criticised even more radically for their oversimplified and empirically inaccurate picture of "*a sharp dichotomy of primary and secondary sectors*" and a "*presumption that differences in primary and secondary sector wages reflect differences either in job content, or in skills or productivity potential of the workers employed*" (Craig *et al*, 1982b). Accepting these criticisms, in analysing our results we still felt it was useful to consider, within the limitations of a survey of women through which details of their jobs were obtained, whether women workers were found in jobs typically described as secondary sector.

[2] In fact there has been surprisingly little criticism of the occupational classification system *per se* compared with criticism of the use made of it in discussions of social class. Hunt (1980) criticises it for being 'heavily male orientated, (often out of date male orientated)' whilst Hakim (1979) points out that occupational classifications do not differentiate and separately list women's occupations as precisely as they do men's occupations. However, generally, criticism focusses on the way married women are allocated to a social class on the basis of their husband's occupational standing rather than their own.

[3] Our schema was designed in 1979. For a more recent occupational classification system for women which differs from ours see Elias (1981).

[4] From January 1984 when the Equal Pay Act was amended a woman has also been able to claim if her work is of equal value to that of a man in the same establishment or company.

[5] We have used similar questions to those asked by A Marsh in his study of women and shiftwork (Marsh 1979) but he did little analysis of this question in his report.

[6] Hakim discusses part time working but, because she is concerned with the degree of segregation in occupations and translates part time into whole time equivalents, she is able to show part time working has virtually no impact on the pattern of job segregation (Hakim, 1979).

33

Chapter 4 Working hours: the length and patterns of working days

Introduction

Nothing epitomizes the impact of domestic responsibilities on women's working lives more than the amount of time women with varying domestic commitments work during the week and the times of day when they work. For many women, this issue is crucial in determining whether they take paid employment at all and indeed, as we will show in Chapter 6, 'convenient hours' often takes priority over all other aspects of a job. At a national level, individual decisions, shaped by local opportunities and domestic constraints, may have a considerable effect on the overall pattern of employment as the dramatic increase in part time working in the 1960s and 1970s illustrates. Overall, 44% of working women in the survey worked part time, as we showed in Chapter 2.

In this chapter we look more closely at the number of hours all working women work and examine the variation in length and pattern of their working day. We focus in particular on how family responsibilities affect women's hours and on the arrangements women make to combine paid work with caring for their children. Most of the analysis of the number and distribution of hours worked in this chapter is based on a detailed account of the hours worked by women in their last full working week before the interview, but we also asked women about their usual hours of work; we begin by describing these.

Women's 'usual' hours of work

Table 4.1 shows the usual number of hours worked per week by full and part time women workers, with the exception of the 4% who worked very irregular hours. On average, full time workers worked 37.4 hours per week compared with 18.5 hours for part time workers. The vast majority of full time workers were working at

least thirty one hours a week which constitutes the official definition of full time work. Of the 8% who were not, over half were teachers who must work a minimum of twenty six hours per week at their place of work to be considered officially full time workers. We do not know how many of the others were in jobs such as school secretary where relatively short hours would also be considered full time. Of the part time workers 6% were working thirty-one hours or more a week, generally in jobs where their own hours were shorter than the normal hours for the job.

Table 4.1 Number of hours usually worked per week by full and part time working women (excluding those working very irregular hours)

Usual number of hours worked per week	Full time	Part time	All working women
	%	%	%
Under 8 hours	–	10	4
8 but less than 16 hours	0	27	12
16 but less than 31 hours	8	57	29
31 hours or more	92	6	55
	100	**100**	**100**
Average number of hours worked per week	37.4 hrs	18.5 hrs	29.2 hrs.
Base	*1,820*	*1,402*	*3,222*

We show in Table 4.2 that the hours of full time workers did not vary much between occupational groups, with the obvious exception of teaching, although clerical workers had somewhat shorter hours than women in other groups. However, there was considerable variation in the hours of part time workers. Looking at these results in relation to the proportion of part time workers in each occupational group (Table 3.6) it appears that, with the exception of teaching, the higher the proportion of part time workers in an occupational group, the shorter the average hours worked by the part time workers.

Table 4.2 Average number of hours usually worked per week by full and part time workers in different occupational groups: women with regular hours of work

Occupational group	Full time		Part time		All working women	
	Average hours per week	*Base*	Average hours per week	*Base*	Average hours per week	*Base*
Professional		*18**		*6**		*24**
Teaching	32.0	*146*	13.0	*43*	27.7	*189*
Nursing, medical and social	39.0	*118*	22.0	*92*	31.6	*210*
Other intermediate non-manual	40.7	*147*	24.1	*31*	37.8	*178*
Clerical	36.4	*722*	19.0	*270*	31.6	*992*
Sales	39.5	*113*	18.3	*174*	26.6	*287*
Skilled manual	37.5	*139*	20.8	*89*	31.0	*228*
Semi-skilled factory	38.6	*248*	23.3	*101*	34.1	*349*
Semi-skilled domestic	39.2	*69*	16.7	*286*	21.0	*355*
Other semi-skilled	39.2	*57*	20.0	*62*	29.2	*119*
Unskilled	38.4	*43*	16.0	*247*	19.4	*290*
All working women	**37.4**	*1,820*	**18.5**	*1,402*	**29.2**	*3,222*

*Base too small to show mean

Although all employees have a number of statutory rights which are not dependent on the number of hours worked a week, much of the employment protection legislation applies only to employees working 16 hours a week or more and may also be conditional on employees having worked for their employer for a qualifying period. For example, for unfair dismissal there is a qualifying period of one year, or two years in firms of 20 or fewer employees, and for redundancy pay and maternity reinstatement rights and pay it is two years.[1] These provisions also apply to people working 8 but less than 16 hours a week who have worked for their employer for five years or more. In order to see how many women in the survey were covered by the main employment protection legislation we looked at their usual number of hours of work in relation to length of service with their employer.

Table 4.3 shows that altogether 64% would be covered by legislation which applies to those working 16 hours or more a week for at least two years and eight hours or more a week for five years; the proportion of full and part time employees covered were 67% and 60% respectively. Thus, just under a third of women working full time were not covered because they had not worked for their current employer for two or more years. By contrast, only 10% of part timers were not covered because they worked less than 8 hours a week, but 30% were not covered because they had not worked for their employer long enough to qualify.[2]

Table 4.3 Proportions of full and part time employees covered by the main employment protection legislation (excluding those working very irregular hours)

Hours of work and length of service with present employer	Full time	Part time	All employees
	%	%	%
Working 16 or more hours per week, 2 or more years with employer	67	52	61
Working 8 but less than 16 hours per week, 5 or more years with employer	–	8	3
Total covered by main legislation	**67**	**60**	**64**
Working 16 or more hours per week, less than 2 years with employer	33	11	24
Working 8 but less than 16 hours per week, less than 5 years with employer	–	19	8
Working less than 8 hours per week	–	10	4
Total not covered by main legislation	**33**	**40**	**36**
	100	100	100
Base	*1,805*	*1,342*	*3,147*

Overtime working

In general women work less paid overtime than men, and this accounts for some of the well known variations in male/female average earnings (Webb 1982). There is no research literature which explains why this is so; we do not, for example, know if it is because fewer women want to work overtime or because they have less opportunity to do so; indeed, data on women's overtime is scarce. Only 5% of women employees in our survey said they regularly worked paid overtime (7% of full time and 3% of part time workers) and a further 23% said they worked overtime occasionally. This compares with 38% for men of working age working full time in 1980 (OPCS, 1982a). Half the women (51%) said it was not possible to work paid overtime in their job. Only 19% said that it was possible to work overtime but they did not in fact do so; there was no difference between full and part time workers in this respect. It is clear therefore that many women have no opportunity to work paid overtime, but we do not know how many of these would want paid overtime if it were available. From many comments during the interviews, particularly during pilot work, it appeared that women saw working overtime as doing their employers a favour by helping out in a busy period, rather than something they particularly sought to do or relied on for the money as many men do. In 1980 two thirds of male employees who did paid overtime said they relied on it to make their pay up to a reasonable amount (*ibid.,* Table 5.23).

The days women work each week and hours worked each day

If we think of a standard working week for full time workers as being about seven or eight hours worked on five days of the week, part time workers may reduce their hours either by working on fewer days or by working fewer hours each day or by a combination of the two (or indeed in rare cases by working alternate weeks). In order to examine in more detail how women's hours of work are arranged, particularly for part time workers, we used the detailed information collected about the last full week's work. Obviously some women's hours vary from week to week but 77% of working women said that they worked on the same days each week and for the same hours each day; for these women 'last week' is a completely typical week. A further 11% said that they always worked on the same days but their starting and finishing times varied, and 6% said that although their starting and finishing times did not vary, the days on which they worked varied. The remaining 6% both worked on different days and had varied starting and finishing times.

Looking first at the number of days women worked last week, Table 4.4 shows that most full time workers (85%) worked for five days but 9% worked on six and 3% on seven days. The remaining 3% of full time workers who appeared to have worked less than five days may be accounted for by a misunderstanding in the interview. Although we asked for details of the last full week's work we suspect in a number of cases incom-

Table 4.4 Number of days worked in the previous week by full and part time working women

Number of days worked	Full time	Part time	All working
	%	%	%
1	–	4	2
2	0	9	4
3	0	13	6
4	3	12	7
5	85	54	71
6	9	6	8
7	3	2	2
	100	100	100
Base	*1,877*	*1,477*	*3,354*

plete weeks were recorded when the Monday was a Bank Holiday (of which there were two in the interviewing period). Part time workers were of course less likely than full time workers to have worked on five days or more, but even so 62% had done so.

From information about the hours worked in the week before the interview we calculated the average number of hours worked per day. Taking 7 hours per day as the minimum to be considered a 'full' working day for full time workers, 81% of full time workers had worked on average at least 7 hours per day in the last week compared with only 10% of part time workers. Relating average hours worked per day to the number of days worked, 60% of part time workers worked on five days but averaged less than 7 hours per day, 8% worked at least 7 hours per day but on fewer than five days and 30% worked both less than 7 hours per day and on fewer than five days. The remaining 2% appeared to be working a full week of five or more days averaging at least 7 hours per day; possibly these part time workers were working alternate weeks or were in jobs where 35 hours per week was still shorter than the normal working week for the job but we have no information about this. Thus the most common pattern of working part time is to work a reduced number of hours per day rather than a reduced number of days per week.

The length of the working day

So far we have been looking at the hours women in the survey actually worked, ignoring any main break in the working day and travelling time both of which increase the time women are away from home. To look at the length of the working day we used details of the hours worked on one day of the week preceding the interview. Although we had collected details for all the days worked in that week, for the majority of women in the sample there was in fact little variation in the hours worked on different days of the week. In addition we have information about the starting and finishing times and the length of any meal break or other break in the work lasting more than 15 minutes.

Over half of the part time women workers (56%) said they did not have a meal break, but more surprisingly neither did 6% of full time workers. The majority of part time workers who did not have a meal break (84%) worked less than 5 hours per day and a further 9% worked 5 but less than 6 hours; only 7% of part timers worked 6 hours or more with no break. However, of the few full timers who had no break 75% worked 6 hours or more. Legislation specifies the length of time for which some women can work without a break, but not all women work in occupations covered by the relevant Acts.[3] Women covered by the Factories Act must have a break of at least 30 minutes if they have worked for 4½ hours or more. Under the Shops Act 1950 shop workers must not work for longer than 6 hours without a twenty minute break. We cannot tell which women in our survey would be covered by this legislation, but many occupations are clearly excluded,

and the self-employed and those working at home would not be covered. Legislation may also, of course, be ignored.

Although most working women in our sample had a break lasting less than 1½ hours, 7% had a break lasting longer than this, sometimes, particularly in the case of part time workers, lasting several hours. These women were presumably working some kind of split shift system. Such an arrangement is particularly common among workers in the catering trades, where staff are required to work at lunch breaks and in the evenings; office cleaners may also work mornings and evenings.

The journey to work may add considerably to the length of the working day, if this is taken to be the total time away from home. Most women who travelled to a regular place of work had fairly short journeys, as Table 4.5 shows; over half had journeys of fifteen minutes or less and only 15% travelled for more than half an hour. Part time workers tended to have shorter journeys than full time workers; two thirds had journeys of fifteen minutes or less compared with just under half the full time workers, but even among full time workers only 20% travelled for more than half an hour to work.

Table 4.5 Length of journey to work for full and part time workers who travel to a regular place of work

Length of journey to work	Full time	Part time	All who travel to a regular place of work
	%	%	%
10 minutes or less	30	51	39
11–15 minutes	17	17	17
16–30 minutes	33	23	29
31–45 minutes	12	6	9
45–60 minutes	5	2	4
Over 60 minutes	3	1	2
	100	100	100
Base	1,794	1,335	3,129

We know from other sources such as the National Travel Survey and from our own pilot work that a high proportion of short journeys are made on foot, and therefore that many women, particularly those working part time, work within very short distances of their homes (Department of Transport, 1983). Indeed as we show in Chapters 6 and 11 an easy journey to work, which means a short distance or a straightforward form of travel, is an important consideration for many women when looking for a job, particularly for those with children, because it is the total time away from home which has to fit in with their domestic arrangements. In general, women working the fewest hours per day had the shortest journeys (although women working very long hours per day also had shorter than average journeys).

Finally we show in Table 4.6, for full and part time workers, how the total working day, from leaving home to returning home, is made up in terms of average time spent working and in breaks, and by adding on travelling time, to the length of the total working day. The travelling time was an estimate because we had not collected exact journey times and so we used the mid-

Table 4.6 Average time spent working and average length of the working day of full and part time workers

	Full time	Part time
Average hours spent working	7.5 hrs	4.4 hrs
Average length of meal break	0.9 hrs	0.6 hrs
Average hours at work	8.4 hrs	5.0 hrs
Average length of working day (including travelling time)	8.8 hrs	5.2 hrs
Base	1,877	1,477

point of each of the bands we had recorded and added this to the hours spent at work to arrive at the length of the total working day. Interestingly, the proportion of the total working day actually spent working was the same for full and part timers (85%); thus breaks and journey times are roughly proportional to hours worked.

The range of patterns of working hours
We turn next to the way in which women arrange their hours of work over the day, and look at how this fits in with their domestic commitments. To do this we devised a classification of arrangements, based on starting and finishing time (ignoring meal breaks). Table 4.7 shows the classification and how both full and part time workers were distributed among the categories. The majority of full time workers worked what we have called a 'standard' day, starting before 10 am and finishing at 4 pm or later, but before 6 pm. A number worked a similar number of hours but started somewhat earlier or later than this and a small proportion (2%) worked at night. Those in the short day (am) category were mainly teachers. The part time workers, of course, showed much more variation in the arrangement of their hours of work. Working in the morning was the most common arrangement, but over half the part time workers had finished work before 4 pm which would enable those with school children to be back when their children returned from school.

Table 4.7 Arrangement of hours and average hours per day worked by full and part time workers on a typical working day

Arrangement of hours		Full time			Part time		
		%	Average hours per day	*Base*	%	Average hours per day	*Base*
Mornings	Starting before 10 am Finishing before 2 pm	2	8.2	*30*	29	3.7	*415*
Short day (am)	Starting before 10 pm Finishing 2 pm or later but before 4 pm	9	6.3	*174*	13	5.3	*192*
Standard day	Starting before 10 am Finishing 4 pm or later but before 6 pm	74	7.4	*1,384*	12	6.2	*178*
Long day	Starting before 10 am Finishing 6 pm or later	8	8.3	*144*	4	6.0	*63*
Mid-day	Starting 10 am or later Finishing before 4 pm	0		*5**	12	3.0	*174*
Short day (pm)	Starting 10 am or later Finishing 4 pm or later but before 6 pm	1		*16**	10	4.3	*146*
Late day	Starting 10 am or later Finishing 6 pm or later	4	7.7	*78*	4	5.2	*57*
Evenings	Starting 4 pm or later Finishing before midnight	0		*6**	13	3.3	*193*
Nights	Starting 4 pm or later Finishing midnight or later	2	9.5	*30*	3	9.5	*39*
All working women		**100**	**7.5**	*1,877†*	**100**	**4.4**	*1,477‡*

*Base too small to show means
†Includes 10 cases whose arrangements of hours were not known
‡Includes 20 cases whose arrangements of hours were not known

Table 4.8 Arrangement of hours of work of full and part time workers at different life cycle stages (excluding women whose arrangement of hours were not known)

Arrangement of hours	Full time						Part time					
	Women aged under 30 with no children	Women with youngest child aged:			Women with no child under 16, aged:		Women aged under 30 with no children	Women with youngest child aged:			Women with no child under 16, aged:	
		0–4	5–10	11–15	30–49	50 or over		0–4	5–10	11–15	30–49	50 or over
	%	%	%	%	%	%		%	%	%	%	%
Morning	1	1	3	3	1	1		17	29	29	31	33
Short day (am)	5	12	15	14	12	10		7	18	16	9	11
Standard day	82	53	63	69	73	72		7	11	13	15	14
Long day	7	11	11	7	8	8		2	2	5	8	5
Mid-day	0	3	–	–	–	1		10	16	9	13	11
Short day (pm)	1	3	1	1	0	1		8	7	11	12	12
Late day	3	6	4	3	5	5		5	3	5	3	5
Evenings	0	1	1	1	–	1		38	12	10	7	7
Nights	1	10	1	2	1	1		6	2	2	2	2
	100	100	100	100	100	100		100	100	100	100	100
Base	725	73	138	204	392	335	26*	196	407	268	205	355

*Base too small to show percentages

We would expect part time workers in particular to fit their hours of work around their domestic commitments, the major one being childcare. Thus, different arrangements are likely to suit women with children of different ages. We therefore compared the arrangements of hours of work for women at different life cycle stages, as defined in Chapter 2 (Table 4.8). There was little variation in the arrangement of hours worked by full time workers at different life stages, although childless women aged under thirty were more likely to be working a standard day than any other group. Night working was more common among those with children under 5 than among any other group. Most of the night workers were in nursing occupations.

Among the part time workers, the most striking feature was the high proportion of evening workers (38%) among those with a child under 5. Indeed 78% of part time evening workers were mothers of children under 16 (77% of all evening workers). Mothers of children under 5 were also more likely than others to be working at night. Overall 69% of part time night workers were mothers of dependent children (60% of all night workers). Once the youngest child is at school arrangements which appear to fit in with school hours become much more common, particularly mornings, short days (am) and mid-day working. The arrangement of hours of part time workers without children under 16 did not differ very much from those of women with older school age children, although of course fewer of the former were working part time as opposed to full time.

Childcare arrangements

As most mothers have the major responsibility for childcare they can only undertake paid work if they can fit it around these commitments or can make arrangements for the care of their children. The issue of 'childcare arrangements' is therefore very important in any study of women's employment (Hunt, 1968; Fonda and Moss, 1975). These arrangements may be formal or informal and of varying cost (Bone, 1977; Equal Opportunities Commission, 1978). Although the absence of suitable childcare facilities may prevent some of the women in our sample with dependent children from taking paid employment, in this chapter we discuss only the way in which those mothers who were currently working coped with childcare. Whether more women would take paid work or go back to work earlier if more childcare facilities were available is discussed in Chapter 7.

Apart from the small minority of mothers who work at

home and look after their own children at the same time or take their children to work with them, there are three main options open to mothers who go out to work which vary with the age of the children. They must either arrange their hours of work so that they are at work only while the children are at school; or they must arrange for someone else to look after the children; or the children can be left to care for themselves once they are old enough. Among the working women, 41% had children under 16 (23% of full time and 63% of part time workers). We asked all of them whether they had to make arrangements for anyone other than themselves to care for their children while they were at work and Table 4.9 shows the proportion of women who needed to do this by the age of their youngest child.

Overall half the working women with a child under 16 needed to make arrangements for their children's care; this was the case for 55% of full time and 47% of part time workers. A further 5% made arrangements only during school holidays. Most women (86%) with a youngest child under five needed to make arrangements (93% of full time and 83% of part time workers); those who did not were generally working at home, although a small minority of part timers took their children to work with them. Once the youngest child was at school the proportion of women who needed to make childcare arrangements fell considerably to 53% overall, though the differences between full and part timers became much larger: 70% of full time and 47% of part time women workers with a youngest child aged 5–10 made childcare arrangements. Full time workers who did not need to make arrangements were mainly teachers or others whose hours fitted in with school hours, whereas part time workers who did not make arrangements were generally only working during the school day. Far fewer women with a youngest child aged 11–15 made any arrangements for their care (29%) because children of this age were generally left to look after themselves. However a significant proportion of the part time workers with children of this age were only working during school hours anyway.

We asked women what type of arrangements they made for the care of their children while they worked. Table 4.10 shows the arrangements separately for those with pre-school and school age children since different options are available. It is clear that a high proportion of women use family based childcare. Overall, husbands were the most frequent source of care, with the child's grandmother being the second most frequent.

Table 4.9 Proportions of full and part time working women with children who make arrangements for their children's care while they work by age of youngest child

Age of youngest child	Full time		Part time		All women with children under 16	
	% who make arrangements for childcare	Base	% who make arrangements for childcare	Base	% who make arrangements for childcare	Base
Under 5	93%	73	83%	203	86%	276
5–10	70%	139	47%	414	53%	553
11–15	34%	223	23%	315	29%	538
All women with children under 16	55%	435	47%	932	50%	1,367

Table 4.10   Arrangements made by full and part time workers for care of pre-school and school age children during term time

Type of arrangements	Women who make arrangements for pre-school children*			Women who make arrangements for school children in term time*		
	Full time	Part time	All working women	Full time	Part time	All working women
	%	%	%	%	%	%
Husband	13	50	47	44	63	57
Child's older brother or sister	4	3	4	13	9	10
Child's grandmother	44	24	34	28	24	25
Other relative	4	10	9	12	9	10
Childminder (in her home)	23	11	16	7	4	6
Person employed in informant's home	6	2	4	4	2	3
Friend or neighbour on an exchange basis	3	3	3	10	8	9
Day nursery or creche run by employer	3	1	1	..	..	..
Day nursery or creche run by local authority and social services	3	2	2	..	..	..
Private day nursery or creche	3	1	1	..	..	..
State nursery school or class	4	3	4	..	..	..
Private nursery school	1	1	1	..	..	..
Playgroup	3	3	3	..	..	..
Other arrangements	–	–	–	4	3	3
Base	66	160	226	196	353	549

*Some women made arrangements for both pre-school and school children
Percentages do not add to 100 because some women made more than one arrangement

The use of formal institutional care such as crèches, day nurseries or nursery classes was relatively rare reflecting their limited availability.

The arrangements women made varied with the hours they worked. Women with pre-school children who worked full time most frequently arranged for their mother or mother-in-law to care for the children, but childminders were used by 23%, and even for full time workers institutional care was very much less frequently used than individual care. Among part time workers with pre-school children, husbands most frequently looked after the children (50%), as opposed to mothers or mothers-in-law (24%), and only 11% used childminders.

For women with school age children the need to make childcare arrangements was obviously related to their own hours and pattern of work in that those who worked only during school hours generally did not need to make such arrangements during term time. Table 4.11

shows the proportions of women who made arrangements for their children during term time and the form of these arrangements according to the organisation of their own hours of work. For full time workers there were too few women working other than a standard day for results to be shown and similarly for part time workers several categories contained too few women with school age children for percentages to be calculated.

As would be expected, among women working part time those working in the mornings or in the middle of the day were least likely to need to make arrangements for their children's care (27% and 20% respectively), while those with evening jobs were most likely to make arrangements (80%). In most groups of part time workers husbands were most likely to look after the children whilst the woman was at work, but in the case of women working short days in the mornings the respondent's mother or mother-in-law was the most common source of care.

Table 4.11   Arrangements made by full and part time workers for the care of school children during term time by arrangement of hours of work

Childcare arrangements	Full time		Part time									
	Standard day	All full time	Mornings	Short day (am)	Standard day (am)	Long day	Mid-day	Short day (pm)	Late day	Evenings	Nights	All part time
	%	%	%	%	%			%		%		%
Husband	37	44	57	35	52			45		90		63
Child's grandmother	31	28	22	47	23			28		13		24
Child's older brother or sister	12	13	7	6	13			14		8		8
Other relative	12	12	12	10	19			10		7		9
Childminder (in her home)	9	7	2	10	–			3		2		4
Person employed in informant's home	2	4	–	–	10			3		3		2
Friend or neighbour on an exchange basis	12	10	12	6	10			10		4		8
Other arrangements	4	4	7	2	3			3		1		3
Base	137	196	61	51	34	11*	21*	30	17*	107	19*	353†
Percentages of all women with school children who make arrangements in term time	55%	50%	27%	37%	40%		20%	41%	57%	80%		41%
Base	250	392	223	138	85	28*	105	74†	30†	134	24*	851‡

*Base too small to show percentages
†Includes 2 cases whose arrangement of hours were not known
‡Includes 10 cases whose arrangements of hours were not known
 Percentages do not add to 100 because some women made more than one arrangement

Table 4.12 Payment for arrangements made by full and part time workers for care of pre-school and school children in term time

	Women who make arrangements for pre-school children			Women who make arrangements for school children in term time		
	Full time	Part time	All working women	Full time	Part time	All working women
Proportion who pay for childcare arrangements	48%	22%	30%	16%	7%	10%
Base	*66*	*160*	*226*	*196*	*353*	*549*
Average amount spent per week by those who pay for arrangements	£12.00	£5.70	£8.70	£9.70		£8.70
Base	*32*	*35*	*68*	*31*	*25**	*55*

*Base too small to show mean

The costs of childcare

We asked women workers about the cost of any child-care arrangements they made. Not surprisingly in view of the amount of childcare provided by the immediate family only a small proportion of women who made any arrangements (16%) incurred any direct financial cost. However, this proportion varied considerably from 48% of those working full time with a child under 5 to 7% of those working part time with school age children, as Table 4.12 shows. Likewise, the amount paid also varied considerably though it averaged £8.70 a week for both pre-school and school age children. Women with pre-school children who worked full time paid the most (£12 per week on average) – twice as much as part time workers with similar aged children.

Quite apart from day to day arrangements for the care of children, women are more likely than men to be expected to look after children if they are ill or need to be taken to see a dentist, a doctor, or other specialist. We asked the mothers in our survey (and the fathers we interviewed: husbands and wives are compared in Chapter 8) whether they could get time off work easily in such circumstances. The majority of mothers (90%) said they could get time off easily, 8% said they would take time off anyway and only 2% said they would not take time off. Since, as we have seen, in many cases the woman's husband or mother was looking after the children while she worked presumably in these 2% of cases they could also cope if a child were ill.

Table 4.13 Arrangements made by full and part time employees with children for taking time off in case of child's illness etc: women who go out to work

Arrangements for time off	Full time	Part time	All working women who go out to work
	%	%	%
Does not take time off	3	2	2
Takes formal leave:	25	12	17
as part of holidays*	17	7	10
as part of own sick leave*	9	6	7
as compassionate leave*	3	1	2
Just takes time off:	69	83	78
gets paid	32	21	24
makes up lost time	9	28	22
loses pay	28	34	32
Doesn't know what would happen	3	3	3
	100	100	100
Base	*363*	*770*	*1,133*

*Percentages do not add to totals as some women made more than one arrangement

Although there was no difference between full and part time workers in how easy it was to get time off work, there was a difference in how this was likely to be arranged, as Table 4.13 shows. Full time workers were more likely than part time workers to be able to use annual holidays or sick leave for this purpose, or to get paid if they took time off. Of the part time workers, 34% said they would lose pay if they took time off, but 28% said they would be able to make up for any time taken off.[4] These differences are a reflection of the general differences in employment conditions between full and part time workers which will be described in the next chapter.

Women's attitudes to their hours of work

We have described the hours that women actually worked on a typical day. We also asked our respondents whether they could choose their starting and finishing times. As Table 4.14 shows, over three quarters said they had to start and finish at fixed times each day, 18% said they could choose or worked a flexitime system and the remaining 6% were either self-ployed or worked at home and could therefore presumably exercise some discretion over when they worked. Full time workers were slightly more likely than part time workers to work at fixed times.

Table 4.14 Whether full and part time working women can choose the time at which they start and finish work

	Full time	Part time	All working women
	%	%	%
Has fixed starting and finishing times	79	72	76
Can choose starting and finishing times	16	19	18
Self-employed or works at home	5	9	6
	100	100	100
Base	*1,877*	*1,477*	*3,354*

Women who worked at fixed times were asked whether they were happy with their present starting and finishing times or whether they would like to change them in any way, without changing the total number of hours worked. The majority (84%) said that they were happy with their starting and finishing times; the part time workers were somewhat more likely than the full time workers to be satisfied (89% compared with 80%). We also looked at women's attitudes to their starting and finishing times in relation to the arrangement of their hours of work (Table 4.15). For full time workers there were only four types of arrangements with sufficient number for comparisons to be made, but it was clear that those working short days were less likely than the others to want to change their starting and finishing times. Among the part timers, those who worked a 'long day', which in most cases was a split shift, and those who worked in the evenings were most likely to want to change their starting and finishing times.

Arrangement of hours of work	Full time		Part time	
	% who would like to change starting or finishing times	Base	% who would like to change starting or finishing times	Base
Morning		20*	4%	276
Short day (am)	10%	157	12%	135
Standard day	21%	1,103	8%	144
Long day	23%	87	28%	40
Mid-day		2*	5%	131
Short day (pm)		10*	14%	106
Late day	24%	60	15%	48
Evenings		5*	21%	147
Nights		29*	11%	38
All who start and finish at fixed times	**20%**	**1,479†**	**11%**	**1,066†**

*Base too small to show percentages
†Includes 7 cases whose arrangements of hours is not known (6 full time and 1 part time)

All women who were employees were also asked whether they wanted to change the number of hours they worked, but 74% said they were happy with their present number of hours. Table 4.16 shows that those who were not happy with their hours generally wanted to work fewer rather than more hours per week (20% compared with 6%), but there was a significant difference here between full and part time employees. Full time employees were less likely than part timers to say they were happy with their present number of hours, and almost all the full time employees who wanted to change their hours wanted to reduce them, whereas of the part time employees who wanted to change, almost twice as many wanted to work more hours as wanted to work fewer.

Table 4.16 Whether full and part time employees would prefer a job with a different number of hours per week

	Full time	Part time	All employees
	%	%	%
Would prefer a job with more hours per week	2	11	6
Would prefer a job with fewer hours per week	31	6	20
Happy with present number of hours	67	83	74
	100	**100**	**100**
Base	1,805	1,407	3,212

In general, most women seemed happy with their present hours of work, but this finding has to be considered in conjunction with the importance they attached to their hours of work compared with other aspects of their job. We discuss this in more detail in Chapter 6, but here we note that for part time workers 'convenient hours of work' was one of the most important things they looked for in a job. However, for full time workers this was much less important, probably because if a woman is able to work full time she is likely to be working a fairly standard day. For part timers, as we have shown, there is much more variation in the arrangement of hours of work and women frequently have to find a job to fit in with their domestic commitments. In some ways it is not surprising that such a high proportion of part time workers were happy with their hours of work; unless they can find a job with suitable hours they are unlikely to be able to work at all. This finding was consistent with the answers working women gave to a question on satisfaction with a number of different aspects of their jobs: when asked how satisfied they were with their hours of work, 91% of all working women said they were very or fairly satisfied (89% of full time and 94% of part time workers).

Summary and conclusions

We have described the hours women worked and the patterns of their working day in considerable detail. No such detailed study has been done for men partly because much less variety in their typical working day would be expected from them as predominantly full time workers and partly because there is generally less interest in how men combine paid work with their domestic commitments.

Over half of all working women in the survey worked more than 31 hours a week; most of these defined themselves as full time workers. The majority of part time workers worked more than 16 hours a week while only 10% of part time workers (4% of all women workers) worked under eight hours a week. Almost two thirds of all working women were covered by employment protection legislation meeting both the weekly hours and length of service criteria, 67% of full time and 60% of part time workers. Amongst those women not covered insufficient length of service, rather than insufficient hours, was the main reason.

The length of a working day is affected not only by the number of hours worked but also by whether overtime is worked and by travelling time. However, very few women in the sample worked overtime regularly and it is clear that while just over half reported they had no opportunity to do overtime, some women who did have the opportunity never took it. Generally journeys to work were short, the majority taking under fifteen minutes, with part time workers having shorter journeys than full timers on average. Consequently an average full time worker's working day including travelling time was 8.8 hours and a part time worker's working day was 5.2 hours.

Most women (77%) regularly worked the same days each week, usually with the same hours and the same starting and finishing times. Only 6% of women varied both the days they worked and their starting and finishing times. For most women, working a five day week was the norm; it was more common for women working part time to reduce the number of hours they worked a day, rather than the number of days they worked a week. There were however, a wide range of types of working day. Although the majority of women working full time worked a standard day, ie they started work before 10 am and finished between 4 and 6 pm, women working part time were particularly likely to work at different times. Working in the morning was the most frequent form of part time working. However, over half the part time workers had finished work before 4 pm, so enabling those with school age children to be home when their children returned from school. As this shows, there is a clear association between the time of day when women work and the ages of their children. This was particularly noticeable for mothers of a child under five, 38% of whom worked in the evenings and 6% at night.

Women are plainly more likely to have to make arrangements for their child to be looked after the younger the child and the more hours they work a week. In most cases care was family based; fathers looked after their children most frequently, while grandmothers were the second most frequent source of childcare overall, and were particularly likely to look after the child when mothers of pre-school children worked full time. Generally mothers did not pay for child care; only 16% incurred any direct cost and this averaged £8.70 a week for mothers of both pre-school and school aged children.

It is clear that for many women working part time, the number of hours and time of day they work is highly interrelated with childcare needs and the availability of alternative care. It is not surprising then, that having found a job which fitted their domestic commitments, a higher proportion of part time women workers (83%) did not want to change their current number of hours compared with 67% of full time workers. More part timers (94%) were very or fairly satisfied with their hours compared with full time workers (89%). Hours of work are a more crucial issue for women working part time than for women working full time and, as we show in subsequent chapters, affect part timers' attitudes to other aspects of their job more generally and indeed, often their choice of occupation.

Notes

[1] The 1978 Employment Protection (Consolidation) Act drew together the bulk of the existing law on individual employee rights. The Employment Act 1980 amended several of these rights and added new rights including one covering time off for ante natal care.

[2] Our use of a two year cut-off undercounts those women who would be entitled to rights where the qualifying period is shorter.

[3] Legislative restrictions on the hours of employment of women are contained in the Hours of Employment (Conventions) Act 1936, the Mines and Quarries Act 1984 and the Factories Act 1961. These provisions do not apply to men. The Health and Safety Executive has the power to grant employers exemption, for up to one year at a time from the first and last of these Acts.

[4] Table 5.27 of the 1980 General Household Survey shows that whilst men and women's absence from work for all reasons are the same, women are more likely than men to be absent from work for their own illness/injury and for 'personal and other reasons' (OPCS 1982a).

Chapter 5 The pay and conditions of employment of working women

Introduction

Chapter 3 showed that women workers tend to be concentrated in particular occupations and industries, and that full and part time workers are differently distributed among occupational groups and industrial groups. It also showed that, at the level of the workplace, the majority of women in the sample worked in segregated jobs. The last chapter showed that part time workers in particular arrange their hours of work to suit their domestic arrangements which may constrain the type of work available to them. In this chapter we look at the pay, working conditions, training and promotion prospects and union membership of working women. We describe differences between women in different occupations in full and part time work, and according to whether women are segregated, that is, are in 'women only' jobs at their workplace. Throughout, we compare the position of full time and part time workers overall. We also compare part time workers who work less than 16 hours a week with those part timers who work more hours to identify to what extent their pay and conditions of employment differ. Where relevant we draw upon Joshi's analysis of the earnings data from this survey (Joshi, 1984).

Earnings

Most discussions of pay are based on weekly or monthly earnings data. However comparisons between men and women's gross earnings are not very informative because of the extensive variation in the number of hours women work. Many women, but a very small minority of men, work part time, and even full time women workers generally work fewer hours a week than full time men workers. As we have shown in Chapter 4 this is partly because women working full time are likely to be in occupations with a relatively short working week and partly because they are less likely to work overtime. Accordingly, while we begin by looking briefly at women's actual weekly earnings, our main measure for comparison will be hourly earnings so that we control for variations in hours worked while examining some of the factors associated with variations in women's pay.

We asked women how much they usually earned each week or month before and after compulsory deductions. Table 5.1 shows the gross weekly earnings of both full and part time workers. Ten per cent of working women either did not know or declined to give their gross earnings and so the distributions are based on those who gave this information. This assumes that the answers of those who did not give the information would be distributed in the same way as the answers of

Table 5.1 Gross and net weekly earnings of full and part time workers who gave information about earnings

Weekly earnings	Full time		Part time		All who gave earnings information	
	Gross	Net	Gross	Net	Gross	Net
	%	%	%	%	%	%
£1–£10	0	0	12	12	6	6
£11–£20	1	1	24	26	11	12
£21–£40	8	24	45	54	24	37
£41–£60	32	51	14	7	24	31
£61–£80	31	17	4	1	19	10
£81–£100	15	5	1	0	9	3
£101–£120	7	1	0	0	4	1
Over £120	6	1	0	0	3	0
	100	100	100	100	100	100
Average weekly earnings	£71	£52	£29	£25	£52	£40
Base	1,677	1,719	1,337	1,368	3,014	3,087

those who did. On average, full time workers earned over twice as much as part time workers: £71 compared with £29. According to the 1980 New Earnings Survey (NES) the average earnings of full time women employees of 18 and over was £78.80 at the time of our survey (Department of Employment, 1980). Our results, however, include 16 and 17 year olds who tend to have lower earnings than adult workers. When we excluded these the figure for full time workers rose to £73. The NES figure for men was considerably higher, the average weekly earnings of full time men aged 21 and over being £124.50 in April 1980 (ibid). Our results show that only 6% of full time working women were earning over £120 a week and 41% had weekly earnings of £60 or less. Over one third (36%) of part time workers earned £20 or less and nearly all (95%) earned £60 or less per week.

Table 5.1 also shows the net earnings of those full and part time workers who gave this information. There is less difference between gross and net earnings among part than full time workers because fewer part time workers pay income tax or national insurance. Overall 77% of working women said they paid income tax, but 96% of full time workers did so compared with only 53% of part time workers, reflecting of course the different proportions earning over the tax threshold. Similarly 80% of all working women paid national insurance contributions, 96% of full time and 60% of part time workers. Over a third of those who paid national insurance contributions (ie 29% of all working women) paid the special reduced rate for married women and widows.

Before discussing hourly earnings we look briefly at the way in which pay was calculated for women. As Table

5.2 shows, only a minority of working women (23%) were actually paid by the hour; the majority (71%) said they were paid the same amount each week or month while a very small group (5%) were paid on a piecework or commission basis. However, part time workers were very much more likely than full time workers to be hourly paid. This difference is a reflection of the different types of jobs done by full and part time workers; women working in the higher level jobs were more likely to be paid a regular weekly or monthly amount whilst those in lower level jobs, which had higher proportions of part time workers, were more likely to be hourly paid. Women paid on a piecework or commission basis tended to be in skilled or semi-skilled factory occupations and were therefore more likely to be paid on a piecework than on a commission basis in practice.

Table 5.2 Basis on which full and part time women employees were paid

Basis of payment	Full time	Part time	All employees
	%	%	%
Same amount per week/month	81	59	71
By the hour	12	36	23
Piecework or commission basis	6	4	5
Other	1	1	1
	100	**100**	**100**
Base	*1,805*	*1,407*	*3,212*

Table 5.3 Hourly earnings of full and part time working women: women who gave information about gross earnings and hours of work

Hourly earnings	Full time	Part time	All working women
	%	%	%
Under £1.00	6	7	6
£1.00–£1.24	8	17	12
£1.25–£1.49	16	30	22
£1.50–£1.74	19	21	20
£1.75–£1.99	16	9	13
£2.00–£2.24	9	6	8
£2.25–£2.49	7	3	6
£2.50–£2.99	8	2	5
£3.00 or more	11	5	8
	100	**100**	**100**
Average earnings	£1.90	£1.60	£1.80
Base	*1,630*	*1,279*	*2,909*

To obtain hourly earnings for all women we divided usual gross weekly earnings by the usual number of hours worked excluding overtime and meal breaks. Table 5.3 shows the resulting distribution of hourly earnings for full and part time workers for whom the relevant information about earnings and hours was available. When differences in hours worked are taken into account, part time workers were still paid on average less than full time workers (£1.60 compared with £1.90 an hour). Part time workers working under 16 hours a week had slightly higher hourly earnings (£1.80) than those working 16 hours or more (£1.60) but the range of earnings in the former group was very wide. Over half of all part time workers (54%) were earning less than £1.50 an hour compared with 30% of the full timers; over twice as many full time as part time workers earned £2.00 an hour or more.

Clearly some of the differences between the earnings of full and part time workers will be due to differences in the kind of work they do, and so we compare hourly earnings of full and part time workers for different occupational groups (Table 5.4). Although these comparisons allow for the different proportions in each occupational group as a whole, it should be remembered that an occupational group contains a variety of occupations and different levels of work and therefore full and part time workers within a group are not necessarily doing the same type of work at the same level and may well be expected to have different pay. In so far as part time workers tend to be concentrated among the lower levels in any particular occupation we would expect their hourly pay to be lower.

In general hourly earnings decrease through the occupational groups. The professional groups and other intermediate non-manual workers had the highest earnings, whilst sales workers not only earned considerably less per hour than their fellow non-manual workers, but were among the least well paid of all women workers, earning the same as women in semi-skilled domestic jobs who were the lowest paid group of manual workers.[1] As Table 5.4 shows, there was surprisingly little difference in the hourly earnings of full and part

Table 5.4 Average hourly earnings of full and part time working women by occupational group: women who gave information about gross earnings and hours of work

Occupational group	Full time		Part time		All working women	
	Average hourly earnings	Base	Average hourly earnings	Base	Average hourly earnings	Base
Professional		*17**		*5**		*22**
Teaching	£3.50	*138*	£3.60	*38*	£3.50	*176*
Nursing, medical and social	£2.10	*103*	£2.20	*80*	£2.10	*183*
Other intermediate non-manual	£2.20	*114*	£1.60	*23*	£2.10	*137*
Clerical	£1.90	*660*	£2.00	*248*	£1.90	*908*
Sales	£1.30	*102*	£1.40	*162*	£1.40	*264*
All non-manual	**£2.10**	*1,134*	**£1.90**	*556*	**£2.00**	*1,690*
Skilled	£1.70	*119*	£1.50	*83*	£1.60	*202*
Semi-skilled factory	£1.60	*226*	£1.50	*92*	£1.60	*318*
Semi-skilled domestic	£1.30	*62*	£1.40	*261*	£1.40	*323*
Other semi-skilled	£1.50	*50*	£1.60	*53*	£1.60	*103*
Unskilled	£1.60	*39*	£1.40	*233*	£1.40	*272*
All manual	**£1.60**	*496*	**£1.40**	*722*	**£1.50**	*1,218*
All working women	**£1.90**	*1,630*	**£1.60**	*1,279*	**£1.80**	*2,909*

*Base too small to show mean

Table 5.5 Average hourly earnings of full and part time working women by length of service with present employer: women who gave information about gross earnings and hours of work

Length of service	Full time		Part time		All working women	
	Average hourly earnings	Base	Average hourly earnings	Base	Average hourly earnings	Base
Less than 6 months	£1.60	170	£1.50	156	£1.50	326
6 months, but less than 1 year	£1.70	185	£1.60	132	£1.60	317
1 year, but less than 2 years	£1.70	207	£1.50	180	£1.60	387
2 years, but less than 5 years	£1.90	436	£1.70	341	£1.80	777
5 years, but less than 10 years	£2.20	345	£1.70	287	£2.00	632
10 years or more	£2.20	287	£1.80	183	£2.00	470
All working women	**£1.90**	1,630	**£1.60**	1,279	**£1.80**	2,909

time workers within an occupational group apart from women in the category of other intermediate non-manual occupations. Thus the overall difference in hourly earnings arose because part time workers were concentrated in occupations with low earnings rather than being paid worse than full timers within an occupational group. Thus our hypothesis that there would be a significant difference within an occupational group was not substantiated.

In some occupations hourly rates of pay depend not only on the job itself but on length of service. Non-manual jobs are more likely than manual jobs to have an incremental salary scale, but even in jobs without this, rates of pay may go up with length of service as people progress to different types of work or take on more responsibility. Table 5.5 shows the relationship between average hourly earnings and length of service. Overall there was an increase in earnings with length of service, but it is noticeable that the increase was considerably more marked for full time than part time workers. Among women with less than six months service part time workers earned 94% of the full time rate, but this declined markedly to 78% among women with five years but less than ten years service.

These differences between full and part time workers overall are likely to be due at least in part to the smaller proportion of part time workers in occupations where some kind of salary progression would be expected. Our sample is not large enough to compare the varia-tion of hourly earnings with length of service for full and part timers in each occupational category, but we can look at all working women in a category and relate the results to the proportion of part timers known to be in that category. This has been done in Table 5.6. The occupational groups with the highest proportion of part time workers – unskilled, semi-skilled domestic, sales – showed little evidence of an increase in hourly pay with length of service, in contrast to teaching, clerical occupations and semi-skilled factory work in which pay increased with length of service. Joshi's analysis of the hourly earnings data from this survey suggests than on average, when allowance for differences between occupations is made, real hourly pay is increased by 2½% per year of experience in any employment and additionally by ½% per year of service with the same employer. The analysis did not allow for these effects of experience and/or seniority to vary between women currently working full and part time, nor between occupations. It did establish, however, that part time employment in the past enhances current pay almost as much as the same number of full time years would have done (Joshi, 1984).

We have already mentioned that women earn significantly less than men overall and have lower average hourly earnings. Many reasons are advanced to explain this in several recent studies (see for example Webb, 1982 and Craig et al 1982b). It is pointed out that men and women have different qualifications and training, a different occupational distribution, length of service,

Table 5.6 Average hourly earnings by length of service with present employer and occupational group: women who gave information about gross earnings and hours of work

Occupational group	Length of service with present employer								All working women		Proportion of women working part time in each occupation	Base
	Less than 2 years		2 years but less than 5 years		5 years but less than 10 years		10 years or more					
	Average hourly earnings	Base	Average hourly earnings	Base	Average hourly earnings	Base	Average hourly earnings	Base	Average hourly earnings	Base		
Professional		4*		9*		8*		1*		2*		26*
Teaching	£3.30	31	£3.30	52	£3.60	51	£3.80	42	£3.50	176	22%	196
Nursing, medical and social	£1.90	51	£2.00	45	£2.30	50	£2.30	37	£2.10	183	43%	223
Other intermediate non-manual	£2.10	33	£1.90	35	£2.30	30	£2.20	39	£2.30	137	19%	204
Clerical	£1.70	334	£1.90	236	£2.00	209	£2.20	129	£1.90	908	29%	1,028
Sales	£1.30	125	£1.40	65	£1.30	48		26*	£1.40	264	60%	290
Skilled manual	£1.40	65	£1.60	52	£1.80	47	£1.70	38	£1.60	202	39%	239
Semi-skilled factory	£1.40	115	£1.60	84	£1.70	54	£1.80	65	£1.60	318	30%	352
Semi-skilled domestic	£1.30	137	£1.40	83	£1.40	62	£1.50	41	£1.40	323	80%	371
Other semi-skilled	£1.50	38		26*		25*		14*	£1.60	103	53%	129
Unskilled	£1.40	97	£1.50	89	£1.40	48	£1.40	38	£1.40	272	85%	295
All working women	**£1.60**	1,030	**£1.80**	777	**£2.00**	632	**£2.10**	470	**£1.40**	2,909	**44%**	3,354

*Base too small to show means or percentages

and labour market experience, all of which will affect their earnings and account for some or most of the variation in earnings. We cannot of course explore this issue in this study, as we have no comparable data for men. However Joshi has looked at the effect of many of these factors, particularly the effect of family formation, on women's lifetime earnings and shows that the low pay of women is partly attributable to the interruptions in their work history and their return to part time work after childbearing (Joshi, 1984).

One factor of considerable interest in attempts to explore variations in hourly earnings between men and women is whether women are working with men doing similar work as themselves. For those that are we might expect their pay to be higher because men's pay in general is higher and under the Equal Pay Act in operation in 1980 men and women doing the same or broadly similar work, or work rated as equivalent on a job evaluation scheme, at a given establishment, must be paid the same rates. We therefore looked at the relationship between hourly pay and our measure of occupational segregation described in Chapter 3, that is whether informants were working in 'women only' jobs or whether men also did the same kind of work at their place of work. We needed to take account of the variation in the proportion of women in 'women only' jobs in different occupations but our sample was not large enough to look at each occupation separately and so we divided the occupational groups into non-manual and manual categories. Table 5.7 shows the average hourly earnings in the resulting groups, separately for full and part time workers.

These results show that among both full and part time workers, women working in 'women only' jobs earned less per hour on average than those working with men as well as women. The greater proportion of women in 'women only' jobs and their lower average earnings in part explains the lower earnings of part time compared with full time workers. Even so, part time workers in non-manual occupations earned less per hour than full timers. There was no difference, however, for women in part time manual occupations between those in 'women only' jobs compared with those working with men and women. Thus, overall, our measure of occupational segregation explained more variation in average rates of pay than whether women worked full or part time.

Conditions of employment
The range of facilities and provisions employees have in their job in the form of 'fringe benefits' has increased over the last few years. We concentrated on three of these, paid holidays, sick pay and occupational pensions in order to see whether any groups of women did not have access to what are increasingly taken to be the 'basic' provisions; in particular we were interested in whether part time workers were significantly disadvantaged in this respect.

Paid holidays
Some paid holiday is an almost universal condition of employment once an employee has been with an employer for a period of time. Of all the women employees in our sample 88% received paid holidays, though there was a significant difference between full and part time employees: 96% of full time, but only 77% of part time employees had some paid holiday (62% of those working less than 16 hours a week). Moreover, part time employees had proportionately shorter paid holidays than full time employees. From Table 5.8, which shows the number of working weeks holiday full and part time employees were entitled to, it can be seen that 78% of full time employees had more than three working weeks paid holiday compared with 46% of part time employees.

All those eligible for paid holidays were asked whether they had to take their holidays at specific times or whether they had some choice about when they could take them. Overall 78% of those with paid holidays said they had some choice, and there was little difference between full and part time women workers in this respect. Teachers were among those who said, in effect, they had no choice because of the educational year.

Table 5.7 Average hourly earnings for full and part time workers by occupation, and whether they work with men and women or women only at their place of work: women who work with others and who gave information about gross earnings and hours of work

Occupation	Works with men and women		Works with women only		All who work with others	
	Average hourly earnings	Base	Average hourly earnings	Base	Average hourly earnings	Base
Full time						
Non-manual	£2.30	499	£1.90	582	£2.10	1,081
Manual	£1.80	143	£1.50	333	£1.60	476
All who work full time	**£2.20**	642	**£1.80**	915	**£2.00**	1,557
Part time						
Non-manual	£2.10	164	£1.70	324	£1.90	488
Manual	£1.50	172	£1.40	474	£1.50	646
All who work part time	**£1.80**	336	**£1.60**	799	**£1.60**	1,135
All who work with others						
Non-manual	£2.30	663	£1.90	906	£2.00	1,569
Manual	£1.60	315	£1.50	807	£1.50	1,122
All who work with others	**£2.10**	978	**£1.70**	1,714	**£1.80**	2,692

Table 5.8 Number of working weeks paid holiday received by full and part time employees

Number of working weeks paid holiday	Full time	Part time	All employees
	%	%	%
1 week or less	0	2	1
More than 1 week, up to 2 weeks	4	9	6
More than 2 weeks, up to 3 weeks	12	16	14
More than 3 weeks, up to 4 weeks	40	23	33
More than 4 weeks, up to 5 weeks	23	12	18
More than 5 weeks	15	11	13
Don't know how much holiday	2	4	3
Total receiving paid holiday	**96**	**77**	**88**
No paid holiday	3	19	10
Don't know whether will get paid holiday	1	4	2
	100	100	100
Base	*1,805*	*1,407*	*3,212*

Sick pay

While 67% of all women employees said they would receive sick pay from their employers, there were again marked differences between full and part time employees in this respect: 80% of full time employees said they would receive sick pay compared with 51% of part timers (34% of those working less than 16 hours a week). However 10% of employees did not know whether they would receive sick pay or not: 7% of full time and 14% of part time employees (Table 5.9).

Table 5.10 shows the reasons women gave for not being entitled to sick pay from their employer. Full time employees were more likely to say this was because their employer did not have a sick pay scheme, although some were not eligible because they had not worked for their employer long enough or their particular job was not eligible. By far the most common reason given by part time employees was that they were not eligible for sick pay because they worked part time.

Table 5.9 Whether full and part time employees are entitled to receive sick pay from their employer

Whether entitled to receive sick pay from employer	Full time	Part time	All employees
	%	%	%
Entitled to sick pay from employer	80	51	67
Not entitled to sick pay from employer	13	35	23
Doesn't know whether entitled to sick pay	7	14	10
	100	100	100
Base	*1,805*	*1,407*	*3,212*

Table 5.10 Reasons given by full and part time workers for not being entitled to receive sick pay from their employer

Reasons for not being entitled to receive sick pay	Full time	Part time	All employees who do not receive sick pay
	%	%	%
Working part time	..	46	32
No sick pay scheme	36	18	24
Informant's type of job not eligible	13	16	15
Paid only for work done	5	14	11
Not worked for employer long enough	17	6	9
Doing temporary work	13	6	8
Don't know why doesn't receive sick pay	16	8	11
Base	*228*	*493*	*721*

Percentages do not add to 100 because some informants gave more than one reason

Table 5.11 Proportions of full and part time employees who are entitled to receive sick pay from their employer by occupational group

Occupational group	Full time		Part time		All employees	
	% entitled to sick pay	*Base*	% entitled to sick pay	*Base*	% entitled to sick pay	*Base*
Professional		*17**		*4**		*21**
Teaching	91%	*150*	42%	*40*	80%	*190*
Nursing, medical and social	93%	*127*	70%	*94*	83%	*221*
Other intermediate non-manual	92%	*122*		*19**	87%	*141*
Clerical	91%	*719*	68%	*291*	84%	*1,010*
Sales	67%	*112*	38%	*173*	49%	*285*
All non-manual	**89%**	*1,247*	**58%**	*621*	**79%**	*1,868*
Skilled	63%	*137*	50%	*82*	58%	*219*
Semi-skilled factory	50%	*248*	48%	*104*	49%	*352*
Semi-skilled domestic	68%	*73*	46%	*289*	50%	*362*
Other semi-skilled	71%	*57*	41%	*62*	56%	*119*
Unskilled	72%	*43*	49%	*248*	52%	*291*
All manual	**59%**	*558*	**47%**	*785*	**52%**	*1,343*
All employees	**80%**	*1,805*	**51%**	*1,407*	**67%**	*3,212*

*Base too small to show percentages

Table 5.12 Proportions of full and part time employees who are entitled to sick pay by length of service with present employer

Length of service with present employer	Full time		Part time		All employees	
	% entitled to sick pay	*Base*	% entitled to sick pay	*Base*	% entitled to sick pay	*Base*
Less than 6 months	50%	*188*	19%	*172*	35%	*360*
6 months, but less than 1 year	71%	*196*	33%	*142*	55%	*338*
1 year, but less than 2 years	76%	*218*	45%	*192*	62%	*410*
2 years, but less than 5 years	84%	*467*	53%	*378*	70%	*845*
5 years, but less than 10 years	88%	*389*	64%	*325*	77%	*714*
10 years or more	87%	*347*	73%	*198*	82%	*545*
All employees	**80%**	*1,805*	**51%**	*1,407*	**67%**	*3,212*

Table 5.13 Proportions of full and part time employees who are entitled to receive sick pay from their employer by occupation, and whether they work with men and women or women only at their place of work

Occupation	Works with men and women		Works with women only		All who work with others	
	% entitled to sick pay	Base	% entitled to sick pay	Base	% entitled to sick pay	Base
Full time						
Non-manual	92%	556	86%	638	89%	1,194
Manual	69%	169	54%	369	59%	538
All who work full time	**87%**	725	**74%**	1.007	**80%**	1,732
Part time						
Non-manual	53%	186	57%	364	56%	550
Manual	46%	186	48%	519	48%	705
All who work part time	**50%**	372	**52%**	884	**51%**	1,256
All who work with others						
Non-manual	83%	742	76%	1,002	79%	1,744
Manual	57%	355	51%	888	53%	1,243
All who work with others	**74%**	1,097	**64%**	1,891	**68%**	3,988

Table 5.11 shows that the differences in proportions of full and part time employees entitled to sick pay was apparent in all occupational groups with the exception of semi-skilled factory workers. Overall 89% of full time employees in non-manual occupations were entitled to sick pay compared with 59% in manual occupations. The corresponding proportions for part time employees in non-manual and manual occupations were 58% and 47%. Thus full time non-manual workers were much more likely to get sick pay than the other groups. In all non-manual occupations, except sales, at least 90% of full time employees were entitled to sick pay, as were around two thirds of part time employees in clerical, nursing, medical and social occupations. The proportion of women who could receive sick pay was much lower among the manual and sales occupations; among full time workers, women in semi-skilled factory occupations were particularly disadvantaged whereas sales and other semi-skilled workers were least likely among the part time workers to get sick pay.

We also looked at how entitlement to sick pay varied with length of service (Table 5.12). The proportion of both full and part time employees who could receive sick pay increased with length of service, but for full time employees there was a sharp rise after 6 months service and thereafter the rise was more gradual, whereas for part time workers there was a general gradual increase with length of service. Overall significantly fewer part time than full time employees with comparable lengths of service could receive sick pay.

We carried out the same sort of analysis as we had done for hourly earnings to find out whether some of the differences in the proportions of women employees who were entitled to sick pay between full and part time employees and non-manual and manual occupational groups were related to whether or not women were working in 'women only' jobs, where working conditions might be expected to be poorer. Table 5.13 shows that overall full time workers were very much more likely to receive sick pay from their employer than part time employees and non-manual workers were more likely to receive sick pay than manual workers. Occupational segregation however seemed to be a more important factor for full than part time workers

but this variable explained less variation than either occupational level or whether women worked full or part time.

Occupational pensions

All women employees in the survey were asked whether their employer ran an occupational pension scheme (apart from the state pension scheme) and if so whether they belonged to it (Table 5.14). Although over half the women worked for an employer who ran a

Table 5.14 Proportions of full and part time employees whose employer has a pension scheme and who belong to a scheme

Whether informant belongs to pension scheme	Full time	Part time	All employees
	%	%	%
Belongs to pension scheme	53	9	34
Employer has pension scheme but informant does not belong	18	34	24
All whose employer has a pension scheme	**71**	**43**	**58**
Employer does not have a pension scheme	22	39	30
Don't know whether employer has a pension scheme	7	18	12
	100	**100**	**100**
Base	1,805	1,407	3,212

Table 5.15 Reasons given by full and part time employees for not belonging to their employer's pension scheme

Reason for not belonging to employer's pension scheme	Full time	Part time	All employees who do not belong to their employer's pension scheme
	%	%	%
Working part time	..	67	40
Not worked for employer long enough	23	6	13
Too young	25	0	10
Informant's type of job not eligible	6	9	8
Doing temporary work	6	4	5
Too old	4	3	4
Did not want to join pension scheme	18	7	12
Don't know why doesn't belong/never thought about it	12	7	9
Base	318	460	778

Percentages do not add to 100 because some informants gave more than one reason

pension scheme, only 34% belonged to it. There were major differences between full and part time employees both in the proportion who worked for an employer who ran a scheme and in the proportion belonging to such a scheme. Amongst those whose employer ran a pension scheme, three quarters of full time employees belonged to it compared with 21% of part time employees (16% of part timers working less than 16 hours). Thus overall only 9% of part time employees belonged to an employer's pension scheme compared with 53% of full timers.

We looked at the reasons women gave for not belonging to their employer's pension scheme to see whether they were unwilling to join the scheme or were not eligible to do so. Table 5.15 shows overwhelmingly that the majority of these women, particularly the part timers said they were not eligible for the scheme, either because they worked part time, or on the grounds of age or length of service. Only 12% overall said they did not want to join the scheme and 9% had not really thought about joining.

The proportion of women whose employer ran a pension scheme varied between different occupational groups, as did the proportion of women belonging to a pension scheme (Table 5.16). In general women in the higher level occupations were more likely both to work for an employer with a scheme and to have joined it, and in almost all occupations part time workers were at

a disadvantage in these respects compared with full time workers.

Lack of service was mentioned particularly by full time workers as a reason for not belonging to their employer's pension scheme. Table 5.17 shows, for those women whose employer ran a scheme, the proportions belonging to the scheme according to their length of service. This factor appeared to be more important for full time than part time workers in determining whether they belonged to the scheme; significant increases in the proportion of full time employees belonging to the scheme occurred after one, two and five years of service. Among part time workers the only significant increase came after two years service, and they were significantly less likely to be members of a scheme than full time workers with comparable lengths of service.

We carried out a similar analysis to that done for hourly earnings and sick pay to see to what extent the likelihood of women belonging to a pension scheme was affected by whether they worked in 'women only' jobs or not. Table 5.18 shows that whether women worked full or part time was by far the most important factor determining whether or not they belonged to an employer's pension scheme, although women in non-manual occupations were more likely to belong to a pension scheme than those in manual occupations; non-manual full time workers were particularly likely to belong to a pension scheme. However, occupational seg-

Table 5.16 Proportions of full and part time employees whose employer has a pension scheme and who belong to a scheme by occupational group

Occupational group	Full time			Part time			All employees		
	% whose employer has scheme	% who belong to scheme	Base	% whose employer has scheme	% who belong to scheme	Base	% whose employer has scheme	% who belong to scheme	Base
Professional			*17**			*4**			*21**
Teaching	96%	91%	150	92%	35%	40	95%	79%	190
Nursing, medical and social	86%	79%	127	73%	21%	94	80%	54%	221
Other intermediate non-manual	72%	52%	122			*19**	68%	45%	141
Clerical	80%	59%	719	52%	13%	291	72%	46%	1,010
Sales	45%	20%	112	27%	6%	173	34%	12%	285
All non-manual	**79%**	**61%**	1,247	**50%**	**13%**	621	**69%**	**45%**	1,868
Skilled	57%	34%	137	39%	11%	82	50%	25%	219
Semi-skilled factory	51%	30%	248	38%	8%	104	47%	24%	352
Semi-skilled domestic	47%	34%	73	43%	7%	289	44%	12%	362
Other semi-skilled	55%	44%	57	30%	10%	62	42%	26%	119
Unskilled	65%	37%	43	32%	3%	248	36%	8%	291
All manual	**54%**	**34%**	558	**37%**	**6%**	785	**44%**	**18%**	1,343
All employees	**71%**	**53%**	1,805	**43%**	**9%**	1,407	**58%**	**34%**	3,212

*Base too small to show percentages

Table 5.17 Proportions of full and part time employees working for an employer who runs a pension scheme who belong to the scheme by length of service with employer

Length of service with employer	Full time		Part time		All employees	
	% who belong to employer's pension scheme	Base	% who belong to employer's pension scheme	Base	% who belong to employer's pension scheme	Base
Less than 6 months	42%	92	14%	44	33%	136
6 months, but less than 1 year	49%	121	14%	43	40%	164
1 year, but less than 2 years	64%	142	15%	68	48%	210
2 years, but less than 5 years	76%	319	25%	150	59%	469
5 years, but less than 10 years	85%	322	26%	170	65%	492
10 years or more	86%	282	23%	128	66%	410
All employees whose employer runs a pension scheme	**74%**	1,278	**22%**	603	**57%**	1,881

Table 5.18 Proportions of full and part time employees who belong to an employer's pension scheme by occupation, and whether they work with men and women or women only at their place of work

Occupation	Works with men and women		Works with women only		All who work with others	
	% who belong to a pension scheme	Base	% who belong to a pension scheme	Base	%who belong to a pension scheme	Base
Full time						
Non-manual	70%	556	53%	638	61%	1,194
Manual	41%	169	31%	369	34%	538
All who work full time	**64%**	725	**45%**	1,007	**53%**	1,732
Part time						
Non-manual	17%	186	13%	364	14%	550
Manual	11%	186	5%	519	7%	705
All who work part time	**14%**	372	**8%**	884	**10%**	1,256
All who work with others						
Non-manual	57%	742	38%	1,002	46%	1,744
Manual	26%	355	16%	888	19%	1,243
All who work with others	**47%**	1,097	**28%**	1,891	**35%**	2,988

regation was also of some importance in that both within occupational categories and among both full and part time workers women working in 'women only' jobs were less likely than those working with men to belong to a pension scheme. In general, there was a smaller difference between women in 'women only' jobs and those working with men than between full time compared with part time workers.

Training and promotion

So far our discussion about women's jobs has focussed chiefly on the extrinsic rewards they offer, the pay and benefits. Jobs are also characterised by the skill and training levels they require and the opportunities they provide for further training and promotion. We examine these aspects in this section and again link the results to the degree of occupational segregation in the workplace in which are respondents were employed.

Training for the current job

To cover the topic of training in any detail would require a survey in its own right; indeed the National Training Survey conducted in 1975 was designed to do just this.[2] In this survey, training is only one of many topics covered and it was therefore not possible to collect full training histories although it was possible to collect some information. We asked women questions about the training their current employer provided for their present job, but no information was collected to assess to what extent women brought relevant skills, qualifications or experience to the job when they started it or to what extent they required training. Jobs differ in the amount of training they require and in the ways these training needs are generally met. For example, in jobs such as teaching or secretarial work initial training is normally acquired at educational institutions before starting the job. In contrast, a much greater amount of initial training is provided in the course of the work in occupations such as nursing, hairdressing and most factory work, although sometimes formal courses are interspersed with formal or informal on-the-job training. The amount of training provided to any particular individual will take account of any previous experience in similar work.

In the interview we distinguished between formal and informal training. By formal training we meant courses and formal on-the-job training, and by informal training we meant being shown what to do, either by a supervisor or by other employees. Table 5.19 shows that over half the women employees in the survey (58%) had received some form of training from their present employer for their present job, although only 39% had received formal training. Full time employees were significantly more likely than part time employees both to have received training and to have received formal training; again, part time employees working under 16 hours per week were less well provided for in these respects than those working longer hours. Formal on-the-job training was the most common type of training, particularly for full time employees; full time employees were very much more likely than part time employees to have attended a training course. There was little difference between full and part timers in the proportion receiving informal training. We asked women who had had formal training how long it had lasted; for 53% it had lasted less than one month and for 25% less than one week. Part time employees had shorter formal training than full timers.

Table 5.19 Proportions of full and part time employees who received different types of formal and informal training from their employer for their present job

Training for present job	Full time	Part time	All employees
	%	%	%
Formal course	24	8	17
Formal on-the-job training	30	18	25
Total who had formal training	**49**	**26**	**39**
Shown by supervisor	17	15	16
Shown by other employees	13	10	12
Total who had informal training	**29**	**25**	**28**
Total who had training	**67**	**46**	**58**
No training	33	54	42
Base	1,805	1,407	3,212

Percentages do not add to totals because some informants had more than one type of training

We looked briefly at the proportions of women in different occupational groups who received any training from their employer for their present job, but as mentioned above, the results are confounded by differing levels of training or qualifications required for starting different occupations. Levels of training were highest in nursing and semi-skilled factory occupations and lowest among unskilled workers and teachers. We show the reasons given by women for not having received training in Table 5.20. Similar proportions said that they had done the same type of work before they started their present job or had learnt the job as they went along (some gave both reasons) and 8% said they were trained before they started working. Part time workers were more likely than full time workers to say they learnt the job as they went along, which can probably be taken as indicating that they were doing jobs which required little or no training.

Table 5.20 Reasons given by full and part time employees for receiving no training from present employer for present job

Reasons for receiving no training	Full time	Part time	Employees with no training
	%	%	%
Had done that kind of work before	61	56	58
Learnt the job as she went along	55	67	62
Was already trained before starting with present employer	14	4	8
Base	595	752	1,347

Percentages do not add to 100 because some informants gave more than one reason

Opportunities for further training

We also looked at the opportunities women felt they had for further training in their jobs, either to improve their skills in their present job or to fit them for jobs requiring new skills or at a higher level (Table 5.21). Less than half the women employees (44%) said that there were any opportunities for further training in their present job. Full time employees were more likely to report having training opportunities than part time employees: 54% of full time employees had opportunities for further training compared with 31% of all part time employees (23% of part timers working under 16 hours a week).

However, not all women were interested in having further training as Table 5.22 shows. Just under half

Table 5.21 Opportunities for full and part time employees to have further training with present employer

Opportunities for further training	Full time	Part time	All employees
	%	%	%
No opportunities	46	69	56
Training opportunities:			
In present job	28	13	21
For jobs with new skills	38	20	30
For higher level jobs	40	20	31
Total with opportunities for further training	**54**	**31**	**44**
Base	1,805	1,407	3,212

Percentages do not add to totals because some informants had more than one type of opportunity

Table 5.22 Whether full and part time employees have opportunities for further training with their present employer and whether they would like further training

Whether women would like further training	Full time	Part time	All employees
	%	%	%
Women with opportunities for further training who:			
Would like training	31	14	24
Would not like training	23	17	20
Total with opportunities for further training	**54**	**31**	**44**
Women with no opportunities for further training who:			
Would like training	19	23	20
Would not like training	27	46	36
Total with no opportunities for further training	**46**	**69**	**56**
	100	100	100
Base	1,805	1,407	3,212

(44%) of all women employees said that they would like further training, but these were not necessarily the women for whom training was available. Those with training opportunities were somewhat more likely to want further training than those without, but this was because full timers were more likely to want training. However, one in five women said they would like training even though no opportunities were available for this in their job.

Because opportunities for further training, whether or not they are desired, can in some sense be considered indicators of the 'quality' of a job we examined how

Table 5.23 Proportion of full and part time employees with training opportunities by occupation, and whether they work with men or women only at their place of work

Occupation	Works with men and women		Works with women only		All who work with others	
	% with training opportunities	Base	% with training opportunities	Base	% with training opportunities	Base
Full time						
Non-manual	77%	556	50%	638	62%	1,194
Manual	45%	169	33%	369	36%	538
All who work full time	**69%**	725	**44%**	1,007	**54%**	1,732
Part time						
Non-manual	46%	186	34%	364	38%	550
Manual	26%	186	28%	519	28%	705
All who work part time	**36%**	372	**30%**	884	**32%**	1,256
All who work with others						
Non-manual	69%	742	44%	1,002	55%	1,744
Manual	35%	355	30%	888	31%	1,243
All who work with others	**58%**	1,097	**37%**	1,891	**45%**	2,988

they were related to the variables we looked at earlier in the chapter in relation to working conditions. In order to consider several factors at once we again divide occupational groups into non-manual and manual categories and examine how training opportunities vary depending on whether women worked with men or only with other women, and whether they worked full or part time.

Table 5.23 shows that overall there were large differences in training opportunities between full and part time employees and also that women in non-manual occupations were more likely to have training opportunities than those in manual occupations; thus full time non-manual women stand out as being particularly likely to have training opportunities. However, women who worked where both men and women do the same work were more likely to have training opportunities than those who worked in 'women only' jobs, and this difference was particularly marked among full time employees and those in non-manual occupations.

Promotion

The prospect of promotion is another dimension of a job's 'quality'. It is often argued that one reason why somewhat fewer women than men have been promoted and are in positions of responsibility is that women are less likely to be working in jobs with promotion prospects. It is also argued that they do not want promotion even when it is available. However, as detailed studies of both employers and women's attitudes to promotion and career advancement show, the situation is more complex than these simple explanations suggest.[3] We cannot, in this study, look at the employers' perspectives or examine the way in which career paths are organised in establishments, nor can we identify to what extent women's current attitudes may be a product of previous discouragement. Rather we focus on women's actual experience of promotion and then discuss their current attitudes to it.

We first asked women who were currently employed whether they had ever been promoted, either in their present job or in any previous job, and found that 44% had had promotion at some time in the past, but our data do not indicate in which job this promotion occurred. Against this background of women's past promotions we looked at women's promotion prospects in their present job. Only 30% of women said they felt there were prospects of promotion for them in their present job, 41% of full time employees compared with 16% of all part time employees and 11% of part timers working under 16 hours per week. These proportions differed significantly among women in different occupations. Table 5.24 shows that in all occupational groups full time employees felt there were more likely to be promotion opportunities than part time employees, but the greater likelihood of opportunities among the higher than lower level occupations was much more apparent for full than part time employees.

As with training we need to take account of whether women in fact want promotion. Overall 49% of women employees said they would like to be considered for promotion (60% of full time and 34% of part time employees) and 46% did not want to be considered for promotion. As Table 5.25 shows 32% were interested in having promotion but were in jobs which they saw as having no promotion prospects.

Both promotion prospects and desire for promotion were more common among women in the higher occupational groups (Table 5.26), as might be expected given the greater likelihood of there being career paths in these occupations. As a consequence the proportion of women who wanted promotion but were in jobs with no promotion prospects did not vary consistently across the occupational groups. The clerical category had a particularly high proportion of women (39%) who wanted promotion but said they were in jobs with no promotion prospects.

Although almost half the women did not want to be considered for promotion at the time of the interview, the reasons they gave suggested this might be a temporary situation (Table 5.27). The most common reason

Table 5.24 Proportions of full and part time employees in different occupational groups whose current job has opportunities for promotion

Occupational group	Full time		Part time		All employees	
	% with promotion opportunities	Base	% with promotion opportunities	Base	% with promotion opportunities	Base
Professional		17*		4*		21*
Teaching	57%	150	22%	40	50%	190
Nursing, medical and social	51%	127	21%	94	38%	221
Other intermediate non-manual	57%	122		19*	52%	141
Clerical	41%	719	15%	291	34%	1,010
Sales	42%	112	21%	173	29%	285
All non-manual	**46%**	1,247	**18%**	621	**37%**	1,868
Skilled manual	34%	137	13%	82	26%	219
Semi-skilled factory	23%	248	16%	104	21%	352
Semi-skilled domestic	29%	73	16%	289	19%	362
Other semi-skilled	32%	57	8%	62	20%	119
Unskilled	30%	43	10%	248	13%	291
All manual	**31%**	558	**13%**	785	**20%**	1,343
All employees	**41%**	1,805	**16%**	1,407	**30%**	3,212

Base too small to show percentages

Table 5.25 Whether full and part time employees have opportunities for promotion in their present job and whether they would like to be considered for promotion

	Full time	Part time	All employees
	%	%	%
Women with opportunities for promotion who:			
Would like to be considered	27	4	17
Would not like to be considered	13	11	12
Don't know	1	0	1
All with opportunities for promotion	**41**	**16**	**30**
Women with no opportunities for promotion who:			
Would like to be considered	33	30	32
Would not like to be considered	24	48	34
Don't know	2	6	4
All with no opportunities for promotion	**59**	**84**	**70**
	100	100	100
Base	*1,805*	*1,407*	*3,212*

given was not wanting more responsibility whilst other reasons mentioned included family commitments, or expecting to leave the job soon. To see whether respondents' views were related to their current position and might therefore change as their situation altered, we compared the proportion of women not wanting promotion, and the reason they gave, by their current life cycle stage (Table 5.28). As one might expect, women with young children were less likely than others to want promotion, and tended to give family commitments as a reason for not wanting promotion. However the proportions changed among women with older children, and so it seems likely that some women who did not want promotion at the time of the survey will hold different views at a later stage in their life; of course, young childless women are likely to change their views in the opposite direction if they start families. The lowest proportion of women wanting promotion was among those in their fifties, many of whom were expecting to retire soon.

Table 5.26 Whether employees have opportunities for promotion in their present job and whether they would like to be considered for promotion by occupational group

	Occupational group											All employees
	Professional	Teaching	Nursing, medical and social	Intermediate non-manual	Clerical	Sales	Skilled manual	Semi-skilled factory	Semi-skilled domestic	Other semi-skilled	Unskilled	
		%	%	%	%	%	%	%	%	%	%	%
Women with opportunities for promotion who:												
Would like to be considered		35	24	37	22	12	12	6	6	11	4	17
Would not like to be considered		15	14	13	11	16	13	14	12	9	8	12
Don't know		–	1	1	1	1	1	1	1	–	1	1
All with opportunities for promotion		**50**	**39**	**51**	**34**	**29**	**26**	**21**	**19**	**20**	**13**	**30**
Women with no opportunities for promotion who:												
Would like to be considered		24	33	29	39	30	32	26	29	33	26	32
Would not like to be considered		24	25	18	25	38	38	47	47	40	53	34
Don't know		2	3	2	2	3	4	6	5	7	8	4
All with no opportunities for promotion		**50**	**61**	**49**	**66**	**71**	**74**	**79**	**81**	**80**	**87**	**70**
		100	100	100	100	100	100	100	100	100	100	100
Base	*20**	*190*	*221*	*141*	*1,010*	*285*	*219*	*352*	*362*	*119*	*291*	*3,212*

* Base too small to show percentages

Table 5.27 Reasons given by full and part time employees for not wanting to be considered for promotion in present job

Reasons for not wanting to be considered for promotion	Full time	Part time	All employees who do not want promotion
	%	%	%
Does not want more responsibility	31	26	28
Have family commitments	12	32	23
Happy in present position	18	18	18
Expect to leave job soon	18	13	15
Would prefer a different job to promotion	9	8	8
Nature of work would change	6	3	4
Not qualified	3	3	3
Other	11	8	10
Base	*664*	*829*	*1,493*

Percentages do not add to 100 because informants could have more than one reason

Lastly we look at whether women working in 'women only' jobs were less likely to have promotion opportunities than those working with men, taking into account their occupation and whether they worked full or part time, as in the previous analyses of this sort. Table 5.29 shows that although fewer women had promotion than training opportunities the pattern of relationships with the other variables is very similar. Full time employees were significantly more likely to have promotion opportunities than part time employees and non-manual than manual. Thus full time non-manual workers were markedly more likely to have promotion opportunities than other women, especially those working with men, and women working with men were more likely to have promotion opportunities than those in women only jobs, especially amongst non-manual workers.

Table 5.28 Reasons given by employees at different life cycle stages for not wanting to be considered for promotion

Reasons for not wanting promotion	Life cycle stage						All employees who do not want promotion
	Women aged under 30 with no children	Women with youngest child aged:			Women with no children under 16, aged:		
		0–4	5–10	11–15	30–49	50 or over	
	%	%	%	%	%	%	%
Does not want more responsibility	29	22	28	32	34	24	28
Has family commitments	4	45	38	36	21	11	23
Happy in present position	20	20	12	17	21	18	18
Expect to leave job soon	8	2	1	6	10	39	15
Would prefer a different job to promotion	19	12	12	6	6	3	8
Nature of work would change	7	2	4	4	6	4	4
Not qualified	6	–	3	3	5	1	3
Other	9	9	10	12	9	10	10
Base	194	129	250	226	255	439	1,493
Proportion of all employees who do not want promotion	26%	50%	48%	51%	44%	67%	47%
Base	749	257	526	444	576	660	3,212

Percentages do not add to 100 because some informants gave more than one reason

Table 5.29 Proportions of full and part time employees with promotion opportunities by occupation and whether they work with men and women or women only at their place of work

Occupation	Works with men and women		Works with women only		All who work with others	
	% with promotion opportunities	Base	% with promotion opportunities	Base	% with promotion opportunities	Base
Full time						
Non-manual	63%	556	33%	638	47%	1,194
Manual	36%	169	25%	369	28%	538
All who work full time	57%	725	30%	1,007	41%	1,732
Part time						
Non-manual	22%	186	18%	364	20%	550
Manual	15%	186	13%	519	14%	705
All who work part time	18%	372	15%	884	16%	1,256
All who work with others						
Non-manual	53%	742	27%	1,002	38%	1,744
Manual	25%	355	18%	888	20%	1,243
All who work with others	44%	1,097	23%	1,891	31%	2,988

Trade union membership and activity

There has been a considerable growth of interest in women's trade union activity over the last few years (Hunt, 1982). This reflects both the increasing number of women trade union members, particularly in service industries, and the view increasingly expressed by women trade union activists in the late 1970s that much more should be done to promote equal opportunities for men and women at work through established industrial relations channels (Robarts, et al, 1981). It is suggested, however, that women are less willing than men to be involved in unions either as members or by taking an active part in union affairs.[4] In this study we cannot make direct comparisons between men and women, but we examine the extent of women's trade union membership and activity. As well as describing the level of trade union membership and activity amongst our sample of working women we also examine the relationship between women's conditions of employment described earlier in the chapter and whether women have access to a trade union at their workplace, since the stated role of trade unions is to promote better pay and working conditions for their members.

Respondents were initially asked whether they belonged to a trade union or staff association and if not whether there was a trade union at their place of work which they could join if they wished. If we assume that those who belonged to a trade union belonged to a union at their place of work (only a very few people belong to a union which is not represented at their place of work) then 61% of all women employees had a union which they could join, but only 41% in fact belonged to a trade union. This is markedly higher than the 28% of women workers in a MORI sample in 1980 reported by Coote and Kellner who said they belonged to a union (Coote and Kellner, 1980). There were significant differences between full and part time employees as Table 5.30 shows. Full time employees were more likely than part time employees to have a union they could join (69% compared with 50% respectively) and much more likely to belong to a union (51% compared with 28%). That is to say, almost three quarters of full time employees who had a union they could join belonged to the union compared with just over half the part timers. Amongst part time employees working less than 16 hours a week, only 41% said they had a union they could join and only 17% were union members.

The proportion of employees with access to a trade union and who were union members varied by occupational group, and between full and part time employees

Table 5.30 Whether full and part time employees belong to a trade union

Whether belongs to a trade union	Full time	Part time	All employees
	%	%	%
Belongs to a trade union	51	28	41
Trade union at place of work but informant does not belong	18	22	20
All with a trade union at place of work	**69**	**50**	**61**
No trade union at place of work	27	39	32
Don't know whether a trade union at place of work	4	11	7
	100	100	100
Base	*1,805*	*1,407*	*3,212*

in many of the groups (Table 5.31). Sales workers were very much less likely to have a union they could join or to be union members than women in other occupational groups, regardless of whether they worked full or part time. Teaching and nursing are known to be highly unionised occupations, which our results confirm. The only manual occupational group which had a high proportion of women having access to and belonging to a union was semi-skilled factory workers. We asked employees who said that there was no union at their place of work whether they would like to have a union they could join. Overall 44% said they would like to be able to join a union, but 51% of full time employees said this compared with only 28% of part timers.

It is an often held view that not only are women less likely to belong to a trade union than men, but that those who do belong are less active in the union. Our results show that regular attendance at union meetings by women members was low; but then this is also true of all ordinary trade union members apart from those holding office (Daniel and Millward, 1983, Table IV.3). Only 13% of union members in our sample said they attended union meetings regularly, although 31% said they attended occasionally, and 56% said they never

attended meetings at all. Among union members full time workers were more likely than part timers to attend union meetings regularly (16% compared with 6%) whereas 49% of full timers and 72% of part timers never attended meetings. Holding office in a union was also rare among women trade union members; only 7% said they had ever held union office (9% of full time and 2% of part timers), but we do not have figures for men for comparison.

A variety of reasons are offered to explain women's relatively low level of trade union activity though, as we have shown, it is difficult to know whether their activity is significantly lower than men's in practice. Some explanations focus on women's lack of interest or time whilst others focus on the union's lack of concern for women members in general, and their specific needs in particular, which in turn ensures that many women remain uninvolved or inactive members (Hunt, 1982; Stageman, 1980). We could not explore this in detail in this survey but we did ask those women who did not attend meetings their reasons for not attending. As Table 5.32 shows a number of women said there were no meetings (or only committee meetings), or they did not know of any meetings, but the main reason given by

Table 5.31 Proportions of full and part time employees who have a trade union at their place of work and proportions who belong to a trade union by occupational group

Occupational group	Full time			Part time			All employees		
	% who have a trade union	% who belong to a trade union	*Base*	% who have a trade union	% who belong to a trade union	*Base*	% who have a trade union	% who belong to a trade union	*Base*
Professional			*17**			*4**	97%	70%	*21**
Teaching	99%	80%	*150*	92%	35%	*40*	97%	61%	*190*
Nursing, medical and social	90%	69%	*127*	84%	49%	*94*	87%	61%	*221*
Other intermediate non-manual	63%	42%	*122*			*19**	59%	38%	*141*
Clerical	62%	41%	*719*	40%	16%	*291*	54%	34%	*1,010*
Sales	41%	27%	*112*	21%	11%	*173*	29%	17%	*285*
All non-manual	**67%**	**47%**	*1,247*	**44%**	**21%**	*621*	**59%**	**38%**	*1,868*
Skilled	67%	53%	*137*	50%	27%	*82*	61%	43%	*219*
Semi-skilled factory	77%	66%	*248*	56%	44%	*104*	71%	60%	*352*
Semi-skilled domestic	60%	48%	*73*	61%	31%	*289*	60%	35%	*362*
Other semi-skilled	61%	52%	*57*	46%	28%	*62*	53%	39%	*119*
Unskilled	84%	72%	*43*	54%	37%	*248*	59%	42%	*291*
All manual	**72%**	**60%**	*558*	**56%**	**34%**	*785*	**62%**	**45%**	*1,343*
All employees	**69%**	**51%**	*1,805*	**50%**	**28%**	*1,407*	**61%**	**41%**	*3,212*

*Base too small to show percentages

Table 5.32 Reasons given by trade union members for not attending trade union meetings by whether informant works full or part time

Reasons given for not attending trade union meetings	Full time	Part time	All trade union members who do not attend meetings
	%	%	%
No meetings are held	22	11	18
Don't know when or if meetings are held	9	13	11
Not interested/haven't got time	38	40	39
Meetings held at inconvenient times	20	20	20
Do not believe in unions	9	12	10
Other reasons	4	6	5
Base	*452*	*285*	*737*

Percentages do not add to 100 because some informants gave more than one reason

both full and part time women was that they did not have, or were not sufficiently interested to make, time to attend meetings. A sizeable minority (20%) mentioned that meetings were held at inconvenient times, and 10% said they did not really want to belong to the union anyway.

As lack of time and/or interest was mentioned most frequently as a reason for union inactivity we investigated whether there were any significant variations in union membership and activity between women at different stages of their life cycle. Since there are different proportions of full and part time workers among women at different life cycle stages we examine the two groups separately. Table 5.33 shows how the proportion of women who belong to a union varies at different life cycle stages.

There were significant differences among women at different life cycle stages in whether they were working in a job where they could join a union reflecting the different occupational distributions of full and part time workers. For this analysis we show the proportion of union members of those with access to a union rather than the overall proportions of union members. Amongst those with access to a union there was a lower proportion of trade union members among part timers than among full timers at all life cycle stages. Although union membership increased among women with older children, the young full time workers with no children

had a smaller proportion of union members (69% of those with access to a union) compared with almost all other groups of full time workers. It is difficult to know whether this is a genuine age effect or a reflection of a different union and occupational distribution. Young women, as Dex has pointed out, may start their working lives in a very different labour market from that experienced by older women when they first entered the labour market (Dex 1984a). Moreover, as we will show in Chapter 6, there is some evidence that young women seem less committed to work in general than older women; they might therefore be expected to show less interest in trade unions, as this would imply a considerable interest in work issues.

Turning to levels of activity as measured by regular attendance at meetings, it is clear from Table 5.34 that women with a youngest child under 5 are more likely than women at other life cycle stages to attend union meetings regularly. At all stages of the life cycle, union members working full time are more likely than those working part time to do this. Among full time workers regular attendance is highest among those women aged 30–59 with no children under 16 followed by women with children aged 5–15. Amongst part time workers there is little variation in attendance among women at different life cycle stages, with the exception of women with a youngest child under 5 who are more likely than others to attend, but why this should be so is not apparent from these findings.

Table 5.33 Proportions of trade union members among full and part time employees with access to a trade union, by life cycle stage

Life cycle stage	Full time		Part time		All employees with access to union	
	% union members	Base	% union members	Base	% union members	Base
Women aged under 30 with no children	69%	445		12*	68%	457
Women with youngest child aged:						
0–4	67%	40	44%	82	52%	122
5–10	72%	90	48%	192	56%	282
11–15	82%	141	57%	135	70%	276
Women with no child aged under 16:						
aged 30–49	78%	283	70%	111	76%	394
aged 50 or over	78%	236	63%	176	71%	412
All employees with access to union	**74%**	1,235	**56%**	708	**68%**	1,943

*Base too small to show percentage

Table 5.34 Proportions of trade union members who attend union meetings among full and part time employees by life cycle stage

Life cycle stage	Full time		Part time		All trade union members	
	% of union members who attend union meetings regularly	Base	% of union members who attend union meetings regularly	Base	% of union members who attend union meetings regularly	Base
Women aged under 30 with no children	13%	308		5*	13%	313
Women with youngest child aged:						
0–4		27*	14%	36	19%	63
5–10	15%	65	5%	92	10%	157
11–15	16%	115	7%	77	12%	192
Women with no children aged under 16:						
aged 30–49	18%	221	5%	78	14%	299
aged 50 or over	19%	183	6%	110	14%	293
All trade union members	**16%**	919	**6%**	398	**13%**	1,317

*Base too small to show percentages

Table 5.35 Proportions of full and part time employees who had trade union representation at their workplace by occupation, and whether they work with men and women or women only at their place of work

Occupation	Works with men and women		Works with women only		All who work with others	
	% who had trade union representation	Base	% who had trade union representation	Base	% who had trade union representation	Base
Full time						
Non-manual	82%	556	56%	638	68%	1,194
Manual	69%	169	74%	369	72%	538
All who work full time	**79%**	725	**63%**	1,007	**69%**	1,732
Part time						
Non-manual	57%	186	42%	364	47%	550
Manual	57%	186	59%	519	59%	705
All who work part time	**57%**	372	**52%**	884	**54%**	1,256
All who work with others						
Non-manual	75%	742	51%	1,002	61%	1,749
Manual	63%	355	65%	888	65%	1,243
All who work with others	**71%**	1,097	**58%**	1,891	**63%**	2,988

We have shown earlier in this chapter that women working in 'women only' jobs had lower average rates of pay and were less likely to have access to a number of job related benefits than women working in jobs done by both men and women. We were interested in whether such women were also less likely to have trade union representation at their place of work, and whether this varied for women in different occupations and for full and part time workers. We therefore carried out a similar analysis to that described earlier, and show in Table 5.35 the proportion of employees with trade union representation at their workplace by these job characteristics.

The results of this analysis are less clear than those previously described but full time employees, particularly those in non-manual occupations, were more likely than part time employees to have trade union representation. Women working with both men and women in non-manual jobs were also more likely to have union representation than those in 'women only' jobs, but among manual workers this relationship was reversed. Among manual employees, particularly those working full time, women in 'women only' jobs were more likely to have trade union representation than those working with both men and women; this might reflect the fact that many of these jobs would be in the public sector where there is a high degree of unionisation (Daniel and Millward, 1983). Thus it is not possible to say that occupational segregation has a direct relationship with union representation in the way it is related to some of the other conditions of employment described earlier.

The inter-relationships between women's conditions of employment and the levels of unionisation at their place of work

So far we have looked in turn at women's access to a number of job related benefits and to training and promotion opportunities. We have seen some common patterns emerge, in that for most of the aspects of employment examined, certain groups of women appear to be advantaged compared with others. Thus in general terms full time workers were more likely than part time workers to have access to job-related benefits and

training and promotion opportunities; non-manual workers were at an advantage compared with manual workers, as were women who worked with both men and women compared with those in 'women only' jobs.

These various factors are often interrelated, so that, for example, women working full time in non-manual jobs particularly if they worked with men as well as women were much more likely to have access to better employment conditions and opportunities. These results of course imply that women who get one type of benefit or opportunity are likely to get others as well. Among full time employees 50% received both sick pay and an occupational pension whereas 17% had neither. However, among part time employees only 8% had access to both and 47% had neither. There were similar associations between training and promotion opportunities: 32% of full time employees had both training and promotion opportunities and 37% had neither. Among part time employees only 11% had both and 64% had neither. There was less correspondence between receiving sick pay or an occupational pension on the one hand and having training or promotion opportunities on the other.

We looked at how many of these four benefits women employees in our sample had access to to see whether there was any relationship between this and the existence of a union at their work place. The results are set out in Table 5.36. Full and part time employees are shown separately since the level of unionisation differs between them. It is clear from the table that full time workers were much more likely than part time workers to have access to all four benefits, but among full time workers with a trade union at their workplace, 28% had access to all four benefits compared with only 7% of those without a trade union. Among the part time employees only 3% of those with trade union representation and 1% of those without had access to all four benefits. Conversely part time employees were much more likely to have none of the four benefits, particularly if their workplace had no trade union representation. Overall, the consequent disadvantage of working part time rather than full time was somewhat greater than that of being in a job with no trade union repre-

Table 5.36 Whether full and part time employees have access to sick pay, occupational pension, training and promotion opportunities by whether there is a trade union at their workplace

How many of 4 benefits (sick pay, occupation pension, training and promotion opportunities) women have	Full time employees			Part time employees		
	With trade union at workplace	No trade union at workplace	All	With trade union at workplace	No trade union at workplace	All
	%	%	%	%	%	%
All four	28	7	22	3	1	2
Three	31	19	27	14	5	10
Two	24	31	27	29	11	20
One	12	30	17	38	41	40
None	5	13	8	16	41	28
	100	100	100	100	100	100
Base	1,166	483	1,649	623	577	1,200

sentation with respect to the four benefits considered. However, it is important to note that it is not possible to say whether the advantages of women with trade union representation at their workplace are a direct effect of having a trade union which can negotiate for better employment conditions or whether the sorts of workplaces which are unionised are also those with better conditions of employment.

The above results go some way to confirm the general picture emerging from the results presented earlier in this chapter, that some groups of women are advantaged compared with others in respect of pay and a number of job related benefits and opportunities. Women working full time in non-manual jobs where men as well as women do the same kind of work tend to be better paid and to have better conditions of employment and opportunities than the majority of women workers.

Summary and conclusions

In this chapter we have described variations in the pay, conditions of employment and trade union activity of working women, showing differences between full or part time workers, women in different occupational groups and between women working only with other women or with both men and women.

Comparison of women's hourly earnings are complex. In general evidence from the survey indicates that hourly earnings decrease through the occupational groups, although sales workers were an exception in that, along with semi-skilled domestic workers they earned the least of all women. On average, part time workers were paid less than full time workers: 54% earned less than £1.50 an hour in 1980 compared with 30% of full time workers. However, within occupational groups in the majority of instances there was no significant difference in the average hourly pay of full and part time workers. Thus, to a large extent, the difference in the hourly rate of pay of full and part time workers can be explained by their being found disproportionately in different occupational groups. When the pay level of full and part time workers was linked to our measure of occupational segregation however, it was also clear that the hourly earnings of part timers work-

ing with men was higher than that of women working full time in 'women only' jobs in the same occupational category. Thus occupational segregation was more closely correlated with hourly earnings than whether women worked full or part time.

Turning to the three basic conditions of employment, paid holidays, sick pay and access to an occupational pension scheme, full time workers in general were more likely to report these as part of their conditions of employment than part time workers. Whilst most working women (88%) had some paid holidays, full time workers were more likely to have them and to have proportionately more than part time workers. Similarly more full time employees (80%) than part time employees (51%) said they would receive sick pay from their employer. Women working full time in non-manual jobs were particularly likely to get sick pay whilst women working part time in manual jobs were least likely to be eligible for this. Occupational segregation was less important a factor in whether a woman got sick pay than her occupational level or whether she worked full or part time.

Many fewer women belonged to an occupational pension scheme (34%) than got sick pay and the differences between full and part time workers was also quite marked: 53% of full time workers belonged compared with 9% of part time workers. In general whether a woman worked full or part time was a more important factor in determining whether she was likely to be in a pension scheme than whether she worked with men or in a 'women only' job, though women in non-manual jobs were more likely than manual workers to be in a pension scheme.

Training opportunities and opportunities for promotion are much less tangible aspects of a job than its fringe benefits. However, the pattern we have described of full time workers being more likely to have experience of or access to these benefits was repeated in these aspects of a job. Full time employees for example were more likely to have been trained by their employers or prior to taking up their job than women working part time. They were also significantly more likely to feel they had training and promotion opportunities than part timers were, though overall fewer women felt they had promotion as opposed to training opportunities. Being in a non-manual job and working with men as well as women were likely to increase a woman's chances of having opportunities for further training or promotion.

A minority of working women belonged to a trade union (41%) and both the level of union membership and opportunity to join a union was higher on average for full time workers. Occupational segregation had less effect on levels of unionisation overall however, for although women in non-manual occupations were more likely to have union representation if they worked with men than in 'women only' jobs, the opposite was true for women in manual jobs. Union representation is associated with better pay, job benefits and opportunities. Whether this is a direct effect of a union presence or because jobs which are likely to be unionised are independently likely to have better conditions of employment is impossible to say.

In conclusion it is clear that some groups of women are advantaged compared with other women in respect of pay and some basic job-related benefits and opportunities. When these benefits and job opportunities are taken together both full time and non-manual employees are much more likely to have access to them than part time or manual employees. Accordingly women working full time in non-manual jobs, particularly those where men as well as women do the same kind of work, tend to be better paid and to have markedly better conditions of employment and opportunities than the majority of women workers. This would lead us to conclude that they can well be seen as belonging to the more protected and rewarded sector of the labour market. These findings provide some empirical support for the view that the labour market is segmented along dual lines for women with the majority of women workers segregated in jobs with secondary characteristics. However, they do not support the idea that all women workers are secondary workers. Women workers, as we have shown, are more heterogeneous in their pay and job conditions than this simple dichotomy of the labour market implies.

Notes

[1] Joshi's analysis also showed that sales occupations were significantly worse paid than other non-manual occupations and the manual categories skilled and semi-skilled factory work. There was no statistically significant difference between pay in these two categories, nor between sales, other semi-skilled and unskilled manual categories. The analysis also established that the nursing, medical and social group could be bracketed together in the pay league with the other intermediate non-manual category and put the small categories of professional and childcare at the top and bottom of the ladder respectively (Joshi, 1984).

[2] This enormous survey is a mine of useful information on both men and women's past and present training as well as containing work history information. Several publications cover aspects of it including Research Services (1976), Claydon (1980), Greenhalgh and Stewart (1982a,b,c,d) and Elias and Main (1982).

[3] For a useful discussion of the general attitudes underlying employers' specific views on women's promotion see Hunt (1975). Certain questions were subsequently repeated in the 1979 study by IFF and a comparison of change over time made (EOC, 1981). For a small scale study within the teaching profession see NUT/EOC (1980). For a booklet based on research into the factors which limit women's opportunities which shows how to tackle career development for women and discusses promotion (and training) policies in some detail see Manpower Services Commission (1981).

[4] This is a popular rather than a serious view. As Richard Brown has pointed out in his useful discussion of research on women as employees in industry the position of women workers *vis-à-vis* union membership or activity is better understood in terms of their work situation rather than their sex (Brown, 1976).

Introduction

In the last three chapters we have looked in detail at the types of jobs women work in and their conditions of employment. We were primarily concerned to describe the factual aspects of women's employment, although we did look briefly at women's views about their hours of work in Chapter 4 and whether or not they were interested in training and promotion opportunities in Chapter 5. In this chapter we focus on working women's attitudes to working in general and to their own jobs in particular and show how they differ among women in different situations. As we pointed out in Chapter 1, we were interested in looking at women's attitudes not least because we were aware that considerably less information was generally available about the attitudes of women as workers in their own right than about men (Brown *et al*, 1983). Most studies have either ignored women workers or tended to study them in terms of the problems they face in combining their dual role as workers and mothers or the problems they pose for employers, rather than treating them as workers as such, albeit with differing perspectives (Beynon and Blackburn, 1972, provide an exception; see also Beechey, 1978 and Brown, 1976). More recently however research on working women's attitudes to working and their jobs has begun to be published (Agassi, 1979; McNally, 1979; Hunt, P, 1980; Pollert, 1981; Wajcman, 1983).

As Brown points out, women's consciousness as workers is likely both to be markedly different from men's, reflecting the differing role paid employment typically has for men compared with women, and to vary according to women's position in the life cycle (Brown, 1976). We would expect women's orientations to work, that is the meaning paid work has for women, its importance as an aspect of their lives and their expectations of and priorities in a job, to differ from men's in certain crucial ways. As they move from school into work girls are much less likely to see their future in terms of an uninterrupted working life. As almost all the studies of adolescent girls show, young women looking ahead see a future dominated by marriage and caring for a family whilst boys' aspirations and plans are almost always job orientated (Maizels, 1970; Sharpe, 1976). Work is not necessarily rejected by girls; often they expect to return after having a family, usually part time, but paid work must always be accommodated to their other home based roles. Once in work their opportunities are usually very different. Not only are men and women often in diverse types of jobs with different prospects, but, where they do similar work, there are often contrasting assumptions about their working lives and cor-

respondingly divergent views about further training needs and promotion opportunities (Hunt, 1975; Fogarty *et al*, 1981). Accordingly women's experience of work may well confirm their view of themselves as different kinds of workers from men and influence their attitudes to work (Feldberg and Glenn, 1984; Curran, 1981).

But of course expectations and attitudes may change as situations and experiences change. Women may find they have to work to support themselves, or that they enjoy having a job more than they anticipated or that they do not want to return to work after having a baby as soon as they intended. In a cross-sectional study asking women about their current attitudes we cannot show this process of change, though we can show how women's attitudes to working and their jobs vary for different groups of women at different stages of their life cycle. Moreover, great care needs to be taken in making inferences about the nature of relationships between women's attitudes and their behaviour. Since attitudes can not only shape behaviour but can be changed as a result of the choices people make, we cannot infer that attitudes expressed after a particular choice has been made are necessarily the same as before the choice.

At any point in time women may vary in their attachment to work, that is, how important it is for them to have a job, why it is important and how committed they are to working. For some women a job is essential for financial reasons and for others, for social or psychological reasons; for still others, a job is not essential, either because financial needs are less pressing, or because other aspects of life are seen to take greater priority. By examining women's general attitudes to work we aimed to establish the relative importance of different orientations towards work for different groups of working women. In addition we look at some of the feelings women express about how they cope with the competing demands of work and home and at different expressions of psychological wellbeing, or its reverse, psychological stress.

As well as asking about their general attitudes to working we also asked them their specific reasons for working. We were particularly interested in identifying the range or variety of reasons women had and how this varied amongst different groups so as to assess the importance of financial reasons as well as the intrinsic attractions of having a job. Finally we asked women to rate how important different aspects of a job would be to them in choosing a job and compared their answers with their satisfaction with these aspects of their current job. We linked some of their general attitudes to their more specific attitudes about jobs to identify whether women with different broad orientations to work valued different aspects of working and dimensions of a job.

Attitudes to working in general
We show in later chapters that the majority of women normally work until the birth of their first child, but after that time there is no expectation by society that they should continue to work and in fact the majority of women give up work for a few years. It is possible therefore to view women who are working after having had children as, in a sense, having chosen to work; this view is dominant officially in that, for example, social security regulations do not require married women or women with children to be available for work before they are eligible for benefit in the way that they do men or single childless women. However we recognise that women in difficult financial circumstances might well not see themselves as having much of a choice about working. Financial circumstances, however, are clearly not the sole determinants of whether or not women work at particular stages of their lives. In this section we examine the extent to which women feel they are financially dependent on working and look at some other attitudes to working which relate to women's motivation to work and how they feel about working.

We explored the topic of women's attitudes to working by asking our informants to look at a number of statements expressing opinions about various aspects of working and to indicate for each one whether it was definitely true, partly true or not true for them. The ten statements, which we show in Table 6.1, were chosen to represent different aspects of working which other studies suggested were relevant to understanding women's attitudes to work. They include both favourable and unfavourable opinions about work, and cover both factors which might motivate women to work and statements about some possible consequences of working.

Women's responses to the individual statements show patterns of interrelationships which can be explained by the existence of underlying attitudes to different aspects of working. The technique of factor analysis was used to analyse the intercorrelations between answers to the ten statements and three independent clusters of statements or factors were identified.[1] Table 6.1 therefore lists the ten statements in three groups according to the factor with which they were mostly closely associated, in the order of the strength of their association with it. The first group of statements appears to be measuring the expression of women's financial dependence on work. The first two statements mention this specifically and since the other two are correlated with them, they too refer to a financial dependence on working. The second group of statements can be seen as being about the intrinsic attractions of work; the stimulation of work and sense of purpose or the lack of attraction of work. These attitudes are independent of views about the financial dependence on work. The third group of statements clearly relate to feelings about the consequences of work in relation to other aspects of life and appear to be an expression of feelings about the demands of work and whether women are able to cope with them in relation to other demands on their time.

If we look at the first group of statements it can be seen that the majority of women express a high financial dependence on working. Only a small minority said they really do not need to work for the money: 11% said this was definitely true, whereas 64% said this was not true for them. However, 30% implied they would be able to manage if they were not earning. The second group of statements showed that the majority of women expressed very positive views about working. Very few women did not find work stimulating and only 6% definitely wished they did not go out to work. Nevertheless the conflicting demands of work and home were expressed by a number of women: 18% said it was definitely true that they had less time than they would like to spend with friends and family while 36% said this was partly true; only 27% said it was not true that they got very tired because of their work; 31% said it was definitely true that they never had enough time for everything and 43% said this was partly true. These statements do not necessarily imply that it is the demands of domestic responsibilities that conflict with work. Men with demanding jobs might respond in simi-

Table 6.1 Proportions of working women rating different statements about working as definitely true, partly true and not true

Statements of attitudes to working		Definitely true	Partly true	Not true	All working women
Financial dependence on work					
I couldn't manage unless I was earning	%	43	27	30	**100**
I don't need to work for the money	%	11	25	64	**100**
If I lost my job, I'd look for another straight away	%	66	18	16	**100**
It wouldn't bother me if I lost my job and couldn't find another	%	12	19	69	**100**
Intrinsic attraction of work					
I like the stimulation of going out to work	%	60	32	8	**100**
I wish I didn't go out to work	%	6	18	76	**100**
Working makes me feel I'm doing something useful	%	61	34	5	**100**
Coping with work and home					
I have less time than I would like to spend with my friends and family	%	18	36	46	**100**
I often get very tired because of my work	%	29	44	27	**100**
I never have enough time for everything	%	31	43	26	**100**

Base: 3,354 working women

lar fashion, but among women we shall show that those with responsibilities for young children are in fact most likely to express difficulties with coping with the demands of work on their time.

In order to simplify the comparison of the attitudes of different groups of women on these dimensions we calculated a score for each woman on the three factors and divided the women according to whether they had high, medium or low scores relative to the average for working women. It is important to note that this method means we can compare one group of working women relative to another, but we cannot say that working women as a whole are high or low on these measures.

The financial need to work

Table 6.2 compares first the financial dependence on working of full and part time workers. Not surprisingly, over twice as many full time workers as part time workers had high scores on the measure, whereas over twice as many part timers as full timers had low scores. We have already shown that married women were very much more likely than non-married women to be working part time and were unlikely to be the sole financial supporter of themselves and their families, and so we would expect them to feel less financially dependent on

work. We therefore compared the financial dependence on work of married and non-married women according to whether they were childless, had dependent children or grown-up children. This is shown in Table 6.3 which gives results for full and part time workers separately.

If we look first at the bottom set of figures, for all working women, it is clear that there is a big difference between married and non-married women overall: 22% of married women are in the high financial dependence category compared with 72% of the non-married women. Comparing the figures for full and part time workers we can see that among both married and non-married women, part timers expressed less financial dependence on work than full timers and among both full and part time workers the non-married women were more financially dependent on work than the married women. In relation to these overall results the impact of children is less significant. There was a tendency for women with children under 16 to express a greater financial dependence on work than either the childless or those with grown-up children. This is particularly true for non-married women who were of course lone parents and likely to be providing the main financial support for their children. We discuss this group in more detail in Chapter 8.

We also compared the financial dependence on work of women in different occupations, but on the whole found few significant differences between them. The exceptions were women in unskilled occupations, whether working full or part time, and women in sales occupations working full time, all of whom had higher proportions than average in the high financial dependence on work category, which is of interest in relation to the findings of the previous chapter that these are amongst the lowest paid occupations.

Table 6.2 Full and part time working women's level of financial dependence on work

Level of financial dependence on work	Full time	Part time	All working women
	%	%	%
1 (High financial dependence)	47	21	36
2	34	35	34
3 (Low financial dependence)	19	44	30
	100	100	100
Base	1,877	1,477	3,354

Table 6.3 Full and part time working women's level of financial dependence on work by marital status and whether they have dependent children

Level of financial dependence on work	Married				Non-married				All working women
	Childless	Youngest child aged:		All married working women	Childless	Youngest child aged:		All non-married working women	
		Under 16	16 and over			Under 16	16 and over		
Full time	%	%	%	%	%	%	%	%	%
1 (High financial dependence)	29	32	24	27	73	91	74	75	47
2	44	41	40	42	26	8	22	24	34
3 (Low financial dependence)	27	27	36	31	1	2	4	1	19
	100	100	100	100	100	100	100	100	100
Base	379	371	339	1,089	628	64	96	788	1,877
Part time									
1 (High financial dependence)	16	19	15	18		61	46	56	21
2	36	37	30	35		27	39	32	35
3 (Low financial dependence)	48	44	55	47		12	16	12	44
	100	100	100	100		100	100	100	100
Base	64	873	409	1,346	15*	59	57	131	1,477
All working women									
1 (High financial dependence)	27	22	19	22	73	76	63	72	36
2	43	38	34	38	26	17	28	25	34
3 (Low financial dependence)	30	40	47	40	1	7	9	3	30
	100	100	100	100	100	100	100	100	100
Base	443	1,244	748	2,435	643	123	153	919	3,354

*Base too small to show percentages

Non-financial attractions of working

In a similar manner to financial dependence, we compared the proportion of women with high, medium and low scores on the measure of the intrinsic attraction of work. We first compared full and part time workers, but found no difference at all between them. Even though women working part time tended to work in lower level jobs, and as we shall show in Chapter 10 had often moved down from higher level jobs, they were overall no less likely than women working full time to find work stimulating or worthwhile.

However, there were differences in the orientations of women at different life stages as Table 6.4 shows. Childless women aged 30 or over were most likely to have high scores on this measure of the intrinsic attraction of work, whereas childless women under 30, most of whom would be in the younger end of the age range, were least likely to have high scores. These younger childless women may be expected to have children in future and no doubt, if financial circumstances permit, those who do not find work stimulating and worthwhile will not continue working. Since working full time until the birth of the first child has become the normal working pattern for young women, as we show in Chapter 9, these women had not yet had a real, socially approved, opportunity to leave the labour market. Moreover they had not had any sustained experience of not working from choice with which to contrast their experience of working. They may, in fact, therefore have been more attracted to not working, given its association with being married and having children, than women who have had time out of the labour market (Brown, 1976).

In contrast, most of the older childless women were married, and some may have delayed childbearing or remained childless because of their interest in work.

We would expect that many of this group and of the women who had had children would have chosen to work because they found working stimulating and therefore it is not surprising to find higher proportions of these women in the high scoring group than of the young childless women. The results show an increase with age of youngest child in the proportions with high scores, which again is probably an indication of increasing proportions choosing to work for other reasons in addition to financial necessity.

Table 6.4 also shows that the lack of difference between full and part time workers is generally maintained for women at different life stages, but there are some exceptions. Among both women with children under 5 and women with grown-up children, those working full time were more likely than those working part time to find work intrinsically attractive. However, women working full time with pre-school children also have a high proportion who did not find working attractive. This fits in with a finding we shall come to later, that women with young children who worked full time tended to fall into two main categories: one group worked because they really needed the money and would not work otherwise; these women tended to be unqualified and work in low level occupations; the second group were committed to careers and were likely to be in professional or semi-professional occupations. This latter group would be likely to find work of greater intrinsic satisfaction, though, of course, they might also be working for financial reasons since they were likely to have earnings well above the average for women and there would be a high opportunity cost in foregoing this high income.

An examination of women's views about the intrinsic attractions of work according to their occupational level lends some support to this suggestion (Table 6.5).

Table 6.4   Full and part time working women's level of intrinsic attraction of work by life cycle stage

Level of intrinsic attraction of work	Life cycle stage							All working women
	Childless women aged:		Women with youngest child aged:			Women with children 16 or over aged:		
	Under 30	30 or over	0–4	5–10	11–15	Under 50	50 or over	
Full time	%	%	%	%	%	%	%	%
1 (High attraction)	28	48	38	36	39	46	48	38
2	42	32	32	36	37	38	31	37
3 (Low attraction)	30	20	30	28	24	17	21	25
	100	100	100	100	100	100	100	100
Base	730	277	73	139	223	186	249	1,877
Part time								
1 (High attraction)		47	31	35	41	42	41	38
2		31	43	38	37	31	34	37
3 (Low attraction)		22	26	27	22	28	25	25
		100	100	100	100	100	100	100
Base	28*	51	203	414	315	176	290	1,477
All working women								
1 (High attraction)	28	48	33	36	40	44	44	38
2	41	32	40	37	37	34	33	37
3 (Low attraction)	31	20	27	27	23	22	23	25
	100	100	100	100	100	100	100	100
Base	758	328	276	553	538	362	539	3,354

*Base too small to show percentages

Table 6.5 Full and part time working women's level of intrinsic attraction of work by occupation

Level of intrinsic attraction of work	Occupational group											All working women
	Professional	Teaching	Nursing, medical and social	Other intermediate non-manual	Clerical	Sales	Skilled	Semi-skilled factory	Semi-skilled domestic	Other semi-skilled	Unskilled	
Full time	%	%	%	%	%	%	%	%	%	%	%	%
1 (High attraction)		57	52	43	34	35	31	30	39	46	36	38
2		33	35	38	37	41	44	35	37	28	37	37
3 (Low attraction)		10	13	19	29	24	25	35	24	26	27	25
		100	**100**	**100**	**100**	**100**	**100**	**100**	**100**	**100**	**100**	**100**
Base	18*	152	127	165	727	115	145	248	75	61	44	1,877
Part time												
1 (High attraction)		57	50	33	46	36	29	23	38	29	36	38
2		27	40	36	32	38	44	38	38	34	37	37
3 (Low attraction)		16	10	31	22	26	27	39	24	37	27	25
		100	**100**	**100**	**100**	**100**	**100**	**100**	**100**	**100**	**100**	**100**
Base	8*	44	96	39	301	175	94	104	296	68	251	1,477
All working women												
1 (High attraction)		57	51	41	37	35	30	28	38	37	36	38
2		32	37	37	36	39	44	36	38	31	37	37
3 (Low attraction)		11	12	22	27	26	26	36	24	32	27	25
		100	**100**	**100**	**100**	**100**	**100**	**100**	**100**	**100**	**100**	**100**
Base	26*	196	223	204	1,028	290	239	352	371	129	295	3,354

*Base too small to show percentages

Overall, a higher proportion of women in the higher level non-manual occupations had an intrinsic orientation to work than women in other occupations, particularly those in semi-skilled factory work who were particularly likely to find little intrinsic attraction in work. There were some differences between full and part time workers in the different occupations, but some of these were at least partly explained by the life cycle differences described above. Full time clerical workers tended to be young and childless and we have seen that these young women did not have a very high intrinsic orientation to work. In contrast part time clerical workers were usually older women with children who were more attracted to working. However, among women in other intermediate non-manual occupations, semi-skilled factory workers and those in other semi-skilled occupations it was the full timers who seemed most attracted to work. This may be a reflection of the heterogeneity of jobs in these occupational categories, with full timers being more likely to be found in the most interesting and stimulating jobs.

Coping with the competing demands of home and work
The first two factors show us how women's motivation to work may vary and we come back to this issue more specifically later in the chapter when we look in detail at women's actual reasons for working. However, the third factor measured a different set of feelings women have about the demands of work in relation to other aspects of their lives. We therefore look next at how well women felt they were coping with the demands of home and work. In so far as full time workers are, by definition, spending more hours at work than part timers, we would expect them to find greater difficulties in coping with the conflicting demands on their time and Table 6.6 shows this to be the case: 34% of full time workers had high scores on this dimension, showing they had difficulty in coping with the demands of work

Table 6.6 Full and part time working women's level of coping with work and home

Level of coping with work and home	Full time	Part time	All working women
	%	%	%
1 (Difficult to cope)	34	21	28
2	44	40	42
3 (Easy to cope)	22	39	30
	100	**100**	**100**
Base	1,877	1,477	3,354

and only 22% had low scores, whereas the corresponding figures for part time workers were 21% and 39%.

Equally the demands of home may vary too. Women with domestic responsibilities, particularly those with dependent children, are likely to have most demands on their time to compete with the demands of work. However, the presence of a partner might make a difference and so we compare married and non-married women in Table 6.7. Although married and non-married women did not differ much overall, there are marked differences within the non-married group according to whether they have had children. The single childless found it easier to cope, but then many of them were still living with their parents and therefore had few domestic responsibilities. Non-married women with either dependent or grown-up children were most likely to find it difficult to cope, more so than any of the married women which is probably indicative of the extra strains of having to cope with all aspects of running a household without a partner. The lack of difference among all working married women according to whether they have children concealed differences between full and part time workers, which were also apparent among non-married women. Among both full and part time workers the childless women generally found it easier to cope; among the full time workers those with dependent children found greater difficulties

Table 6.7 Full and part time working women's level of coping with work and home by marital status and whether or not they have dependent children

Level of coping with work and home	Married				Non-married				All working women
	Childless	Youngest child aged:		All married working women	Childless	Youngest child aged:		All non-married working women	
		Under 16	16 or over			Under 16	16 or over		
Full time	%	%	%	%	%	%	%	%	%
1 (Difficult to cope)	32	46	38	39	21	52	47	27	34
2	47	41	46	44	44	42	39	43	44
3 (Easy to cope)	21	13	16	17	35	6	14	30	22
	100	**100**	**100**	**100**	**100**	**100**	**100**	**100**	**100**
Base	*379*	*371*	*339*	*1,089*	*628*	*64*	*96*	*788*	*1,877*
Part time									
1 (Difficult to cope)	10	22	20	21		24	23	24	21
2	46	40	40	40		41	44	43	40
3 (Easy to cope)	44	38	40	39		36	33	33	39
	100	**100**	**100**	**100**		**100**	**100**	**100**	**100**
Base	*64*	*873*	*409*	*1,346*	*15**	*59*	*57*	*131*	*1,477*
All working women									
1 (Difficult to cope)	29	29	29	29	21	38	38	26	28
2	46	40	42	42	44	42	41	43	42
3 (Easy to cope)	25	31	29	29	35	20	21	31	30
	100	**100**	**100**	**100**	**100**	**100**	**100**	**100**	**100**
Base	*443*	*1,244*	*748*	*2,435*	*643*	*123*	*153*	*919*	*3,354*

*Base too small to show percentages

than those with grown-up children; this was particularly the case for non-married women.

Clearly differences in how well women feel they are coping with the demands of work in relation to their lives may relate to the amount of freedom of choice they have had about working. Married women, for example, are more likely to be able to choose to work part time than non-married women because they have the economic support of a partner. We shall show in Chapter 8 that, although lone mothers are no more or less likely to work than married mothers, if they do work, they are much more likely to work full time. However, these results show that many women who work full time with dependent children find it difficult to cope with the competing demands of home and work, the married only marginally less so than the non-married.

Perceived stress
Difficulty in coping with conflicting home and work demands may be one cause of stress for women; financial or social problems may be another. It is possible that in attempting to solve one problem which may cause stress, such as shortage of money or loneliness at home, women may put themselves into an equally or more stressful position. We therefore included in this survey a general measure of reported psychological stress derived from that used by Marsh in a survey which looked at women and shiftwork (Marsh, 1979). We also use this measure again in Chapter 7 to compare the experiences of non-working and working women.

We presented the women in the survey with eight bipolar statements about how people feel and asked them to indicate which of five positions along a continuum between the two opposing statements most closely described the way they felt at the time of the interview.

The statements were:

Exhausted and tired out	–	Full of energy
No worries about the future	–	Often worried about the future
Irritable and touchy	–	Even tempered
Lots of self-confidence	–	Losing my self-confidence
Often depressed	–	Never depressed
Able to cope with life	–	Things get on top of me
Anxious and worried	–	Calm and unworried
Generally not feeling well	–	Usually in good health

Thus, for example, the position nearest the left hand of the first pair of statements indicated that the woman felt exhausted and tired out whereas the position nearest the right hand statement indicated that she felt full of energy. The intermediate positions could be used to express feelings between the two extremes. Previous analysis had shown that the eight pairs of statements were measuring a single dimension which we called psychological stress. We therefore combined women's answers to the eight separate items to give an overall score of psychological stress.

This is a general measure of psychological stress which was used in both Marsh's and our study with working and non-working women and for our sample of husbands. The causes of the symptoms of stress may lie in the working or non-working parts of women's lives, or in the interaction between the two. Since the measure of coping with conflicting demands of work and home was necessarily directed at the interaction, we would not expect all the women who showed evidence of psychological stress necessarily to have difficulties in coping with the demands of work and home, because, for some, the causes of their stress would lie elsewhere. Nor would we expect all those who had difficulties in coping necessarily to show psychological stress. In order to examine the relationships therefore, we divided women according to whether their scores on the measure of psychological stress were high, medium or low, as we did with the attitude measures described earlier.

We compared first full and part time workers and found little overall difference in their levels of psychological stress, despite the differences on the measure of coping with the demands of home and work described above.

Table 6.8 shows that there is in fact a relationship between the two measures: women who found difficulty in coping with the demands of work were more likely to have high stress levels than those who felt they could cope with the demands. In general the relationships were very similar for full and part time workers. It is noticeable however, that part time workers were more likely to have high stress scores than full time workers who had either comparable difficulty in coping or scores which indicated they could cope.

Table 6.8 Level of psychological stress by level of coping with the demands of home and work

Level of psychological stress	Level of coping with the demand of home and work			All working women*
	1 (Difficult to cope)	2	3 (Easy to cope)	
Full time	%	%	%	%
1 (High stress)	32	22	14	23
2	44	44	38	43
3 (Low stress)	23	34	48	34
	100	**100**	**100**	**100**
Base	623	817	414	1,854
Part time				
1 (High stress)	39	28	15	26
2	40	46	47	45
3 (Low stress)	21	26	38	29
	100	**100**	**100**	**100**
Base	306	592	567	1,465
*All working women**				
1 (High stress)	34	25	15	24
2	43	44	43	44
3 (Low stress)	22	31	42	32
	100	**100**	**100**	**100**
Base	929	1,409	981	3,319

Excluding 35 women for whom one or both measures were not available

These results may reflect differences in the circumstances which affect women's decisions to work or not, and whether to work full or part time. Since this is related to the presence and ages of children we looked at psychological stress levels for women at different life stages, comparing married and non-married women. Table 6.9 shows that although there was little difference overall in the level of stress among married and non-married women, the presence of children made a difference, particularly for non-married women. Among the married women, those who had had children had slightly higher levels of stress than the childless, but among the non-married women, those with dependent children, the lone mothers, had much higher levels of stress than any other group; 39% of lone mothers had high stress scores whereas the next highest proportion, among non-married women with grown-up children, was 28%. Surprisingly, when we compared lone mothers working full and part time, it was the part timers who showed the highest level of stress, possibly because their children were younger or because they were more likely to have financial difficulties. Apart from this there was little difference between full and part time workers.

Table 6.9 Level of psychological stress of full and part time working women by marital status and whether or not they have dependent children

Level of psychological stress	Married				Non-married				All working women
	Childless	Youngest child aged:		All married working women	Childless	Youngest child aged:		All non-married working women	
		Under 16	16 or over			Under 16	16 or over		
Full time	%	%	%	%	%	%	%	%	%
1 (High stress)	20	22	25	22	24	33	26	25	23
2	45	47	40	44	40	45	46	41	43
3 (Low stress)	35	31	35	34	36	22	27	34	34
	100	100	100	100	100	100	100	100	100
Base	379	371	339	1,089	628	64	96	788	1,877
Part time									
1 (High stress)	16	26	23	24		46	32	37	25
2	49	45	43	45		39	51	46	45
3 (Low stress)	35	29	34	31		15	17	17	30
	100	100	100	100		100	100	100	100
Base	64	873	409	1,346	15*	59	57	131	1,477
All working women									
1 (High stress)	20	25	24	24	24	39	28	27	24
2	45	46	41	44	41	42	48	42	44
3 (Low stress)	35	29	35	32	35	19	24	31	32
	100	100	100	100	100	100	100	100	100
Base	443	1,244	748	2,435	643	123	153	919	3,354

Base too small to show percentages

Table 6.10 Level of psychological stress of full and part time working women by occupation

Level of psychological stress	Occupation											All working women
	Professional	Teaching	Nursing, medical and social	Other intermediate non-manual	Clerical	Sales	Skilled	Semi-skilled factory	Semi-skilled domestic	Other semi-skilled	Unskilled	
Full time		%	%	%	%	%	%	%	%	%	%	%
1 (High stress)		20	15	19	21	30	22	36	33	20	33	23
2		41	49	42	43	40	53	39	40	37	37	43
3 (Low stress)		39	36	39	36	30	25	25	27	43	30	34
		100	100	100	100	100	100	100	100	100	100	100
Base	18*	152	127	165	727	115	145	248	75	61	44	1,877
Part time												
1 (High stress)		16	16	13	19	25	24	35	25	29	37	25
2		48	44	38	47	46	46	42	47	43	42	45
3 (Low stress)		36	40	49	34	29	30	23	28	28	21	30
		100	100	100	100	100	100	100	100	100	100	100
Base	8*	44	96	39	301	175	94	104	296	68	251	1,477
All working women												
1 (High stress)		19	15	18	20	27	23	36	27	25	36	24
2		43	48	41	44	43	50	40	45	40	41	44
3 (Low stress)		38	37	41	36	30	27	24	28	35	23	32
		100	100	100	100	100	100	100	100	100	100	100
Base	26*	196	223	204	1,028	290	239	352	371	129	295	3,354

*Base too small to show percentages

Although these results indicate that non-work factors are likely to be important determinants of psychological stress, the demands of the job itself may also be relevant. We therefore looked at the levels of stress women reported in relation to the occupation they worked in. Table 6.10 shows that manual workers tended to have higher levels of stress than non-manual workers, although, as we might expect given our earlier finding that they are more like manual workers, the sales workers were similar to the manual workers in this respect. The highest proportions of women with high stress scores were amongst semi-skilled factory and unskilled workers. This held for both full and part time workers, although among full time workers those in semi-skilled domestic work also had high levels of stress. Our findings are similar to those reported in a study of factory workers (Shimmin *et al*, 1981) which showed that high levels of mental stress and ill health among married women with dependent children were linked both to women's negative feelings about having to work and dislike of their job, coupled with heavy domestic responsibilities. We examine women's feelings about their own jobs as opposed to working in general later in the chapter, but next we examine the reasons women gave for working.

Women's reasons for working

A central aim of the survey was to investigate why women do or do not work. Although, as we have shown in Chapter 2, personal characteristics provide an explanation at the aggregate level, it is also important to ask individual women this question directly, whilst recognising that it is a question rarely asked of men (Brown *et al*, 1983). However, it is because a large proportion of women, unlike men, are not working at any one point in time and an even larger proportion of women have spent or will spend some time in their lives out of the labour market, that we can ask women why they are working currently, even though not all women will see themselves as having made a choice between working or not working.

We said earlier in this chapter that we were interested in women's financial motivation to work. However, although in some sense everyone works for money, men and women alike, work fulfils a variety of needs and people's reasons for working will vary according to their situation. Because we wished to identify how important a reason money was, we needed to distinguish women whose primary motivation to work was financial from those for whom it was secondary. In addition, among those who said they were working mainly for financial reasons, we wanted to distinguish those who really were dependent on their earnings for basic necessities from those who were not. This latter distinction is rather hard to make.

Objective measures, even if they are possible to establish, require detailed income information and almost become a study of their own. We therefore decided to see what reasons emerged from the open questions we asked in our pilot work, and to use whatever subjective distinctions in types of financial need women volunteered. Accordingly, in pilot work we questioned women in detail about all their reasons for working and then at the main stage respondents were shown a card listing a number of the most commonly mentioned reasons and were asked to say which applied to them. This approach enabled us to compare the importance of financial incentives to work with other reasons which are commonly held to be important for women such as social contact.[2] It also enabled us to distinguish sub-categories within the overall financial incentive to work. The card presented to respondents listed three different possible financial reasons for working: 'need money for basic essentials such as food, rent or mortgage', 'to earn money to buy extras' and 'to earn money of my own', though this last reason may be seen as expressing a desire for autonomy or financial independence rather than a financial need to work.

We initially asked women to look at the statements and select all those which best described their reasons for working and to mention any others not listed on the card. In this way we hoped to identify all the reasons women have for working. In so far as very few women gave other reasons for working than the ones on the card so that we only added one new category in the analysis, the list of reasons seems comprehensive. On average women gave between 2–3 reasons, women working full time being more likely to mention more reasons than women working part time.

As Table 6.11 shows, the most frequently selected reason, mentioned by 52% of women, was 'enjoy working'. Financial reasons were also given by high proportions of women: 'need to earn money for basic essentials' and 'to earn money for extras' were each mentioned by 47% of women. The next most commonly mentioned reasons were 'for the company of other people' (44%) and 'to earn money of my own' (37%). The other reasons were less frequently mentioned overall, although they were sometimes mentioned frequently by particular sub-groups of women as we shall show. Women working full time gave rather different reasons for working from those given by women working part time. It was particularly noticeable, although not perhaps surprising, that full time workers were more likely to say they were working to earn money for basic essentials rather than for extras whereas the reverse was true of part time workers. 'Enjoy working' was frequently mentioned by both groups, but more so by full than part time workers, while 'for the company of other people' was more often mentioned by part time workers. 'Working is the normal thing to do' and 'to follow my career' were very much more likely to be mentioned by full time workers, as might be expected.

The importance of financial reasons

When asked to select a main reason for working from those mentioned, respondents showed clearly the importance of financial reasons, whether this was because of the actual money or the greater autonomy earning

her own money gave a woman. Table 6.11 shows that 35% gave as their main reason for working 'need money for basic essentials', a further 20% said 'to earn money to buy extras' and 14% said 'to earn money of my own'. Thus 69% mentioned a financial reason as their main reason for working. The proportion of women giving 'enjoy working' as a main reason (14%) was considerably smaller than the proportion mentioning it as one of their reasons (52%), showing that, for most women, this is subsidiary to a financial reason for working. Likewise working 'for the company of other people' was only given as a main reason by 7% compared with the 44% who mentioned it as one of their reasons.

We compared women's scores on our measure of financial need to work (discussed earlier in this chapter) with their main reason for working and, as we expected, found a very high correlation. Women whose general attitudes towards working showed they had a high financial need to work were particularly likely to say they worked for financial reasons. Whilst the proportions of full and part time workers giving one of the three financial reasons as their main reason for working were the same (69%), there were differences in the type of financial reason given. Among full timers, 41% gave 'need money for basic essentials' as their main reason for working compared with 13% mentioning 'to earn money to buy extras' while equal proportions of part timers (28%) mentioned these two reasons. Although the differences between full and part timers in this respect are to be expected, it is important to note that a substantial minority of part time workers (28%) were working because they needed the money for basic essentials. Our study provides confirmatory evidence at a subjective level of those studies which, using objective measures, show that wives' earnings are often a vital supplement in some families to keep them above the official poverty line (Hamill, 1979). We have no way of knowing, however, whether the women who said they worked to earn money for 'extras' were in fact meeting basic needs too. It is also the case that some people's basic needs are other people's extras (Hunt, P, 1980).

Table 6.11 All reasons and main reason for working of full and part time working women

Reasons for working	All reasons			Main reason		
	Full time	Part time	All working women	Full time	Part time	All working women
				%	%	%
Working is the normal thing to do	20%	7%	14%	4	1	3
Need money for basic essentials such as food, rent or mortgage	55%	35%	47%	41	28	35
To earn money to buy extras	35%	51%	47%	13	28	20
To earn money of my own	38%	36%	37%	15	13	14
For the company of other people	40%	49%	44%	4	11	7
Enjoy working	55%	48%	52%	15	14	14
To follow my career	24%	7%	17%	7	2	5
To help with husband's job or business*	1%	2%	1%	–	2	1
Other reasons	2%	2%	2%	1	1	1
				100	100	100
Base	1,877	1,477	3,354	1,877	1,477	3,354

*Not listed on the prompt card
Percentages for all reasons do not add to 100 as women could have more than one reason for working

To simplify further comparisons of different groups of women, we compared three of the most frequently mentioned main reasons for working, as these showed the most significant differences. We did not include 'to earn money of my own' because, while this measured a wish for financial independence, it appeared to have rather different meanings for different groups of women. It was most frequently mentioned by young single women in the context of earning so as to be self-supporting and financially independent of their parents. It was also sometimes mentioned by married women working part time. In this context women viewed their earnings as money of their own which they could choose to spend as they wished, as opposed to their husband's income.

We expected women's reasons for working to be affected by both marital status, because married women have additional sources of economic support, and the presence of dependent children, who inevitably make financial demands on parents. Table 6.12 shows how the proportion of women giving as a main reason for working 'need money for basic essentials', 'to earn money for extras' and 'enjoy working' varies for married and non-married women at different life stages. Looking first at the bottom part of the table, which gives the results for all working women, it can be seen that married women were less likely to say they were working for money for basic essentials than non-married women. We would expect this since most married women are either actually less reliant on their own earnings to buy basics or possibly less willing to admit to working mainly for essentials as this might reflect badly on their husband as a breadwinner.

It was clear that non-married women with dependent or grown-up children were most likely to say they were working for basic essentials. About three quarters said this compared with about a quarter of their married counterparts. They were also less likely to say they were working for extras or because they enjoyed working than their married peers. In fact, hardly any non-married women (3%) said they worked for extras whilst 26% of married women said they did and women with children were more likely to say this than childless married women.

The low percentage of non-married childless women who said they were working for essentials (36%) is partly attributable to the higher incidence of 'other reasons' given by this group; many said they were working to earn money of their own or because it was the normal thing to do. When we compared women working full and part time, it was clear that the general trend we have described was maintained. Regardless of their work status, non-married women were more likely than their married counterparts to say they were working for essentials. However, work status was also important. Non-married women with children who worked full time were most likely to say they worked for essentials. Similarly, whilst part time workers overall were more likely than full timers to say they worked for extras, married women working part time were more likely to say this than non-married part time workers.

Table 6.13 compares the reasons given for working by women in different occupational groups. When we look at all working women, it is clear that while just over a

Table 6.12 Proportions of full and part time working women who are working mainly because they 'need money for essentials', 'want to earn money for extras' or because they 'enjoy working' by marital status and whether or not they have dependent children

Main reason for working	Married				Non-married				All working women
	Childless	Youngest child aged:		All married working women	Childless	Youngest child aged:		All married working women	
		Under 16	16 or over			Under 16	16 or over		
Full time	%	%	%	%	%	%	%	%	%
Need money for basic essentials	44	34	33	38	36	87	80	46	41
To earn money for extras	19	25	23	22	1	3	2	2	13
Enjoy working	16	18	20	17	13	5	4	11	15
Other reasons	21	24	24	23	50	5	14	41	31
	100	100	100	100	100	100	100	100	100
Base	379	371	339	1,089	628	64	96	788	1,877
Part time									
Need money for basic essentials	23	26	20	24		57	68	65	28
To earn money for extras	19	31	28	30		–	14	8	28
Enjoy working	25	12	18	14		21	3	6	14
Other reasons	33	31	34	32		22	15	21	30
	100	100	100	100		100	100	100	100
Base	64	873	409	1,346	15*	59	57	131	1,477
All working women									
Need money for basic essentials	41	28	26	30	36	78	74	48	35
To earn money for extras	19	29	25	26	1	8	3	3	20
Enjoy working	17	14	19	16	13	4	5	11	14
Other reasons	23	29	30	28	50	10	18	38	31
	100	100	100	100	100	100	100	100	100
Base	443	1,244	748	2,435	643	123	153	919	3,354

*Base too small to show percentages

Table 6.13 Proportions of full and part time working women who are working mainly because they 'need money for basic essentials', 'want to earn money for extras' or because they 'enjoy working' by occupation

Main reason for working	Occupational group											All working women
	Professional	Teaching	Nursing, medical and social	Other intermediate non-manual	Clerical	Sales	Skilled	Semi-skilled factory	Semi-skilled domestic	Other semi-skilled	Unskilled	
Full time		%	%	%	%	%	%	%	%	%	%	%
Need money for basic essentials		35	31	30	43	37	44	52	34	39	66	40
To earn money for extras		6	13	13	14	11	14	18	18	18	14	13
Enjoy working		25	28	24	12	17	11	6	12	15	9	15
Other reasons		34	28	33	31	35	31	24	36	28	11	32
		100	100	100	100	100	100	100	100	100	100	100
Base	18*	152	127	165	727	115	145	248	75	61	44	1,877
Part time												
Need money for basic essentials		9	37	18	16	27	28	41	26	27	41	28
To earn money for extras		11	17	13	27	28	29	34	26	27	37	28
Enjoy working		32	20	35	20	9	20	4	12	13	4	14
Other reasons		48	26	34	37	36	23	21	36	33	18	30
		100	100	100	100	100	100	100	100	100	100	100
Base	8*	44	96	39	301	175	94	104	296	68	251	1,477
All working women												
Need money for basic essentials		29	34	28	35	30	38	49	27	32	45	35
To earn money for extras		7	14	13	18	22	20	22	25	22	33	20
Enjoy working		27	25	26	15	12	14	5	12	14	5	14
Other reasons		37	27	33	32	36	28	24	36	32	17	31
		100	100	100	100	100	100	100	100	100	100	100
Base	26*	196	223	204	1,028	290	239	352	371	129	295	3,354

*Base too small to show percentages

third (35%) said their main reason for working was for money for basic essentials, women in semi-skilled factory and unskilled jobs stood out as being much more likely to say this (49% and 45% respectively), which ties in with them being more likely to have a high financial dependence on their earnings as we saw earlier. This pattern held when we compared full and part time workers although overall, full timers were more likely than part timers to say they were working to earn money for essentials: 40% compared with 28%. However, in one occupational group, nursing, medical and social, there was a marked divergence from the trend. Among women working in nursing, medical and social jobs, part timers were more likely than full timers to say they were working for basic essentials: 37% said this compared with 31% of full timers. It is not easy to explain this difference; it may be that because this occupational category covers a range of jobs of different skill levels many of which offer shift and night work, it is particularly attractive to mothers of young children who are working chiefly because of high financial need, but who need to work at different times when husbands can care for children.

The importance of non-financial reasons
When we looked at the proportions of women saying they worked because they enjoyed working, women in semi-skilled factory and unskilled jobs again stood out. They were very much less likely overall than other groups to give this as their main reason for working (5% for each group). In contrast, about a quarter of women in the three higher non-manual occupational

groups (teaching, nursing, medical and social and intermediate non-manual) reported they worked because they enjoyed working, but noticeably fewer women, between 12%–15%, said this in their other non-manual groups or in the manual level jobs. When we compared women working full and part time in the three non-manual groups, the group containing nursing, medical and social occupations again stood out. For, unlike women working part time in teaching or intermediate non-manual jobs, women working part time in this group were less likely than full timers to say they worked because they enjoyed working: 20% said this compared with 32% and 35% respectively of the other two non-manual groups. In fact, the same proportion of women working part time in nursing, medical and social occupations gave 'enjoying working' as their main reason for working as women working part time in clerical or skilled manual occupations. Paradoxically though, a high proportion of women in the former group, as we shall see later in the chapter, reported that they were very satisfied with their current job.

Because we could not examine the details of women's actual jobs in a survey of this kind, it is impossible to know from this study to what extent those women who said that they worked because they enjoyed working were working in more enjoyable or intrinsically rewarding jobs or were able to emphasise 'enjoyment' because their financial need for work was less, so enabling them to emphasise non-financial orientations to working. It is worth noting, however, that the three occupations with the highest proportions of women giving 'enjoy working' as a main reason for working are also the three highest paid occupational groups for women, as we showed in Chapter 5. Furthermore, as Table 6.13 shows, the proportion of women saying they worked to earn money to buy extras tended to rise as the level of the job fell: only 7% of teachers overall gave this as their main reason compared with 18% and 22% of clerical and sales respectively and 33% of the unskilled. Women working part time were more likely to say this than full time workers. Among part timers, however, women in the higher non-manual groups were less likely to say they worked to earn money for extras (between 11% and 17% compared with over a quarter of women in all other groups). We looked at how the reasons women gave for working related to their attitudes towards work in general and found the kind of associations that we would expect. Women who said they are working mainly for enjoyment or to follow a career were least likely to have a high financial dependence on their earnings.

The link between women's reasons for working and psychological stress

When we looked at whether women's levels of psychological stress varied with their reasons for working, we found, as Table 6.14 shows, a strong relationship. Among all working women, a third of those working to get money for basic essentials expressed relatively high levels of psychological stress compared with 23% of those working for money for extras and only 13% of women working for enjoyment. It is not possible to say, however, whether financial pressure among women working for basic necessities leads directly to feelings of high psychological stress or whether psychological stress results from several factors including financial pressures for a woman to work.

Table 6.14 **Level of psychological stress of full and part time working women who are working mainly because they 'need money for basic essentials', 'to earn money to buy extras' or because they 'enjoy working'**

Level of psychological stress	Main reason for working			All working women
	Need money for basic essentials	To earn money to buy extras	Enjoy working	
Full time	%	%	%	%
1 (High stress)	30	20	15	23
2	44	49	38	43
3 (Low stress)	26	31	47	34
	100	**100**	**100**	**100**
Base	*763*	*253*	*282*	*1,877**
Part time				
1 (High stress)	38	25	12	25
2	43	44	45	45
3 (Low stress)	19	31	43	30
	100	**100**	**100**	**100**
Base	*406*	*408*	*199*	*1,477**
All working women	%	%	%	%
1 (High stress)	33	23	13	24
2	44	46	41	44
3 (Low stress)	23	31	46	32
	100	**100**	**100**	**100**
Base	*1,169*	*661*	*481*	*3,354**

Including women who gave other main reasons for working

Looking at the stress levels of full time and part time workers in Table 6.14, we can see that both groups follow the same overall trend. However, among women working because they need money for basic essentials, a higher proportion of part time than of full time workers expressed relatively high levels of psychological stress. One of the reasons why women who need money for basic essentials may work part time as opposed to full time is that they have domestic constraints which prevent them from doing full time jobs; we know for example that a relatively high proportion of part time workers are women with dependent children. Full time workers in contrast, particularly those working for money for basic essentials, include larger proportions of young childless women who normally have very few domestic responsibilities. This, together with the fact that full time workers may be under less financial pressure because of their higher earnings, may account for the higher levels of psychological stress among those working part time.

Women's priorities in choosing jobs

Most studies of workers' orientations to work, as we have noted earlier, have focused on men, usually manual workers in manufacturing industry (Brown *et al*, 1983). They begin by looking at the characteristics workers think desirable or important about jobs in general and so identify those aspects of a job to which workers give priority. As we have shown, this is a second stage in any study of women's orientations to work as their general attitudes to and their reasons for working also reflect their priorities.

We look next, therefore, at the relative priority women assigned to a number of different features of their jobs, in order to find out which aspects they consider to be the most important in a job, and whether different groups of women have different priorities in choosing a job. In particular, we wanted to know whether intrinsic factors in a job, such as 'work you like doing', 'the opportunity to use your abilities', or 'good prospects' were important to women and what importance they accorded to 'a good rate of pay' as compared with extrinsic factors like 'convenient hours' or 'an easy journey to work'. We asked women to think about what they looked for in a job and to rate each of eight aspects as 'essential', 'very important', 'fairly important' or 'not very important'. We used the answers on each aspect to represent a score on a four point scale with 'essential' as 1 and 'not important' as 4. From these ratings we computed the average level of importance of each aspect for different groups of women.

Table 6.15 shows the average importance ratings assigned by women to each of the eight aspects of their jobs. Overall, 'work you like doing' was considered most important, followed by 'friendly people to work with'. 'Good prospects' was considered the least important aspect of a job. Full and part time workers differed in their priorities for some aspects, although 'work you like doing' was considered most important by both full and part time workers. However, for part timers 'con-

Table 6.15 Proportions of full and part time working women rating as essential or very important eight different aspects of jobs, and their average importance rating* for each aspect

Aspects of jobs	Full time		Part time		All working women	
	% rating as essential or very important	Average importance rating*	% rating as essential or very important	Average importance rating*	% rating as essential or very important	Average importance rating*
Work you like doing	93%	1.6	88%	1.8	91%	1.7
The opportunity to use your abilities	78%	2.0	62%	2.3	71%	2.1
Good prospects	58%	2.4	37%	2.8	49%	2.6
A good rate of pay	79%	1.9	68%	2.2	74%	2.0
A secure job	83%	1.9	68%	2.2	76%	2.0
Friendly people to work with	85%	1.9	88%	1.9	86%	1.9
Convenient hours of work	65%	2.2	88%	1.8	75%	2.1
An easy journey to work	53%	2.4	66%	2.2	59%	2.3
Base	1,877	1,877	1,477	1,477	3,354	3,354

*1 = essential, 2 = very important, 3 = fairly important, 4 = not very important

venient hours of work' was rated of equal importance. For full time workers 'a good rate of pay', and 'a secure job' were considered to be of equal importance to 'friendly people to work with', whereas for part time workers the first two of these aspects were of lesser importance. The intrinsic factors 'good prospects' and 'the opportunity to use your abilities' were considered less important than other aspects by both full and part timers, although they were of greater priority to full than part time workers.

We examined the priorities given to different aspects of jobs by women at different life stages, but found that most of the differences could be attributed to the differing priorities of full and part time workers and the differences in the relative proportions of the two at different life stages. However, as might be expected, women with dependent children as opposed to the childless or those with grown-up children attached particular importance to convenient hours of work. Younger childless women attached somewhat greater priority than other women to 'good prospects' and 'a secure job'.

As there are very few published studies of women's job priorities it is difficult to make comparisons of this sample of women with other groups. However, it is of note that women in our study placed less importance on 'a good rate of pay' or 'a secure job' than the various studies of male workers suggest men do. Brown, Curran and Cousins show that economic considerations (pay, security, etc) predominate for men in these studies, whereas amongst women in our survey interesting work is accorded most importance overall. It is impossible to know, however, whether this is a genuine difference between men and women workers or a consequence of comparing different groups. A nationally representative sample of working men which includes more men in white collar and professional and managerial jobs than studies to date have done, for example, might show less priority given to pay, not least because this would be taken as a corollary of having interesting or responsible work. Our study does confirm however the importance attached to or emphasis placed on 'convenience' factors by part timers which other studies have noted (Hunt, 1968; Beynon and Blackburn, 1972).

Once we had identified women's job priorities, we examined whether there was any relationship between the importance they attached to these eight different job aspects and their main reasons for working and we summarise the results here (see tables in technical report, Martin and Roberts, 1984). Women whose main reason for working was that they enjoyed work or wanted to follow a career attached more importance than other groups to the intrinsic features of a job such as 'work you like doing' and 'the opportunity to use your abilities'. However, women who gave some kind of financial reason as their main reason for working saying they worked to earn money for 'basic essentials', or for 'extras' or for 'money of my own', generally considered a 'good rate of pay' only slightly more important than average and rated other features of jobs as of equal or greater importance.

It may well be that, for women who need to work for financial reasons, the desire for a well-paid job has to be balanced against other factors when looking for a job. For example, among part time workers who said their main reason for working was for money for basic essentials, 'convenient hours' was considered more important than 'a good rate of pay'. This suggests that these women need a job that fits in with their domestic arrangements in order for them to be able to work at all, and therefore the rate of pay has to be a secondary consideration; Beynon and Blackburn (1972) and Craig et al (1982a) have also found this. However, it is also very important to note that women who were working for financial reasons considered 'work you like doing' as important an aspect in choosing a job as 'a good rate of pay'.

Women's satisfaction with their jobs
The approach to the measure of job satisfaction used on this survey was relatively unsophisticated since to cover such a complex topic fully would have required far more detailed questioning, (for example about the woman's type of work), than we could undertake in the course of a survey designed to look at many other aspects of employment. We also recognised that people responding to job satisfaction questions rarely say they are dissatisfied with their jobs, though they might have varying levels of satisfaction with particular aspects of their jobs.

Table 6.16 Proportions of full and part time working women rating themselves very or fairly satisfied with eight different aspects of jobs, and their average satisfaction rating* for each aspect

Aspects of jobs	Full time		Part time		All working women	
	% rating as very or fairly satisfied	Average satisfaction rating*	% rating as very or fairly satisfied	Average satisfaction rating*	% rating as very or fairly satisfied	Average satisfaction rating*
The sort of work you do	88%	1.7	89%	1.7	88%	1.7
The opportunity to use your abilities	76%	2.2	72%	2.3	75%	2.2
Your prospects	73%	2.2	65%	2.2	69%	2.2
Your rate of pay	75%	2.2	83%	2.0	79%	2.1
How secure your job is	86%	1.8	84%	1.8	85%	1.8
The people you work with	92%	1.6	90%	1.4	91%	1.5
Your hours of work	89%	1.8	94%	1.4	91%	1.6
The ease of your journey to work	85%	1.7	87%	1.4	86%	1.6
Base	*1,877*	*1,877*	*1,477*	*1,477*	*3,354*	*3,354*

1 = very satisfied, 2 = fairly satisfied, 3 = neither satisfied nor dissatisfied, 4 = a little dissatisfied, 5 = very dissatisfied

We asked women how satisfied they were with each of eight aspects of their present job. They were asked to rate their satisfaction on a four point scale: 'very satisfied', 'fairly satisfied', 'a little dissatisfied', and 'very dissatisfied'. Their answers were scored 1, 2, 4 and 5, with a score of 3 given to those few women who expressed no opinion on a particular aspect. Average ratings of satisfaction with each aspect of women's jobs were then computed.

Table 6.16 shows the average levels of satisfaction women expressed with different aspects of their jobs. The most satisfactory aspect was 'the people you work with', followed by 'your hours of work' and 'the ease of your journey to work'. Women overall were least satisfied by 'the opportunity to use your abilities' and 'your prospects'. Differences between the satisfaction ratings of full and part time workers were less apparent for these intrinsic aspects of jobs than for some of the extrinsic factors. Part timers were most satisfied with 'the people you work with', 'your hours of work' and 'the ease of your journey to work'; more so than full timers in the case of all three. It is not very useful, however, to know how satisfied women are with particular aspects of their jobs unless we also know how important these aspects were; high satisfaction scores on job aspects of little importance will not mean very much.

To show how the importance and satisfaction ratings of full and part time workers compare the average ratings for each aspect are plotted side by side in Figure 6.1. It

Figure 6.1 Average importance ratings assigned by full and part time working women to eight different aspects of jobs and average satisfaction ratings with those aspects of their current job

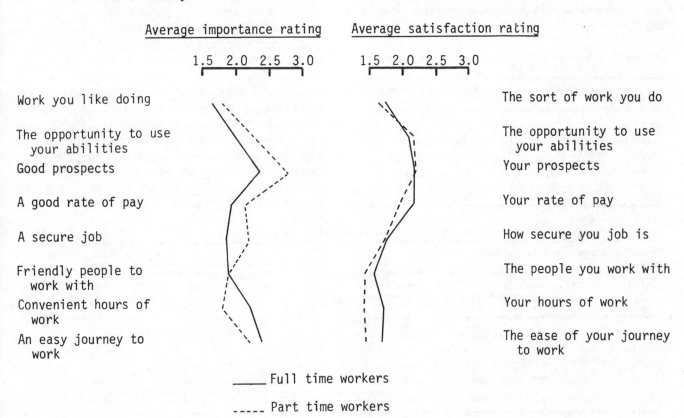

_____ Full time workers

- - - - - Part time workers

is not possible to compare importance and satisfaction ratings directly however, because they are based on different scales, but it is of interest to compare the relative ordering of the different aspects and to look at the difference between full and part time workers.

For most features of jobs examined there was a fairly high degree of congruence between importance and satisfaction ratings; on the whole the more important aspects tended to be rated as most satisfactory and vice versa. However, it is noticeable that the extrinsic factors such as 'hours of work', 'journey to work' and 'people you work with', were considered more satisfactory in relation to their importance than the intrinsic factors 'use of abilities', 'prospects' and the 'nature of the work'. For full time workers the biggest discrepancy between importance and satisfaction related to rate of pay. This was an important aspect of a job for these workers and they were not very satisfied with the rate of pay they received in their jobs, whereas for part time workers it was less important compared with other factors and they were more satisfied.

The congruence between the importance women attach to various aspects of their jobs and their satisfaction with them may be reflecting to some extent their expectations. It is commonly found that people's job aspirations are shaped by experience and by their knowledge of the kind of jobs available to them (Blackburn and Mann, 1979). As we have seen, the priorities of part time workers are rather different from those of full timers. They often face such considerable domestic constraints on the kind of job they can take that factors such as convenient hours become of overriding importance. For many part time workers the choice is not between this job or that job but between working in any job that fits in with these constraints and not working at all.

After women had been asked to rate their satisfaction with specific aspects of their jobs they were asked to rate how satisfied they felt overall with their job. Table 6.17 shows that 55% said they were very satisfied and a further 36% said they were fairly satisfied. Part time workers were slightly more likely to say they were 'very satisfied' rather than 'fairly satisfied' but there was little difference in the proportions expressing some degree of dissatisfaction, a minority in any event. This compares with similar results on other surveys or studies using similar measures. All show high proportions of people expressing satisfaction with their job with women generally being more satisfied than men and part timers more satisfied than full timers, a finding the discussion on job satisfaction in the General Household Survey, 1980 also shows (OPCS, 1982a). However, there are differences between groups of people in their level of satisfaction and we go on to distinguish how these vary for different groups of women in our survey.

Variations in levels of job satisfaction
From Table 6.18 we can see how levels of job satisfaction vary among women at different life stages. The job satisfaction levels of full and part timers did not differ significantly for women at different life stages and so they were not shown separately. Childless women under 30 were least satisfied with their jobs. This may be because, as we have suggested earlier in the chapter, this group is likely to contain women who for a variety of reasons were less attached to working, whereas the other groups were likely to contain higher proportions of women who had chosen to work. However, our results, like those of other studies, show some evidence of an increase in job satisfaction with age. It is rather difficult to say whether this is a genuine trend or a reflection of the extent of choice about working among women at different life stages or of a process of accommodation. Older women, for example, may have had more opportunity to find a job that they liked or may have changed their expectations and adapted to their job over time in much the same way as men who also show greater levels of satisfaction with age. The exception to the general increase in satisfaction with age was that women with pre-school children were slightly more likely to be very satisfied with their jobs than women with slightly older children, although the proportions expressing dissatisfaction were the same. This result may relate to differences in the type of women who work when their children are young: those who are

Table 6.17 Full and part time working women's overall satisfaction with their present jobs

Overall satisfaction with present job	Full time	Part time	All working women
	%	%	%
Very satisfied	53	58	55
Fairly satisfied	37	34	36
A little dissatisfied	7	6	6
Very dissatisfied	3	2	3
	100	100	100
Base	1,877	1,477	3,354

Table 6.18 Working women's overall satisfaction with their present jobs by life cycle stage

Overall satisfaction with present job	Life cycle stage							All working women
	Childless women aged:		Women with youngest child aged:			Women with all children 16 or over, aged:		
	Under 30	30 or over	0–4	5–10	11–15	Under 50	50 or over	
	%	%	%	%	%	%	%	%
Very satisfied	45	51	54	50	60	62	67	55
Fairly satisfied	42	41	38	41	31	31	27	36
A little dissatisfied	8	5	7	6	7	6	5	6
Very dissatisfied	5	3	2	3	2	2	2	3
	100	100	100	100	100	100	100	100
Base	758	328	276	553	538	362	539	3,354

committed to the intrinsic aspects of work on the one hand and those working from financial necessity on the other.

If this is the case we might also expect women in different occupations to express different levels of job satisfaction. Table 6.19 shows that there are differences, but not a consistent relationship with level of occupation. Looking first at the ratings for all working women it is clear that semi-skilled factory workers were less likely than other workers to say that they were very satisfied: 16% expressed dissatisfaction, compared with around

Table 6.19 Full and part time working women's overall satisfaction with their present jobs by occupation

Overall satisfaction with present job	Occupational group											All working women
	Professional	Teaching	Nursing, medical and social	Other intermediate non-manual	Clerical	Sales	Skilled	Semi-skilled factory	Semi-skilled domestic	Other semi-skilled	Unskilled	
		%	%	%	%	%	%	%	%	%	%	%
Full time												
Very satisfied		54	61	64	48	63	53	49	59	65	48	53
Fairly satisfied		39	35	30	41	28	37	36	31	25	43	37
A little dissatisfied		6	4	6	8	7	6	8	5	5	7	7
Very dissatisfied		1	–	1	3	3	4	7	4	5	2	3
		100	100	100	100	100	100	100	100	100	100	100
Base	18*	152	127	165	727	115	145	248	75	61	44	1,877
Part time												
Very satisfied		45	64	58	64	59	54	43	61	54	54	58
Fairly satisfied		46	34	37	30	31	35	39	33	39	37	34
A little dissatisfied		9	2	3	5	7	9	10	5	5	6	6
Very dissatisfied		–	–	3	1	2	1	9	1	2	3	2
		100	100	100	100	100	100	100	100	100	100	100
Base	8*	44	96	39	301	175	94	104	296	68	251	1,477
All working women												
Very satisfied		52	62	63	52	61	53	47	60	60	53	55
Fairly satisfied		40	35	31	38	30	37	37	33	32	38	36
A little dissatisfied		7	3	5	7	7	7	9	5	5	6	6
Very dissatisfied		1	–	1	3	2	3	7	2	3	3	3
		100	100	100	100	100	100	100	100	100	100	100
Base	26*	196	223	204	1,028	290	239	352	371	129	295	3,354

*Base too small to show percentages

Table 6.20 Full and part time working women's overall satisfaction with their present jobs by their main reason for working

Overall satisfaction with present job	Main reason for working									All working women
	Normal thing to do	Need money for basic essentials	To earn money to buy extras	To earn money of my own	Company	Enjoy working	To follow my career	To help with husband's job	Other reasons	
	%	%	%	%	%	%	%	%	%	%
Full time										
Very satisfied	55	47	58	49	53	69	54			53
Fairly satisfied	38	42	34	38	39	26	34			37
A little dissatisfied	4	8	5	8	6	4	10			7
Very dissatisfied	3	3	4	5	3	1	2			3
	100	100	100	100	100	100	100			100
Base	75	763	253	281	72	282	126	9*	11*	1,877†
Part time										
Very satisfied		48	53	62	68	75	55	70		58
Fairly satisfied		40	39	32	28	20	33	15		34
A little dissatisfied		7	7	5	3	4	12	12		6
Very dissatisfied		5	2	1	1	1	–	3		2
		100	100	100	100	100	100	100		100
Base	18*	406	408	189	165	199	33	33	20*	1,477†
All working women										
Very satisfied	53	47	55	55	64	72	54	67	45	55
Fairly satisfied	40	41	37	35	31	23	33	21	48	36
A little dissatisfied	5	8	6	7	4	4	11	10	3	6
Very dissatisfied	2	4	2	3	1	1	2	2	3	3
	100	100	100	100	100	100	100	100	100	100
Base	93	1,169	661	470	237	481	159	42	31	3,354†

*Base too small to show percentages
†Includes 11 cases where main reason for working was not known

6–10% of women in all other occupations except those in nursing, medical and social occupations of whom only 3% expressed any dissatisfaction. Differences in the job satisfaction of full and part timers in different occupations were generally not great and showed no consistent pattern.

Among full time workers those in clerical, unskilled and factory occupations were least likely to say they were very satisfied while those in other semi-skilled occupations, other intermediate non-manual occupations and sales occupations were most likely to say this. Among part timers, semi-skilled factory workers and, perhaps surprisingly, teachers were least likely to say they were very satisfied while clerical workers and those in nursing, medical and social occupations were most likely to be very satisfied with their jobs even though, as we have shown, fewer women in these last two groups said they worked because they enjoyed working. The lack of any obvious pattern of results suggests that factors other than occupation itself, such as the age structure of women in different occupations, women's different labour market experiences or the reasons women in different occupations have for working, may be of relevance in explaining the differences we observed, though of course variations in the type of work done within an occupational group which we could not take into account are likely to be important too (Agassi, 1979; Feldberg and Glenn, 1984).

We examined women's overall ratings of satisfaction with their jobs in relation to their main reason for working on the basis that those whose main reason indicated they had a sense of choice about working would be more likely to be in a position to find a satisfying job. Table 6.20 provides evidence of this. Women who said they were working because they enjoyed working were most likely to say they were very satisfied, whereas those working because they needed money for basic essentials were least likely to say they were very satisfied. These two groups were the extremes among both full and part timers, but among women who were working because they enjoyed working, 75% of part timers said they were very satisfied compared with 69% of full timers.

Among women working for the company of other peo-

ple, the part timers again expressed greater satisfaction than the full timers, possibly reflecting either the greater degree of choice these part timers had about whether or not to work or their lower expectations about a job. Differences between full and part time workers working 'to earn money of my own' probably reflects the differences in the interpretation of this reason for different women which we referred to earlier. Most of these women who were working full time were young and single and therefore had to work to support themselves whereas those working part time were mainly married women with children who wanted some financial independence from their husbands, but were less likely to be totally financially dependent on their own earnings.

To determine whether the differing levels of satisfaction among groups of women working for different reasons were associated with particular features of their jobs or a more generalised feeling, we looked at the average satisfaction ratings these groups gave to individual aspects of their jobs (Table 6.21). Looking at the averages for all working women, it is clear that the high levels of satisfaction among women working because they enjoyed work is particularly attributable to their satisfaction with the intrinsic aspects of their jobs, the sort of work they were doing and the opportunity to use their abilities. However they were also slightly more satisfied than average with most of the other features, suggesting that they have a generally favourable view of their jobs, but were particularly satisfied with its intrinsic aspects. Women working for basic essentials, who are the least satisfied group, tended to give relatively low ratings to most features but only in the case of their prospects did they give a lower rating than any other group, suggesting that they have a fairly generalised dissatisfaction with their jobs.

Dissatisfaction with one's job may contribute to feelings of psychological stress and we saw earlier, for example, that one of the most dissatisfied groups, women working for money for basic essentials, expressed relatively high levels of stress. Table 6.22 shows directly the relationship between feelings of psychological stress and overall job satisfaction. We can see that among all working women there is a marked trend for the relative level of stress to increase as overall satisfaction with the

Table 6.21   Average satisfaction ratings* assigned by working women to eight different aspects of their jobs by their main reason for working

Aspects of jobs	Main reason for working							All working women
	Normal thing to do	Need money for basic essentials	To earn money to buy extras	To earn money of my own	Company	Enjoy working	To follow my career	
The sort of work you do	1.8	1.8	1.7	1.8	1.6	1.4	1.7	1.7
The opportunity to use your abilities	2.1	2.3	2.2	2.3	2.2	1.9	2.2	2.2
Your prospects	2.2	2.4	2.1	2.2	2.1	2.1	2.2	2.2
Your rate of pay	2.2	2.2	1.9	2.1	1.9	2.1	2.3	2.1
How secure your job is	1.6	1.9	1.8	1.9	1.8	1.6	1.7	1.8
The people you work with	1.5	1.5	1.5	1.5	1.4	1.5	1.6	1.5
Your hours of work	1.4	1.7	1.6	1.5	1.4	1.5	1.7	1.6
The ease of your journey to work	1.6	1.7	1.4	1.5	1.5	1.6	1.6	1.6
Base	93	1,169	661	470	237	481	159	3,354†

*1 = very satisfied, 2 = fairly satisfied, 3 = neither satisfied nor dissatisfied, 4 = a little dissatisfied, 5 = very dissatisfied
†Includes 84 women who gave other reasons

Table 6.22 Level of psychological stress of full and part time working women by overall satisfaction with their present job

Level of psychological stress	Overall job satisfaction				All working women
	Very satisfied	Fairly satisfied	A little dissatisfied	Very dissatisfied	
	%	%	%	%	%
Full time					
1 (High stress)	17	27	36	53	23
2	41	47	38	29	43
3 (Low stress)	42	26	26	18	34
	100	100	100	100	100
Base	989	691	126	61	1,877*
Part time					
1 (High stress)	22	27	39	55	25
2	42	51	44	32	45
3 (Low stress)	36	22	17	13	30
	100	100	100	100	100
Base	847	504	87	31	1,477*
All working women					
1 (High stress)	20	27	37	54	24
2	41	49	41	30	44
3 (Low stress)	39	24	22	16	32
	100	100	100	100	100
Base	1,836	1,195	213	92	3,354*

*Including 18 women for whom job satisfaction was not known

job decreases. Over a half (54%) of women who were very dissatisfied with their jobs expressed relatively high psychological stress compared with 20% of very satisfied women. Full time and part time workers showed the same pattern, although among women who were very satisfied with their jobs a higher proportion of part time than of full time workers were in the relatively high stress category (22% and 17% respectively), suggesting that non-occupational factors such as the presence of children and domestic constraints are also likely to contribute to feelings of stress.

After they were questioned about their satisfaction with their particular jobs, women were asked to think more generally about working and to say whether they liked working very much, reasonably well, not much or not at all. Over a half (54%) said that they liked working very much and only a very small proportion (5%) expressed an unfavourable opinion. We looked at the answers to this question in relation to other aspects of the women's situations but found that they showed very similar relationships to those of responses to the overall job satisfaction question and so we have not described any further analyses of this question.

Summary and conclusions
This chapter has dealt with the attitudes of working women towards working in general, their reasons for working and their views about their jobs in particular. Throughout, we have been concerned to identify differences between groups of women, whether this be between women working full or part time, women at different stages of the life cycle or different occupational levels, though these are often interrelated.

It was clear from their general attitudes that the majority of working women in the survey had a high financial dependence on working and that the vast majority enjoyed working; only 6%, for example, definitely wished

they did not go out to work. Women's reasons for working also showed this multifaceted approach. On average, they gave between 2–3 reasons for working, full timers giving slightly more reasons than part timers, and the most frequently selected reason, mentioned by 52% of women, was 'enjoy working'. However the salience of financial reasons rose when women were asked to select their main reason for working, as 69% chose one of three financial reasons.

There were some important differences between groups of women, particularly between women at different life stages. Non-married women were more likely both to have a high financial dependence on work and to say they were working for basic essentials than married women, and non-married women with children were most likely of all to say they worked for basic essentials. To a certain extent differences between full and part time workers in their attitudes mirrored these differences. Full time workers were more likely than part timers to say they were working for basic essentials though a substantial minority of part time workers (28%) gave this as their main reason for working.

There was no significant difference, however, between full and part time workers in the proportions finding work stimulating or worthwhile overall though there were differences of attitudes between women at different life cycle stages. Childless women under 30, for example, were least likely to find work stimulating, whereas childless women over 30 were most likely to rate highly the intrinsic attractions of working. However, when we compared the non-financial reasons women gave for working, there was a difference between full and part time workers. The former were more likely to endorse 'working is the normal thing to do' or 'to follow my career' as reasons for working whilst the latter mentioned 'the company of other people' more often.

The notion that women who are more intrinsically committed to paid work will work full time is partially borne out by the findings. For when we compared women at the same stage of their life cycle, women working full time with a pre-school child and those with grown-up children were more likely to rate work as intrinsically attractive than comparable women working part time. However within the group of mothers of pre-school children who worked full time there were two distinct sub-groups. One sub-group, who tended to be in higher level occupations, appeared to be more career minded and showed higher intrinsic attachment to work, while women in the other group worked because they really needed the money and would not work at that stage otherwise.

It was clear that full time and part time workers had different job priorities. Whilst both endorsed 'work you like doing' as the most important, women working part time also voted 'convenient hours' of equal importance. Indeed, our study confirms what small scale studies have already shown, that convenient hours are of such priority to part time workers that they override other considerations. Even women working part time for 'essentials' rated 'convenient hours' more important than 'a good rate of pay'.

Overall, high proportions of working women said they liked working and were very or fairly satisfied with their jobs. However, they were more satisfied with the extrinsic features such as 'hours of work', 'people you work with' than with the intrinsic aspects and there was a difference between full and part time workers. Full timers for example were less satisfied than part timers with their rate of pay which was a more important dimension of a job for them. On the whole, our results show, unsurprisingly, higher satisfaction in the older age groups and some variation in levels of satisfaction according to occupational level. Semi-skilled factory workers were markedly less satisfied with their jobs than other workers for example. Young childless women, and those working from financial necessity also tended to view work as less intrinsically attractive than other women and were less satisfied with their jobs. It was also true that women who said they were working because they enjoyed working were more satisfied with the intrinsic dimensions of their job than women working for basic essentials.

Since for most women paid work has been fitted in with domestic work we looked at how women coped with these potentially conflicting demands. Full time workers were more likely to report difficulty in coping with the demands of a job. However many part timers have more domestic demands made upon their time and life cycle variations were therefore important. Amongst the factors established in the survey, the presence of children was the single most important factor in whether a woman had difficulty in coping or not. Lone parents were more likely to find it difficult to cope than married mothers, particularly if they had dependent children and worked full time; however many of the married women who worked full time whilst responsible for dependent children also said they found it difficult to cope with the competing demands of home and work.

One possible consequence of having difficulties in coping is psychological stress. We found that women who had difficulty in coping with the demands of home and work were more likely to have high stress scores than those who felt they could cope. Part time workers, however, were more likely to have high stress scores than full timers with comparable levels of coping ability. Again it was the presence of children which overall raised stress scores. There also appears to be a link with job dissatisfaction as there is a tendency for the relative level of stress to be higher among women with somewhat lower job satisfaction. However, even when they were very satisfied with their jobs, more part timers showed high stress than full timers, yet again revealing the non-work or domestic causes of stress.

Notes

[1] See the technical report for a full account of the method and the system of scoring.

[2] The emphasis on 'social contact' as a reason for working for women is found frequently and the implication often is that women are different from men in this respect; work has rather different functions. This is possible, but a more important explanation is that most women unlike most men have the experience of being without social contact on a daily basis for considerable periods. The very absence of human (adult) contact whilst they are housewives makes social contact a desirable feature of working. Men might well have a similar response if they had had a similar experience. Studies of unemployed or retired men show they miss the social contacts which work produces (Harrison, 1976).

Chapter 7 Unemployment and economic inactivity: the concepts, extent and consequences for women

Introduction

As we showed in Chapter 2, just over a third of women of working age in our sample were not working in a paid job at the time of the interview. (For convenience we describe this group in the rest of the chapter as currently not working.) We describe in later chapters, particularly Chapter 9, how for most women the experience of not working is a temporary phase. Almost all of the women in the study either had experienced, or will experience, non-working phases during the course of their working lives as they move in and out of employment. Non-working women were a very heterogenous group and were currently not in employment for a variety of reasons. Some had chosen not to work, either permanently or temporarily, whilst others in varying degrees, wanted a job. We explore this continuum of states of economic activity and inactivity in more detail in this chapter.

We explained in Chapter 1 that an important reason for undertaking this survey was the growing interest in the extent and consequences of unemployment for women. We designed the survey knowing that existing definitions of unemployment, based on administrative statistics and male concepts of lifetime economic activity, were not necessarily appropriate for studying female unemployment in the nineteen eighties.[1] In this chapter we discuss the conceptual and methodological problems underlying various ways of defining and measuring female unemployment and distinguish it from economic inactivity. We describe the circumstances at the time of the survey of all currently non-working women, identifying how many would be counted as unemployed according to different criteria, and compare the characteristics of non-working women. Having considered how women came to be not working, we look at the consequences of this, focussing in particular on women's attitudes to not having a paid job and whether or not they were experiencing financial and psychological stress. As the survey was in part designed to be one of three research projects funded by the Department of Employment to explore the issue of unemployment amongst women, we draw on the findings of the two other studies at points in this chapter.

Defining the unemployed and economically inactive

In Chapter 2 we identified amongst the non-working women (35% of women in our sample) those who were initially classed as 'unemployed' (5%) on the basis of their answers to a question asking for their reasons for not having a paid job. These women were defined as 'unemployed' if they gave one of the following as their main reason for not having a paid job:

i) waiting to take up a job already obtained
ii) looking for work
iii) prevented from looking for work by temporary sickness or injury

These categories, but somewhat different questions are used in household surveys to identify both men and women who are unemployed, regardless of whether or not they are registered as such. The remaining women who were without paid jobs (30%) were classed as economically inactive.

Although we have used the above definition of 'unemployment' in Chapter 2 to discuss women's activity rates and for some preliminary comparisons of the characteristics of women in the different categories of economic activity, it was never intended that this survey should confine itself to the use of one particular definition of unemployment. Rather we aimed to examine the situations of all women without paid employment in order to find out which of various different definitions are appropriate to women. We thought, initially, in terms of a continuum with the registered unemployed, who comprised the official count of the unemployed, at one end and those with no paid work and no intention of ever working again at the other end, although we knew from other surveys of registered unemployed that this was problematic (Daniel, 1974; White, 1983). Women with different employment plans such as those currently looking for work or those not currently looking but who expected to work again sometime would be at different points along this continuum, and we set out to explore their situations and characteristics. This approach meant that we needed to ask all non-working women about their present situations and future plans so as to place them in different groups along the continuum.

Questions to identify different groups of non-working women

In Figure 7.1 the sequence of questions asked of different groups of non-working women is set out. At an early point in the interview all non-working women were asked their main reason for not being in a paid job. Somewhat later, they were asked whether they would ever do a paid job again. This question, however, was not asked of those who had already said that they were permanently unable to work because of sickness or disability, nor was it asked of childless women under 40 who were not working. We found at the pilot stage that this latter group of women was almost invariably looking for work and found it rather odd to be asked such a question. The childless women under 40

Figure 7.1 Questions non-working women were asked about their current and future employment plans and their route through the questionnaire according to their answers

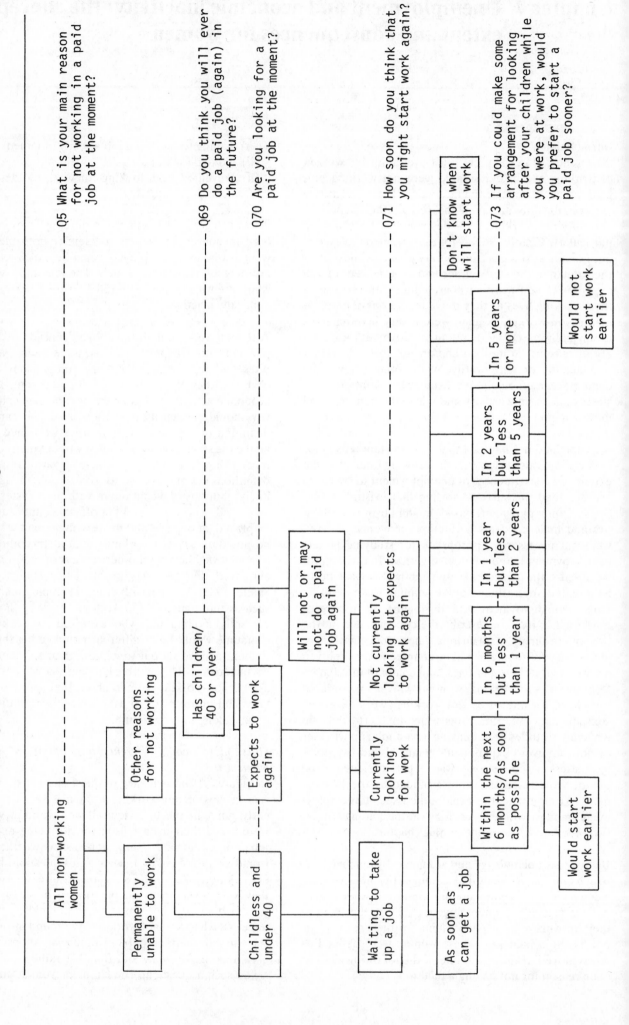

and all those who said they thought they would do a paid job again were asked whether they were looking for work at the moment. Those who said they were not looking for a job and who had not already found a job were asked how soon they thought they might start work again. Women with children were then asked if they would start paid work sooner if they could make some arrangement for their children to be looked after.

If we look first at women's reasons for not having a paid job, shown in Table 7.1, it is clear that the vast majority of non-working women (75%) were currently economically inactive for domestic reasons, while only 15% would be defined as 'unemployed' (5% of all women interviewed) on our survey question. Table 7.2 summarises the future employment plans of women without a paid job from their answers to the later questions in the questionnaire. If, using these different questions, we now define as unemployed anyone who was waiting to start a paid job they had found or said they were currently looking for work, the proportion of women who might be defined as unemployed rises to 18%.

In order to examine this difference we compared the answers given to the two sets of questions to see what degree of congruence existed between them. Table 7.3 shows that 90% of non-working women answered in the same form at both questions: 12% said at both questions that they were either looking for a job or waiting to start a job and 78% said they were not working for domestic or other reasons and at the later question that they were not looking for work. The remaining 10% gave apparently discrepant answers, but this was probably a consequence of differences in the wording of the relevant questions (Figure 7.1). The first focussed on the main reason why women were currently not working (Q5), the other questions asked more directly about women's labour market intentions (Q69) and then very precisely whether they were currently looking for a paid job (Q70). Thus, 6% said initially that they were not working for domestic or other reasons, but, nevertheless, later said they were looking for a job (and a few had, in fact, found a job which they were waiting to start). Most of these women were looking after children and had given this as their main reason for not having a paid job at our initial question.

A further 4% of women with no paid job had initially said they were not working and were either looking for a job or were prevented from looking by temporary sickness or injury. However, they said subsequently in answer to later questions that they either did not expect to work again or were not currently looking for work. There appeared to be three different groups of women in this situation. The first group (1%) were looking for work but did not expect to find a job and thus did not expect to work again. Most of these women were over 50 and/or suffered from disability or health problems.

Table 7.1 Reasons given by non-working women for not having a paid job

Reasons for not having a paid job	% of non-working women	% of all women
Waiting to take up a job already obtained	1	0
Looking for work	11	4
Prevented from looking for work by temporary sickness or injury	3	1
Total 'unemployed'	**15**	**5**
Permanently unable to work because of sickness or disability	6	2
Looking after children	52	18
Looking after other relatives — Domestic reasons	3 } 75	1 } 26
Keeping house	20	7
Other reasons	4	2
Total economically inactive	**85**	**30**
Total not working	**100**	**35**
Base	*1,941*	*5,588*

Table 7.2 Summary of current positions of women without a paid job

Current position	% of non-working women	% of all women
Waiting to start a job already obtained	2	0
Looking for a job	16	6
Total waiting to start or looking for a job	**18**	**6**
Expecting to start work:		
Within the next 6 months	5	
In 6 months but less than 1 year	3	
In 1 year but less than 2 years	3	
In 2 years but less than 5 years	11	
In 5 years or more	14	
Don't know how soon will start	10	
Total expecting to start work (but not currently working)	**46**	**16**
Don't know whether will work again	9	3
Does not expect to work again	21	8
Permanently unable to work	6	2
Total who will not or may not work again	**36**	**13**
Total not working	**100**	**35**
Base	*1,941*	*5,588*

Table 7.3 Relationship between reason for not working and current position of women with no paid job

Current position	% of non-working women	
Apparently congruent answers		
Looking for work/waiting to start work at both questions	12	'unemployed'
Not looking for work and not waiting to start at either question	78	economically inactive
All congruent answers	**90**	
Apparently discrepant answers		
Not working for domestic reasons, but looking for work/waiting to start	6	?economically inactive or 'unemployed'
Looking for work but not expecting to work (because of age, health etc)	1	'unemployed'
Prevented from looking for work by temporary sickness or injury:		
Will look when better	1	'unemployed'
Will not look when better	2	economically inactive
All discrepant answers	**10**	
	100	
Base	*1,941*	

All the remaining women said they were prevented from looking for work by temporary sickness or injury. More detailed inspection of their answers on the questionnaires suggested that they could be classified into two further groups, those who were temporarily ill and expected to look for work as soon as they were better (1%), and the remainder (2%); these appeared to have interpreted the initial question about reasons for not working wrongly and whilst they suffered from some form of illness or injury, in fact, were not planning to look for work even when they recovered. Accordingly, this last group should probably not be considered unemployed. Some of them would in practice have been excluded from the 'unemployed' category on the General Household Survey definition as they appeared to have been ill for longer than 28 days. When this group is excluded from the unemployed, the proportion of non-working women who were 'unemployed' falls from 16% to 14%, which is still 5% of all women of working age.

Five categories of non-working women
The answers to the two sets of questions enabled us to categorise most of the non-working women as either currently unemployed or economically inactive, as Table 7.3 shows. The only women who were difficult to categorise were those who gave domestic reasons for not working and therefore were defined as economically inactive on our initial definition, but, in fact, later said they were looking for work or in some cases were waiting to take up a job offer. We decided to keep them as a separate group on the continuum between the two main groups of unemployed and inactive women and to examine subsequently the extent to which they had characteristics and attitudes which were more similar either to the unemployed or economically inactive women.

The large category of currently economically inactive women comprised women with very different plans and expectations with regard to their future employment. We therefore sub-divided them on the basis of how permanent their economic inactivity seemed to be, into those who did not expect to work again (or who were unsure of whether they would work again) and those who did expect to work. We also subdivided those who

expected to work again, but were not currently looking for work according to how soon they thought they would start. We then compared those who expected to start work in the next year with the rest. One reason for choosing this division was that only those women who expected to start work at least within the next year, were asked a series of detailed questions about the sort of job they would look for and how they would set about finding a job. This is because it is difficult to ask women who do not expect to start work for at least a year questions about job seeking which are almost hypothetical at this stage. As a result of these divisions we created the five sub-groups of non-working women which are shown in Table 7.4. This summarises the definitions of each group and shows the proportions of the non-working women in each. We show also in Figure 7.2 how we placed these groups along our continuum of economic activity and inactivity.

It is important, however, to remember that these groups are conceptual artefacts created to enable us to look at degrees of economic activity and inactivity. The situation is in reality more fluid in two main ways. First

Table 7.4 Five categories of non-working women along the unemployed–permanently economically inactive continuum

Categories of non-working women	% of non-working women	% of all women
Unemployed Not working because: Waiting to take up job Looking for work Prevented from looking for work by temporary sickness or injury *unless* not expecting to start work for 6 months or more	14	5
Others looking for work Not working for domestic or other reasons, but looking for work or found a job	6	2
Planning to start work in the next year Not currently looking for work but expecting to start within the next year	5	2
Planning to start work in a year or more Planning to start work again but not for at least a year	39	14
Will not/may not work again Does not expect to work again or not sure whether will work again	36	12
All non-working women	**100**	**35**
Base	*1,941*	*5,588*

Figure 7.2 The position of non-working women along the economically active - economically inactive continuum

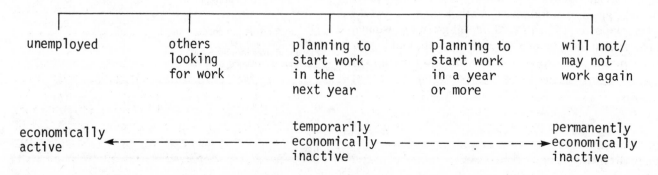

it is fluid in terms of time, for women will change positions as their circumstances change. For example, we asked women with children intending to work if they would return to work sooner if they could make arrangements for the care of their children. A minority (22%) said they would, citing family based care as their preferred arrangement in most cases. Second it is conceptually fluid in that we have created the groupings by the definitions we have used; so, for instance the proportion of unemployed women amongst non-working women will vary according to the definition used. If only women in the first group on Table 7.4 are included, then 14% of non-working women (or 5% of all women of working age) were unemployed. If the second group is included as well, on the grounds that these women were in fact looking for work, then 20% of non-working women (or 7% of all women of working age) were unemployed. For the rest of the chapter we keep the two groups distinct so as to see whether there are major differences between them and to establish more clearly the extent and meaning of unemployment for women.

Registration and the unemployed woman

So far we have taken no account of whether or not women were registered as unemployed in our attempt to categorise them into the five groups along the continuum, though technically the registered unemployed are seen as economically active and would therefore be at that end of our continuum. We wanted to see what proportion of non-working women said they were registered as unemployed, and in particular, where the registered women were placed along the continuum.[2] Overall 10% of women without a paid job said they were currently registered as unemployed and in addition, a further 3% said they had been registered since they last worked but were so no longer. Women, like men, in 1980 were most likely to be registered as unemployed when they were eligible for benefit.[3] Many women, however, were not eligible, either because they had been out of the labour market for a while and had not paid their national insurance contributions or because when they worked they paid the reduced married women's contributions, (a system which since April 1978 is being phased out). In addition married women are not eligible for Supplementary Benefit. This means therefore that women are most likely to be registered if they are single and at the start of a period of not working when they are entitled to benefit.

The 10% of women who said they were currently registered were found in all groups along the continuum as Table 7.5 shows. Although about two thirds (66%) of all registered unemployed women were found in the unemployed group, only 54% of this group said they were registered as unemployed. Altogether 79% of the registered unemployed were in the two economically active groups; however, 21% were inactive. Some of these (7%) had, in effect, retired and thought they were unlikely to work again because of ill health or age, in much the same way as some men near retiring age may effectively drop out of the labour market whilst

still being registered (White, 1983). Amongst the 10% who were planning to work in a year or more, some had recently left the labour market but were not expecting to work in the near future usually because they had had a child meanwhile.

Table 7.5 **Proportion of non-working women in different current positions who were registered unemployed**

Current position	Proportion of registered unemployed in each group	Proportion of all non-working women who were registered unemployed in each group	Base
	%		
Unemployed	66	54%	267
Others looking for work	13	22%	115
Planning to start work in next year	4	7%	104
Planning to start work in a year or more	10	2%	762
Will not/may not work	7	1%	693
All non-working women	**100**	**10%**	**1,941**
Base	*198*		

Looking at the proportions of women registered as unemployed in each group along our continuum, it is clear that, while women were less likely to be registered the more inactive they were, whether they were registered as unemployed or not cuts across our categories to some extent. We therefore decided not to use registered unemployed as an additional group on our continuum. However, we looked at the effect on estimates of female unemployment of including all registered unemployed women (even though some clearly were not currently looking for work). This is shown in Table 7.6. The broader the definition of unemployment used, the less difference it makes to the estimates to add the registered unemployed to our other economically active groups. If we add the registered unemployed to our group of unemployed women a further 3% of non-working women are included making 17% in all. If we then broaden the definition to include all other women looking for work then 21% of non-working women (7% of all women) would be included.

Table 7.6 **Proportions of non-working women who would be classified as unemployed using different definitions**

Various definitions of unemployed women	Proportion of non-working women	Proportion of all women
Registered unemployed	10%	4%
Unemployed	14%	5%
Either registered unemployed or unemployed	17%	6%
Either registered unemployed or unemployed or others looking for work	21%	7%
Base	*1,941*	*5,588*

Self-definitions of unemployment

So far we have been using information about what women said they were doing in order to classify women as unemployed or economically inactive. It is, however, also interesting to explore women's own perception of their employment status and see whether they identify with the label 'unemployed'. Although we did not ex-

83

plore this topic in depth in this survey, the experience and meaning of unemployment for women were examined in a qualitative follow-up study (Cragg and Dawson, 1984). The study was based on a sub-sample of non-working women from the Women and Employment Survey defined very broadly as 'unemployed' who were re-interviewed some time after our original interview. It explored the women's subsequent labour market experience and their reactions to being without employment.[4]

In the current survey we asked all women without paid jobs (except those permanently unable to work) whether at present they thought of themselves as unemployed or just as not having a paid job.[5] We followed this by asking women who did not think of themselves as unemployed why this was so. The proportions who thought of themselves as unemployed in each of the five groups of non-working women are shown in Table 7.7. The proportion of women thinking of themselves as unemployed was clearly related to their position on the continuum, as we would expect. But there were some discrepancies; only 54% of the unemployed group thought of themselves as unemployed and as many as 13% of the least active group also identified with this label. Women who thought of themselves as unem-

ployed were not necessarily the same women as those who were registered unemployed, as the right hand column of Table 7.7 shows. Overall only 6% of women both thought of themselves as unemployed and were registered unemployed; even among the group of women we have classed as unemployed, the proportion was only 36%.

When we asked women why they did not think of themselves as unemployed it was clear that for a sizeable majority 'being unemployed' meant having nothing to do which was manifestly not the case for them. As Table 7.8 shows, two thirds of these women (65%) saw working in the home as a full time job in its own right which kept them fully employed. The Cragg and Dawson study supplements this by showing very clearly that many women, despite looking for work, rejected the idea that they were 'unemployed' explicitly because they had so much to do, though they did not know what to call themselves (ibid). The second reason why women did not consider themselves unemployed is straightforward – they were not currently looking for work. Whilst this is unexceptional for the three economically inactive of our five groups it seemed surprising that 19% and 5% respectively of the two groups of women we knew to be looking for work could give this answer. Further investigation showed that most of these women had either found a job and were waiting to start work or were temporarily unable to look for work for health reasons.

Some women rejected the label 'unemployed' because they associated it with 'official' dimensions of unemployment, namely being registered or in receipt of benefit (5%); twice as many of the women in the 'unemployed' and 'others looking for work' group as women in inactive groups said this. Not having had recent or regular employment was another reason advanced by 5% of women for not seeing themselves as 'unemployed' even for the 5% and 7% respectively of the two groups of women who were currently looking for a job.

It is clear from this, that the terms 'unemployment' and 'unemployed' have somewhat different associations

Table 7.7 **Proportions of non-working women in different current positions who think of themselves as 'unemployed' and who are also registered unemployed (excluding permanently unable to work)**

Current position	% who thought of themselves as 'unemployed'	% who both thought of themselves as 'unemployed' and were registered unemployed	Base
Unemployed	54%	36%	267
Others looking for work	31%	11%	115
Planning to start work in next year	19%	5%	104
Planning to start work in a year or more	14%	0%	762
Will not/may not work again (except permanently unable to work)	13%	0%	571
All except permanently unable to work	**21%**	**6%**	1,819

Table 7.8 **Reasons why non-working women with different current positions did not think of themselves as unemployed**

Reasons why non-working women did not think of themselves as 'unemployed'	Current position					All who do not think of themselves as unemployed
	Looking for work		Not looking for work			
	Unemployed	Others looking for work	Planning to start work in next year	Planning to start work in 1 or more years	Will not/may not work again	
	%	%	%	%	%	%
Fully employed working in the home	50	76	54	72	60	65
Not looking for work/do not want a job/already found a job	19	5	29	20	25	22
Not registered unemployed or not claiming benefit	10	11	5	4	4	5
Haven't been employed regularly/haven't worked for ages	5	7	5	3	8	5
Other reasons	9	3	1	1	2	2
Don't know	8	3	5	3	4	4
Base	119	76	79	644	478	1,396

Percentages do not add to 100 as women could give more than one reason.

and meanings for many women from those they have for men. Certainly, as Cragg and Dawson argue, most men looking for work would define themselves as 'unemployed' (*ibid*). However, most men would be primary wage earners and looking for full time work. We have not looked as yet at women's self-perceptions in terms of the type of job they want and their breadwinner status.

Characteristics of women with different future employment plans

The next three tables (Tables 7.9–7.11) show the main demographic characteristics of non-working women grouped according to their current employment position. It is clear that the currently unemployed tended to have a much larger proportion in the 16–19 age group than the other groups and although the majority were married this group contained the highest proportion of single women (30%). The currently unemployed were

Table 7.9 Age of non-working women by their current position

Age	Current position					All non-working women
	Looking for work		Not looking for work			
	Unemployed	Others looking for work	Planning to start work in next year	Planning to start work in 1 or more years	Will not/may not work again	
	%	%	%	%	%	%
16–19	18	3	10	3	1	4
20–29	28	42	27	44	9	28
30–39	22	29	32	41	15	28
40–49	15	22	17	8	22	16
50–59	17	4	14	4	53	24
	100	**100**	**100**	**100**	**100**	**100**
Base	*267*	*115*	*104*	*762*	*693*	*1,941*

Table 7.10 Marital status of non-working women by their current position

Marital status	Current position					All non-working women
	Looking for work		Not looking for work			
	Unemployed	Others looking for work	Planning to start work in next year	Planning to start work in 1 or more years	Will not/may not work again	
	%	%	%	%	%	%
Married	58	83	75	88	86	82
Cohabiting	2	2	6	2	0	2
All married or cohabiting	**60**	**85**	**81**	**90**	**86**	**84**
Single	30	5	10	3	4	7
Widowed	4	2	1	1	6	3
Divorced	4	7	4	4	3	4
Separated	2	1	4	2	1	2
All non-married	**40**	**15**	**19**	**10**	**14**	**16**
	100	**100**	**100**	**100**	**100**	**100**
Base	*267*	*115*	*104*	*762*	*693*	*1,941*

Table 7.11 Life cycle stage of non-working women by their current position

Life cycle stage	Current position					All non-working women
	Looking for work		Not looking for work			
	Unemployed	Others looking for work	Planning to start work in next year	Planning to start work in 1 or more years	Will not/may not work again	
	%	%	%	%	%	%
Women aged under 30 with no children	34	1	10	3	1	7
Women with youngest child aged:						
0–4	14	61	45	66	14	39
5–10	13	21	16	19	13	16
11–15	10	9	12	5	7	7
Women with no children aged under 16:						
aged 30–49	12	5	3	3	11	7
aged 50 or over	17	3	14	4	54	24
	100	**100**	**100**	**100**	**100**	**100**
Base	*267*	*115*	*104*	*762*	*693*	*1,941*

much more likely than all the other groups to be childless. (The registered unemployed were even more likely to be young, single and childless. Over half (56%) were under 30, over a third were single (35%) and 44% were childless.)

The majority of women in the three middle groups – those looking for work but not unemployed and those planning to look for work either in the next year or at some time further in the future – were married women with dependent children. However, those planning to start work in the next year were somewhat less likely to have dependent children and tended to be older than women in the other two groups. It is striking though not unexpected that the last group, women who did not think they would work again or were not sure whether they would work again, were generally much older than women in the other groups: 53% were 50 or over with no children under 16. Many of this group considered themselves to be retired or to be too old to start work again, particularly if they had not worked for many years.

Routes into unemployment and economic inactivity
The unemployment – economic inactivity continuum described above can be seen as part of a wider continuum encompassing employment as well. So far we have looked at non-working women's current position on the continuum, but it is also of interest to explore how women have arrived at this position. In this section we examine the variety of routes by which non-working women came to be in their present situation; this contrasts with and supplements the emphasis of Chapter 9 in which we look in more detail at the frequency with which women move in and out of employment over their lives and their reasons for doing this.

Women may have arrived at their current position on the non-working continuum either directly from previous employment or full time education or by moving between the different categories of non-working. For example, they may move from 'unemployment' to 'not intending to work again' or, as probably occurs more

frequently as women move back into the labour market, from 'planning to start work in one or more years' to currently 'looking for a job'. Our data did not allow us to look in depth at the processes of these transitions from one employment situation to another; this is best done by a longitudinal study in which women are re-interviewed at intervals. However, our study did allow us to use the data collected about women's past work histories to examine whether the current period of not working was preceded by employment or full time education, how long this period had lasted and what women saw as their main reason for not working during this period in relation to their current employment situation. This means we can look at certain aspects of the transition process into 'non-working'. We begin by describing how long women had been out of employment and then consider their main reason for not working during this period and, where they had previously had jobs, the reasons why they left these.

The length of time out of employment
Table 7.12 shows the length of time since the non-working women last worked by their current employment situation. Overall just over half (54%) had worked within the last five years, 15% had not worked for more than 15 years and 4% had never worked. However, there were marked differences between the groups. In general the length of time out of work was related to the women's position along the unemployment – economic inactivity continuum. For example, unemployed women were much more likely than other women to have worked recently or to have never worked: over half had worked within the past year and 11% had never worked, most of these being recent school leavers. By contrast, very few unemployed women (2%) had not worked for 15 years or more. Amongst the three groups of women who were either looking for work or expecting to work again, women who were currently either looking for work or planning to start work in the next year were more likely to have spent shorter times out of employment than women whose return to employment was seen to be further in the future. About a third of women currently looking for

Table 7.12 Length of time since women with no paid job last worked by their current position

Length of time since last worked	Current position					All non-working women
	Looking for work		Not looking for work			
	Unemployed	Others looking for work	Planning to start work in next year	Planning to start work in 1 or more years	Will not/may not work again	
	%	%	%	%	%	%
Less than 1 year	52	31	35	15	7	20
1 yr, but less than 5 yrs	25	41	29	46	24	34
5 yrs, but less than 10 yrs	7	16	20	24	19	19
10 yrs, but less than 15 yrs	3	7	3	7	11	8
15 yrs or more	2	3	8	4	36	15
Never worked	11	2	4	4	3	4
	100	100	100	100	100	100
Base	267	115	104	762	693	1,941
Average time since last worked, for those who have ever worked	2yrs 4mths	3yrs 10mths	4yrs 9mths	4yrs 10mths	13yrs 0mths	7yrs 5mths
Base	238	112	99	735	672	1,856

work or expecting to start work in the next year had been in work within the last year compared with 15% of the women planning to start work in one or more years. It is difficult to know precisely what this means; however, it suggests that women fall broadly into two groups, some returning (relatively) quickly to work whilst others take a longer period out. Analysis of women's patterns of return in Chapter 9 confirms this broad distinction. Fewer women in the group currently looking for work have shorter periods out of employment than among those intending to start work in the next year (placed further along our economic activity–inactivity continuum). However, this is because this group contains both those women returning to work quickly and those returning after a longer absence.

Women's reasons for not working and for leaving their last job

Women's reasons for not working may vary during any one non-working period reflecting the processes of transition through the non-working continuum that may occur. However retrospective data collection cannot properly capture this.[6] Instead we asked women their main reason for not working over the whole of their not working period and, for those who had left a job, the main reason why they left and then compared these. Table 7.13 shows the main reason women gave for not working since they last worked. We show the individual reasons, but have also grouped them into two broad categories of non-domestic and domestic reasons.

Although the majority (80%) of all non-working women gave domestic reasons, chiefly looking after their children, as their main reason for not working over the period this was strikingly not the case for the unemployed women. They were alone amongst non-working women in having a majority (74%) who were not working for non-domestic reasons. Women who were not planning or expecting to work again were the next most likely to give non-domestic reasons for not working: 20% did so. However, unlike the unemployed, overwhelmingly these reasons concerned illness or injury reflecting the fact that older women, like older men workers, often leave jobs and indeed stop working early for health reasons (Parker, 1978). Clear-

Table 7.13 Main reasons for not working during period since last worked (or left school/college) given by non-working women by current position

Main reasons for not working in period since last worked	Current position					All non-working women
	Looking for work		Not looking for work			
	Unemployed	Others looking for work	Planning to start work in next year	Planning to start work in 1 or more years	Will not/may not work again	
	%	%	%	%	%	%
Looking for work or waiting to take up a job	65	10	8	1	1	11
Illness or injury	9	3	2	3	19	9
All non-domestic reasons	**74**	**13**	**10**	**4**	**20**	**20**
Looking after children	14	76	57	83	39	56
Looking after sick or elderly relatives	3	2	7	2	6	4
Looking after the home	3	3	14	6	28	14
Other reasons	6	6	12	5	7	6
All domestic reasons	**26**	**87**	**90**	**96**	**80**	**80**
	100	**100**	**100**	**100**	**100**	**100**
Base	*267*	*115*	*104*	*762*	*693*	*1,941*

Table 7.14 Main reason for leaving last job given by non-working women by their current position

Main reason for leaving last job	Current position					All non-working women who have worked
	Looking for work		Not looking for work			
	Unemployed	Others looking for work	Planning to start work in next year	Planning to start work in 1 or more years	Will not/may not work again	
	%	%	%	%	%	%
Temporary job finished	11	11	7	6	4	6
Redundant	18	3	6	5	6	7
Dismissed	6	2	–	1	1	2
Didn't like job	21	8	7	8	7	9
(grouped totals)	56	24	20	20	18	24
Illness/injury	12	4	2	4	19	10
Went to college	1	–	1	1	0	0
All non-domestic reasons	**69**	**28**	**23**	**25**	**37**	**34**
Pregnancy	12	46	37	54	29	38
Marriage	1	1	3	4	13	7
Moved because of husband's job	3	3	4	3	5	3
Moved for other reasons	5	3	1	2	2	3
To look after children	3	13	12	7	3	6
To look after other relatives	2	4	7	2	5	4
Other reasons	5	2	13	3	6	5
All domestic reasons	**31**	**72**	**77**	**75**	**63**	**66**
	100	**100**	**100**	**100**	**100**	**100**
Base	*238*	*112*	*99*	*735*	*672*	*1,856*

ly the domestic reasons given by women in the different groups are broadly as might be expected from what we already know about the main characteristics of non-working women. The women in the three middle groups are likely to have young children and give this as a reason for not working. Those who were not planning nor expecting to work again tended to be older and to have grown-up children. This no doubt partly accounts for the high proportion of this latter group who mention looking after the home as a reason for not working.

As might be expected the dominance of non-domestic factors for unemployed women was also apparent when women were asked their main reason for leaving their most recent job. Unemployed women were the only group of the five where the majority (69%) gave a non-domestic reason for leaving their last job as is shown in Table 7.14. The same broad pattern of difference between the reasons given by women in the five groups is apparent here as in the previous table. For example, the women who were not planning to work again had the second highest proportion (37%) of non-domestic reasons for leaving their last job, just over half of which were health related.

Overall, women giving domestic reasons outnumbered those giving non-domestic reasons two to one and pregnancy was by far the most common reason given for leaving their most recent job: 38% gave this as their main reason. However, only 12% of the unemployed gave this reason compared with more than twice as many women in all the other groups. Women gave a range of other domestic reasons for leaving their last job such as looking after their children or other relatives, moving house or getting married, though it is very noticeable that this last reason was mentioned most commonly by those women who did not now expect to work again (13%), who were older than the other women. This no doubt reflects a phenomenon that is becoming increasingly rare among more recent generations, whereby a woman leaves a job and the labour market for good on marriage.

Women's non-domestic reasons for leaving a job were varied. Some reasons appeared involuntary; women were either dismissed, made redundant, their temporary job finished or they left a job for health reasons. Other reasons were more likely to be a result of choice; women left a job they did not like or in a very few cases went to college.[7] Unemployed women were more likely than other groups of women to have left jobs for non-domestic reasons: 21% for example had left their last job because they did not like it. Higher proportions of women in this group (18%) had been made redundant than in any other group whilst the proportion of women leaving a job because of illness or injury (12%) was only surpassed by those who were not planning nor expecting to work again (19%).

The picture we present here, of the majority of non-working women having left jobs for domestic reasons is, of course, only a partial view of women's job changes and subsequent labour market behaviour because the analysis has focussed on those job changes which take women out of employment. However, not all women who change jobs leave the labour market or experience a period of unemployment as we shall show in Chapter 11. When these women are included the ratio of domestic to non-domestic job reasons for changes is different, showing that more women leave jobs for non-domestic than for domestic reasons, though more women leave employment for domestic than non-domestic reasons as we might expect.

It is clear from the above tables that two sets of factors operate to take women out of a job. Some are job-related and 'push' women out: women are made redundant or dismissed or there are features of the job a woman dislikes and so she leaves. Others are domestically based and 'pull' women out, whether willingly or unwillingly, such as having a baby and rearing children or moving house. Women may, however, leave a job for one reason but stay out of employment for other reasons. We wanted to find out to what extent women's reasons for leaving a job and reasons for not working were congruent. We therefore compared the reasons

Table 7.15 Main reason for leaving last job and main reason for not working in the period since the last job given by non-working women by their current positions (excluding those who have never worked previously)

Main reason for leaving last job and main reason for not working in current period*	Current position					All non-working women who have worked
	Looking for work		Not looking for work			
	Unemployed	Others looking for work	Planning to start work in next year	Planning to start work in 1 or more years	Will not/may not work again	
	%	%	%	%	%	%
Left last job mainly for domestic reasons, hasn't worked since mainly for:						
Domestic reasons	18	68	73	75	60	62
Non-domestic reasons	13	4	4	1	3	3
Left last job mainly for non-domestic reasons, hasn't worked since mainly for:						
Domestic reasons	10	20	19	21	21	19
Non-domestic reasons	59	8	4	3	17	16
	100	**100**	**100**	**100**	**100**	**100**
Base	238	112	99	735	672	1,856

*See Tables 7.13 and 7.14 for types of reasons classified as 'domestic' and 'non-domestic'

women gave for leaving a job with their main reason for not working in the succeeding period. To do this we used our two broad categories, dividing reasons into the domestic and non-domestic as shown in Table 7.15. It is clear that overall there is a high degree of apparent congruence (78%) particularly for those 62% of women who both left and stayed out of employment for domestic reasons. It is also clear that most discrepancy occurs when women leave a job for non-domestic reasons but stay out of employment for domestic reasons. This occurred for 19% of all non-working women but markedly less so for the 'unemployed' group (10%). Only 3% of women left their last job mainly for domestic reasons but gave a non-domestic reason for staying out of employment.[8]

Consequences of and attitudes towards not working

As well as comparing and contrasting the women in our five categories in terms of their demographic and labour market characteristics we also looked at their reactions to not working. Similar or different attitudinal responses to or consequences of not being in paid work amongst women in different categories might challenge or substantiate the usefulness of the categories. Accordingly in this section we compare women's levels of financial stress as a measure of the financial consequences of not working. We also look at women's attitudes to not working, identifying both the financial dimensions and non-financial dimensions of this and we compare briefly how women in different groups appeared to be coping in their current position. Throughout we compare working women's situation and attitudes with that of the five groups of non-working women.

Financial stress associated with not working

The financial consequences to an individual and her/his family of not having a paid job are discussed very comprehensively in most studies of unemployment. There are several ways of measuring these using either objective or subjective measures or a mixture of the two. Objective measures were not very suitable in this survey for several reasons. Some non-working women had not had a previous 'in work' income or for some of those that had it was too long ago to compare meaningfully with their current 'out of work' income. The other 'objective measure', which sets current total family income (including benefits and rebates etc) against family composition, financial commitments and expenditure, required more extensive financial data collection and manipulation than we could undertake on this survey.[9] So, although we discuss factual information about women's financial situation at various points in this report, in this chapter we use subjective measures, looking at how women who were not working viewed their financial situation and how they appeared to be managing financially. Thus we compare the subjective financial situation of women who were currently looking for work with those who were not, as well as with women who were working.

We asked women to think about their financial situation generally and say whether they managed without any difficulty; managed, but with not much money to spare; found it very difficult to manage; or did not really manage at all. Table 7.16 shows that the proportion of women giving these different answers varied according to their current employment situation. About a third of both the unemployed and other women looking for work said they found it very difficult to manage or did not really manage at all, suggesting they had a very strong financial incentive to look for work and that paid work was of considerable financial importance to them. This proportion fell across the remaining groups to 13% of those who did not intend to or might not work again suggesting there was little financial incentive to work for this group.

It is very important to note, however, that on this measure there was no evidence that the women we have categorised as unemployed were in a significantly worse financial situation than other women looking for work. As would be expected almost all working women were generally managing better than non-working women; only 9% found it difficult to manage or did not really manage at all. If just over a third of women who were not working but wanted a job said they felt financial hardship in this way and about half of all working women either found it financially very difficult to manage or said they managed but with not much money to

Table 7.16 How well non-working women manage financially by their current position

How well informant manages financially	Current position					All non-working women	Working women
	Looking for work		Not looking for work				
	Unemployed	Others looking for work	Planning to start work in next year	Planning to start work in 1 or more years	Will not/may not work again		
	%	%	%	%	%	%	%
Manages without any difficulty	14	18	22	26	37	28	49
Manages but with not much money to spare	49	50	51	54	49	51	42
Finds it very difficult to manage	28 } 36	27 } 32	23 } 26	18 } 20	11 } 13	18 } 21	8 } 9
Does not really manage at all	8 }	5 }	3 }	2 }	2 }	3 }	1 }
Don't know	1	–	1		1	0	0
	100	100	100	100	100	100	100
Base	267	115	104	762	693	1,941	3,354

spare then, it is clear, that for a large number of women their earnings were not seen as simply 'pin money'.

We also asked women how often they worried about money: almost all the time, quite often, only sometimes or almost never. Table 7.17 shows a similar pattern of response to those of the previous table with women not expecting to work again showing little evidence of worrying and working women worrying least of all. Again there was no significant difference between the unemployed and other women looking for work; a sizeable proportion of them (43% and 45% respectively) worried about money almost all the time or quite often.

Another indicator of a family's financial circumstances is whether or not they manage to save money. We looked therefore at the proportion of women who said they (and their partner) did not manage to save any money at the moment (Table 7.18). Although the re-

sponses show the same general pattern across the groups as the two previous tables, there was a difference in this instance between the unemployed and other women looking for work: 75% of the unemployed said they did not save compared with 68% of other women looking for work. Thereafter the proportion who did not save was lower in successive groups falling to 52% among those who did not plan to work again and 33% of working women. It is difficult to know whether this variation in the saving behaviour of the two groups of women wanting work stemmed from either greater ability to save, ie more surplus, or reflected a different attitude to saving, with young single women (found in the unemployed group) being less saving conscious.

Finally, we looked at women's overall financial stress by compiling a composite score based on responses to

Table 7.17 How often non-working and working women worry about money by their current position

| How often informant worries about money | Current position | | | | | All non-working women | Working women |
| | Looking for work | | Not looking for work | | | | |
	Unemployed	Others looking for work	Planning to start work in next year	Planning to start work in 1 or more years	Will not/may not work again		
	%	%	%	%	%	%	%
Almost all the time	19	22	19	14	11	14	7
Quite often	24	23	18	19	12	18	16
Only sometimes	38	39	47	44	40	42	44
Almost never	19	16	16	22	37	26	33
Don't know	–	–	–	1	0	0	–
	100	**100**	**100**	**100**	**100**	**100**	**100**
Base	*267*	*115*	*104*	*762*	*693*	*1,941*	*3,354*

Table 7.18 Whether non-working and working women (and their husbands/partners) manage to save any money by their current position

| Whether informant (and partner) manages to save any money | Current position | | | | | All non-working women | Working women |
| | Looking for work | | Not looking for work | | | | |
	Unemployed	Others looking for work	Planning to start work in next year	Planning to start work in 1 or more years	Will not/may not work again		
	%	%	%	%	%	%	%
Manages to save money	25	32	36	39	48	40	67
Does not manage to save money	75	68	64	61	52	60	33
	100	**100**	**100**	**100**	**100**	**100**	**100**
Base	*267*	*115*	*104*	*762*	*693*	*1,941*	*3,354*

Table 7.19 Overall levels of financial stress* of non-working and working women by their current position

| Financial stress scores* | Current position | | | | | All non-working women | Working women |
| | Looking for work | | Not looking for work | | | | |
	Unemployed	Others looking for work	Planning to start work in next year	Planning to start work in 1 or more years	Will not/may not work again		
	%	%	%	%	%	%	%
Low financial stress (scores 3–5)	32	31	35	45	62	47	68
Medium financial stress (scores 6–7)	38	41	41	37	25	34	25
High financial stress (scores 8–10)	30	28	24	18	13	19	7
	100	**100**	**100**	**100**	**100**	**100**	**100**
Base	*267*	*115*	*104*	*762*	*693*	*1,941*	*3,354*

*Based on questions about how often informants worried about money, how well they managed financially and whether they saved money (see Tables 7.16–7.18)

the three questions about how often women worried about money, how well they managed financially and whether they saved money. A low score indicates low stress and, as Table 7.19 shows, women in the category of 'unemployed' were overall the most stressed, closely followed by the other women looking for work. There was also a declining level of stress along the unemployed – economically inactive continuum. Again, we show for contrast the financial stress scores of working women, 68% of whom had low stress scores. Overall, perceived financial need or stress is closely correlated with a desire for paid employment. Women who were unemployed were most likely to experience financial stress, though in many instances the other women looking for work showed very similar levels of financial stress. We therefore conclude from the answers to the various financial questions, that not having a job may result in feelings of considerable financial distress and hardship for a sizeable minority of women who want one. Moreover there is not much difference between our two categories of women looking for work in this respect.

Women's attitudes to not working
There have been many studies of male unemployment which have aimed to examine the social and psychological consequences of unemployment, both for the men concerned and sometimes also for their wives and families (Harrison, 1976; Turner and Dickinson, 1978; Sinfield, 1981). Studies have also increasingly been made recently of the effects of unemployment on young people (Carroll, 1981; Roberts *et al*, 1981; Warr *et al*, forthcoming). Relatively little however, has been done to find out whether the way women feel as a consequence of unemployment is similar to or different from the feelings of men. Indeed, at the time we began our study in 1979 there was little material published specifically on women other than a section in the classic 1930s study by the Pilgrim Trust (1938). Women had occasionally been included in general studies of the unemployed but were either ignored as a particular group or added into the general analysis of men in the sample.[10]

In this study, however, we could not directly address questions about the similarity or difference between men and women's experience of unemployment. Firstly, we did not have a comparable sample of men with which to contrast the women in the survey. Secondly, we did not want to ask questions which would only be relevant to women who would be defined as unemployed on the same basis as men; we wanted our questions to be appropriate to all non-working women so that we could then compare the answers of non-working women in different categories. The study therefore investigated women's attitudes to not having a paid job in general, rather than to being unemployed specifically. Within this context we tried to cover some of the attitudes found to be important in other studies of unemployment, but also included questions designed to reveal the attitudes of the economically inactive women.

We asked all non-working women to look at a number of statements of attitudes to not working and to indicate for each one whether it was definitely true, partly true or not true for them. In addition, women who were currently working were asked to imagine they had lost their job and had not been working for a couple of months. They were asked to think about how they would feel in that situation and to rate the attitude statements. The statements used had been selected from a much larger number of statements included in the pilot study. Answers to all the statements were analysed using factor analysis.[11] In the analysis eleven of the statements could be grouped into two factors. We found that one statement was not associated with either factor. This statement, 'There aren't many jobs around for people like me', has not been included in any further discussion of the factors. The statements within the factors can be viewed as being associated with two distinct and independent attitude dimensions related to feelings about not having a job and the financial need to work. We show in Table 7.20 the statements, grouped according to the factor with which they were most clearly associated, and arranged in order of their strength of association with that factor.

To make it easier to compare the answers of so many groups of women to the statements we show in Table 7.20 only the proportion of women who said each statement was definitely true for them, and discuss responses to the individual statements briefly before looking at the results of the factor analysis as a whole. Two statements stand out as showing the high attachment to having a job of unemployed women as compared with other non-working women. Most (84%) endorsed 'I would start work straight away if I could find a job' as definitely true, whilst over three quarters of them (77%) said 'I wish I was earning some money' was definitely true for them. Other women looking for work also had relatively high attachment compared with economically inactive women, though it was lower than the unemployed: 63% and 58% for the two statements respectively. Both groups, however, endorsed equally the statement 'There aren't many jobs around for people like me' suggesting the same proportion of the two groups experienced similar difficulties in looking for work. Comparison of working women with women wanting work was particularly interesting. The unemployed, for example, resembled women working full time in their responses to particular statements whilst part time workers and other women looking for work had similar attitudes. This is shown further in the discussion of the factor analysis.

Turning to discussion of the attitudes as a whole, it is clear that the two factors identified here are broadly consistent with findings from other studies of attitudes to unemployment. We did not identify any extra dimensions by covering attitudes to not working in general, although clearly the range of women's responses along these dimensions is likely to be greater as a result of including all non-working women. The statements included were designed to cover both feelings

Table 7.20 Proportions rating different statements about not working as 'definitely true' and mean factor scores for full and part time working women, and non-working women by their current position

Statements of attitudes to not working	Current position								All non-working women
	Working women			Non-working women					
				Looking for work		Not looking for work			
	Working full time	Working part time	All working women	Unemployed	Others looking for work	Planning to start work within 1 year	Planning to start work in 1 or more years	Will not/ may not work again	
Feeling about not having a job									
I feel out of things not having a job	44%	29%	37%	33%	23%	15%	7%	9%	13%
I often get depressed about not having a job	56%	31%	45%	34%	23%	15%	8%	9%	13%
I get bored being at home	56%	43%	51%	50%	37%	31%	14%	13%	21%
Not having a job makes me feel rather useless	37%	23%	30%	31%	19%	15%	5%	8%	11%
I really look forward to starting work	72%	56%	65%	68%	48%	41%	14%	6%	22%
I would start work straight away if I could find a job	83%	65%	75%	84%	63%	24%	7%	6%	21%
I find being at home very satisfying	10%	17%	13%	9%	14%	15%	37%	55%	37%
Not having a job is making me lose my confidence about ever going back to work	37%	28%	33%	25%	19%	13%	8%	8%	11%
Mean factor score	−0.49	−0.15	−0.34	−0.28	0.04	0.25	0.77	0.88	0.60
Financial need to work									
I find it difficult to manage	54%	31%	44%	43%	33%	28%	21%	14%	22%
I wish I was earning some money	77%	59%	69%	77%	58%	61%	36%	25%	41%
I don't need to go out to work for the money	8%	18%	13%	10%	15%	10%	18%	30%	20%
Mean factor score	−0.34	−0.07	−0.16	−0.22	−0.04	0.04	0.26	0.57	0.27
Other statement									
There aren't many jobs around for people like me	23%	33%	27%	53%	53%	25%	24%	36%	34%
Base	1,877	1,477	3,354	267	115	104	762	693	1,941

about not having a paid job and feelings about being at home (for example 'I find being at home very satisfying', 'I get bored being at home'). In theory, attitudes to the 'pull' of paid employment may be distinct from attitudes towards the 'pull' of home. However, in practice we did not find this to be the case. Women's answers to these sorts of statements were interrelated and appeared to be measuring one general dimension of feelings about not having a job.

The mean factor scores for the two factors are shown below each group of statements on Table 7.20. These scores were calculated from women's answers to the attitude statements and have a mean of zero for the whole sample of women. High negative scores on Factor I indicate a strong dissatisfaction with not having a paid job whereas high positive scores indicate the opposite: satisfaction with not having a paid job. On Factor II high negative scores indicate a strong financial need to work whereas high positive scores indicate the absence of a financial need to work.

Looking first at overall differences between the attitudes of working and non-working women it is clear that the working women anticipated they would have strong negative feelings about not having a job if they were to lose their present job whereas the non-working women in general had positive attitudes to not having a paid job. However, there were large differences amongst the different groups of non-working women, and amongst the working women. Among the latter for example those working part time appeared to be less

firmly attached to working both in terms of the social/psychological dimensions of not having a job and in terms of financial need than women working full time.

Amongst the non-working women differences were very marked. The unemployed had the strongest negative feelings about not having a paid job and the greatest financial need to work. In fact their scores on both factors were in between those of the full and part time working women. The women who were looking for work but not classified as unemployed were somewhat more positive than the unemployed about not having a job, and their scores on the second factor indicated a weaker financial need to work than that of unemployed women and women working part time. Moving along the continuum through the remaining three groups of non-working women to the permanently economically inactive, the results show increasingly positive attitudes towards not having a job and a decrease in the financial need to work. The last two groups, those planning to start work in a year or more and those who did not expect to work again, differed much less in their feelings about not having a job than in their financial need to work, which was low for both groups but particularly so for the group of women not expecting to work again.

Overall the results show that for working women, the more attached they were to working in terms of working full rather than part time the stronger their anticipated attitudes to the consequences of losing their jobs both in social/psychological and financial terms. Similarly for the non-working women, those who would be considered to be in or on the edge of the labour market, in terms of being unemployed or at least looking for work, tended to express the sort of attitudes to not having a job that have commonly been identified in other studies of unemployment covering men as well as women.

What is of interest is the similarities in the patterning of the scores across the groups. Unemployed women in their responses were more like women working full time while the other women looking for work resembled the part time workers in their reactions. We shall show in Chapter 11 that, in fact, this attitudinal similarity is shared by the two non-working groups looking for different jobs. The unemployed on the whole wanted full time jobs whilst the vast majority of the other women looking for work wanted part time jobs.

Some caution, however, should be used in interpreting these results in that they do not imply any causal relationships between women's attitudes and their employment circumstances. For example, women with positive attitudes to staying at home and little financial need to work may choose not to work, but equally women who see little prospect of being able to find a job may as a consequence adopt positive attitudes to staying at home, adapt to the financial consequences of not working and thus express little financial need to work.

Perceived stress
As well as asking women directly about their attitudes to not working we used a measure of psychological stress to compare working and non-working women. This measure was described in the last chapter. As we showed in Chapter 6, non-work factors are likely to be important determinants of levels of stress. In Table 7.21 we compare the levels of psychological stress expressed by the different groups of working and non-working women. Overall non-working women scored higher on this measure of stress than working women. However, as we know from Chapter 6, there is some evidence of an association between high stress scores and the presence of dependent children. Clearly more non-working than working women have dependent children, and this, in part, explains their higher stress scores; but even when allowance is made for the presence or absence of dependent children, non-working women still had higher stress scores than working women (see also Brown *et al*, 1978).

When we compared groups of non-working women the picture was less clear. There is some indication that women looking for work score higher on this measure of stress than other non-working women, although there was not such a clear trend across the different groups of non-working women as when we compared their attitudes to not working. The highest levels of stress were expressed not by unemployed women but by the other women who were looking for work; the unemployed differed little from women planning to work within the next year. In some ways this measure

Table 7.21 Level of psychological stress of full and part time working women and non-working women by their current position

Current position		Level of psychological stress				Base
		1 (High stress)	2	3 (Low stress)		
Working full time	%	23	43	34	100	1,877
Working part time	%	26	45	29	100	1,477
All working women	%	**24**	**44**	**32**	**100**	3,354
Unemployed	%	34	42	24	100	267
Others looking for work	%	34	51	15	100	115
Planning to start work within 1 year	%	33	43	24	100	104
Planning to start work in 1 or more years	%	32	42	26	100	762
Will not/may not work again	%	32	36	32	100	693
All non-working women	%	**32**	**41**	**27**	**100**	1,941

of women's reactions to their current employment situation is less subject to the type of reservations we expressed about our more direct measures of women's attitudes to not working. But because (as we discussed in Chapter 6) psychological stress is so obviously related to other circumstances in a women's life beside her employment situation it is impossible to say precisely which set of circumstances has more effect. The differences in stress between unemployed women and other women looking for work is likely to be because the latter are more likely to have children and domestic commitments.

Summary and conclusions
In this chapter we have explored the issue of unemployment amongst women and some of its complexity. We have shown that the 35% of women who were not working at the time of the survey were a fairly heterogeneous group. For most of them, 'not working' was a temporary phase; they were either currently looking for work or intended to return when their children were older. We identified five categories of women along an unemployed – permanently economically inactive continuum by their answers to a series of questions about their current employment status and their future work intentions. Two groups of women were considered to be economically active, those in our unemployed category (14%) and a smaller category of women (6%) who had said they were looking for work, but said they were not currently working for domestic reasons. The third and fourth categories contained women who, though not looking for work currently, expected to work again, either within a year (5%) or not for at least a year (39%). Our final category covered those 36% of non-working women who either did not expect to or were not sure whether they would work again.

We compared our categories both with official registration as an unemployed person and women's self-definition of whether they were unemployed or not. Overall 10% of non-working women said they were registered as unemployed and 21% thought of themselves as unemployed, but only 6% were both registered and defined themselves as unemployed. As we would expect there was a broad concordance between a woman's position along our continuum and whether she was registered and/or saw herself as unemployed.

There were marked demographic differences between the five groups. The currently unemployed tended to be younger than other groups, have the highest proportion of single women and be least likely to have children. At the other end of the continuum, women who did not expect to work again were generally much older with no dependent children. Women in the three middle groups tended to have similar demographic characteristics; the majority were married with dependent children, though women in the third group, who were planning to be back in work within a year, were a slightly more mixed group. They were less likely to be married or have dependent children and had a wider age spread.

There were also differences between the groups when we examined the length of time women had not been working and their reasons for not working. Unemployed women were more likely to have worked recently than all other groups and to give a non-domestic reason for leaving their last job and for not currently working. By contrast about three quarters of the women in the three middle groups had left their last jobs for domestic reasons, chiefly pregnancy, and between 87% and 96% of them gave domestic reasons for not currently working. The responses of women in the fifth group were more diverse suggesting a greater heterogeneity of labour market experience.

When we looked at the financial stress scores and attitudes to not working of these groups of women, the pattern of differences between the groups was slightly different. Women looking for work, and therefore in either of our first two groups, were much more likely to say they were finding it very difficult or impossible to manage financially or that they worried about money, and there was no significant differences in the proportion of unemployed women and other women looking for work who said this. Unemployed women, however, were more likely not to save money and to have overall higher financial stress scores than the other women looking for work and the level of financial stress declined steadily across our unemployed – economically inactive continuum. It is clear therefore that perceived financial need or stress is closely correlated with a desire for paid employment.

Though non-working women overall had positive attitudes in general to not having a job, there were marked differences between the different groups. Unemployed women showed the strongest negative feelings towards not working and a greater financial need to work than other non-working women. However, in both cases this was less than for women working full time, who anticipated stronger negative feelings and higher financial need were they to lose their job than the currently unemployed. The other group of women looking for work showed slightly more positive attitudes to not working than the unemployed or either group of working women. Attitudes to not working became progressively more positive along the continuum and this was accompanied by a decreasing financial need to work. Generally, working women showed less psychological stress than non-working women even when the presence of children was controlled for, but among the non-working women, those who were looking for work were most stressed.

We can see, therefore, from these findings, that the group of non-working women comprises a range of labour market situations. Women in the unemployed category are different in most respects from other non-working women and react to being without paid employment in much the same way as studies show unemployed men do. The other category of women who were looking for work were different from the unemployed in that they were mostly returning to work after a period of domestic absence; that is they were re-entering the labour market. Despite having different demographic characteristics and a different type of labour market attachment from the unemployed, as measured by their attitudes to working, their perceived financial need for work was as great as that shown by the unemployed. We look in further detail at the job priorities and job search behaviour of the two groups in Chapter 11.

Notes

[1] The limitations of registered unemployment figures as a measure of female unemployment was well known by the mid to late 1970s when use of sample surveys, in particular the General Household Survey, had increased and their different counting of the unemployed was more frequently referred to (Showler and Sinfield, 1980; Sinfield, 1981).

[2] At the time the fieldwork was conducted in 1980 the rules governing registration and claiming benefit were different from the time of writing (1983). The text therefore refers throughout to the 1980 situation. Since 1982 registration has been voluntary for those aged 18 and over.

[3] Insofar as in 1980 registering for work and claiming benefit were distinct, though sequential activities, it was possible to register and then not claim though not possible to claim without registering.

[4] Cragg and Dawson were concerned to explore what 'being unemployed' meant for women, how they defined their position, whether it had changed in the intervening months since their OPCS interview, (that is had they become discouraged and withdrawn, or just withdrawn from the labour market) and the financial and social effects of being without paid work (Cragg and Dawson, 1984).

[5] The exact wording of the question was: 'some people when they are not working think of themselves as being unemployed, while others just think of themselves as not having a paid job; which of these best describes how you think of yourself at present . . .
  unemployed
  or not having a paid job?'

[6] Several interviews conducted over a period of time are necessary if this process of transition is to be captured. This methodology was used in a study of unemployment amongst women after redundancy funded by DE (Martin and Wallace, 1984).

[7] It is, of course, very difficult to know how voluntary or involuntary actions may be in reality. For example, some employees may opt to be made redundant; likewise some people may resign from jobs rather than be dismissed. Degrees of choice cannot be captured easily in interviews. For a discussion of the 'voluntary' nature of redundancies see Wood and Dey, (1983).

8 It is difficult to explain precisely, without a longitudinal study, why this discrepancy occurs more frequently when women leave jobs for non-domestic rather than domestic reasons. This survey did not explore the extent to which women's reasons for not having a paid job change over the course of a period of not working, which would lead to their being defined as unemployed or economically inactive at different points in time over such a period; nor did it look at what leads them to change their status at different times. The Cragg and Dawson follow-up study of unemployed women looked at these issues in greater detail, but it did not cover all types of non-working women. We therefore do not have a complete picture of the routes by which non-working women arrived at their current point on the continuum from unemployment to economic inactivity, whether from another point on the continuum or from employment.

9 Some of this was looked at in a specific study of incomes in and out of work by the DHSS Cohort Study of Unemployed Men (Wood, 1982 and Davies et al, 1982).

10 Daniel (1974) included women in his survey only insofar as women were on the register and while some initial breakdowns of the sample on particular issues were done by sex, most of the study ignored gender, treating men and women together. By contrast in an earlier study (Daniel, 1972) women were the subject of a separate analysis and chapter. Women were ignored completely in the North Tyneside COP study (Turner and Dickinson, 1978). By and large studies which rely on the register as a sampling frame are likely to get a distorted view of female unemployment and thus even in more recent studies the issue of women's unemployment is problematic (Daniel, 1981; White, 1983).

11 See technical report for details of the method used (Martin and Roberts, 1984).

Chapter 8 Domestic demands and women's employment

Introduction
Women's employment cannot be studied separately from the unpaid work most women do at home, in their roles as wives and mothers, running a house and looking after a husband, children and sometimes sick or elderly dependants. Indeed the interaction of paid and unpaid work over the course of a woman's lifetime is a central theme of this study. We have already looked in general terms in earlier chapters at how women's participation in employment varies by their position in the lifecycle, though we also showed that domestic circumstances are not the only factors affecting a woman's decision whether or not to work.

In this chapter we turn to look more precisely at the domestic circumstances of different women in our sample and how these affected their working lives. In particular we consider how husbands and wives shared domestic and paid work, identifying who was the primary wage-earner and houseworker. We look also at husbands' and wives' attitudes to their own arrangements and men and women's roles in general. In addition we examine the consequences of not having a partner for those women who were lone parents, comparing their employment position and attitudes to work with married mothers with comparable aged children. As well as the normal care of young children, some women have extra responsibility for disabled or elderly relatives and our final section considers this and its impact on women's employment. We start by examining the composition of the households in which women lived and discussing who was a houseworker in the household.

The composition of women's households
All women were asked who else lived in their household with them, and we have used this information to classify the composition of their households. Since many of our analyses look particularly at women with children under 16 we distinguish in our classification women who had at least one child under 16 living with them from those whose children were all sixteen or over. The classification is designed primarily to show the different combinations of husband, children and parents women lived with since this covers the majority of situations. It is of course possible for women to live in households with other adults in addition to husbands, parents and grown-up children (ie aged 16 or over), but apart from non-married women sharing with other adults, these situations were not very common and have not been distinguished in our classification. In fact the only situation in which other adults were present in more than a few cases was where non-married women were living with their parents and may have had

grown-up siblings in the households who would not be distinguished by our classification.

Table 8.1 shows the distribution of women living in the different types of household according to this classification, with both the proportion of all women in each category and the proportions of married and non-married women shown separately. The majority of married women (71%) lived in a nuclear family, with their husband and children, and a further 26% lived

Table 8.1 Composition of households of married and non-married women

Household composition	% of all women	% of married women	% of non-married women
Married women			
Living with:			
Husband only*	19	26	
Husband and children			
– some under 16*	41 } 51	57 } 71	
– all 16 or over	10	14	
Husband and parents (in-law)*	1	1	
Husband, parents (in-law) and children			
– some under 16*	1 } 2	2 } 2	
– all 16 or over*	1	0	
All married women	**73**	**100**	
Non-married women			
Living alone	4		16
Living with children:			
– some under 16*	4 } 6		14 } 21
– all 16 or over*	2		7
Parents	14		53
Parents (in-law) and children			
– some under 16*	1 } 1		3 } 3
– all 16 or over*	0		0
Other adults	2		7
All non-married women	**27**		**100**
All women	**100**		
Base	*5,588*	*4,079*	*1,509*

*Household included other adults in a few cases

Table 8.2 Composition of households of single and widowed, divorced or separated women

Household composition	Single	Widowed, divorced or separated
	%	%
Living alone	11	29
Living with:		
Children		
– some under 16*	3 } 3	37 } 60
– all 16 or over*	0	23
Parents	75	4
Parents and children		
– some under 16*	2 } 2	5 } 6
– all 16 or over	0	1
Other adults	9	1
	100	100
Base	*1,036*	*473*

*Household included other adults in a few cases

just with their husband. Extended families, where a woman lived with both her husband and his or her parents, were rare. Over half the non-married women (53%) were living with their parents (and possibly also their siblings), but 21% lived with their own children and 16% lived alone.

Table 8.2 looks at the situation of non-married women in more detail and compares the position of single women with the widowed, divorced and separated, showing marked differences in their living arrangements. The majority of single women (who were concentrated in the younger age bands) lived with their parents (77% including 2% who also had their own children), although a minority either lived alone (11%) or with other adults (9%). Most of the widowed, divorced and separated women lived just with their own children (60%), but 29% lived alone and 11% lived with their parents or other adults and some of these also had children. We look in more detail at the circumstances of non-married women with children under 16, the lone mothers, later in the chapter.

'Housewife' or 'houseworker'
Many surveys employ the concept of a 'housewife', who is usually defined as the person responsible for the majority of domestic tasks in a household, either carrying them out personally or being responsible for their being carried out by others. Rather than ask questions directly to determine who is the 'housewife', surveys often apply a rule that in households with a married couple the wife is automatically defined as the 'housewife'. Similarly, when two women share the domestic tasks the elder is defined as the 'housewife' irrespective of how the responsibilities are shared. We rejected the use of the term in this way, because of its assumptions about the division of domestic work between men and women, an issue we wished to investigate (Nissel, 1980; Oakley, 1974). Instead, we defined as a 'houseworker' anyone responsible for at least half the domestic tasks in the household. This meant that anyone in the household could be a 'houseworker' and a household could have two houseworkers if domestic responsibilities were shared equally.[1] Almost all the married women interviewed (99%) were houseworkers in that they said they were responsible for at least half the domestic tasks in their household so it was very rare for the husband to assume more than half the share of the domestic responsibilities. However only 46% of non-married women were houseworkers. Those women who were not houseworkers were generally living with their parents and were predominantly young single women. Among the non-married women only 25% of the single women were houseworkers compared with 93% of the widowed, divorced and separated. Altogether 85% of all women were houseworkers.

Clearly once they have left their parental home the majority of women are responsible for at least half the domestic tasks in their households. Those living in households with no adults other than their own grown-up children are likely to bear the major part if not the whole responsibility, whereas for married women the husband is potentially available to share the responsibility for, and carrying out of domestic work. We look at the domestic arrangements of wives and husbands in detail next when we consider how husbands and wives divide paid and unpaid work between them.

Wives and husbands
In this section we look in more detail at the effect 'being married' has on women's employment. We have touched on various aspects of this issue in earlier chapters. We showed, for example, in Chapter 2 that marital status alone does not affect whether a women works or not, though it may have some effect on whether she works full or part time. We also pointed out that we were only able to ask working women their reasons for working, discussed in Chapter 6, because the assumption is still current in our society that married women have a choice about working. Married women regardless of their own employment status are often seen as dependent, economically at least, upon their husbands, who in turn are seen as the sole or primary wage earner in the family. Wives' work is regarded as secondary in financial terms as well as less important than a husband's while their primary contribution is seen as being in the sphere of domestic work. Indeed this view is embodied in our tax structure and social security system (Land, 1978).

We decided to look at the basis for this set of assumptions by comparing husbands and wives and contrasting their share of paid work and domestic work. We asked all the 73% of women in the study who were married two types of questions, firstly factual questions about their husband's employment situation, job, earnings, hours of work, and qualifications; secondly questions about their own views on how housework and childcare were shared with their spouse and what they thought were their husband's views about their working or not working. We also asked the sub-sample of husbands we interviewed the same factual and attitudinal questions. In cases where husbands' answers to factual questions differed from their wives we used the husband's answer in the analysis. Where husbands' and wives' attitudes have been contrasted in our analysis, we have only used the responses of our sub-sample of husbands and their wives.

Wives' and husbands' employment
The vast majority of husbands (92%) were in paid work. Of the 8% who were not, half were unemployed so 96% of husbands were economically active. This compares with 65% of married women who were economically active. The majority of the remaining husbands were either retired or permanently unable to work because of sickness or disability. When we looked at husbands and wives together, we found that working husbands were more likely to have a working wife than either unemployed or economically inactive husbands: 62% of the wives of working husbands worked compared with 33% of the wives of unemployed men and 40% of the wives of economically inactive men (Table

8.3). Moreover the wives of unemployed men were more likely to be unemployed than the wives of either working or economically inactive men; 12% of such wives were, compared with 4% for the other two groups.

Table 8.3 Wife's economic status by husband's economic status

Wife's economic status	Husband working	Husband unemployed	Husband economically inactive
	%	%	%
Wife working	62	33	40
Wife unemployed	4	12	4
Wife economically inactive	34	55	56
	100	**100**	**100**
Base	*3,747*	*164*	*167*

The question arises then as to whether wives' unemployment is a consequence of husbands' unemployment. This issue has aroused considerable interest even though in very few couples are both husband and wife unemployed; one per cent in our study. Analysis from the DHSS Cohort Study of the Unemployed has shown that a range of factors were associated with wives' likelihood of being unemployed when their husbands were unemployed. Moreover, husbands and wives usually share similar social and educational characteristics and both are likely to be affected by a high local unemployment rate. In addition, part of the explanation, it is also suggested, lies in the rules governing social security benefit which have low earning ceilings for wives of unemployed men receiving social security ie provide a financial disincentive for wives in these circumstances to work (Moylan *et al*, 1984). In her analysis Joshi looks at the effect of a non-working husband on a wife's participation in the labour market in more detail. She shows that whilst having a non-working husband, other things being equal, reduces both a woman's economic activity and her likelihood of working, having an unemployed husband (in receipt of unemployment benefit) is associated with larger reductions in labour market participation. Joshi argues her results favour both a 'demand side' interpretation of the 'unemployed husband effect' as well as the 'unwillingness to work hypothesis', that is, both husband and wife are affected by a local scarcity of jobs as well as the wife being affected by the earnings rules (Joshi, 1984).

Husbands' and wives' employment status determined the proportion of wives who were joint wage earners with their husbands and the proportion who were completely economically dependent on their husbands at the time of our interview. When we compared husbands' and wives' employment status directly it was clear that the most common pattern was the two earner couple: in 57% of couples husbands and wives were both working. If we included those partners who were unemployed the proportion of couples where both were economically active rose to 62%. The second most common pattern, as might be expected, was the one earner couple where the husband worked and his wife was economically inactive: 31% of couples. The proportion of couples with other combinations of employ-

ment status was very small: 2% of husbands and wives were both economically inactive and most of these tended to be older couples. This was also the case in the small proportion (2%) of role reversal couples where the wife worked and her husband was economically inactive (see tables in technical report Martin and Roberts, 1984). Thus in 1980 only a minority of husbands were the sole wage earner in the family and, as we know from Chapter 7 and will show again in Chapter 9, this is likely to be a temporary phase for most couples while dependent children are young.

Nevertheless, it is clear that husbands are more likely to work than their wives; they are also much more likely to work more hours in the week than their wives. The overwhelming majority of husbands in paid work worked full time whereas only 27% of wives were in full time employment and 33% worked part time. On average husbands worked 45.1 hours per week if overtime is included. We saw in Chapter 4 that even women working full time averaged only 37.4 hours per week, so most husbands worked considerably longer hours than their wives even when both worked full time. Only 4% of wives worked longer hours than their husbands and 11% worked the same number of hours. The fact that in the majority of cases (85%) husbands worked longer than their wives reflects both the degree of part time working among wives and the shorter hours worked by full time working wives (see tables in technical report Martin and Roberts, 1984).

There was very little difference overall between the hours worked by the husbands of working and non-working wives. Husbands of wives working part time worked the longest hours on average, 46.4 hours per week; husbands of non-working wives worked 44.7 hours a week on average, while husbands of women working full time worked the least, 43.9 hours on average (see tables in Martin and Roberts, 1984). It is impossible to tell whether husbands' and wives' hours were substitutable, that is whether husbands worked more if their wives were unable to work, though the higher hours of husbands with wives working part time or not at all suggests this might be happening.[2] However many men, particularly those in non-manual jobs, work fixed hours with no opportunities for paid overtime. Women working full time and fixed hours are particularly likely to be married to such men; this may, in part, explain the lower average hours of the husbands of women working full time.

Wives' and husbands' pay
We also compared husbands' and wives' earnings. However, we only had information about this for 66% of husbands since, apart from those husbands not in paid employment, many wives could not or would not tell us their husbands' earnings. For the husbands about whom information was available, the average gross hourly earnings were £3.00, which compares with averages of £1.90 and £1.60 for women working full time and part time respectively, quoted in Chapter 5. Table 8.4 shows that a husband's hourly pay did not vary very much according to his wife's working status.

Table 8.4 Husband's gross hourly earnings by wife's work status

Wife's work status	Husband's gross hourly earnings	Bases
Wife working full time	£2.90	707
Wife working part time	£3.10	809
Wife not working	£2.90	876
All wives*	**£3.00**	2,403

Including 11 in full time education

If we look at husband's gross earnings, there is some evidence that longer hours of work and lower rates of pay went together, in that despite some differences in their hours of work the gross earnings of husbands with wives working full time and wives working part time were identical at £115 per week. However, the gross earnings of the husbands of non-working women were somewhat higher at £123 per week. But the difference is very small in relation to the average earnings of the working women which were £52 for all working women and £71 and £29 for full timers and part timers respectively (see table in technical report, Martin and Roberts, 1984). It does not appear, therefore, that overall the husbands of women who do not work or work part time compensate for not having a wife who works full time through earning more themselves.

If we compare the earnings of husbands and wives at the level of individual couples rather than overall, working wives earned on average only half of what their husbands earned. Only 7% of wives earned the same as or more than their husbands. As might be expected the differences are partly due to the wives' shorter hours of work. On average, wives' hourly earnings were 75% that of their husbands, virtually the same proportion that the hourly earnings for all women constitutes of that of all men. However, the earnings of wives who worked full time were 79% of their husbands' compared with 71% for women working part time. Only 15% of wives had the same as or higher hourly earnings than their husbands, and even among those working full time, who as we saw in Chapter 5 generally had higher pay than part timers, only 20% had the same as or higher hourly earnings than their husbands.

Explanations of the differential in men and women's earnings are necessarily complex and it is impossible here to give a full explanation of this difference. Various econometric studies have shown that much of the earnings differential between men and women can be accounted for by the fact that men have, on average, better qualifications and greater work experience than women, and work in occupations and industries with higher rates of pay (Greenhalgh, 1980; Siebert and Sloane, 1981; Zabalza and Arrufat, 1983). Certainly when we compared the educational qualifications of the husbands and wives in our sample we found that husbands were more likely to be better qualified than their wives even though they were slightly more likely to have left school sooner: 34% of husbands were better qualified than their wives in contrast to 17% of wives who were better qualified than their husbands. (See

tables in the technical report, Martin and Roberts, 1984).

Joshi has used the data in this study to quantify the effect of family formation on women's earnings and her findings explain some of the variation in husbands' and wives' earnings. She argues that the effect of family formation is felt not only through the career break, described in Chapter 9, but in terms of women's reduced participation subsequently when they work part time and, as we show in Chapter 10, are often occupationally downwardly mobile as a result. Thus family formation has a lasting effect for, as she estimates, it depresses women's lifetime earnings on average by between 25–50% (Joshi, 1984).

Interaction of husbands' employment with wife's employment

The fact that husbands' hourly earnings are higher in part reflects the fact that they are primary wage earners, continuously economically active over their lifetime, whilst most wives are not. Therefore a husband's employment needs may well be seen as more important than a wife's. We attempted to explore this by asking whether wives thought that their husband's employment (or lack of it) directly affected their own employment situation, either in terms of the sort of work they could do or the hours they could work or indeed whether they could work at all. We asked the question in neutral terms so that wives who thought their husband's employment situation facilitated rather than constrained their own situation would also be able to respond positively.

Only a minority (20%) of wives said that their husband's employment situation affected their own. Table 8.5 shows that this proportion did not vary overall very much as between wives of working or non-working husbands. However, amongst wives with working husbands women working full time were least likely to say their employment was affected, while those who were not working were most likely to say this. In contrast, amongst wives of non-working husbands there was little variation according to whether the wife worked or not.

Table 8.5 Proportion of wives who feel that their husband's employment situation affects their own by husband's and wife's work status

Wife's work status	Husband working		Husband not working	
	% of wives whose employment is affected	Base	% of wives whose employment is affected	Base
Working full time	12%	1,033	18%	56
Working part time	18%	1,284	16%	62
All working	**15%**	2,317	**17%**	118
Not working	28%	1,414	18%	211
Full time student		16*		3*
All married women	**20%**	3,747	**18%**	332

Base too small to show percentages

Table 8.6 Ways in which wives of working husbands feel that their husband's employment situation has affected their own

Ways in which wives feel their employment has been affected	Wife's work status				All wives of working husbands whose employment is affected
	Working full time	Working part time	All working	Not working	
	%	%	%	%	%
Husband's hours of work are inconvenient	32	61	51	76	64
Husband's hours of work facilitate wife's employment	23	21	22	2	11
Helps with husband's job or works for husband	12	7	8	8	8
Has to work because of husband's low earnings	19	6	10	–	5
Other answers	17	9	11	19	15
Base	*120*	*234*	*354*	*385*	*739*

Percentages do not add to 100 because women gave more than one answer

All the wives who said their employment was affected were asked in what ways it was affected. However, since the numbers of wives with non-working husbands were very small we only show in Table 8.6 the answers given by the wives of working husbands. Husband's hours of work were most often mentioned as affecting the wife's employment, usually in that they constrained the hours she could work or prevented her from working at all: 64% of wives of working husbands whose employment had been affected said this. However, among the working wives a sizeable minority of the women (22%) said their husbands' hours facilitated their working. Looking at the answers given by the wives of non-working husbands (details in Martin and Roberts, 1984) some said that they were prevented from working because their husband was sick or disabled and needed their care. A few said that it would not be economically worthwhile for them to work because the state benefits they received would be affected, while a small number said their husband's not working meant they needed to work instead. The numbers, however, were too small to be statistically reliable.

In addition to asking this question of all married women we also asked the same question of the husbands who were interviewed so we can compare their answers with their wives' responses. The majority (82%) of husbands and wives gave the same answers to the questions about whether the husband's employment affected his wife's, but for 11% of couples the husband thought his employment did affect his wife's although she did not think so, and for 7% the wife thought her employment was affected but her husband did not. Thus husbands seemed to be generally aware of the effect of their employment situation on that of their wives.

The share of domestic work and responsibilities between husbands and wives

Having seen how husbands take the greater share of paid work we looked next at how wives and husbands share domestic work and responsibilities. We saw at the beginning of this chapter that the vast majority of married women were 'houseworkers' in the sense that they were responsible for at least half the domestic tasks in their households. Their husbands could also be considered houseworkers on this basis if the responsibilities were split equally between the couple. The degree to which men are 'houseworkers' in this sense clearly

has consequences for women's domestic and employment roles (Oakley, 1974; Hunt, P, 1980; Porter, 1983). This led us to examine in what proportion of couples wives and husbands share the housework and childcare and what both thought about their current arrangements.

Housework

We asked all the married women to think about all the jobs that need to be done to keep a home running, such as shopping, cooking and cleaning and to say how much of this work was shared with their husband. Table 8.7 shows the categories from which they had to choose their answer and the distribution of answers according to the wife's working status. Just over a quarter of wives overall said that they shared the housework equally with their husband or that he did more than they. The majority (73%) said that they did all or most of the housework. However, there were important differences according to the wife's working status: wives who worked full time were much more likely than those who did not work to say they shared the housework equally with their husband; 44% did so, while 23% of wives who worked part time said they shared housework equally. Nevertheless, even among women working full time 13% said they did all the housework and 41% that they did most of it. So 54% of women working full time were combining paid work with the major share of housework at home.

It is likely in fact that these figures understate women's share of domestic work. At the pilot stages of the survey we had asked in much greater detail about an extensive range of tasks required to keep a home running. These covered daily household jobs as well as the regular or occasional work needed to maintain homes, gardens and cars. We found many women who gave long lists of what they did, and whose husbands appeared to do relatively little of this work, who nevertheless said that they shared the housework equally. There seemed to be common feeling among many women that if the tasks were shared equally when husband and wife were both at home this constituted equal shares overall even if she was doing additional work when he was not there.

The husbands who were interviewed were also asked how much they thought they shared the housework with their wives, and their views, according to their wife's working status, are also shown in Table 8.7. The husbands were less likely than the wives to think she did all the housework, but more said that she did most of it. Interestingly similar proportions of husbands and wives thought they shared the housework. Comparing the answers of the husbands who were interviewed with the answers of their own wives there appeared to be a large amount of agreement: two thirds gave the same answers and the most common disparity was when the wife said she did all the housework whereas her husband said she did most of it.

It is rather difficult to ask wives and husbands in a meaningful way in a structured interview if they feel this division of labour between them is satisfactory; answers to most questions about satisfaction show that people usually tend to give responses indicating that they are satisfied with their current situation. On the whole, wives were satisfied with the amount of housework that their husbands did, as Table 8.8 shows, but 20% said they did not think their husbands did enough. Working wives were slightly more likely to think this than non-working wives. Like the wives, the majority of husbands were satisfied with the status quo. Just over three quarters felt they did about the right amount of housework, 3% said they did too much and 20% said they did not do enough. Their views were not related to whether or not their wives worked.

Childcare

Married women with children were then asked about the share of childcare between themselves and their husbands in a similar manner to the question about housework. Their answers, shown in Table 8.9, indicate that a higher proportion of wives considered that childcare was shared equally than was the case with housework; 50% compared with 26%. Oakley also found that wives felt husbands participated more in childcare than with other household work (Oakley, 1974). A small minority (9%) of wives in our study felt they did all the childcare and 40% felt they did most of it. As with housework, working women, particularly those working full time, were more likely than non-working women to consider that childcare was shared equally.

Comparisons are made complex, however, because the amount and nature of the childcare work to be done will vary for couples with children of differing ages. Non-working women with very young children will be involved in a considerable amount of care while their husbands are out at work, so they therefore inevitably provide most of the care. However, as with housework, some women discounted this, saying that they and their husbands shared the childcare equally, ignoring times

Table 8.7 Wives' and husbands' views about how the housework is shared between them by wife's work status

Views about share of housework	Wife's work status								All married women*	
	Working full time		Working part time		All working		Not working			
	Wife's view	Husband's view	Wife's view	Husband's view	Wife's view	Husband's view	Wife's view	Husband's view	Wife's view	Husband's view
	%	%	%	%	%	%	%	%	%	%
Wife does it all	13	9	26	15	20	13	32	22	25	16
Wife does most of it	41	46	51	61	47	54	49	58	48	56
Shared half and half	44	43	23	24	32	32	17	19	26	27
Husband does most of it	2	2	0	0	1	1	1	0	1	1
Husband does it all	0	–	–	–	0	–	1	1	0	0
	100	100	100	100	100	100	100	100	100	100
Base	1,062	190	1,327	250	2,389	440	1,592	269	4,000†	712‡

*Excludes women with disabled husbands and cases where most of the housework is done by someone else
†Includes 19 full time students
‡Includes husbands of 3 full time students

Table 8.8 How wives and husbands feel about the amount of housework done by husbands, by wife's work status

Feelings about amount of housework done by husband	Wife's work status								All married women*	
	Working full time		Working part time		All working		Not working			
	Wife's view	Husband's view	Wife's view	Husband's view	Wife's view	Husband's view	Wife's view	Husband's view	Wife's view	Husband's view
	%	%	%	%	%	%	%	%	%	%
Amount of housework done by husband is:										
Too much	4	4	2	3	3	3	3	2	3	3
About right	74	76	75	78	75	77	80	76	77	77
Not enough	21	20	23	19	22	20	17	22	20	20
	100	100	100	100	100	100	100	100	100	100
Base	1,062	190	1,327	250	2,389	440	1,592	269	4,000†	712‡

*Excludes women with disabled husbands and cases where most of the housework is done by someone else
†Includes 19 full time students
‡Includes husbands of 3 full time students

Table 8.9 Wives' and husbands' views about how the childcare is shared between them by wife's work status

Views about share of childcare	Wife's work status								Married women with children under 16*	
	Working full time		Working part time		All working		Not working			
	Wife's view	Husband's view	Wife's view	Husband's view	Wife's view	Husband's view	Wife's view	Husband's view	Wife's view	Husband's view
	%	%	%	%	%	%	%	%	%	%
Wife does it all	5	2	8	5	7	4	11	6	9	5
Wife does most of it	24	24	36	44	32	39	48	64	40	51
Shared half and half	67	72	55	51	59	57	41	30	50	44
Husband does most of it	4	2	1	–	2	0	0	0	1	0
Husband does it all	0	–	–	–	0	–	–	–	0	–
	100	**100**	**100**	**100**	**100**	**100**	**100**	**100**	**100**	**100**
Base	370	63	867	158	1,237	221	1,119	191	2,366†	414‡

*Excludes women with disabled husbands and cases where most of the childcare is done by someone else
†Includes 10 full time students
‡Includes husbands of 2 full time students

Table 8.10 How wives and husbands feel about the amount of childcare done by husbands by wife's work status

Feelings about amount of childcare done by husband	Wife's work status								Married women with children under 16*	
	Working full time		Working part time		All working		Not working			
	Wife's view	Husband's view	Wife's view	Husband's view	Wife's view	Husband's view	Wife's view	Husband's view	Wife's view	Husband's view
	%	%	%	%	%	%	%	%	%	%
Amount of childcare done by husband is:										
Too much	2	2	0	–	1	0	1	–	1	0
About right	88	87	87	82	87	84	83	74	85	79
Not enough	10	11	13	18	12	16	16	26	14	21
	100	**100**	**100**	**100**	**100**	**100**	**100**	**100**	**100**	**100**
Base	370	63	867	158	1,237	221	1,119	191	2,366†	414‡

*Excludes women with disabled husbands and cases where most of the childcare is done by someone else
†Includes 10 full-time students
‡Includes husbands of 2 full time students

when he was at work and she was at home. Husbands however, appeared less likely to take this into consideration. As Table 8.9 shows, a much smaller proportion of husbands with non-working wives said they shared childcare equally than did the wives themselves. Comparing the answers of individual couples this was apparent. Although there was a fair amount of agreement on how much childcare was shared, the main disparity occurred when wives thought it was shared equally but their husbands thought their wives did most of it. In addition as our pilot work showed husbands and wives tended to be involved in rather different aspects of their children's care. Wives were more likely to be involved in the routine basic care such as feeding, dressing, washing and so on, while husbands spent time playing with the children or taking them out. Perhaps, therefore, husbands' views of how much childcare work they do more accurately reflects wives' and husbands' share of this activity.

The high proportion (85%) of wives who felt that the amount of childcare that their husbands did was about right (Table 8.10), is probably also a reflection of their expectation that his contribution will be limited (Hunt, P, 1980). It is noticeable that non-working wives were slightly more likely than working wives to feel that their husbands did not do enough, although for housework the reverse was the case. This may be partly attribut-

able to the fact that non-working wives are more likely than the working mothers to have very young children and so well might need more help with childcare from their husbands. Husbands were less likely than wives to feel that the amount of childcare they did was about right. Whilst the majority (79%) felt it was, a sizeable minority (21%) felt they did not do enough. Husbands of non-working wives were most likely to say this: 26% did so thereby confirming the views of their wives.

A problem which has to be faced by couples with children when both go out to work is how to cope when a child is ill or has to be taken somewhere such as to the doctor or dentist. We asked both husbands and wives who were working and who had children whether they could get time off easily for this sort of reason. Of the working wives, 90% said they could get time off work easily and a further 8% said they would take time off anyway. Of the husbands, 83% said they could take time off easily and a further 12% said they would take time off anyway. Thus only a tiny minority of either husbands or wives appeared to have difficulties taking time off in connection with their children. Moreover, when we compared the answers of the husbands who were interviewed with the answers of their own wives (rather than all the wives in the survey), those who could not take time off easily tended to have wives who could and vice versa. Only 2% of couples said one or other could not take time off work easily and there were no couples at all where neither the husband nor the wife said they would not take time off anyway. It seems that not only can most couples take time off work fairly easily to cope with sick children and similar problems, but husbands are only slightly less likely than wives to be able to do this, although we did not ascertain whether the husbands did so in practice. Aggregate sickness statistics as we indicated in Chapter 4 suggest women take time off for their children's sickness more often than men (OPCS, 1982a).

We went on to ask both husbands and wives about the arrangements they had at work for taking time off. Table 8.11 shows that the majority of wives (54%) were not paid for such time off, but some (22%) could make up the time subsequently. Husbands however were significantly more likely than wives to be able to take paid leave (44%) and also to be able to use their holiday leave, whilst as we saw in Chapter 5 many women, particularly those working part time, did not have paid holidays, or if they did, could not choose when to take them. Similar proportions of both husbands and wives (6% and 7% respectively) were able to use their own sick leave. Only 8% of husbands could make up for any time taken off compared with 22% of wives. So, altogether more husbands than wives could take time off to cope with sick children in one way or another without losing pay.

Table 8.11 Types of arrangements for taking time off work made by working wives and husbands when their children are ill or need to be taken somewhere: employees working outside the home who had children under 16

Type of arrangement	All wives	Husbands
	%	%
Takes holiday	11	18
Takes sick leave	7	6
Other arrangements:		
Is paid for time off	25	44
Not paid, but makes up time taken	22	8
Not paid, can't make up time taken	32	21
Don't know	3	3
	100	100
Base	1,108	361

Wives' and husbands' attitudes to their financial situations

There are many aspects of a family's finances which are difficult to research, particularly if a researcher wants to investigate the detail of family income levels and money handling strategies and consider how couples share their money and view the wife's earnings or see whether both wives and husbands have a measure of financial control or financial independence. Many of these issues, moreover, are not amenable to direct questions or structured interviewing. As Pauline Hunt's work shows, the subtleties and ambivalences women feel about having or not having their own money, or what sharing money equally really means only becomes apparent through discussion and observation over time (Hunt, P, 1980). We decided to concentrate therefore on two main issues: firstly, how husbands and wives viewed their current financial situation and, where

wives worked, how important the wife's contribution was seen to be; secondly, the views working and non-working women had about financial independence.

We have already described in Chapter 7 the questions we used in the survey to assess women's views of their current financial situation, and have shown how answers to these questions were combined to give an overall measure of financial stress. We also showed that working women in general, as might be expected, expressed a lower level of financial stress than non-working women in answer to the three individual questions about how they managed financially, whether they saved money, and how often they worried about money, and on the overall measure which combined the answers to these three questions. Here we look specifically at how married women answered these questions.

Levels of financial difficulty or stress

Various studies show that even though working wives' earnings only account on average for about 25% of their gross household income, the contribution they make to raising the family's living standards may be considerable (Hamill, 1979). We know for example from the Royal Commission on the Distribution of Income and Wealth that, but for wives' earnings, three times as many families would be living below the official poverty line (Layard *et al*, 1978). Consequently, we would expect non-working wives, reliant on one income, to show more evidence of financial difficulty than working wives.

Table 8.12 shows that this is undoubtedly the case. A large minority of wives overall (44%) said they could manage without difficulty but over half (52%) of the working women said they managed without difficulty compared with 30% of non-working women. Only 6% of working women said they found it very difficult to manage or did not manage at all compared with 14% of non-working women who found it very difficult and a further 2% of non-working women who said they did not really manage at all.

Similarly on the question of saving money (Table 8.13), whilst 59% of wives said they and their husbands managed to save, 69% of working women saved compared with 45% of non-working women. Employment status had much less effect on whether a wife worried about money as is shown in Table 8.14. Overall, working women were only slightly less likely to worry about money than non-working wives, though 11% of the latter said they worried almost always compared with 6% of working wives.

All three tables show differences between married women working full or part time, with the full time women showing less evidence of financial pressure than the part timers. These differences between working and non-working married women and between full and part time working women are also apparent in the overall financial stress scores shown in Table 8.15. (We used the same financial stress score as in Chapter 6.) Just under three quarters of wives working full time had a low financial stress score (74%) compared with 66% of wives working part time and just over half of non-working wives (53%).

When we looked at women's financial stress scores by whether they had dependent children or not it became clear that wives with children under 16 were most likely to have high financial stress scores: 45% did overall.

Wives with children over 16 by contrast were much more likely to have a low financial stress scored: 75% did. Childless wives came in between: 70% of them had low stress scores. Within these groups the differential between wives of differing work status was maintained; being in work reduced a wife's financial stress score in all groups (see tables in technical report Martin and Roberts, 1984).

Table 8.12   Views of working and non-working married women about their financial situation

| Views about financial situation | Working | | All Working | Not Working | All married women |
	Full time	Part time			
	%	%	%	%	%
Manage without any difficulty	60	46	52	30	44
Manage but with not much money to spare	35	47	42	54	46
Find it very difficult to manage	5	7	6	14	9
Do not really manage at all	0	0	0	2	1
	100	**100**	**100**	**100**	**100**
Base	*1,089*	*1,346*	*2,435*	*1,625*	*4,079**

*Includes 19 in full time education

Table 8.13   Whether working and non-working married women and their partners manage to save any money

| Whether saves any money | Working | | All Working | Not Working | All married women |
	Full time	Part time			
	%	%	%	%	%
Saves	72	66	69	45	59
Does not save	28	34	31	55	41
	100	**100**	**100**	**100**	**100**
Base	*1,089*	*1,346*	*2,435*	*1,625*	*4,079**

*Includes 19 in full time education

Table 8.14   How often working and non-working married women worry about money

| How often do you worry about money? | Working | | All Working | Not Working | All married women |
	Full time	Part time			
	%	%	%	%	%
Almost always	5	7	6	11	8
Quite often	14	16	15	17	16
Only sometimes	44	46	45	44	45
Never or almost never	37	31	34	28	31
	100	**100**	**100**	**100**	**100**
Base	*1,089*	*1,346*	*2,435*	*1,625*	*4,079**

*Includes 19 in full time education

Table 8.15   Overall financial stress scores of working and non-working married women

| Financial stress scores* | Working | | All Working | Not Working | All married women |
	Full time	Part time			
	%	%	%	%	%
Low financial stress (score 3–5)	74	66	70	53	63
Medium financial stress (score 6–7)	22	27	24	33	28
High financial stress (score 8–10)	4	7	6	14	9
	100	**100**	**100**	**100**	**100**
Base	*1,089*	*1,346*	*2,435*	*1,625*	*4,079†*

*The scores were based on answers to the 3 questions shown in Tables 8.12 – 8.14
†Includes 19 in full time education

Since we asked the same three questions of the sample of husbands who were interviewed we can compare their answers with those of their wives to see whether they both viewed their financial situation in the same way, though we recognised that wives and husbands might not have comparable financial situations.[3] There was most agreement to the straightforward question of whether the couple managed to save or not; 83% of husbands and wives agreed they did. In contrast only 49% of couples agreed on how often they worried about money, reflecting perhaps, both differing predispositions to worry as well as the likelihood of them as individuals having different financial roles and facing different financial situations.

Although only 38% of couples had exactly the same overall financial stress score, a further 39% were within one point of their partner's score (the scoring ranged from 3 to 10), and only 6% had differences of 3 or more points. There was no bias in the direction of the differences. Thus the majority of couples had similar perceptions of their financial situation and there was no difference in this respect between couples where the wife was working and those where the wife was not working, although, as already mentioned, the latter had higher levels of financial stress.

Importance of wives' earnings
As well as asking all wives about their financial situation in general we asked working wives more specifically whether, if they were not working, they would 'be able to get by alright'; 'have to give up a lot' or 'not be able to manage at all' without the money they themselves earned. We recognised that this was a difficult question to ask in that although, as Land has pointed out, women's earnings make an essential contribution to the incomes of many households (Land, 1978), the financial arrangements husbands and wives make are often based on the notion that the family's basic needs or 'unavoidable expenses' will be met by the husband's income (Hunt, P, 1980). In this sense therefore many families will 'manage' or 'get by' on one income. For, as Hunt has argued, they do this in practice whilst the wife is at home and once she returns to work the notion that the husband is the (chief) breadwinner is unlikely to be challenged as few wives earn enough to be able to support the family's basic needs on their own (*ibid*).

Thus, we have the paradox that wives' earnings are both 'extra' and also for many families essential. This can be seen from the fact that a large minority of working wives (46%) said they could get by alright if they were not working (Table 8.16). Not surprisingly, those working full time were much more likely than those working part time to expect that it would be difficult to manage without their earnings. Overall, only 14% of wives said they would not be able to manage at all, 18% of wives working full time and 11% of part time, workers. However 60% of working wives anticipated having to give up a lot; 47% and 33% for full and part time workers respectively.

Table 8.16 How well working married women would manage financially if they were not working

If you weren't working would you . . .?	Working		All working married women
	full time	part time	
	%	%	%
Get by alright	35	56	46
Have to give up a lot	47	33	40
Not be able to manage at all	18	11	14
	100	**100**	**100**
Base	*1,089*	*1,346*	*2,435*

To a certain extent we would expect this measure of the importance of the wife's earnings to be related to the proportion of the family income which she contributes. We therefore looked at answers to this question in relation to the proportion of the joint gross earnings the wife's earnings represented (excluding non-earning husbands). From Table 8.17 we can see that the higher the proportion of the joint earnings contributed by the wife the less likely she was to say that they could manage financially if she was not working. Whilst nearly half (46%) of all working wives said they would get by alright without their earnings, women contributing over 30% of the gross earnings of their husband and themselves were less likely to say this. Indeed, as Table 8.17 shows, even among wives contributing less than 20% of the joint earnings (who comprise 25% of working couples who told us their income), a quarter did not feel they would get by alright if they did not work and 6% felt they would not be able to manage at all.

Financial independence
For many wives, earning money has an importance over and above the income it generates; their own earnings may give them some financial independence as opposed to their being totally dependent financially on their husbands (Oakley, 1974). Indeed, as we showed

Table 8.17 How well working women would manage financially if they were not working by the proportion of the joint gross earnings of husband and wife contributed by the wife's gross earnings

If you were working would you . . . ?	Wife's gross earnings as a percentage of joint gross earnings of husband and wife						All working married women
	Less than 10%	10% less than 20%	20% less than 30%	30% less than 40%	40% less than 50%	50% or more	
	%	%	%	%	%	%	%
Get by alright	89	68	51	40	26	16	46
Have to give up a lot	11	26	40	49	53	52	40
Not be able to manage at all	–	6	9	11	21	32	14
	100	**100**	**100**	**100**	**100**	**100**	**100**
Base	*90*	*311*	*381*	*395*	*324*	*132*	*2,435**

*Excludes women whose husbands were not employed or for whom details of earnings were not available

in Chapter 6, for some women this is one of their reasons for working. We attempted to measure the extent to which this financial independence was important to both working and non-working women by asking them to look at four statements and indicate whether each was definitely true, partly true or not true for them. Slightly different wording was used in the statements for working and non-working women so as to be appropriate to their situations. We chose statements which other studies showed reflected different aspects of the desire for financial independence covering, for example, the wish for some money to control entirely and spend as they chose or the wish to contribute to family income and by implication to have more say in household financial decisions.

Our final statements were chosen from a larger number used in the pilot study on the basis of the results of a factor analysis similar to that described in Chapter 6 to identify attitudes to not working. In this case all four statements were designed to measure one dimension, an attitude to financial independence. Table 8.18 shows the proportions of women saying each statement was definitely true for them. The statements are shown in order of their contribution to the overall measure of financial independence; the mean factor scores derived from the answers to the individual statements are shown below. High negative scores indicate a greater desire for financial independence whereas high positive scores indicate a low desire for financial independence.

Clearly, working married women, and in particular those working full time, have a greater desire for financial independence than those who do not work. However, we cannot tell from these cross-sectional data whether such attitudes determine whether or not women work or are a consequence of whether or not they work. What is interesting is that women were more likely to endorse as definitely true statements about liking to contribute to family income or to spend money as they choose, rather than more obvious financial independence statements. Only a minority of women, even amongst full time workers agreed it was definitely true that they did not 'like being dependent on my husband for money'.

Husbands' attitudes to their wives' employment
In 1965 Hunt found, in her survey, that, whilst in general the majority of wives had husbands who had no objection to them working, some wives (10% of those working full time for example) were working despite their husband's apparent disapproval (Hunt, 1968). Fifteen years on we did not feel we could ask this question in quite the same way.[4] However, we did want to get some idea of what wives felt their husbands' attitudes were to them working or not. For we would expect wives and husbands, in varying degrees, to discuss a wife's decision to work or not, particularly once they have started a family. We wanted, however, to go beyond the approval/disapproval dichotomy which presents too crude a view of the dynamics of a couple's decision making process. We know, for example, from in-depth studies that often husbands, whilst approving in general, explicitly or implicitly place constraints on their wives' participation in paid work, not wanting it to conflict with their other domestic duties or impinge on their role as wife and mother. At the same time, many husbands also recognise that wives often need to work both for financial and for social or psychological reasons.

Women were presented with six statements, shown in Table 8.19, which aimed to cover different aspects of husbands' attitudes to their wives' working or not and were asked to say whether each was definitely true, partly true or not true of their husband. As with the statements about financial independence described above, these statements had been chosen, on the basis of a factor analysis, from a larger number of statements used at the pilot stage. All were designed to contribute to an overall measure of a woman's view of her husband's attitude to her working. However, one statement did not correlate well with this and so is placed below the mean factor scores on Table 8.19.

On the whole, as the mean factor scores show, there are predictable differences between the answers of working and non-working women, and between full time and part time working women. Working married women, particularly those working full time, were more likely than non-working women to think their husband was in favour of their working and less inclined to think that he would feel that home should take priority over work. The picture presented by these results is that the husbands of working women were seen as moderately supportive of their wife's working, but the husbands of the non-working women appeared to be rather more against their wife's working.

Table 8.18 Proportions of working and non-working married women rating different statements about financial independence as 'definitely true' and mean factor scores

Statements of attitudes towards financial independence	Working		All working	Not working	All married women
	Full time	Part time			
Earning my own money gives me a feeling of independence/I miss the feeling of independence earning my own money would give me	61%	58%	60%	29%	47%
I don't like being dependent on my husband for money	44%	38%	40%	23%	33%
I like to feel I am/would like to be contributing to the family income	75%	62%	68%	36%	55%
I like to have some money to spend as I choose	74%	71%	72%	63%	69%
Mean factor score	−0.33	−0.23	−0.27	0.41	0.00
Base	*1,089*	*1,346*	*2,435*	*1,625*	*4,079**

*Includes 19 in full time education

Table 8.19 Proportions of working and non-working married women rating different statements about their husbands' attitudes to whether or not they worked as 'definitely true' and mean factor scores

Statements about husbands' attitudes to whether or not their wives worked	Working		All Working	Not Working	All married women
	Full time	Part time			
My husband is pleased that I work/would be pleased if I got a job	52%	36%	43%	14%	32%
My husband would prefer me not to work	14%	17%	16%	40%	25%
My husband feels my main job is to look after the home	10%	22%	17%	46%	28%
My husband thinks I would be unhappy if I didn't work/would be happier if I went out to work	37%	29%	32%	11%	24%
My husband likes me to be at home when he is	46%	49%	48%	65%	55%
Mean factor score	−0.47	−0.19	−0.31	0.48	0.00
Other statement					
My husband is only happy for me to work if it fits in with family life/would only be happy for me to work if it filled in with family life.	38%	57%	49%	54%	51%
Base	1,089	1,346	2,435	1,625	4,079*

Includes 19 in full time education

Table 8.20 Proportions of working and non-working married women with dependent children rating different statements about their husbands' attitudes to whether or not they worked as 'definitely true'

Statements about husbands' attitudes to whether or not their wives worked	Working		All Working	Not Working	All married women with children under 16
	Full time	Part time			
My husband is pleased that I work/would be pleased if I got a job	48%	37%	40%	15%	28%
My husband would prefer me not to work	18%	18%	18%	35%	26%
My husband feels my main job is to look after the home	11%	23%	20%	46%	32%
My husband thinks I would be unhappy if I didn't work/would be happier if I went out to work	36%	28%	30%	10%	21%
My husband likes me to be at home when he is	46%	47%	47%	64%	55%
My husband would only be happy for me to work if it fitted in with family life	48%	60%	56%	60%	58%
Base	371	873	1,244	1,125	2,379

When we look at individual statements however, a greater complexity is apparent. We show only the proportions of wives endorsing each statement as 'definitely true' for them. This is a much firmer level of agreement than 'partially true' which, in a sense, allows for the ambivalence some husbands express. We can see therefore that, amongst wives working full time, 14% felt their husband would prefer them not to work and only a small majority (52%) felt their husbands were pleased they worked. Interestingly, whereas we might expect a minority of all wives to say their husband felt their main job was to look after the home, even among non-working wives less than half (46%) also said this was definitely true for them. Whether this is because husbands and wives were distinguishing between looking after the home and looking after children is impossible to say, however, though it seems likely they were. Whilst a majority of wives (55%) felt their husbands liked them to be at home when they were, slightly fewer endorsed the more restrictive version of this where a husband was only happy for a wife to work if it fitted in with family life. Women working part time were most likely to say this was true of their husbands (57%).

It is likely that a husband's (and indeed a wife's) attitudes to whether or not his wife worked would be affected by whether they had dependent children. We therefore show in Table 8.20 wives' views of their husband's attitudes for those wives who have children under 16. In fact there is not a major difference when the results of Tables 8.20 and 8.19 are compared. Wives

working full time with dependent children were slightly more likely to say their husband would prefer them not to work whilst fewer non-working wives were likely to say their husband preferred them not to work (no doubt, partly a generational effect as we have, *de facto*, excluded older wives in Table 8.20). When we looked in more detail it was clear that, regardless of a woman's family situation, husbands were more likely to endorse her working if she was working and to endorse her being at home if she was not working. Her family situation did affect her husband's views however, in that in general, husbands of wives with dependent children were less likely to be very supportive of their working wives and more likely to endorse home orientated views than husbands of childless wives or wives with children over 16 (see tables in technical report, Martin and Roberts, 1984).

So far we have looked only at wives' reports of their husband's attitudes. However, for the sample of husbands who were interviewed we can find out what the husbands actually thought and compare their views with those reported by their wives. We show this in Table 8.21 which compares the husband's and wife's answers on each of the six statements. For each statement, approximately half of the wives gave identical answers to their husbands and for only a minority of couples (around 10%) was there complete disagreement, with one partner saying 'definitely true' and the other 'not true'. In general, the husbands were more likely than their wives to rate statements as 'definitely

Table 8.21 Comparison of husbands' and wives' reports of the husbands' attitude to whether or not his wife works

Wife says:	Husband says:			All husbands	Base (= 100%)
	Definitely true	Partly true	Not true		
	%	%	%	%	

Statement (i) 'My husband is/would be pleased that I have/if I got a job'

Definitely true	20	10	2	**32**	
Partly true	16	20	7	**43**	
Not true	2	8	15	**25**	
All wives	**38**	**38**	**24**	**100**	781

Statement (ii) 'My husband would prefer me not to work'

Definitely true	13	6	4	**23**	
Partly true	8	11	11	**30**	
Not true	7	12	28	**47**	
All wives	**29**	**29**	**42**	**100**	778

Statement (iii) 'My husband feels my main job is to look after the home'

Definitely true	16	10	1	**27**	
Partly true	12	19	7	**38**	
Not true	6	15	14	**35**	
All wives	**34**	**44**	**23**	**100**	778

Statement (iv) 'My husband thinks I would be unhappy if I didn't work/happier if I went out to work'

Definitely true	16	7	3	**26**	
Partly true	13	11	8	**32**	
Not true	8	14	20	**42**	
All wives	**38**	**32**	**30**	**100**	782

Statement (v) 'My husband likes me to be at home when he is'

Definitely true	43	11	3	**56**	
Partly true	18	12	3	**34**	
Not true	5	4	1	**10**	
All wives	**66**	**27**	**7**	**100**	777

Statement (vi) 'My husband is/would only be happy for me to work if it fits/fitted in with family life'

Definitely true	30	15	5	**50**	
Partly true	19	10	4	**33**	
Not true	8	4	5	**17**	
All wives	**57**	**29**	**14**	**100**	775

true' while the wives were relatively more likely to say statements were 'not true', but this was the case irrespective of whether this statement was worded positively or negatively. Thus there was no evidence of any general tendency for husbands to be more less favourable towards their wives' working than the wives themselves believed them to be.

The evidence presented so far in this chapter about the division of labour between husbands and wives shows that, in 1980, husbands' and wives' primary roles were different. This has important consequences for their employment participation and the rewards they obtain from paid work over their lifetime. In one sense, of course, individual couples will have 'chosen' the arrangements they individually make to share paid and unpaid work, but the choice will be made in terms of the structure of expectations and opportunities afforded to men and women in our society.

Our study confirms that almost all wives are (and therefore almost all women are or expect to be) primary housekeepers and secondary wage workers whilst the opposite is the case for their husbands. This is not necessarily predicated on the marital relationship itself, but on the economic and social roles associated with it. Several implications of this division of labour need to be considered. Firstly, women are unlikely to see themselves or be seen by employers as competing in the labour market on the same or equal terms as men even when atypically they are older and single. In addition, because women's wages are seen by many women and employers as secondary or 'component' wages, they are in general rarely adequate to support fully a single adult, even less a woman with dependants.[5] As a result, for a woman, the economic consequences of not being married can be severe and the economic effects of marital breakdown particularly so, as, increasingly, formerly married women are expected to return to employment and support themselves (and dependants) on a secondary wage which is often further depreciated by their earlier absence from the labour market (Zabalza and Arrufat, 1983). We turn now to look at the position of lone mothers in more detail.

Lone mothers: their domestic circumstances and employment position

During the 1970s there has been a large increase in the numbers of lone parents, the majority of whom are women (Popay *et al*, 1983). The increase in breakdown of marriage and the change in the divorce law in 1972 has resulted in the majority of lone mothers being divorced or separated, although there has also been some increase in the numbers of single mothers. Thus the characteristics of non-married women and lone mothers in particular, has changed over time (Popay *et al*, 1983; Moss, 1980). As we shall show, the characteristics and situations of single mothers differ in many respects from those of widowed, divorced and separated mothers and so, wherever numbers permit, we show results for the two groups separately and contrast the situation of both groups with those of married women with children.

The characteristics of lone mothers

Altogether just under half (47%) of all women interviewed had at least one child under 16. The majority (90%) were married and thus lone mothers constituted

Table 8.22 Marital status of lone mothers

Marital status		% of all women with children under 16	% of lone mothers
Single		2	22
Widowed	} Formerly married	1 } 8	10 } 78
Divorced		5 }	47 }
Separated		2 }	21 }
All lone mothers		**10**	**100**
Base		*2,632*	*253*

10% of women with children under 16 in our sample. Within this group 22% were single and 78% had been married formerly; 10% were widowed, 47% divorced and 21% were separated (Table 8.22). Because we are focussing on mothers of dependent children, we are excluding from this category any lone mothers whose children were all 16 or older.

Table 8.23 shows the household composition of lone mothers compared with married women with children under 16. Almost half the single mothers (48%) lived only with their children, as did 86% of the widowed, divorced and separated mothers. All the lone mothers were more likely than married women with children to be living with their parents or with other adults, and this was particularly the case for single mothers 41% of whom lived with their parents and 11% of whom lived with other adults. Although the age distribution of all lone mothers was not very different from that of married women with children under 16, the single mothers were very much younger than the widowed, divorced and separated mothers: 75% of single mothers were under 30 compared with 25% of widowed, divorced and separated mothers (Table 8.24).

Table 8.23 Household composition of lone mothers and married women with children under 16

Household composition	Single mothers	Widowed, divorced or separated mothers	All non-married mothers	Married or cohabiting mothers
	%	%	%	%
Living with own children (and partner) only*	48	86	78	96
Living with parents (-in law) and children*	41	12	18	3
Living with other adults and children	11	2	4	1
	100	100	100	100
Base	56	197	253	2,379

*Household included other adults in a small number of cases

Table 8.24 Age distribution of lone mothers and married women with children under 16

Age	Single mothers	Widowed, divorced or separated mothers	All non-married mothers	Married or cohabiting mothers
	%	%	%	%
16 – 19	23	0	6	1
20 – 29	52	25	31	25
30 – 39	14	43	36	47
40 – 49	7	27	23	23
50 – 59	4	5	4	4
	100	100	100	100
Base	56	197	253	2,379

Lone parenthood is for many women a temporary state which they leave on marriage or remarriage. This is particularly so for single mothers, many of whom marry within a few years of their first birth. The majority of single mothers were not only young themselves but were likely to have a young child, as Table 8.25 shows. Most single mothers (90%) had only one child, and

Table 8.25 Number of children under 16 and age of youngest child of lone mothers and married women with children under 16

	Single mothers	Widowed, divorced or separated mothers	All non-married mothers	Married or cohabiting mothers
Number of children under 16:	%	%	%	%
1	90	48	57	40
2	5	34	28	42
3	5	13	11	14
4 or more	–	5	4	4
	100	100	100	100
Age of youngest child:				
0 – 2	44	13	20	28
3 – 4	13	13	13	12
5 – 10	30	41	38	33
11 – 15	13	33	29	27
	100	100	100	100
Base	56	197	253	2,379

over half (57%) had a child under 5. In contrast, women who had been married and had become lone parents through marital breakdown or the death of a spouse were likely to be older and to have more than one child. Their children were likely be correspondingly older too. Thus the formerly married mothers had fewer children under 16 than married mothers; many in fact had grown-up children in addition to the children under 16 shown in Table 8.25.

Economic activity rates of lone mothers

We particularly wanted to look at the employment status of lone mothers because there is considerable interest in whether these mothers are able to undertake paid work. We might expect them to be more likely than married women to go out to work because they lack the financial support of a partner. Nevertheless most studies of lone parents have found that lone mothers are less likely to work than their married counterparts (Popay *et al*, 1983; Rimmer and Popay, 1982). We have already shown in Chapter 2 that among women of the same age with a youngest child of the same age, married and non-married women were equally likely to be working. We did not, however, distinguish between the single and formerly married women among the non-married.

Looking first at the overall rates of economic activity, shown in Table 8.26, there is little difference between the lone mothers and the married mothers. However,

Table 8.26 Economic activity of lone mothers and married women with children under 16

Economic activity	Single mothers	Widowed, divorced or separated mothers	All non-married mothers	Married or cohabiting mothers
	%	%	%	%
Working full time	21	26	25	16
Working part time	13	26	24	37
Total working	**34**	**52**	**49**	**53**
'Unemployed'	14	5	7	4
Total economically active	**48**	**57**	**56**	**57**
Economically inactive	48	41	42	43
Full time student	4	2	2	0
	100	100	100	100
Base	56	197	253	2,379

only 48% of the single mothers were economically active compared with 57% of both the formerly married and the married mothers. Moreover, proportionately fewer of the single mothers were actually working – 34% compared with just over half of both the other groups of mothers – the difference being due to the very high rate of unemployment (14%) among single mothers. Many of these were registered unemployed. This difference may reflect the fact that the single mothers were more likely to have been working recently and would therefore be entitled to unemployment benefit.

One very important factor in explaining the lower economic activity rate of single mothers is that they were more likely than other mothers to have a child under 5, and such mothers as we saw in Chapter 2, generally had lower activity rates than those with older children. There were too few single mothers in the survey to show separately the economic activity rates for those whose youngest children were in different age ranges, but we were able to standardise for the differences in age of youngest child between the single and married mothers.

By applying the proportions of married women who were economically active with youngest children in different age ranges to the numbers of single women with youngest children in the same age ranges we calculated the proportion of married women who would be expected to be economically active if the ages of their youngest children had the same distribution as those of the single women. On this basis we estimated that only 47% of the married mothers would be expected to be economically active as opposed to the 57% who actually were. This estimate, that 47% of married mothers could be expected to be economically active if the ages of their youngest children were the same as that of the single mothers, compares with 48% of single mothers who were in fact economically active. Thus there were no differences in economic activity between single and married mothers once differences in the ages of their youngest children are taken into account.

We carried out the same standardisation in order to compare the economic activity rates of the widowed, divorced and separated mothers with that of the married mothers. We estimated that if married mothers had youngest children of the same age as those of the widowed, divorced and separated mothers (whose children tended to be older), 64% would be expected to be economically active compared with the 57% who actually were. But 57% of the widowed, divorced and separated mothers were in fact economically active, a slightly lower rate than married mothers would be expected to have if their youngest children were of the same ages. However, because of the small numbers involved this difference between the two groups was not statistically significant and so we cannot conclude that there was a real difference in economic activity between widowed, divorced and separated mothers and married mothers when differences in the ages of their youngest children were taken into account.

Although there was no difference in overall economic activity between lone mothers and married mothers, it is clear from Table 8.26 and from Chapter 2 that lone mothers who worked were much more likely to be working full time than married mothers, a finding other studies report too (Moss, 1980; Popay et al, 1983). Half the lone mothers worked full time compared with one third of the married mothers. It is not possible to explain why this was so from our data. But, as one recent study has pointed out: *'the system of income support for lone parents is so complex'* that it is unlikely that lone mothers are able *'to make a "rational" choice about whether to claim benefit, work full time or combine receipt of benefit with part time work'* (Popay, et al, 1983).

The financial position of lone mothers
The primacy of financial need was confirmed when we looked at women's reasons for working. All working women were asked their reasons for working at the moment and were then asked which was their main reason. Table 8.27 shows both all the reasons and the main reason lone mothers and married mothers gave for working. (There were too few working lone mothers for single and formerly married mothers to be shown separately.) Overwhelmingly the lone mothers were working from financial necessity: 85% of lone mothers gave working to earn money for essentials as one of their reasons for working compared with 37% of married mothers. Even more striking, when asked to give their main reason for working, 78% were working to earn money for essentials, whereas this reason was given by only 28% of the married mothers. This is not to say that other reasons for working were not valued as well. On average non-married women gave between 2–3 reasons for working and as Table 8.27 shows a large minority (43%) said they enjoyed working whilst a third said they worked 'for the company of other people'. Interestingly 11% said 'working is the normal thing to do'.

Table 8.27   All reasons and main reason for working for non-married and married mothers with children under 16

Reasons for working	All reasons		Main reason	
	Working non-married mothers	Working married mothers	Working non-married mothers	Working married mothers
			%	%
To earn money for basic essentials	85%	37%	78	28
To earn money to buy extras	29%	54%	8	29
To earn money of my own	17%	33%	2	11
For the company of other people	34%	46%	7	8
Enjoy working	43%	49%	4	14
To follow my career	14%	13%	1	4
Working is the normal thing to do	11%	6%	–	2
To help with husband's job or business	–	3%	–	2
Other reasons	–	3%	–	2
			100	100
Base	*123*	*1,244*	*123*	*1,244*

We looked at the total net incomes of lone parents according to their work status (Table 8.28). We have not shown the net incomes of the married mothers because, although they were in most cases much higher than those of the lone parents, since they included the husband's earnings, they provided support for at least two adults and one or more children, whereas those of the lone parents support only one adult and at least one child. Comparisons therefore would not be meaningful. Moreover comparisons among lone parents are affected by the fact that those receiving Supplementary Benefit in 1980 have their housing costs paid directly whereas others would be paying housing costs out of their net income. Nevertheless, it is clear that lone parents who worked full time had significantly higher incomes that those who worked part time, and both groups had higher incomes than the non-working lone parents 60% of whom had a net income of £40 or less at the time of the survey with which to support a woman and at least one child even if housing costs had been met.[6]

Table 8.28 Weekly net income of lone mothers by work status

| Weekly net income | Working | | All working | Not working | All lone mothers |
	Full time	Part time			
	%	%	%	%	%
£20 or less	–	2	1	7	4
£21 – £40	2	20	11	53	31
£41 – £60	33	47	40	30	34
£61 – £80	36	22	29	8	19
£81 – £100	20	2	11	–	6
£101 or more	6	7	6	–	4
Income not known	3	–	2	2	2
	100	**100**	**100**	**100**	**100**
Base	64	59	123	124	253*

Includes 6 women in full time education

The income of lone mothers came from a number of sources, partly depending of course, on their work status. First we show in Table 8.29 the main sources of income for single and formerly married mothers. For most lone mothers the main source of income was either earnings or Supplementary Benefit. Single mothers were more likely than formerly married mothers to be receiving Supplementary Benefit because they were less likely to be working, as we have seen. Almost all mothers received Child Benefit. It is not clear why a few said they did not, as presumably all these mothers would be entitled to it. It might be expected that more of the formerly married than of the single mothers would be receiving maintenance payments from the children's father, but even so, only 42% of the formerly married received such payments despite the fact that most of this group were divorced or separated rather than widowed.

Some sources of income, such as Child Benefit, are paid regardless of a mother's working status, but the income maintenance benefits, namely Supplementary Benefit and FIS, are dependent on working status and earnings. A lone mother earning below a certain amount, which depends on the number of children she is supporting, would be eligible for FIS. We found that

Table 8.29 Main sources of income of lone mothers

Source of income	Single mothers	Widowed/divorced/ separated mothers	All lone mothers
	%	%	%
Earnings	34	53	49
Supplementary benefit	66	44	49
Family income supplement	4	10	8
Unemployment benefit	9	1	3
Widows pension	–	8	6
Child benefit	95	98	97
Maintenance from children's father	29	42	39
Student grant	4	2	2
Base	56	197	253

Percentages do not add to 100 as most mothers had more than one source of income

20% of lone mothers in full time work and 10% of those in part time work were receiving FIS. A further 36% of lone parents in part time work were receiving Supplementary Benefit, as were 80% of the non-working lone parents. Among the formerly married mothers 51% of those in work were receiving maintenance payments from the children's father compared with 31% of those not in work.

Whilst, as we have said, it is difficult to compare the actual financial situations of the different groups of lone mothers with that of the married mothers, we can compare their subjective views of their financial situations. Table 8.30 shows how the financial stress scores, derived from three questions about women's current financial situation described previously, vary between the different groups of mothers. Almost half the single mothers (48%) and 41% of the formerly married mothers came into the high financial stress category compared with only 11% of the married mothers. By contrast over half the married mothers were in the low financial stress category compared with only 18% of the lone mothers, thereby emphasising the large disparity between the two groups. Lone parents were much more likely to feel under financial strain than their married equivalents.

Table 8.30 Financial stress scores of lone mothers and married women with children under 16

Financial stress scores*	Single mothers	Widowed/divorced/ separated mothers	All lone mothers	Married mothers
	%	%	%	%
Low stress (score 3 – 5)	20	18	18	55
Medium stress (score 6 – 7)	32	41	39	34
High stress (score 8 – 10)	48	41	43	11
	100	**100**	**100**	**100**
Base	56	197	253	2,379

The scores were based on answers to the three questions shown in Tables 8.12 – 8.14

We have focussed on the financial circumstances of lone parents in this chapter because we wanted to illustrate the particular problems lone parents face in combining paid employment with their domestic commitments and the economic consequences of their not being able to do this satisfactorily. Lone mothers are just as likely to work as married mothers with similar aged children but are more likely to work full rather than part time, to work from financial necessity for 'essentials', and to have higher levels of financial stress. A minority, only 39%, get any financial support from their children's father.

Women's responsibility for and care of the elderly, sick or disabled

Women's domestic work sometimes extends beyond the everyday activities involved in running a home and the normal care of children to include the extra responsibilities involved in caring for elderly, sick or disabled relatives or friends. The extent of the caring involved may range from occasional visits to a neighbour to provide social contact or to help with shopping, to the constant care required by a severely disabled member of the family. Such care may of course be provided by men or women, but other studies have shown that the majority of carers are women (Rossiter and Wicks, 1982). This survey looked at the extent of caring responsibilities among women of working age and the employment position of the women who had this domestic responsibility.

Incidence of caring responsibility

All women in the survey, with the exception of those who themselves were permanently unable to work because of sickness or disability, were asked whether, in addition to looking after the family in the normal way, there was anyone such as a sick or elderly friend or member of the family who depended on them to provide some regular service. Altogether 13% of all the women in the sample said that there was someone who depended on them for some form of care. This figure is slightly higher than the 11% found by Hunt in her 1965 survey (Hunt, 1968). However, the wording of the questions differed somewhat from Hunt's survey. Hunt asked 'Are there any elderly people or invalids that you have to look after to any extent, living here or elsewhere?' Not only might this form of words focus attention on older people but care provided for a friend or neighbour might be excluded if a woman feels she has chosen to help rather than *has* to help someone. Nevertheless, the proportion of elderly people in the population has risen since 1965 and, since most of the care is provided for the elderly, this may have contributed to an increase in the proportion of women of working age who have this caring responsibility.

From Table 8.31 we can see that most women cared for members of their near family. Women most frequently reported they were caring for a parent or parent-in-law (68%), whilst 3% cared for their husband, 6% for their own child and 15% for other relatives. Only 8% of women were caring for non-relatives. The fact that most of these women were caring for parents or parents-in-law, the majority of whom would be fairly elderly, is reflected in the proportion of women in different age groups who provided this sort of care (Table 8.32). The proportion of such women increased with age and was highest among women aged 40 and over.

Table 8.31 Relationship of the person cared for to the woman providing this care

Relationship	% of women with a dependant
	%
Husband	3
Child	6
Parent (in-law)	68
Other relative	15
Friend/neighbour	7
Other person	1
	100
Base	*736*

Table 8.32 Proportion of women who provide care for sick or elderly dependants by age

Age	% who care for dependants	*Base*
16 – 19	3%	*576*
20 – 29	5%	*1,297*
30 – 39	12%	*1,414*
40 – 49	21%	*1,142*
50 – 59	21%	*1,159*
All women	**13%**	*5,588*

In fact two thirds of women who cared for a sick or elderly dependant were aged 40 or over.

Considerable interest has focussed on the problems of single women caring for dependants; indeed it has sometimes been assumed that single women are particularly likely to be caring for elderly dependants (Nissel and Bonnerjea, 1982). Possibly the problems such women face are greater than those faced by married women in the same situation especially in the longer term, but in numerical terms it is married women who are most likely to be caring for dependants. Our results show that 84% of the women providing care for someone were married, and 15% of all married women were caring for someone compared with 8% of non-married women. This is not surprising if one remembers that most of the non-married women in the survey were in their teens or early twenties and so their parents would still be quite young. In fact, when we compare the proportions of married and non-married women caring for someone separately for different age groups (Table 8.33), we find that there is very little difference between single, previously and currently married women, although among women in their forties and fifties, the previously married were less likely to be caring for a dependant than single or currently married women.

Table 8.33 Proportions of women who provide care for sick or elderly dependants by age and marital status

Age	Women who care for dependants					
	Single women		Widowed/divorced or separated women		Married women	
	%	*Base*	%	*Base*	%	*Base*
Under 30	3%	*864*	8%	*63*	5%	*946*
30 – 39	12%	*67*	8%	*106*	12%	*1,241*
40 – 49	24%	*51*	17%	*120*	21%	*971*
50 – 59	22%	*54*	14%	*184*	23%	*921*
All women	**6%**	*1,036*	**12%**	*473*	**15%**	*4,079*

Employment and caring

The nature of the relationship between women's employment and providing care for sick or elderly dependants is not easy to establish. Some women's opportunity to have a job at all or the number of hours they can work will be restricted by the need to look after someone. Alternatively, women who are not working may be in a position to take on such responsibilities initially, because they are at home anyway. With this in mind we look at how the proportion of women providing care for someone varies according to their work status, and in Table 8.34 compare our results with those from Hunt's study in 1965. There was little difference in the proportion of women providing care for a dependant between working and non-working women (13% and 15% respectively) but women working part time were more likely to provide this sort of care than those working full time (16% compared with 11%). In all groups the results from this survey are slightly higher than those from the 1965 survey, the largest difference being among women working full time of whom 7% in 1965 were caring for a dependant, compared with 11% in 1980.

Table 8.34 Proportions of women providing care for sick or elderly dependants by work status (1980 compared with Hunt 1965)

Work status	% providing care 1980	% providing care 1965 (Hunt)*
Working full time	11%	7%
Working part time	16%	15%
All working women	13%	10%
Not working	15%	13%
Full time student	3%	..
All women	13%	11%
Base	5,588	7,391

*Excludes women in full time education

Regardless of whether they worked or not, all women who were caring for a dependant were asked about the effect of this responsibility on their work or their opportunity to work. Working women were asked whether the work they did or the hours they worked were affected by having to look after someone and non-working women were asked whether this had affected whether or not they worked. Table 8.35 shows, rather surprisingly perhaps, that of all the women providing care for someone only 19% thought this affected their employment; thus 3% of all the women in the total sample said their employment was affected by their undertaking this additional domestic responsibility. However, non-working women were much more likely than working women to say that their employment had been affected; 29% of non-working and 12% of working women who were caring for dependants said their employment was affected, which represents 4% and 2% of these two groups in the sample as a whole.

All women who said their employment was affected were asked about the way in which it was affected and Table 8.36 shows the answers of working and non-working women. The majority of non-working women (79%) said that caring for someone prevented them

Table 8.35 Proportions of women in different work status categories who feel that their work opportunities have been affected by their having to care for a sick or elderly dependant

Current work status	Women with a dependant		All women	
	% whose work was affected	Base	% whose work was affected	Base
Working full time	11%	201	1%	1,877
Working part time	14%	230	2%	1,477
All working women	12%	431	2%	3,354
Not working	29%	297	4%	1,941
Full time student	–	8	–	293
All women	19%	736	3%	5,588

Table 8.36 Ways in which working and non-working women felt that their employment was affected by caring for a sick or elderly dependant: women whose work was affected

Ways in which women felt their work opportunities were affected	Working women whose employment was affected	Non-working women whose employment was affected	All whose employment was affected
	%	%	%
Prevented from going out to work	9	79	51
Number of hours or times of work restricted	51	15	29
Has to take time off to look after dependant	25	1	10
Affected in other ways	21	5	11
Base	53	85	140*

Percentages do not add up to 100 because some women mentioned more than 1 effect
*Includes 2 full time students

going out to work. This answer was also given by 9% of working women some of whom were working at home while the others appeared to be referring to periods of time in the past. The most frequent answer given by 51% of working women was that the number of hours they could work or the times at which they could work was affected. When this was mentioned by non-working women they were usually referring to reasons why they had to stop work or would find it difficult to get a job. One quarter of the working women mentioned having to take time off work in connection with caring for dependants. These reasons, given in answer to an open question, are very similar to those found in other studies such as Nissel's and Bonnerjea's recent in-depth study (ibid). This focussed on the effect on a family of caring for a handicapped elderly person and shows clearly the enormous effect giving this kind of constant care has on the family in general and the wife, who is almost always the chief carer, in particular.

We asked a number of questions about the amount of contact women had with the person being cared for and the sort of care provided, to give some indication of the extent of the work this involved and the burden on the person providing the care. Table 8.37 shows that 24% of the women lived with the person for whom they were caring and a further 24% saw that person every day. Only 6% saw the dependent person less than once a week. Confirmation that provision of this sort of care is fairly demanding is indicated by the amount of time

113

Table 8.37 Frequency with which women with sick or elderly dependants had contact with the person they cared for

Frequency of contact	Women with a dependant
	%
Dependant lives with informant	**24**
Dependant lives elsewhere and is seen:	
Every day	24
Several times a week	22
Once or twice a week	22
Less than once a week	6
Varies	2
Total with a dependant living elsewhere	**76**
	100
Base	736

women said they spent caring for someone. Over one quarter (26%) said they gave constant attention and a further 13% said they spent at least 15 hours a week. Only 21% said they spent less than 5 hours a week caring for a dependant.

Assessment of the impact of this caring on women's employment is difficult for several reasons. Firstly, as we have shown, the direction of the causal relationship is impossible to establish without more longitudinal information. Secondly, whilst it is true that overall only a relatively small proportion of all women of working age have these extra responsibilities, more older women have them. One in five women between the ages 40–59 was undertaking this extra caring work. Similarly whilst the vast majority of women who cared in this way said it did not affect their employment, for some the amount of care they undertook was quite considerable and for a sizeable minority affected whether they could undertake paid work at all or the kind of work they could do.

Summary and conclusions

In this chapter we have focussed on the unpaid work which has to be done in our society if homes are to be run, children cared for, and families generally maintained. There are several issues here concerning firstly, the diversity of family or household types, secondly the amount of domestic/caring work to be done, which varies with family composition and circumstances, and thirdly the division of responsibility between paid and unpaid work between family members, chiefly husbands and wives. Whilst much of this information is interesting in itself, the real thrust of interest is the extent to which domestic responsibilities and work impinge on women's employment and how breadwinning is shared between husbands and wives. In this sense this chapter complements the data in Chapter 2 on the relationship between demographic characteristics and economic activity by detailing more of the nature of domestic activity, particularly of couples.

Almost all women of working age in our sample lived in a family; only 4% lived alone and 2% lived with unrelated adults. Though the range of family types in our survey was fairly wide, 51% of all women and 71% of all married women at the time of interview were living

in a traditional nuclear family comprising a wife, husband and their children. More of the women in our sample will experience this during their lifetime as they marry and have children whilst some, now lone parents, as married women have lived in a nuclear family. It is important to stress this because current discussion of the changing nature of family structure and the consequent diversity of family types can lead to an understating of the extent to which the 'normal' family pattern is experienced over their lifetime by the vast majority of women and men (Barrett and McIntosh, 1982).

We have argued in this chapter that an important part of the explanation of men and women's different labour market positions lies in their differing balance of home and paid work. The vast majority of husbands were primary wage earners, working full time and earning more than their wives in most cases. Only 15% of wives had the same or higher hourly earnings than their husbands and the discrepancy was even larger when gross earnings were compared. By contrast women undertook most of the domestic work in the family. This, sometimes coupled with the demands of their husbands' jobs affected their employment in several ways, almost always to reduce it. Only a minority of wives, 27%, worked full time, whilst 33% worked part time and 35% were economically inactive. In all only 15% of wives worked the same or longer hours than their husband.

Our survey confirmed what many small scale studies have shown: namely that husbands are more likely to help with childcare than housework and to do more of the latter if their wife works. Even so 54% of wives working full time said they did all or most of the housework whilst 77% of wives working part time said this. Some caveats need to be entered here, however, based on findings from pilot work. Firstly it is clear that wives often understated their contribution by ignoring the work they did when their husband was out of the home at work. Secondly, particularly when thinking about childcare, they often included less onerous activities too, which husbands did disproportionately. More husbands and wives reported they shared childcare but in practice the wife often did most of the routine physical care whilst husbands played with children or took them out. In general, however, the majority of wives and husbands, about 80%, said they were satisfied with the way they shared housework and childcare between them, though husbands were slightly more likely than wives to say they themselves did not do enough. A survey is a blunt instrument by which to explore people's satisfactions with and expectations about situations however and so these results should be interpreted with care.

To show that for the majority of wives market or paid work was secondary to domestic work is not necessarily to imply that it was unimportant to them. Our findings show very clearly that paid work was important for a sizeable proportion of wives both in financial and social terms. Non-working wives were more likely to have higher financial stress scores than working wives, especially if they had dependent children: 26% of wives working full time had medium to high financial stress scores compared with 47% of non-working wives. Amongst working wives the importance of their earnings can be gauged by whether they felt they could get by or not on their husband's earnings. Whilst only a small minority (14%) felt they would not be able to manage at all without their earnings, 60% anticipated they would have to give up a lot. This reaction was not always straightforwardly related to the proportion of total income the wife's earnings provided. Some families where wives contributed less than 20% of the total income, relied on this to the extent that a majority of these wives reported they would not get by alright without their earnings. It is clearly fallacious therefore to assume that because a wife is working part time and contributing less than a quarter of the total income of the couple this is necessarily 'pin money'. Money is also a source of financial independence which wives working full time were particularly likely to value, though, whether they were working because they valued their independence or valued it because they had it we cannot tell from our analysis.

Despite evidence from the wives in our sample which suggests that on the whole they were making a useful contribution to the family income, husbands could not be described as enthusiastic supporters of their wives working. Just 14% of wives working full time said their husbands would prefer them not to work, but only a minority, 43% of working wives, agreed it was definitely true that their husbands were pleased that they worked. Husbands of working wives, however, rarely felt wives should not work or that their wives' main job was to look after the home. The overriding impression our findings give is that husbands of working wives in varying degrees tolerated their wives' working though in many cases they did not want it to interfere or conflict with their own work or domestic life. Women's part time working may in part be seen as an accommodation to this view of the desirable balance between paid and unpaid work.

Women without a partner or with extra caring responsibilities may find it harder to balance employment and domestic work however. Lone parents usually lack both the financial support of an ex-spouse as well as the childcare support we have seen husbands often give working mothers. Consequently, they are doubly disadvantaged and had both a higher financial need to work and higher financial stress scores than married mothers. They were however just as likely to be in paid work as married mothers with similar aged children but, if working, were more likely to work full time. Lone parenthood is probably more of a problem in terms of a woman's employment than caring for a sick or elderly dependant, for whilst slightly more women were likely to have this responsibility, only a small minority of women who undertook this extra work said it had affected their employment in any way. For some

of these women, however, the restrictions will be severe especially if they are caring for handicapped dependants. Moreover it is a problem particularly associated with older women.

This chapter has documented the impact of domestic demands on women's employment. However, whilst we can point to the incidence of domestic work and the corresponding levels of employment women with these domestic commitments, we cannot always say what the direction of causality is. In some instances, as with childcare, it is fairly clear that wives and husbands have a limited range of choices and that the arrival of children intensifies the domestic division of labour as most wives stay at home at least for a time to bring them up. However, not all couples make this trade-off. A very few remain childless, as we discuss in more detail in the next chapter, whilst for others the division of labour is more or less marked depending on the time wives take off work and whether they return to full or part time work. More research, however, remains to be done on why women in apparently comparable domestic situations make different employment decisions. The direction of causality, as we have shown, is also a problem with both lone parents and the impact of caring for elderly relatives. What cannot be denied, however, is that the vast proportion of domestic and caring work which has to be done in our society is done by women, is unpaid, and affects women's ability or willingness to compete as workers on equal terms with men. In the next two chapters we look in more detail at the lifetime effect of domestic work on women's labour market behaviour.

Notes

[1] This is a different use of the term than that employed by Hunt, P (1980), where 'houseworker' referred to a spouse working full time in the home (p5).

[2] A national study which looks at household labour supply behaviour and the effects of taxation may provide some further evidence about this (Brown et al, 1982).

[3] This can arise because not only do husbands and wives often have differential access to money as a resource, they also often have different roles in the household's money management. Wives solely responsible for all housekeeping may worry more about money (and be poorer) than their husbands; for example see Pahl (1980) and Oakley (1974). Thus, to a certain extent, the proportion of husbands and wives giving the same answer to a question will depend partly on the number of different answers from which they can choose, as well as the nature of the question itself and the extent to which a husband or wife's perception may differ, reflecting either a difference in their reaction or a different reality.

[4] Hunt asked one open question 'What is your husband's attitude to your working outside the home?' followed by 'Would you say on the whole he strongly approves . . . . strongly disapproves' (on a five point scale). Questions E4 and E5 (Hunt, 1968).

[5] The phrase 'component wage' comes from Dr A Stewart, Department of Applied Economics, University of Cambridge. Research on women's pay by other researchers at DAE illustrates the issue of secondary wages particularly well (Craig, Garnsey, and Rubery, 1984).

[6] Moss (1980) quotes GHS data which show 'that 87% of lone-parent families had an income below 140% of their SB entitlement where the parent was not working, compared with 37% where she/he had a job'.

Chapter 9 Lifetime patterns of movement in and out of employment

Introduction

As we explained in Chapter 1 the most important in-novation of this study was the collection of complete retrospective work histories from all the women in the survey who had completed their full time education. It is, of course, not unusual for social scientists studying people's work behaviour to collect details of the jobs individuals have had, the reasons they leave them, the ways they find them and the ways they evaluate their various jobs. Generally, however, such studies are small scale, fieldwork is undertaken by the researchers themselves or a small team and there is the opportunity for direct interaction between the informant and the researcher, making data collection a particularly rich if perhaps less systematic process.

Prior to this study there had been few large scale stu-dies in Britain which set out to collect and analyse work history data systematically. The largest of these, the National Training Survey conducted in 1975, covered the training and outline work history of a nationally representative sample of over 54,000 men and women (Research Services, 1976; Claydon, 1980). Other stu-dies either focussed on particular groups or were less comprehensive in their coverage of previous employ-ment (Marsh and Heady, 1981; Cousins, Curran and Brown, 1983). In the USA more work had been carried out, chiefly the various panel studies of the American National Longitudinal Study (NLS) (Jusenius and Shortlidge, 1975; Parnes, 1975; Shaw, 1983). However in 1979, when we planned our study, although there had been a resurgence of interest in life history analysis more generally (Balan *et al*, 1973; Bertaux, 1981; Gold-thorpe, 1980; Plummer, 1983) little had been published and was known in Britain about existing data sets and techniques of analysis.

This study differed from previous studies not only in its scale but also in its scope. We set out to collect full work histories covering all periods of employment and non-employment up to the time of the interview and, for each period of employment, the details of jobs held. The study aimed to provide both an employment and an occupational history. This meant we were relying on women's powers of recall and memory of events occur-ing over 40 years previously in the case of our oldest respondents. Full details of the methodology used to collect the work histories are given in the technical re-port (Martin and Roberts, 1984), but a brief account is essential here before we discuss the main analysis.[1]

Women's work histories may well be supposed to be influenced by their domestic lives and their marital and fertility histories. However we did not want to prejudge the types of events which would interact with and shape women's employment so we collected these two histor-ies separately. The marital and family history was taken first. Women were asked to give dates of all marriages, ends of marriages,[2] births of children, adoptions or ac-quisition of stepchildren and deaths of children. The women in the sample were also asked to give their date of birth and the date they left full time education. From this information we could deduce at any given date the age of the woman, whether she was married or not, how many children she had and what their ages were.

The work history was collected in chronological order from the time the woman left continuous full time education. Two steps were involved in the collection of the data. Women were initially asked to give an outline structure of their work history in terms of the periods of time when they worked full time, worked part time, were not in paid employment or were in full time education. A period was defined as one month or lon-ger. This was a much shorter duration than the work history periods (of one year or longer) counted in the National Training Survey. The starting dates of all periods were recorded, as was the total length of each period and apparent discrepancies were reconciled in the interview. Once the outline work history had been obtained the interviewer asked further detailed ques-tions. For each period of full or part time work women were asked the occupation, industry and duration of each job they had had within the period and why they left each job. For each period when they were not working women were asked their main reason for not working over the whole period, whether they were reg-istered unemployed at any time during the period and, for those women who had started work again after a period of not working, their reasons for starting work again and the age of their youngest child at the time they started. In addition women who had changed be-tween full and part time work were asked their reasons for doing this.

When women were asked to give their reasons for leav-ing jobs, returning to work or not working during a period they were presented with cards showing a range of reasons that had been generated from pilot work. They were initially asked to select all the reasons on the card that applied to them. Then they were asked to choose their main reason from among those they had selected. We cannot, of course, know to what extent these were the reasons women had at the time or reasons that they have developed retrospectively. Col-lecting attitudinal data retrospectively is much more problematic than collecting factual information and is one of the reasons why we have done little analysis of women's reasons for their actions in these two chapters, though Dex has looked at this (Dex, 1984a).

Leaving aside the validity of retrospective attitudinal data, the validity of factual information is easier to establish. Firstly the data can be checked for internal consistency; we cannot know whether the detail of women's jobs is accurate, (though we did not find any very incongruous occupational histories), but the outline information makes a coherent account in virtually all cases. Moreover, we know from our interviewers that this was achieved more easily than they expected. Secondly, as we point out below and describe in the technical report, our data agree with general employment trends over the period, which Dex's work in matching our data to macro-economic data confirms (Dex, 1984a and 1984b). There is a final issue, however, namely whether the act of collecting domestic events prior to work events and in some cases using them as prompts for details of the work history influenced women's recall by over-emphasising marriage or pregnancy as a cause of an employment action. We cannot know the answer to this though to a degree it might have had this effect. However, Dex has looked at the effect of non-domestic factors on women's work histories and identified disruptions to women's employment which were not domestic (*ibid*).

This and the following chapter set out some of the main analyses of the life history data. This chapter concentrates on women's movements into and out of employment and between full and part time work during the course of their lives, and shows how labour market participation is related to childbearing.

Changes over time in the proportion of women working

A number of sources of data are available to show how women's economic activity has changed over time, both overall and for different age groups. Census data provides the longest time series, but is only available at ten yearly intervals (apart from the mid-term Census in 1966). The Family Expenditure and General Household Surveys provide annual figures from 1956 and 1970 respectively, while the Labour Force Survey, based on much larger samples, provides biennial figures from 1971. National Insurance card counts were also a source of regular employment data until 1974 but have now ceased (Joshi, Layard and Owen, 1981). The results from this survey can be analysed to show what proportion of women were working at different dates in

Table 9.1   Proportions of women* working full and part time at different dates by age

Age at date	Work status	Date (end December)								
		1939	1944	1949	1954	1959	1964	1969	1974	1979
		%	%	%	%	%	%	%	%	%
15–19	Full time	89	88	89	93	90	89	86	84†	75†
	Part time	1	1	1	–	1	1	2	1†	3†
	All working women	90	89	90	93	91	90	88	85†	78†
20–24	Full time		70	60	62	61	56	60	57	57
	Part time		1	3	3	5	4	6	11	6
	All working women		71	63	65	66	60	66	68	63
25–29	Full time			35	31	33	30	29	30	32
	Part time			5	8	6	11	12	20	17
	All working women			40	39	39	41	41	50	49
30–34	Full time				24	27	23	25	23	22
	Part time				13	13	16	21	27	34
	All working women				37	40	39	46	50	56
35–39	Full time					27	30	28	29	30
	Part time					19	21	23	36	39
	All working women					46	51	51	65	69
40–44	Full time						29	33	34	32
	Part time						26	29	36	41
	All working women						55	62	70	73
45–49	Full time							34	37	36
	Part time							29	33	37
	All working women							63	70	73
50–54	Full time								34	31
	Part time								32	34
	All working women								66	65
55–59	Full time									26
	Part time									29
	All working women									55

	Size of cohort on which percentages are based‡								
Period of birth	1920–24	1925–29	1930–34	1935–39	1940–44	1945–49	1950–54	1955–59	1960–64
	534	566	543	583	647	749	703	560	372

*Excluding full time students
†Age 16–19
‡Since full time students are excluded, cohort sizes are smaller for the younger age groups

Figure 9.1 Proportion of women of different ages working at five year intervals from 1954

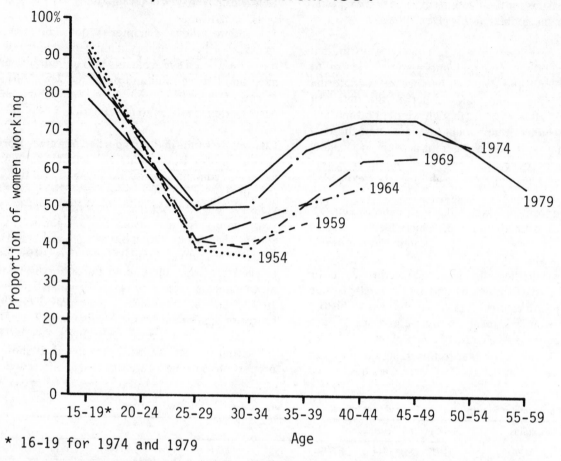

* 16-19 for 1974 and 1979

Figure 9.2 Proportion of women working at given dates by age at date (up to 44)

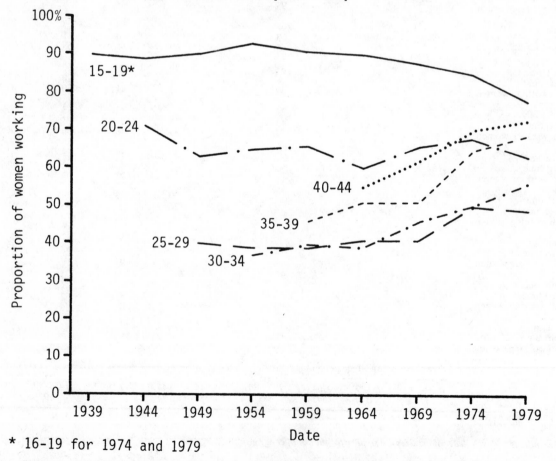

* 16-19 for 1974 and 1979

118

the past and can be compared with figures from time series data collected contemporaneously. The general trends agree very well with contemporary data sources and validates out restrospectively collected information.

Table 9.1 shows the proportion of women working at different dates who were in different age groups at the specified date and illustrates three different kinds of trend that can be examined using retrospective work histories: age, period and generational trends. The effect of *age* on women's labour force participation is seen by looking down the columns. By comparing successive columns we can see how the age profiles change over time. This trend is illustrated in Figure 9.1. A high proportion of women in the 15–19 age group were working at all dates shown, although the rather lower figures for 1979, partly due to rising unemployment in the 16–19 age group, are apparent. The proportion of women working falls as women enter the peak child-bearing age and rises again as they reach their thirties and increasing proportions return to work. However, the bottom of the trough is not as low in 1974 and 1979 as it was in earlier years, and for women in their thirties differences in different years are even more apparent, showing the rise in employment in this age group over

time. Looking at the figures in Table 9.1 split by full and part time working it is apparent that this rise is largely due to the increase in the proportion of women working part time.

Secondly, we can examine *period* effects using these data. By looking along the rows of Table 9.1 we can see for each age group in turn how the proportion of women working changes between particular dates. (Figure 9.2 illustrates the trends for the first six age groups.) The proportion of 15–19 year olds working stays fairly steady until the late 1960s and the steep drop between 1974 and 1979 due to both young people staying on longer in educaton and also rising unemployment among 16–19 year olds can be seen clearly. A smaller drop over this period is apparent among women in the 20–24 year old group. Among women aged 25–29 a sharp rise between 1969 and 1974 is apparent, followed by a levelling off, whereas among women aged 30–34 the rise starts earlier and continues. Similar rises in the recent years are seen amongst women in their late thirties and early forties, and between 1969 and 1974 for the 45–49 age group (not shown on figure). Again, examination of the table shows the importance of the rise in part time working in explaining the results.

Figure 9.3 Proportion of women working at different ages by birth cohort

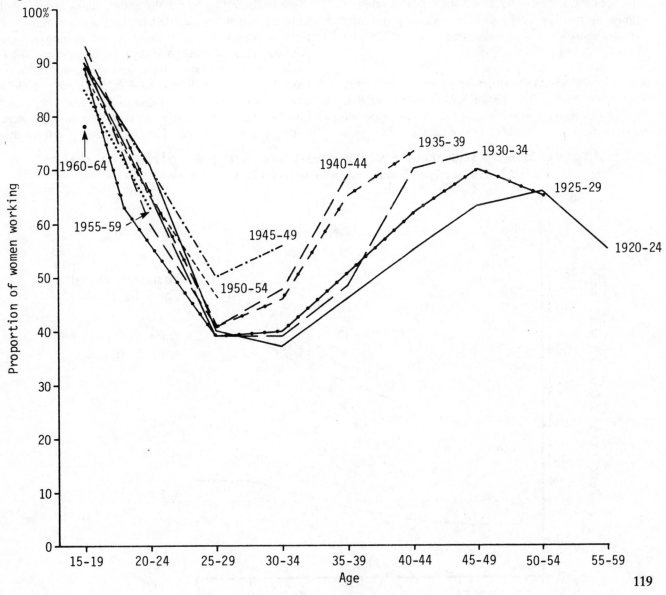

Table 9.2 Proportions of women with dependent children working full and part time at different dates by age of youngest child

Age of youngest child	Work status	Date (end December)						
		1949	1954	1959	1964	1969	1974	1979
		%	%	%	%	%	%	%
0–4	Full time	9	6	8	8	8	6	7
	Part time	5	8	7	10	14	20	19
	All working women	14	14	15	18	22	26	26
	Base	*449*	*710*	*909*	*1,157*	*1,227*	*1,151*	*1,047*
5–10	Full time		21	20	21	23	22	18
	Part time		19	24	30	33	43	45
	All working women		40	44	51	56	65	63
	Base		*215*	*403*	*533*	*707*	*909*	*896*
11–15	Full time			36	33	31	31	31
	Part time			30	32	29	42	47
	All working women			66	65	60	73	78
	Base			*116*	*263*	*389*	*514*	*698*

Figures for the earliest dates in each row will be biased because women in these groups are younger than average for women with a youngest child of the given age at the date in question.

Thirdly, *generational or cohort* effects can be seen by looking along the diagonals of Table 9.1. This shows, for women born in the same five year period (a birth cohort), how the proportion working changes as they reach particular ages. Figure 9.3 illustrates the trends in the proportion of women working at different ages for successive birth cohorts, enabling us to see generational trends. From their late twenties onwards each successive cohort has a higher proportion of women working than the previous one. If these trends continue we would expect, for example, that a higher proportion of women born in 1940–44 will be working by the time they are aged 40–44 than women born in 1935–39 who were that age in 1979.

Although the results shown above by age are available from other sources, information is not always available about other relevant variables, so limiting the types of analyses that are possible. For example, the main

trends by age are normally explained by the relationship between women's age and childbearing patterns, but relevant information about the presence of children and more particularly their ages is not always available. While the general pattern of an earlier return to work is well known, from this survey it has been possible to undertake analysis by the age of a woman's youngest child at particular dates in the past rather than her own age. The results are shown in Table 9.2. Some caution must, however, be expressed in interpreting them because figures for the earlier dates are derived only from women included in the survey rather than from a representative sample of all women with a youngest child of that age at the date in question. Some women now aged 60 or more, and therefore excluded from the survey, will also have had a youngest child aged under 5 in 1949. Our figures for the earlier dates are therefore based on groups of women who were younger than average. However, this problem dis-

Figure 9.4 Proportion of women working at different dates by age of youngest child

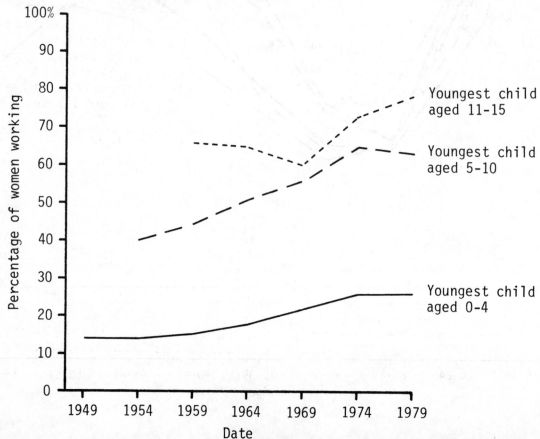

appears as we move forward in time and cover more representative groups of women.

Figure 9.4 illustrates the main trends that can be seen from Table 9.2. Among women with a youngest child under 5 the proportion working rose from 15% in 1959 to 26% in 1974, after which there was no further rise. A steeper rise can be seen among women with a youngest child aged 5–10, from 40% in 1954 reaching 65% in 1974. Among those with a youngest child aged 11–15 the proportion stayed between 60% and 66% until the 1970s, when it rose to 78% in 1979. Looking at the figures in Table 9.2 for full and part time working it is apparent that the rise over time in the proportion of women working is attributable to the rise in part time working. The proportion of women working full time has changed very little over the years in question.

Women's work over a lifetime

The previous section showed the proportions of women working at particular times in the past and enabled us to examine changes over time in aggregate. But we cannot infer from such data the lifetime patterns of work for individual women. While it might be tempting to look at the cross-sectional results for women at different stages in their life cycle and conclude that most women start by working full time, stop work for a time when their children are very young, and return first to part time and then to full time work, this is to simplify reality. For, in fact, the employment patterns of individual women which go to make up the cross-sectional picture are considerably more complex than this simple interpretation suggests. If we know from the cross-sectional results that higher proportions of women work full time rather than part time as the age of their youngest child increases we cannot necessarily infer that individual women are changing from part time to full time work. Some may behave in this way, but others may be returning to work directly in a full time capacity. As we shall show, the aggregate results are the net sum of a large variety of different patterns of work. In so far as opposite individual effects cancel each other out the variety of patterns are not apparent from the aggregate results.

In order to understand what lies behind the aggregate picture we need to take account of how individual women's work histories change over time. We start in this section by summarising employment patterns over women's complete working lives until the time of the survey and then in succeeding sections we look at the patterns by particular stages of their lives. This approach is necessarily limited by the fact that we do not have complete work histories for all women; by definition we only know what had happened up until the time they were interviewed. So for the youngest women we know only about a small fraction of their potential working lives. For the purposes of analysis we have taken a woman's possible working life as being the time between leaving full time education and the interview, and have considered this separately for women of different ages. Using information from their work histories we know how long women have spent working, both full time and part time, and not working. We divide periods of not working according to whether the main reason women gave for not working was domestic (for example, looking after children, keeping house) or non-domestic (for example, looking for work, own illness).

Table 9.3 shows the average number of years spent on these activities between leaving full time education for women born in successive 5 year periods. While we would expect the average number of years spent working, both full and part time, and not working for domestic reasons, to decrease for successive birth cohorts as the time available decreases, the time spent not working for non-domestic reasons however does not vary much for women born since 1940. This means that the proportion of their time spent on this activity is rising for successive cohorts, chiefly as more young women experience unemployment.

The general picture can be seen more clearly if the results are expressed as the percentage of the time between leaving full time education and the interview spent on the different activities (Table 9.4). It is apparent that the proportion of time spent working varies remarkably little among the first five cohorts of women, most of whom are past the main childbearing or child rearing stage. Women born before 1946, that is, those

Table 9.3   Average number of years that women have spent working and not working since leaving full time education by period of birth and age

Activity between leaving full time education and interview	Period of birth (and age)									All women who have finished full time education
	1921–25 (55–59)	1926–30 (50–54)	1931–35 (45–49)	1936–40 (40–44)	1941–45 (35–39)	1946–50 (30–34)	1951–55 (25–29)	1956–60 (20–24)	1961–64 (16–19)	
Working full time	17.9	16.2	14.4	11.6	9.8	8.5	6.7	4.4	1.4	11.7
Working part time	7.2	6.0	5.5	4.7	3.0	2.1	0.9	0.2	0.0	2.6
Total working	**25.1**	**22.2**	**19.9**	**16.3**	**12.8**	**10.6**	**7.6**	**4.6**	**1.4**	**14.3**
Not working for non-domestic reasons*	1.7	1.5	0.6	0.5	0.4	0.3	0.3	0.4	0.3	0.9
Not working for domestic reasons	15.8	14.0	11.6	9.5	8.1	5.2	2.8	0.9	0.2	6.8
Total not working	**17.5**	**15.5**	**12.2**	**10.0**	**8.5**	**5.5**	**3.1**	**1.3**	**0.5**	**7.7**
Average years since leaving FT education	42.6	37.7	32.1	26.3	21.3	16.1	10.7	5.9	1.9	22.0
Base	598	570	553	587	653	763	680	578	333	5,315

Looking for work, waiting to take up a job, illness

121

Table 9.4 Proportion of time that women have spent working and not working since leaving full time education by period of birth and age

Activity between leaving full time education and interview	Period of birth (and age)									All women who have finished full time education
	1921–25 (55–59)	1926–30 (50–54)	1931–35 (45–49)	1936–40 (40–44)	1941–45 (35–39)	1946–50 (30–34)	1951–55 (25–29)	1956–60 (20–24)	1961–64 (16–19)	
	%	%	%	%	%	%	%	%	%	%
Working full time	42	43	45	44	46	53	63	75	73	53
Working part time	17	16	17	18	14	13	8	3	2	12
Total working	**59**	**59**	**62**	**62**	**60**	**66**	**71**	**78**	**75**	**65**
Not working for non-domestic reasons*	4	4	2	2	2	2	3	6	17	4
Not working for domestic reasons	37	37	36	36	38	32	26	16	8	31
Total not working	**41**	**41**	**38**	**38**	**40**	**34**	**29**	**22**	**25**	**35**
	100	100	100	100	100	100	100	100	100	100
Base	598	570	553	587	653	763	680	578	333	5,315

Looking for work, waiting to take up a job, illness

aged 35 and over in 1980, had worked for around 60% of their possible working lives so far, 43% in full time work and 17% in part time work. By contrast the proportion of time spent not working for non-domestic reasons (mainly unemployment) was much greater for the last two cohorts, particularly the 16–19 year olds. It is clear from the previous table, however, that this represents an average of three or four months; although this is a small amount of time it is a significant proportion of the time these women have spent in the labour market since leaving full time education.[3]

Because of the overall rise in women's employment in recent years women currently in their thirties or forties have worked for a greater proportion of the time available than women now in their fifties would have done at younger ages. From the proportion of available time spent working so far we can calculate for younger age groups what proportion of their working lives up to age 60 we would expect them to work on various assumptions. Table 9.5 shows the resulting proportions based on the assumption that the employment rates women would experience as they pass through successive ages are those currently experienced by women of those ages in 1980; that is on the assumption that there is no further rise in women's employment, despite the cohort trends noted earlier.[4] This allows, to some degree, for

the effect of the recession in that the rise in employment among women in the older age groups is assumed to have stopped, but it does not assume an actual fall in employment for these women. The results show, for example, that women currently in their early forties can be expected to have worked for 63% of their potential working life up to age 60 while women in their early thirties can be expected to have worked for 67% of their lives by the same age. Thus an assumption of a significant fall in women's employment is required for the total proportion of time worked not to excede the level of 59% experienced by women in their late fifties, because the younger women have already worked for significantly greater proportions of their lives so far.

Table 9.5 Estimates of proportion of time that women would have spent working by age 60 if 1980 employment rates prevail

Age	Proportion of time spent working between leaving full time education and 1980	Estimated proportion of time worked by age 60 if 1980 employment rates prevail
20–24	78%	67%
25–29	71%	68%
30–34	66%	67%
35–39	60%	64%
40–44	62%	63%
45–49	62%	62%
50–54	59%	59%
55–59	59%	59%

Table 9.6 Summary indices of women's employment since leaving full time education by period of birth and age

	Period of birth (and age)									All women who have finished full-time education
	1921–25 (55–59)	1926–30 (50–54)	1931–35 (45–49)	1936–40 (40–44)	1941–45 (35–39)	1946–50 (30–34)	1951–55 (25–29)	1956–60 (20–24)	1961–64 (16–19)	
Proportion currently working (1980)	53%	67%	73%	74%	67%	56%	49%	64%	74%	63%
Proportion who have ever worked	99%	99%	100%	100%	99%	100%	98%	98%	94%	98%
Proportion who have always been economically active	9%	9%	11%	12%	11%	16%	32%	61%	88%	25%
Average proportion of working life worked	59%	59%	62%	62%	60%	66%	71%	78%	75%	65%
Mean number of working periods	2.9	2.9	2.8	2.9	2.7	2.4	2.0	1.6	1.2	2.4
Mean number of periods not working for domestic reasons	1.7	1.7	1.6	1.7	1.6	1.4	1.1	0.5	0.2	1.3
Mean number of periods not working for non-domestic reasons	0.7	0.5	0.5	0.4	0.4	0.4	0.4	0.6	0.7	0.5
Base	598	570	553	587	653	763	680	578	333	5,315

We have looked at the length and proportion of time so far that women of different ages have spent working and not working, but there are many other possible summary indices of women's employment, some of which are shown in Table 9.6. Although not all women were currently working, almost all had worked at some time, the lowest proportion being among the youngest women, some of whom had been unemployed since leaving school. If we define always being economically active as having had no breaks in employment for domestic reasons (apart from maternity leave, that is, an absence of up to 6 months around the birth of a child) then 9% of the oldest women had always been economically active.[5] The proportions were slightly higher among the next three cohorts and were of course much higher among the younger women, many of whom had yet to have children.

Women aged 25 and over had had on average two or more periods of working in their lives so far, but the averages did not rise further for women aged 35 and over, reflecting the fact that most interruptions in work are caused relatively early in a working life by child-bearing. We look at this in more detail later in the chapter. The highest average numbers of breaks for non-domestic reasons were among the youngest women, who were most likely to have experienced unemployment, and among the oldest women for whom absence from work through illness was likely to be an increasingly important factor (Dex, 1984a).

Work before the birth of children

The picture of women's work over a lifetime is obviously to a considerable extent influenced by the rela-

tionship between employment and responsibility for children. But the amount of work experience women have had before the birth of any children also varies, and this may in turn affect their subsequent employment as Dex shows (ibid). We looked separately at women's work before the birth of any children and since the birth of the first child. This is not to imply that the birth of a child inevitably interrupts employment, although it usually does; as we shall show, most women leave the labour market for several years following childbirth. Accordingly it is useful to consider separately the phases of women's lives before and after the start of childbearing. In looking at the pre-childbearing phase we consider data not only from women who have had children but also from those who at the time of the interview were childless.

Most of the childless women were young (three quarters were under 35) and the majority expected to have children at some time in the future and might therefore be viewed as being in the pre-childbirth phase of their lives. We cannot know how long this phase will last and we can only look at their work experience up to the time of the interview; in contrast for women with children we can look at the complete period up to the birth of the first child.

Table 9.7 shows the proportion of time childless women had spent working and not working since leaving school. Overall 87% of their time was spent working, 83% in full time work and 4% in part time work. Not working for non-domestic reasons accounted for 8% of the time, this proportion being highest amongst those who left school in the five years before the survey and

Table 9.7 Proportion of time that childless women have spent working and not working since leaving full time education by length of time since leaving full time education

Activity between leaving full time education and interview	Time between leaving full time education and interview							All childless women who have finished full time education
	Up to 5 years	Over 5 up to 10 years	Over 10 up to 15 years	Over 15 up to 20 years	Over 20 up to 30 years	Over 30 up to 40 years	Over 40 years	
	%	%	%	%	%	%	%	%
Working full time	82	90	90	89	83	76	68	83
Working part time	2	2	5	4	5	8	7	4
Total working	**84**	**92**	**95**	**93**	**88**	**84**	**75**	**87**
Not working for non-domestic reasons	14	5	3	3	3	4	10	8
Not working for domestic reasons	2	3	2	4	9	12	15	5
Total not working	**16**	**8**	**5**	**7**	**12**	**16**	**25**	**13**
	100	**100**	**100**	**100**	**100**	**100**	**100**	**100**
Base	521	296	131	85	123	123	84	1,364

Table 9.8 Proportion of time that women with children have spent working and not working before the first birth by length of time between leaving full time education and first birth

Activity between leaving full time education and first birth	Time between leaving full time education and first birth					All women with children who have finished full time education
	Up to 5 years	5 years up to 10 years	Over 10 up to 15 years	Over 15 up to 20 years	Over 20 years	
	%	%	%	%	%	%
Working full time	77	87	85	85	84	84
Working part time	1	2	3	3	4	2
Total working	**78**	**89**	**88**	**88**	**88**	**86**
Not working for non-domestic reasons	3	1	2	2	1	2
Not working for domestic reasons	19	10	10	10	11	12
Total not working	**22**	**11**	**12**	**12**	**12**	**14**
	100	**100**	**100**	**100**	**100**	**100**
Base	921	1,876	886	221	52	3,956

who were therefore affected by the general rise in unemployment among school leavers. Conversely, not working for domestic reasons was highest amongst women who left school over 20 years ago. These older women were most likely to have spent time caring for sick or elderly relatives. In general these results show that childless women had spent most of their working lives in full time employment.

Women who had had children had also spent most of the time before childbirth in full time employment as Table 9.8 shows. Overall, 86% of the time was spent working, 84% in full time and 2% in part time employment. The proportion of time spent not working for domestic reasons, 12%, is much higher than the equivalent figure for childless women because almost all these women gave up work during their first pregnancy and therefore spent some time not working for this reason immediately prior to the first birth. The shorter the time between leaving school and the first birth the larger the proportion of time such absence from work represents. Apart from this difference, it is clear that, like the childless women, women with children had spent most of the time prior to childbearing in full time work.

The oldest women in our sample got married at times when it was still socially acceptable for women to stop work on marriage. We might therefore expect women whose first births occurred at earlier dates to have worked for a smaller proportion of the time up to the first birth than those whose first birth occurred in recent years. To some extent this was the case, but the differences are not very great. For example, Table 9.9 shows that women whose first birth occurred between 1940 and 1954 had worked on average for 83%–84% of the time before their first birth compared with 87%–88% for women whose first birth occurred between 1950 and 1974. For women with first births in 1975–1979, 85% of the time before their first birth was spent working, but this group had spent the highest proportion of time not working for non-domestic reasons, generally unemployment.

The actual number of years worked before the first birth are obviously influenced by the age at which a woman finishes full time education and her age at the start of childbearing. These are related in that women who stay in education beyond the minimum age tend to start childbearing somewhat later. However the delay in starting childbearing does not completely compensate for extra years in education and so women who have stayed longest in education tend to have worked for the shortest length of time before their first birth. Thus women who stayed in education beyond 18 worked on average for 6.1 years before the birth of a first child compared with an average of 7.7 years for those who left school between 15 and 17. These figures vary somewhat over time, reflecting changes in the minimum school leaving age and in the timing of the first birth, the former having the greater effect. The net result is that the length of time between leaving full time education and the first birth has generally declined over time as Table 9.9 shows.[6]

Table 9.9 Proportion of time that women with children have spent working and not working before first birth by period of first birth

Activity between leaving full time education and first birth	Period of first birth								All women with children
	1940–44	1945–49	1950–54	1955–59	1960–64	1965–69	1970–74	1975–79	
	%	%	%	%	%	%	%	%	%
Working full time	82	83	81	84	86	86	85	82	84
Working part time	1	1	2	2	2	2	2	3	2
Total working	**83**	**84**	**83**	**86**	**88**	**88**	**87**	**85**	**86**
Not working for non-domestic reasons*	2	1	2	1	1	1	2	4	2
Not working for domestic reasons	15	15	15	13	11	11	11	11	12
Total not working	**17**	**16**	**17**	**14**	**12**	**12**	**13**	**15**	**14**
	100	100	100	100	100	100	100	100	100
Average years between leaving education and first birth	6.3	8.4	9.4	9.2	8.7	7.6	7.7	7.6	8.2
Base	*111*	*366*	*449*	*502*	*628*	*635*	*617*	*588*	*3,956†*

*Looking for work, waiting to take up a job, illness
†Includes births before 1940 and in 1980

Table 9.10 Whether or not women worked between marriage and first birth by period of first birth

Whether worked between marriage and first birth	Period of first birth								All women with first birth after marriage
	1940–44	1945–49	1950–54	1955–59	1960–64	1965–69	1970–74	1975–79	
	%	%	%	%	%	%	%	%	%
Worked	62	63	69	76	79	85	88	88	79
Did not work	38	37	31	24	21	15	12	12	21
	100	100	100	100	100	100	100	100	100
Base	*102*	*357*	*435*	*483*	*598*	*587*	*564*	*520*	*3,693**

*Including 55 women with first births before 1940 or in 1980

Looking more directly at the proportion of women stopping work on marriage, we show in Table 9.10 that the proportion working at all between marriage and the first birth rose from 62% for women with first births in 1940–45 to 88% for those with first births in the last ten years. Thus only 12% of women with first births in the last ten years stopped work completely on marriage and further analysis revealed that a high proportion of these were pregnant at marriage. In fact overall only 8% of women who had a first birth more than 2 years after their marriage stopped work on marriage, compared with 43% of those who gave birth within 8 months of marriage.

In summary, the data from the survey indicate that women spend around 7 of the average of 8 years between leaving full time education and their first birth working, generally full time. In 1965 Hunt showed that marriage had a decreasing relationship to withdrawal from the labour market (Hunt, 1968). Marriage is even more unlikely nowadays to be associated with stopping work (although some women change jobs on marriage, particularly if they move to a different area) and so unemployment is likely to be the major cause of interruption to work prior to the first pregnancy. These retrospective data reinforce the picture formed from the cross-sectional data described in Chapter 2 and from Joshi's analysis that women who have not had children are likely to be in paid work whether or not they are married (Joshi, 1984).

Employment after childbirth

Employment in the pre-childbearing phase is relatively uncomplicated to describe – almost all women work full time. The picture becomes rapidly more complex once women begin to have children. In analysing these data different, but complementary, strategies were adopted by Dex and ourselves. Dex distinguishes two post-childbirth phases which she calls 'the family formation phase' and 'the final work phase' (Dex 1984a). She develops a range of employment profiles generated from individual women's work histories and examines how different groups of women combine employment and paid work during the 'family formation phase'. Subsequently she examines whether women with differing degrees of attachment to work, as measured by their employment profile, have different labour market behaviour in their final work phase. We have not made these distinctions in post-childbirth employment.

Rather we are particularly concerned to show how women's employment has changed at the aggregate level over time. Thus we focus on how quickly women return to work; whether they make more than one return (that is whether the bimodal pattern of women's lifetime employment still holds); how much of their post-childbearing lives they work; whether this is in full or part time employment and what movements they make between full and part time employment over this phase of their lives.

Returning to employment

For most women in the survey the birth of their first child was associated with a period out of the labour force. As we shall show, some women returned to work before a second child was born while others stopped work until after all their children were born; only a minority stayed in the labour market throughout their childbearing period. If we assume that an absence from work of 6 months or less around the time of a birth does not really constitute leaving the labour market but is official or unofficial maternity leave, then 8% of women in our study whose latest birth was at least six months before the interview had returned to work within 6 months of each birth so far. However, for two thirds of these women this was their first birth. Fewer of them are likely to return to work within 6 months of subsequent births, for although 16% of women with one birth had returned within 6 months of this birth, only 3% of women with more than one birth had returned within 6 months of each birth.[7]

It is interesting to see whether the proportion of women who do not leave the labour force at the time of their first birth has changed over time, in order to identify whether younger women are more attached to working. Table 9.11 shows that although overall 14% of women had returned to work within six months of their first birth, the proportion has risen significantly from 9% of women with a first birth in 1945–49 to 17% of those with first births in 1965–69 after which the rate has remained almost constant. The table also shows for women returning to work within 6 months of their first birth that increasing proportions returned first to part time work in recent years. However there is no clear trend with regard to returning to work full time.

Nor does any very strong pattern emerge of the factors associated with an early return to work after a first birth

Table 9.11   Whether women returned to work full or part time within 6 months of first birth by period of first birth

	Period of first birth							All women with children*
	1945–49	1950–54	1955–59	1960–64	1965–69	1970–74	1975–79	
	%	%	%	%	%	%	%	%
Returned to full time work	5	6	10	8	11	6	8	8
Returned to part time work	4	4	4	5	6	10	9	6
Total who returned within 6 months	**9**	**10**	**14**	**13**	**17**	**16**	**17**	**14**
Did not return within 6 months	91	90	86	87	83	84	83	86
	100	**100**	**100**	**100**	**100**	**100**	**100**	**100**
Base	366	449	502	628	635	617	588	3,785

*Excluding those whose first birth was within 6 months of interview

though analysis by occupation and education provides some pointers. Table 9.12 shows that women in other intermediate non-manual occupations were most likely to return within 6 months of their first birth. However, they are rather a small group of women. Other semi-skilled workers, teachers, skilled and unskilled manual workers were all more likely than average to return within 6 months. However, only 10% of the large groups of clerical and sales workers returned within 6 months of their first birth. These results confirm the trend identified by Daniel in his study of new mothers and maternity leave (Daniel, 1980). Not surprisingly, women who had not worked before their first birth were least likely to return within 6 months.

We also looked at the process of returning within 6 months of the first birth in relation to women's highest qualification (Table 9.13). Women with the highest level qualifications, 'A' levels or above, were most likely to return within 6 months. There is some indication that women with lower level qualifications were less likely to return quickly than those with no qualifications

at all, that is, women at both ends of the qualification hierarchy and the occupational ladder returned more quickly than those in the middle, a finding also reported by Daniel (*ibid*).

Clearly a number of factors influence whether women return to work almost straight after their first birth. Women in higher level occupations or with higher qualifications may be established in a career that they do not want to interrupt. They are also likely to be in better paid jobs and therefore will suffer greater absolute economic loss if they do not return to work; they can also pay for childcare if they need to without losing all financial gain from working. Other women in lower level occupations and with no qualifications may not be able to manage financially if they do not return to work as they are likely to have husbands in less well paid occupations or to have no financial support from a partner. Dex provides a fuller discussion based on regression analysis of the factors affecting the duration of time before women return (Dex 1984a). In addition, she shows that unsupported mothers are particularly likely to return to work straight after the first birth and these women tend to have been in the lower level occupations before the first birth (*ibid*). It should also be noted that women returning to work within 6 months of the first birth frequently returned to full time work, and the occupations with high rates of early returns have relatively low proportions of women working part time.

It is clear from the results presented above that most women leave the labour market following their first birth. For the majority however this is a temporary withdrawal. From women's work histories we know that 78% of women with children had returned to work at some time since their first birth, but many women who had not returned still had young children and may be expected to return when their children are older. To get a better idea, therefore, of the proportion of women likely to return eventually we looked only at women whose children were all 16 or over and found that 90% had returned to work at some time since their first birth (Table 9.14). This table also shows that the proportion has increased over time from 87% of women whose first birth occurred in 1940–44 to 95% of those whose first birth occurred in 1960–64 and whose children were all 16 or over.

Women who started childbearing more recently will still have dependent children and so many have yet to return to work. We show later that they have been returning to work sooner after childbirth than women

Table 9.12 Proportion of women returning to work within 6 months of first birth by last occupation before first birth

Last occupation before first birth	Proportion of women who returned to work within 6 months of first birth	Base
Professional		17*
Teaching	22%	149
Nursing, medical and social	14%	210
Other intermediate non-manual	26%	80
Clerical	10%	1,259
Sales	10%	483
Skilled manual	20%	307
Semi-skilled factory	15%	917
Semi-skilled domestic	15%	183
Other semi-skilled	23%	175
Unskilled	19%	53
Did not work before first birth	6%	109
All women with children	**14%**	3,956

Base too small to show percentages

Table 9.13 Proportion of women returning to work within 6 months of first birth by highest qualification

Highest qualification	Proportion of women who returned to work within 6 months of first birth	Base
'A' levels or above	17%	556
'O' levels or equivalent	12%	593
CSE or equivalent	13%	579
No qualifications	14%	2,228
All women with children	**14%**	3,956

Table 9.14 Whether women whose children are now all 16 or over have worked at all since first birth by period of first birth

	Period of first birth					Women whose children are all 16 or over
	1940–44	1945–49	1950–54	1955–59	1960–64	
	%	%	%	%	%	%
Worked at some time since first birth	87	89	88	90	95	90
Not worked at all since first birth	13	11	12	10	5	10
	100	**100**	**100**	**100**	**100**	**100**
Base	114	342	389	366	216	1,442*

Including 15 women with first births before 1940 or after 1964

Figure 9.5 Proportion of women who have made a return to work within varying intervals of first birth: women with first births in five year periods from 1950 to 1979

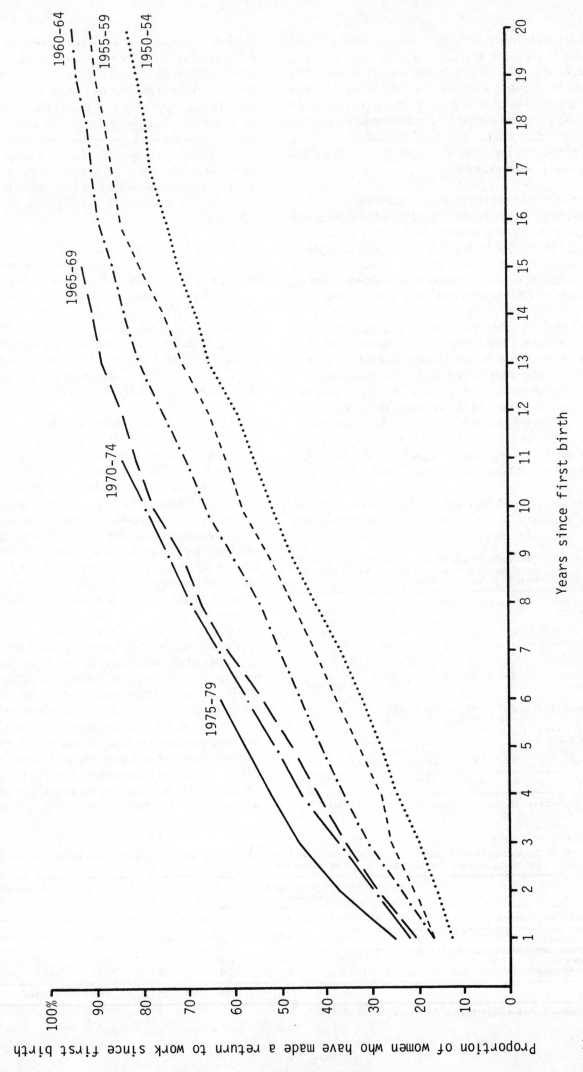

Proportion of women who have made a return to work since first birth

Years since first birth

whose final births occurred in earlier periods and so it is likely that at least as many if not more will return to work eventually. The recession may of course affect their behaviour, but even so the proportion of women returning to work at all after childbirth could continue to rise even if an overall reduction in women's employment occurs; returns may be delayed or women who have returned may stop work again or move in and out of work to a greater extent.[8]

Timing of the return to work after childbirth

Since most women return to work eventually, what is of interest is how long women in the survey spent out of the labour market having children and caring for them, and how this is changing over time. We start by looking at the length of the first break in employment following childbirth. Of course some women will return to work before they have another child while others do not return until all their children have been born. Whilst we discuss this in more detail later, we show in Table 9.15 the proportion of women who had returned to work at various times since the first birth for women whose first births occurred in different five year periods. To allow for the fact that not all the women in the group had the relevant length of time between their first birth and the interview the last figures for each of the later four periods have been estimated by life table techniques (described in Martin and Roberts, 1984).

It is clear from both Table 9.15 and Figure 9.5 that there is a rise in the proportion of women with first births in successive five year periods who had made an initial return to work by any given interval after 1 year since their first birth. The differences between women with first births in the first four of the five year periods since 1950 are particularly marked. The trends can be seen clearly by comparing the median time before the initial return to work for women with first births in successive five year periods. Thus for women with a first birth in 1950–54, half had made an initial return to work by 9.7 years after the first birth while the comparable time for women with first births in 1975–79 was 3.7 years.

Moreover, these changes over time are almost entirely attributable to increasing proportions of women returning initially to part time work since there was little difference in the proportion of women whose first return was to full time work, regardless of when they had their first birth. In general, women returning initially to full time work did so quite soon after the first birth compared with those whose initial return was to part time work. Returns within 6 months of the first birth were more likely to be to full time than to part time work.

After one year women were more likely to return initially to part time work; so, for example, of the 40% of women who had made a return within five years after the first birth, 17% had returned initially to full time and 23% to part time work. By ten years after the first birth the differences were greater: 23% had returned initially to full time work and 39% to part time work. Thus in general, the longer the initial break from work following the first birth a woman had, the more likely she was initially to return to part time work. This has important consequences for the likelihood of her returning to a lower level occupation as we shall show in Chapter 10.

As one might expect the total length of time women spend out of the workforce in connection with childbearing and childcaring is significantly related to the number of children they have and the time period over which the births occur, a finding Joshi confirms (Joshi, 1984). Overall, 37% of women with two or more children had returned to work at some time between the births of their first and latest child. The way in which this proportion has changed over time can be seen from Table 9.16. There is a rise in the proportion of women who had returned to work before their latest birth

Table 9.15 Cumulative proportion of women who have made an initial return to work by varying intervals since first birth by period of first birth

Time since first birth	Period of first birth					
	1950–54	1955–59	1960–64	1965–69	1970–74	1975–79
	%	%	%	%	%	%
1 year	13	17	17	21	22	(25)
2 years	20	21	24	30	30	(37)
5 years	28	33	41	47	51	(58)
10 years	51	58	66	77	(79)	
15 years	71	80	86	(92)		
20 years	82	90	(94)			
Median years to initial return to work	9.7	8.7	7.0	5.5	4.8	3.7
Base	449	502	628	635	617	588

Figures in brackets have been estimated by life table techniques

Table 9.16 Proportion of women with two or more children who returned to work between first and latest birth, time between first and latest birth and average number of children born, by period of latest birth

	Period of latest birth					All women with two or more births
	1955–59	1960–64	1965–69	1970–74	1975–79	
Proportion who returned to work between first and latest birth	25%	35%	38%	40%	47%	37%
Average number of years between first and latest birth	6.2	6.8	6.2	5.7	5.3	5.8
Average number of children born	2.8	3.0	2.9	2.8	2.6	2.8
Base	322	466	599	585	641	2,946*

Including births before 1955 and in 1980

Figure 9.6 Proportion of women who have made a return to work within varying intervals of latest birth: women with latest births in five year periods from 1950 to 1979

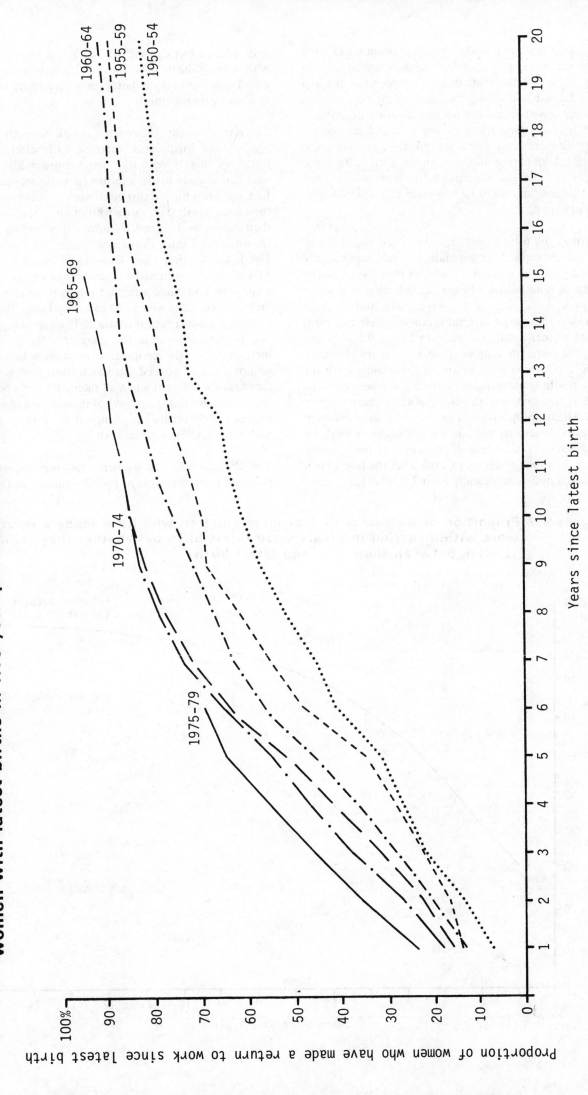

suggesting that the bimodal pattern of women's lifetime employment is an increasingly less common experience. However the length of time between the first and latest birth has declined for latest births occurring in 1965–69 onwards and the average number of children born is also falling which may in part explain the results. The fact that some women have not yet completed childbearing did not significantly affect the figures; the analysis was repeated for women who considered their families to be complete and a similar picture emerged.

Although the total length of time women spend out of the labour force having children varies significantly according to the number of children they have and the length of time between births, an indicator of rates of return to work which is not directly affected by these factors is the length of time following their last birth before women return to work. In Figure 9.6 we compare the cumulative proportions of women who have made a return to work following their latest birth for women with latest births in successive five year periods. Like Figure 9.5 this shows significant changes over time. Higher proportions of women with latest births in successive five year periods are returning to work by any given interval since their latest birth. Consequently the median time of return to work after the latest birth has fallen quite dramatically from 7.7 years for women

with a latest birth in 1950–54 to 3.4 years for women with a latest birth in 1975–79, although it should be noted that some of the latter group are likely to go on to have further children.

There is, as might be expected, a link between returning between births and returning early after a latest birth. Amongst women with two or more children those who had already made a return to work between their first and latest birth returned to work again sooner after their latest birth than those who did not work between their births as Figure 9.7 shows; this finding is also shown in the Family Formation Survey (Ní Bhrolcháin, 1983). By the time their latest child was 3 years old, 54% of women who had worked between their births at some time had made a further return to work whereas only 17% of those who had not worked since their first birth had made a return to work. The gap between the two groups narrowed as the years since the latest birth increased, but the proportion of women in the two groups who had worked since their latest birth were still significantly different when all their children were aged 16 or over. By this stage 96% of those who had worked between their births had returned to work compared with 87% of those who had not.

The characteristics of women who returned to work between their births were broadly similar to those of

Figure 9.7 Proportion of women with 2 or more children who have made a return to work within varying intervals since latest birth by whether they returned to work between their first and latest birth

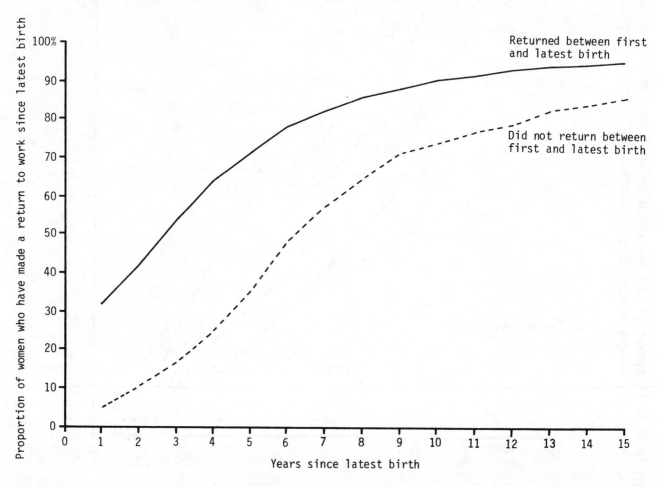

130

women who returned to work within six months of their first birth. Obviously there is overlap between the groups in the case of women who returned within six months of their first birth and then went on to have further children. Moreover women with one child who returned within six months of their first birth but expected to have more children would fall into the second

Table 9.17 Proportion of women returning to work between first and latest birth by last occupation before first birth: women with 2 or more children

Last occupation before first birth	Proportion of women who returned to work between first and last birth	Base
Professional		13*
Teaching	38%	113
Nursing, medical and social	38%	158
Other intermediate non-manual	43%	51
Clerical	29%	926
Sales	40%	356
Skilled manual	39%	229
Semi-skilled factory	47%	684
Semi-skilled domestic	37%	142
Other semi-skilled	40%	134
Unskilled	44%	43
Did not work before first birth	28%	86
All women with 2 or more children	37%	2,946

*Base too small to show percentages

Table 9.18 Proportion of women returning to work between first and latest birth by highest qualification: women with 2 or more children

Highest qualification	Proportion of women who returned to work between first and latest birth	Base
'A' levels or above	37%	409
'O' levels or equivalent	31%	437
CSE or equivalent	28%	407
No qualifications	41%	1,693
All women with 2 or more children	37%	2,946

group in due course and so it is not surprising that they should be similar. Tables 9.17 and 9.18 show in a similar manner to Tables 9.12 and 9.13 the proportions of women with two or more children who returned to work between their first and latest birth by their occupation before the first birth and their highest qualification. Although the patterns are broadly similar to those of women returning within six months of their first birth, there are larger proportions of women who were in lower level occupations and without qualifications who returned to work between their births.[9]

This section has shown that a number of factors affect how soon after their first and latest births women return to work. Overall there has been a trend over time for women to return increasingly soon after the first birth

Figure 9.8 Proportion of women with children currently working or who have made a return since first birth by the age of their youngest child

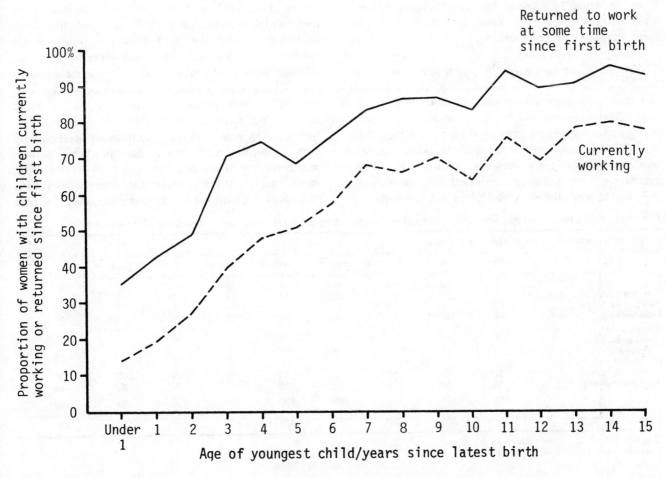

which Dex, for example, has shown is not explained solely by women having smaller families spread over shorter periods of time (Dex, 1984a). The trend is associated with the increased proportion of women who return to part time work. However, those women who return soonest after births are the most likely to return to full time work, although women returning to full time work are in the minority. Women have become increasingly likely to return to work before completing their families and those who do so return sooner after their last birth than women who do not work until childbearing is complete.

Total time worked after childbirth

While, as we have seen, most women withdraw temporarily from work following their first birth and return to work eventually, they do not necessarily continue to work on their return without interruption. Women who return to work following each birth may have more periods of not working but a shorter total time not working than those who do not return until after their last child's birth; in effect they may work more of their possible working life than the latter group. In addition, some women may stop work temporarily for reasons other than childbirth later in life and women may cease working and consider themselves retired before they reach the official retirement age. This is documented extensively by Dex in her account of women's 'final work phase' (Dex, 1984a). Consequently the proportion of women with children working at any one point in time is never as high as the proportion who have worked at all since starting a family, even among women whose children are all grown up. This is illustrated in Figure 9.8. Approximately 20% more women have returned to work at some time since their first birth than are currently working.

Clearly both the timing of the initial return to work following childbirth and subsequent movement in and out of work determine how much of their lives following childbirth women eventually spend working. Table 9.19 summarises the proportion of time since their first birth that women have so far spent working and not working. Many of the women who started childbearing recently will not yet have completed their families or returned to work following childbirth and so results are

presented by period of the first birth. Figure 9.9 shows the actual lengths of time women with children have spent working and not working both before and since the first birth. The percentages shown in Tables 9.9 and 9.19 are also shown on each column of Figure 9.9.

Significant proportions of women whose first birth occurred in the 1970s have not yet completed their families and therefore can be expected to spend further time not working for domestic reasons. Even among those women whose families are, in fact, complete many, whose children are still young, may not return to work for some time yet. It is therefore more useful in looking at Figure 9.6 to focus on the results for women with first births before 1965 since almost all have completed their families and have secondary school age, if not grown-up, children. If women had a fairly constant length of time out of the labour force following childbirth and stayed in work once they returned, the actual length of time not worked for domestic reasons should stabilise once the main childbearing period has passed, while the proportion of time would decrease. It is interesting to see therefore that the length of time not worked for domestic reasons was highest amongst women who started childbearing in the earliest period, and the proportion of time this represents remains more or less constant for all women with first births before 1965. This could be either because women have had a shorter break for childbearing in more recent years or because women move out of the labour market again later in their working lives.

Finally in this section, we summarise women's lives following childbirth in a different way. Table 9.20 shows the average number of periods since the first birth women have spent working full and part time, and not working for domestic and non-domestic reasons. Women with first births in all but the most recent period have averaged more than one period working and nearly two periods not working for domestic reasons. We have shown that returning to work between births was more common among women with more recent first births; the greater number of periods of not working for domestic reasons amongst those with more distant first births shows that many women have periods of not working for domestic reasons other than

Table 9.19 Proportion of time that women with children have spent working and not working since first birth by period of first birth

Activity between first birth and interview	Period of first birth								All women with children
	1940–44	1945–49	1950–54	1955–59	1960–64	1965–69	1970–74	1975–79	
	%	%	%	%	%	%	%	%	%
Working full time	25	22	21	19	18	14	7	8	15
Working part time	19	24	24	26	27	25	21	12	22
Total working	**44**	**46**	**45**	**45**	**45**	**39**	**28**	**20**	**37**
Not working for non-domestic reasons*	4	5	4	2	2	2	1	3	3
Not working for domestic reasons	52	49	51	53	53	59	71	77	60
Total not working	**56**	**54**	**55**	**55**	**55**	**61**	**72**	**80**	**63**
	100	100	100	100	100	100	100	100	100
Base	*111*	*366*	*449*	*502*	*628*	*635*	*617*	*588*	*3,956†*

*Looking for work, waiting to take up a job, illness
†Includes births before 1940 and in 1980

Figure 9.9 Mean lengths of time and proportion of time women with children have spent working before and after first birth by period of first birth

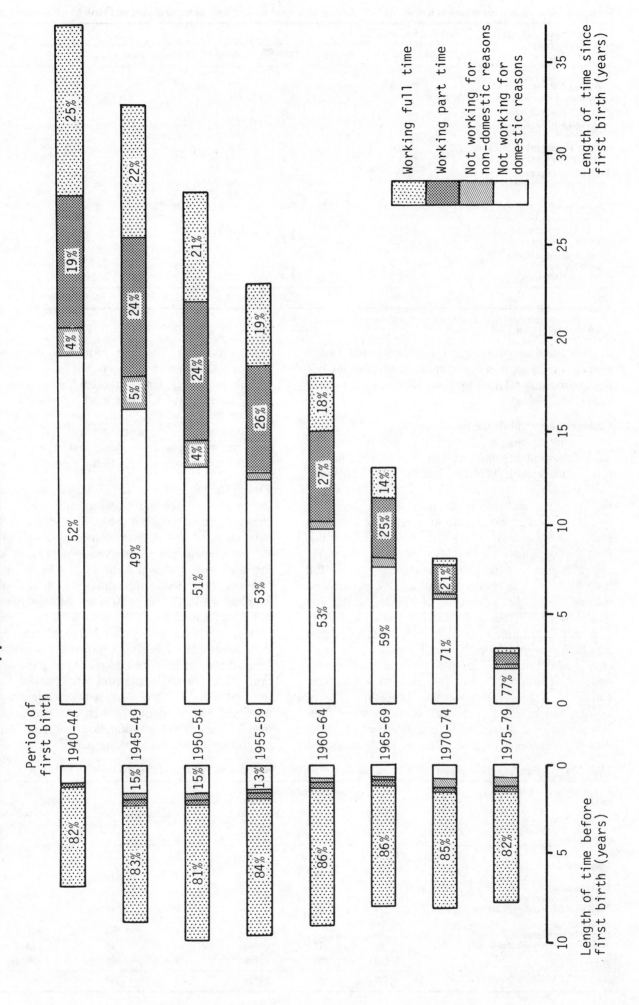

Table 9.20 Average number of periods that women with children have spent working and not working since first birth by period of first birth

Activity between first birth and interview	Period of first birth								All women with children
	1940–44	1945–49	1950–54	1955–59	1960–64	1965–69	1970–74	1975–79	
Average no. of periods working full time	1.2	1.0	0.9	0.8	0.7	0.6	0.3	0.2	0.6
Standard deviation	*1.6*	*1.1*	*1.1*	*1.0*	*0.9*	*0.9*	*0.6*	*0.5*	*1.0*
Average no. of periods working part time	1.2	1.4	1.2	1.3	1.3	1.2	0.9	0.4	1.1
Standard deviation	*1.4*	*1.3*	*1.1*	*1.2*	*1.2*	*1.0*	*1.0*	*0.7*	*1.1*
Average no. of periods working*	2.1	2.0	1.8	1.8	1.8	1.6	1.2	0.6	1.5
Standard deviation	*1.9*	*1.5*	*1.4*	*1.4*	*1.3*	*1.2*	*1.1*	*0.7*	*1.3*
Average no. of periods not working for non-domestic reasons	0.5	0.5	0.4	0.3	0.2	0.2	0.1	0.1	0.2
Standard deviation	*0.8*	*0.8*	*0.8*	*0.7*	*0.6*	*0.6*	*0.5*	*0.3*	*0.6*
Average no. of periods not working for domestic reasons	2.1	1.9	1.7	1.7	1.7	1.6	1.5	1.1	1.6
Standard deviation	*1.4*	*1.2*	*1.0*	*1.1*	*1.1*	*0.9*	*0.8*	*0.5*	*1.0*
Average no. of periods not working	2.6	2.4	2.1	2.0	1.9	1.8	1.6	1.2	1.8
Standard deviation	*1.8*	*1.5*	*1.3*	*1.3*	*1.2*	*1.2*	*0.9*	*0.7*	*1.2*
Base	*111*	*366*	*449*	*502*	*628*	*635*	*617*	*588*	*3,956†*

*Consecutive periods of full and part time work count as one working period
†Includes births before 1940 and in 1980*

childbirth and the period immediately following. In fact women display a variety of patterns of working and not working both in relation to childbirth and later in their lives (Dex, 1984a).

Changes between full and part time work

In our sample most women returned first to part time work following childbirth and women who did not return to work until all their children were born were particularly likely to return part time at first. However, the cross-sectional results described earlier show that the proportion of women working full time rose with the age of the youngest child. One interpretation of this is that women have a two stage re-entry to paid work, returning first to part time work and changing to full time work as their children get older. We particularly wanted to see what proportion of women did this and so examined whether women did in fact change from part time to full time work in this way. We looked first at whether women's most recent job since having a child was full or part time in relation to whether they had first returned to full or part time work following childbirth. Table 9.21 shows that altogether 27% of women had changed their work status between their first job after childbirth and their most recent job; 11% had changed from full to part time and 16% from part

to full time work. However, more than twice as many women return to part time as to full time work (52% to 21% respectively). Thus of those whose first return was to full time work, 34% were working part time in their most recent job, while of those whose first return was to part time work, 23% were working full time in their most recent job; women whose first return was to full time work were more likely to have made a change.

Clearly the longer a women has worked since her initial return to work the more opportunity she has had to change work status. That she was in fact more likely to have changed can be seen from Table 9.21. Overall 86% of women who had worked for 5 years or less had the same work status in their first and most recent job following their first birth compared with 60% of those who had worked for over 20 years. Most of the change can be accounted for by women whose first return was to part time work having changed to full time work by their most recent job; the proportion of women working part time in both jobs decreased with the length of time worked whereas the proportion having changed from part to full time work between these two jobs increased, except among women who had worked for over 20 years. This last group, however, had the highest proportion of women working part time in their most

Table 9.21 Changes in work status between first and most recent job following first birth by length of time worked since first birth

Comparison of first and most recent job following first birth	Length of time worked since first birth					All women who have worked since first birth
	Up to 5 years	Over 5, up to 10 years	Over 10, up to 15 years	Over 15, up to 20 years	Over 20 years	
	%	%	%	%	%	%
First job full time, most recent job part time	9	11	12	11	17	11
First job part time, most recent job full time	5	17	24	27	23	16
Total with different work status	**14**	**28**	**36**	**38**	**40**	**27**
Both jobs full time	20	17	22	25	31	21
Both jobs part time	66	55	42	37	29	52
Total with same work status	**86**	**72**	**64**	**62**	**60**	**73**
	100	100	100	100	100	100
Base	*1,129*	*764*	*518*	*335*	*307*	*3,053*

recent job who returned initially to full time work. There is some evidence of a rise with the length of time worked in the proportion of women who were working full time in both the first and most recent job following their first birth, but women who had worked longest were most likely to have returned first to full time work. As we have seen these women tended to return to work earlier than women who returned part time.

Although this analysis ignores changes in work status occurring between the first and most recent job after childbirth, further analysis at an individual level by Dex shows that the majority of women (63%) who returned to work following childbirth had not changed their work status at all by the time of the interview: 18% had always worked full time and 47% had always worked part time since their first birth (*ibid*). Although 27% had had one change of work status, only 10% had made more than one change. Overall women were almost as likely to change from full to part time work as from part to full time, but there was a life cycle effect. Women who returned to work between their births were more likely than other women to change work status, particularly from full to part time work: 18% of these women changed from full to part time compared with only 6% of those who did not return to work between their births or who returned after one birth only. Although women who returned to work between their births were

more likely than other women to return first to full time work, as many changed subsequently to part time as remained working full time (*ibid*).

It seemed a likely hypothesis that the changes from full to part time work occurred particularly during the childbearing period and would be less likely to occur once all the children were born. We therefore looked at changes in work status following the latest birth for women who had returned to work after the latest (and in most cases their last) birth. Table 9.22 shows that altogether 22% of women had changed work status between the first and the most recent job following their latest birth. The same proportion, 16%, had changed from part to full time as had changed since the first birth, but only 6% had changed from full to part time compared with 11% making this change following the latest birth. Since women were much more likely to return to part than full time work initially following their latest birth it is interesting to note that exactly the same proportion (22%) of those returning full and part time had changed work status between their first and most recent job.

If we look at how the changes vary with the length of time worked we see in Table 9.22 a similar pattern to the previous table: a decrease in the proportion of women working part time in both the first and the most

Table 9.22 Changes in work status between first and most recent job following latest birth by length of time worked since latest birth

Comparison of first and most recent job following latest birth	Length of time worked since latest birth					All women who have worked since latest birth
	Up to 5 years	Over 5, up to 10 years	Over 10, up to 15 years	Over 15, up to 20 years	Over 20 years	
	%	%	%	%	%	%
First job full time, most recent job part time	4	5	6	8	11	6
First job part time, most recent job full time	6	16	24	28	22	16
Total with different work status	**10**	**21**	**30**	**36**	**33**	**22**
Both jobs full time	18	18	22	24	32	21
Both jobs part time	72	61	48	40	35	57
Total with same work status	**90**	**79**	**70**	**64**	**67**	**78**
	100	100	100	100	100	100
Base	*934*	*743*	*510*	*335*	*306*	*2,828*

Table 9.23 Summary of changes in women's work status since returning to work after latest birth by length of time worked since latest birth

Changes in work status since latest birth	Length of time worked since latest birth					All women who have worked since latest birth
	Up to 5 years	Over 5, up to 10 years	Over 10, up to 15 years	Over 15, up to 20 years	Over 20 years	
	%	%	%	%	%	%
Returned initially to full time work:						
Currently working full time and has only worked full time	11	10	14	15	23	13
Currently working full time but has worked part time	0	2	4	4	3	2
Currently working part time	3	4	5	6	10	5
Not working currently	8	7	5	7	6	7
Returned initially to part time work:						
Currently working full time	5	14	22	26	20	14
Currently working part time and has only worked part time	47	48	35	27	23	40
Currently working part time but has worked full time	1	2	4	6	5	3
Not working currently	25	13	11	9	10	16
	100	100	100	100	100	100
Base	*934*	*743*	*510*	*335*	*306*	*2,828*

recent job since the first birth and, in general, an increase in the proportion changing from part to full time with length of time worked. If we allow for the fact that women who had worked longest since their latest birth were most likely to have returned to full time work initially, there is no evidence of these women being increasingly likely to have changed to part time work in the most recent job by length of time worked.

This analysis has ignored other changes in work status between the first job after the latest birth and the most recent job, but Table 9.23, which summarises these changes, shows that the majority of women had not changed their work status. The largest group, 40%, returned to part time work and had only worked part time since, while 13% returned to full time work and continued to work full time. A further 23%, while not currently working, had not changed between full and part time work: 7% had only worked full time and 16% had only worked part time. Thus altogether three quarters of women who had worked since their latest birth had made no change between full and part time work. Of those who had changed, the most common change was from part to full time work (14%); only 5% had changed from full to part time work.

Looking at how these results vary by the length of time worked since the latest birth it is apparent that the proportion of women who had only worked part time decreased with the length of time worked while the proportion changing from part to full time increased generally, suggesting that women changed from part to full time work as their children got older. The proportion of women who had always worked full time since their latest birth was highest among those who had worked for over 20 years. This may be a generational effect since older women who had worked longest would have returned to work at a time when less part time work was available. The highest proportion of women changing from full to part time was also found among women who had worked for over 20 years since their last birth. This suggests that some women changed to part time work as retirement approached, possibly because of health problems or because the financial need to work was less once their children were independent. The proportion of women who although they had returned to work since their latest birth were not currently working was highest amongst those who had worked the shortest time. These women may have had less attachment to work than others or, more probably, may have been women whose children were still young and who may have had difficulty combining work and childcare.

This section has shown that the majority of women do not change work status between full and part time working following childbirth, although the likelihood of making a change increases with the length of time worked. Women who return to work part time initially are increasingly likely to change to full time work the longer they work. This type of change generally takes place after all births have occurred and the children are

growing older. Women who work between their births are more likely than others to change work status, particularly from full to part time work. This type of change is less common after the last birth, although some of the women who had worked longest appear to change to part time work before retirement.

Summary and conclusions

This chapter is the first of two describing results from the complete retrospective work histories collected from all women in the survey who had finished their full time education. It shows the changes that have occurred over time in women's economic activity by analysing the proportion of women in different age groups working at different dates; this illustrates three trends.

Firstly, the *age* profiles of women's labour force participation have been changing over time. Whilst in each time period there is a pattern of high participation rates for non-student women in their teens and lower rates for women in their late twenties followed by a rise as women move out of the main childbearing age, in more recent years the initial decline is smaller, and there are higher rates among women in their thirties and forties. Secondly a *period* effect was demonstrated by looking at the way in which the proportion of women working in a particular age group has been changing over time. This again showed the steep rise in participation rates for women in their thirties and forties since the 1960s. Thirdly, *cohort or generational* effects were examined by showing how the proportion of women in a particular birth cohort changes as women move through successive ages. For ages of 30 and over, each cohort that could be examined showed a higher participation rate at a given age than the preceding cohort. These results confirm trends established from other sources which show that the increase in women's participation in recent years is due mainly to increased participation among women in their thirties and forties, and is largely in part time rather than full time working.

As well as describing changes over time in aggregate terms, the work histories enabled us to summarise the employment patterns of individual women. On average all women born since 1941 (aged 35 or over at the time of the survey) had spent around 60% of their lives working. Without supposing any further increase in women's participation, this implies that women now in their late thirties will have spent at least 64% of their lives since leaving school in work by the time they reach retirement age, while younger women can be expected to work for about 67% of their potential working lives. If the trends towards increased participation among women in their thirties and forties were to continue, these figures would be expected to be higher.

The relationship between childbearing and labour market participation was then examined. Childless women spent the major part of their lives since leaving school in full time employment – 87% of this time on average. Women who had had children also worked full time throughout most of the period of their lives prior to childbearing, though women whose first birth occurred before the mid-1950s worked for a slightly lower proportion of time since leaving school. Stopping work on marriage would have still been fairly common among the older women in the sample and may have contributed to this. In fact the proportion of women who did not work at all between marriage and their first birth fell from around 37% of those with a first birth in the 1940s to 12% of those whose first birth occurred since 1970. Moreover, a significant proportion of all women who recently said they stopped work on marriage were also pregnant.

For most women their first birth was associated with the start of a period out of the labour market lasting several years. Overall 14% of women returned to work within six months of their first birth, but only 3% of women who had had more children returned to work within six months of each birth. However, the proportion of women returning to work within six months of their first birth was shown to be rising over time; this proportion varied according to occupation and level of qualification: clerical and sales workers were least likely to return to work within six months of having a first baby and the most highly qualified women (with 'A' levels or above) returned sooner than others.

Although most women stopped work for a time following their first birth they did not leave the labour force permanently. We showed that 78% of women had already returned to work at some time since their first birth although some of these still had very young children. Amongst women with grown-up children, 90% had returned to work at some time and this proportion was rising over time.

The survey also provided clear evidence of changes over time in the rates at which women returned to work following childbearing. For example, half of all the women who had their first baby between 1975-79 had returned to work for at least a time within four years of the birth while it was almost ten years before a comparable proportion of women with first births in 1950-54 had returned to work. These changes were almost entirely attributable to increasing proportions of women returning initially to part time work.

Although in aggregate women in the survey appeared to show a bimodal work profile (an initial period of work followed by a withdrawal from work for childbearing and then a return to work) our data illustrates that for many women the picture was more complex. Women increasingly tend to return to work between births and to return to work sooner after childbearing is finished, particularly if they have worked between births.

Both the timing of the initial return to work following childbearing and subsequent movement in and out of work affect the proportion of their lives women eventually spend working following childbearing. All women whose first baby was born before 1965, and who

therefore had in general completed their families had worked for at least 45% of the time since their first birth. It is therefore likely that women who have started families more recently will work for a significantly higher proportion of their lives than this by retirement. Women whose first births were in 1940-44 had worked on average for 17 years since childbearing so at a conservative estimate we can expect younger women to work for around 20 years following childbearing unless there is a significant fall in women's participation.

Most women who had returned to work had not changed their work status since returning, though they were more likely to the longer they had worked. Similar proportions of women changed from part to full time work as from full to part time work. This rather surprising result is partly explained by the different timing of these changes. An initial return to full time work was more common among women who returned to work between births than among those who waited till their families were complete, but early returners were particularly likely to change their work status subsequently. Women who returned to work part time after their latest birth, were increasingly likely to change to a full time job the longer they worked. However, in addition there was some evidence that women who had worked longest appeared to change to part time work in the years leading up to retirement. The changes between full and part time work described in this chapter were often associated with changes in occupation; these are discussed next.

Notes

[1] This survey provides a very comprehensive source of data about women's working lives which can be analysed in many different ways. The analyses presented in this report are by no means exhaustive. Additional tables are given in the technical report, and other researchers, as we described in Chapter 1, are involved in further analysis of the data.

[2] End of marriage was the point at which the couple separated rather than the legal end of the marriage.

[3] Because we are using a different length of time to constitute a period for the purposes of this analysis from that used on the National Training Survey, and are looking at all women of working age not just women at work, we get different results from Elias and Main (1982).

[4] Estimates provided by H Joshi.

[5] The lower proportion of women over 50 compared with those in their 40s who had been continuously economically active is partly explained by the fact that some older women who had in fact retired from the labour market said that they were not working for domestic reasons.

[6] The group of women with first births in 1940-44 is probably rather atypical because only the youngest women having first births in this period will be included in our sample and patterns of births were also distorted by the war.

[7] Dex also shows that it becomes increasingly rare for women to return immediately after successive births; very few women work continuously over the family formation phase. Moreover, only when a first birth precedes marriage is it more often associated with remaining in the labour market (1984a).

[8] Dex (1984a) looks at an unemployment effect in her analysis and shows that labour market conditions affect some women's inflow into the labour market. Women who are least affected are those who worked most.

[9] Both Joshi and Dex discuss in greater detail how to interpret the early returns of women who work between births. The statistical difficulty of establishing whether this is because of 'state dependence' or 'fixed effects' is discussed by Joshi (1984).

Chapter 10   Job changes and occupational mobility

Introduction
This chapter examines women's mobility within the labour market, in contrast to their movement in and out of the labour market which was described in Chapter 9. We look at the extent to which women in the sample changed employers and their reasons for doing so, and the extent to which they changed occupations, particularly on returning to work after childbirth and in relation to changes between full and part time work.

Job changing arouses a considerable amount of interest and concern from different quarters. It is often argued that women are less stable employees than men, that they are liable to leave jobs for domestic reasons and consequently it is not worth employers investing resources in training them. It is also argued that women returning to work after a period out of the labour market bringing up children cannot find jobs which use their skills and experience, particularly if they want part time employment, and so are often underemployed (Elias and Main, 1982). Employers are also often seen as reluctant to retrain these women although they may have some twenty or thirty years of working life ahead of them.

Popular discussion of women's job mobility tends to ignore internal movement within an employing organisation. As a result 'changing jobs' is seen as synonymous with 'changing employer'. Women, like men, however, may be promoted, or move into a different occupation and stay with the same employer. Alternatively they may change employer but do the same type of work or job. They may also leave a job, an employer and the labour market at the same time, so that a 'job quit' is simultaneously an 'employment quit'. Although we collected data on job changes with an employer we

do not discuss these here. We do attempt to explore in this chapter, however, the proportion of 'job quits' which in fact result in women leaving the labour market rather than in mobility within the labour market.

We also examine in this chapter the reasons women gave for leaving past employers and distinguish between domestic and job related or non-domestic reasons. It is important to know, for example, whether domestic reasons are given disproportionately when women leave employers to stop work (which is what we would expect) or whether women also frequently change jobs for domestic reasons too. In a sense we are identifying to what extent women behave differently from men as workers, though we cannot make direct comparisons as no nationally comparable data have been collected for men (Curran, 1982).

In the latter part of the chapter we look at those job moves which involve a change of occupation. Initially we look at the extent and type of occupational moves our respondents made and then consider the direction of the occupational change. This allows us to show in broad terms the extent to which women experience downward occupational mobility on returning to work following childbirth and whether they recover from such movement subsequently in their working lives.[1]

The extent of changes of employer over women's working lives
The work histories collected on this survey provide a record of each episode of employment women have had; this covers, by occupation and industry, all the jobs women had had in each period of employment and their duration and, for women who had left employers, their reasons for leaving each employer. We can there-

Table 10.1   Distribution and average number of employers worked for since leaving school by years worked since leaving school

Number of employers	Years worked since leaving school					All who have worked
	Up to 5 years	Over 5 up to 10 years	Over 10 up to 15 years	Over 15 up to 20 years	Over 20 years	
	%	%	%	%	%	%
1	32	12	6	2	2	11
2	28	20	10	7	7	15
3	18	18	17	13	10	15
4	12	17	16	16	13	15
5	5	14	18	14	17	14
6	3	8	12	15	13	10
7	1	5	7	9	12	7
8	1	2	5	8	7	4
9	0	2	4	6	7	4
10 or more	0	2	5	10	12	5
	100	100	100	100	100	100
Average number of employers	2.5	3.8	4.8	5.7	6.1	4.6
Average number of years worked per employer	1.4	2.8	3.5	4.0	6.2	3.6
Base	973	1,286	1,021	729	1,228	5,237

fore examine the extent to which women changed employers over the whole of their working lives and at particular stages. We can also look at their reasons for leaving employers at different stages of their lives and so identify what proportion of 'job quits' were also 'employment quits'.

We start by looking at the extent to which women had changed employers over their whole working lives up to the point at the survey. The number of employers they have worked for is likely to be related to the length of time they have been working and so we show the results by the number of years worked since leaving school in Table 10.1. On average women had worked for just under 5 employers (4.6) in the course of their working lives. This figure varied from 2.5 employers for women who had worked for five years or less to around 6 employers for those who had worked for over 15 years. There was considerable variation in the number of employers worked for by women with working lives of comparable lengths. Thus, among women who had worked for 5 years or less, 32% had worked for only one employer while 5% had had 6 or more employers. Among women with the longest working lives, over 20 years, only 2% had worked for just one employer, while 12% had worked for 10 or more.

However, the rate at which women change employers slows down as working life progresses. Women who had been working for five years or less had worked on average for only 1.4 years with each employer. The length of time spent on average with an employer rose with the number of years worked so women who had worked for over 20 years averaged 6.2 years with each employer. These averages, however, conceal a lot of individual variations as the distributions of numbers of employers women had worked for, shown in Table 10.1, indicate.

Changes of employer before childbearing
If we expect at least some of women's changes of employment to be associated with movement in and out of the labour market in relation to childbearing and childcare responsibilities, it is of interest to look at the phase of women's lives before children are born so that we can establish how often women change employers during this phase and then go on to look at the effect on employment changes of having children.

We examined the number of employers all women had worked for during the childless phase of their lives in relation to the number of years they had worked while childless. We did this by looking at the number of employers childless women had worked for, and the number of employers those women who had subsequently had children had worked for in their childless phase. Results for these two groups of women were analysed separately. We found no significant differences between childless women and those who had gone on to have children in the numbers of employers worked for whilst childless, once differences in the numbers of years they had worked had been taken into account.

Table 10.2 shows that women had worked on average for 3 employers while childless. Although the average number of employers worked for increased with the length of time worked it did not increase very sharply. Women who had worked for five years or less had worked for just over 2 employers on average, while those who had worked for more than 20 years (the majority of whom are unlikely now ever to have children) had worked for around 5 employers. This suggests that women change employers most frequently during the early years of their working life. That this is so is shown clearly by looking at the average length of time worked per employer. Women had worked on average for 3.6 years per employer during the childless phase of their lives, but those who had worked for five years or less had worked for only 1.7 years per employer compared with an average of 9 years among those who had worked for over twenty years.

These results confirm findings of other studies which show that people change jobs most frequently at the start of their working lives (Brannen, 1975; Cherry, 1976). They become less likely to change employers as their working lives proceed. These job changes moreover rarely involved a break in employment since for many women the first interruption to their working

Table 10.2 Distribution and average number of employers worked for while childless by years worked while childless

Number of employers	Years worked while childless					All women who have worked while childless
	Up to 5 years	Over 5 up to 10 years	Over 10 up to 15 years	Over 15 up to 20 years	Over 20 years	
	%	%	%	%	%	%
1	37	20	16	13	8	24
2	30	28	19	14	13	25
3	8	21	20	17	13	19
4	9	14	15	15	15	13
5	4	8	12	13	13	8
6	1	4	7	9	11	4
7	1	3	4	5	11	3
8	0	1	3	5	8	2
9	0	1	2	4	4	1
10 or more	0	0	2	5	4	1
	100	100	100	100	100	100
Average number of employers	2.2	3.0	3.6	4.5	4.8	3.0
Average number of years worked per employer	1.7	3.4	4.9	6.0	9.1	3.6
Base	*1,652*	*2,114*	*815*	*239*	*296*	*5,116**

Excluding 47 women where years worked not known

Table 10.3 Distribution and average number of employers worked for since first birth by years worked since first birth: women with children

Number of employers since first birth	Years worked since first birth					All who have worked since first birth
	Up to 5 years	Over 5 up to 10 years	Over 10 up to 15 years	Over 15 up to 20 years	Over 20 years	
	%	%	%	%	%	%
1	56	26	20	14	12	34
2	25	30	22	24	20	25
3	11	19	17	16	20	16
4	4	11	16	14	14	10
5	2	6	11	9	13	6
6	1	4	7	8	8	4
7	1	2	3	6	4	2
8	0	1	2	4	2	1
9	0	1	1	1	2	1
10 or more	0	0	1	4	5	1
	100	**100**	**100**	**100**	**100**	**100**
Average number of employers since first birth	1.8	2.7	3.3	3.8	3.9	2.7
Average number of years worked per employer since first birth	1.4	3.8	5.5	6.8	9.4	4.1
Base	1,141	764	518	335	307	3.065

life occurred with the arrival of their first child. However, before this event women who subsequently went on to have children were no more or less likely to change employers than women who at the time of the survey had not had children.

Changes of employer after childbearing
Having established how often women without children changed employers we now look at women with children. We examined the whole of their working lives since the birth of the first child, which meant that for many women we were covering the period in which other children were born. Table 10.3 shows that women with children had worked on average for just under three employers since their first birth, but those who had worked for 5 years or less had averaged just under 2 employers. This figure rose to nearly 3 employers for those who had worked between 5 and 10 years and thereafter rose slowly so that women who had worked for over 20 years since their first birth had had on average just under 4 employers. The average number of years worked for each employer rose steeply with the number of years women worked since the first birth, indicating that women had become less likely to change employers the longer they stay in the labour market after their childbearing phase.

If we compare these results with the extent to which women changed employers before the birth of any children, it is the lack of difference between them which is striking (Tables 10.2 and 10.3). Women with children were not significantly more likely to change employers than those without. Overall, women in the childless phase of their lives had worked for slightly more employers and had averaged slightly fewer years with each employer than women in the period after the birth of a child. However, if we compare women who had worked for the same lengths of time it is apparent that among those who had worked the shortest periods of time, women with children were more likely to have changed employers than those without. This group includes women who had moved in and out of the labour market and changed employers between births. Among those who had worked for longer periods of time,

however, the women who had children appeared to be the more stable employees. This was mainly because of job mobility among those who had just started work who were mostly childless. To throw more light on the differences and similarities between women with and without children we go on to examine not only the extent to which they changed employers but their reasons for doing so.

Reasons for leaving employers
We were particularly interested in comparing the extent to which women left jobs for reasons that are likely to apply to all workers: redundancy or dismissal, moving to a better job, illness or injury, as opposed to the domestic reasons which we would expect to be given predominantly by women, particularly those who had children.

Table 10.4 looks at all the employers women have left over the course of their working lives and shows the proportion left for different reasons. It also shows whether the women left the employer to start straight away with a new employer, or whether they stopped work, that is left employment. The sample of over 5,000 women who had worked since leaving school had each left four employers on average, and so the results are based on some 20,000 instances of women leaving employers.

Table 10.4 shows that for 44% of the occasions when women left employers they left for domestic reasons (such as pregnancy or to look after children); thus for just over half (56%) such occasions employers were left for non-domestic reasons which might be given by any employees, male or female, with or without children. The most common of these reasons, (39%), was to go to a better job or because of dissatisfaction with a job. Reasons such as redundancy or dismissal were given in 13% of cases and illness or injury accounted for the remaining 4%. Interestingly, there was little variation in the reasons women gave for leaving employers regardless of the length of time they had worked, apart from those women who had worked for less than five years. This category had a much higher proportion of cases where women had left because of redundancy or dismissal and fewer instances of domestic reasons for leaving. It contained many of the recent school leavers who were particularly likely to be affected by the recession and as short service employees may be vulnerable to redundancy. Moreover many were still childless and therefore unlikely to leave for domestic reasons.

When they left an employer, our respondents in the majority (56%) of cases went straight to a new employer; in 44% of cases they stopped working, becoming either unemployed or economically inactive. Stopping work was less common the longer women had worked, both because unemployment was affecting younger women most at the time of the survey and because the longer women had worked the more likely it was that the childbearing period had passed. While there was some congruence between leaving an employer for domestic reasons and stopping work this was not completely so as Table 10.4 shows.

Looking separately just at childless women, we can see in Table 10.5 that although non-domestic reasons were given for leaving the majority of employers, 28% were left for domestic reasons; this may seem high considering these women did not have children. However, these reasons included stopping work or changing jobs to be able to care for a relative and (frequently) job changes made to fit in with the husband's employment; this, as Dex shows, happened more to women in higher non-manual jobs (Dex, 1984b). Amongst the non-domestic reasons, leaving an employer voluntarily (for a better job) accounted for 43% of all 'job quits' and was the most common type of reason irrespective of the number of years women had worked. Having to leave jobs because of redundancy, dismissal etc accounted for 23% of occasions on which women left employers, but this figure was much higher (37%) among women who had worked for five years or less. In contrast, illness or injury, not surprisingly, (though it was not a very frequent reason overall), was most often mentioned among women who had worked longest who were also older women.

In 60% of cases childless women leaving employers went straight to another job, but in 40% of cases they stopped work either to be unemployed or to be inactive.[2] Stopping work was less likely among women who had worked longest, presumably because the youngest women were most vulnerable to redundancy and unemployment. However, even childless women sometimes stopped work for domestic reasons, and could do so at any stage of their life.

Turning to look at the women who had had children,

Table 10.4 Proportion of employers left for different reasons, and left to go to a new employer or to stop work, by years worked since leaving school

	Years worked since leaving school					All who have worked
	Up to 5 years	Over 5 up to 10 years	Over 10 up to 15 years	Over 15 up to 20 years	Over 20 years	
	%	%	%	%	%	%
Reason for leaving employer	*Proportion of employers left*					
Left involuntarily (eg redundant, dismissed)	22	12	12	11	14	13
Left voluntarily (eg for a better job)	37	39	40	39	39	39
Left through illness or injury	3	4	3	5	5	4
Left for domestic reasons	38	45	45	45	43	44
All employers left	**100**	**100**	**100**	**100**	**100**	**100**
Destination						
Went straight to new employer	50	53	55	56	60	56
Stopped work	50	47	45	44	40	44
All employers left	**100**	**100**	**100**	**100**	**100**	**100**
Average number of employers left	*1.9*	*3.3*	*4.2*	*5.0*	*5.3*	*3.9*
(Number of women	*973*	*1,286*	*1,021*	*729*	*1,228*	*5,237)*

Table 10.5 Proportion of employers left for different reasons, and left to go to a new employer or to stop work, by years worked since leaving school: childless women

	Years worked since leaving school					All childless women who have worked
	Up to 5 years	Over 5 up to 10 years	Over 10 up to 15 years	Over 15 up to 20 years	Over 20 years	
	%	%	%	%	%	%
Reason for leaving employer	*Proportion of employers left*					
Left involuntarily (eg redundant, dismissed)	37	21	16	2	20	23
Left voluntarily (eg for a better job)	43	47	43	46	41	43
Left through illness or injury	3	5	5	9	8	6
Left for domestic reasons	16	27	36	33	31	28
All employers left	**100**	**100**	**100**	**100**	**100**	**100**
Destination						
Went straight to new employer	53	57	60	64	64	60
Stopped work	47	43	40	36	36	40
All employers left	**100**	**100**	**100**	**100**	**100**	**100**
Average number of employers left	*1.3*	*2.4*	*3.4*	*4.3*	*4.1*	*2.5*
(Number of women	*509*	*300*	*147*	*94*	*266*	*1,316)*

we can see from Table 10.6 these women left employers before their first birth for domestic reasons in almost half the cases (48%). This is not surprising since the majority of them left their employer during their first pregnancy. Nevertheless, leaving employers because of dissatisfaction or to go to a better job were almost as frequently cited (40%). There was very little difference in the type of reason given according to how long women had worked before the first birth. Moreover these women were no more likely to stop work in the period before they had children than were childless women. In only 40% of cases did they stop work on leaving an employer, and in most cases this occurred because they stopped work in pregnancy. But as Table 10.6 shows, domestic reasons also caused some women to change employers rather than to stop work altogether.

A similar picture emerges if one looks at the reasons women gave for leaving employers once they had returned to work after having had one or more children (Table 10.7). Again domestic reasons were given less frequently than other reasons although some of these women left work with later pregnancies and others left employers because they had problems associated with their children. Women left employers for domestic reasons in 35% of cases, but this was not much higher than the figure for childless women (28%) shown in

Table 10.5. Domestic reasons did not become less common as the number of years worked since the first birth increased, probably because they cover not only the care of children but also the care of sick or elderly relatives. As we showed in Chapter 8, this category of domestic caring is most likely to affect women in their fifties.

Women who left employers after the start of childbearing were almost as likely to stop work as go to a new employer, particularly amongst those who had worked fewest years since their first birth. Some of these younger women will have stopped and started work again with later births. At the other end of the age scale, some of those who had worked longest since their first birth but had now stopped work were women in their fifties who considered they had retired.

This section has shown that in the majority of cases women left employers for job-related or non-domestic reasons, the single most important of which was to go to a better job. Domestic reasons, as might be expected, were more frequently given by women with children, but nevertheless also account for a significant minority of the reasons why childless women left employers. When women left employers they were more likely to go straight to a new employer than to stop work. With this evidence, it is clear that the common

Table 10.6 Proportion of employers left for different reasons, and left to go to a new employer or to stop work, by years worked before first birth

	Years worked before first birth					All who worked before first birth*
	Up to 5 years	Over 5 up to 10 years	Over 10 up to 15 years	Over 15 up to 20 years	Over 20 years	
	%	%	%	%	%	%
Reason for leaving employer	*Proportion of employers left*					
Left involuntarily (eg redundant, dismissed)	10	8	10	11	7	9
Left voluntarily (eg for a better job)	38	40	42	43	41	40
Left through illness or injury	3	3	2	1	5	3
Left for domestic reasons	49	49	46	46	47	48
All employers left before first birth	**100**	**100**	**100**	**100**	**100**	**100**
Destination						
Went straight to new employer	56	60	64	65	66	60
Stopped work	44	40	36	35	34	40
All employers left before first birth	**100**	**100**	**100**	**100**	**100**	**100**
Average number of employers left before first birth	*1.5*	*2.3*	*2.8*	*3.1*	*3.6*	*2.9*
(Number of women	*1,143*	*1,814*	*668*	*145*	*30*	*3,800)*

Excludes 47 cases where years worked before first birth not known

Table 10.7 Proportion of employers left for different reasons and left to go to a new employer or to stop work, by years worked since first birth

	Years worked since first birth					All who have worked since first birth
	Up to 5 years	Over 5 up to 10 years	Over 10 up to 15 years	Over 15 up to 20 years	Over 20 years	
	%	%	%	%	%	%
Reason for leaving employer	*Proportion of employers left*					
Left involuntarily (eg redundant, dismissed)	22	16	19	20	14	18
Left voluntarily (eg for a better job)	37	37	40	39	43	40
Left through illness or injury	6	8	7	7	6	7
Left for domestic reasons	35	39	34	34	37	35
All employers left since first birth	**100**	**100**	**100**	**100**	**100**	**100**
Destination						
Went straight to new employer	47	49	54	54	56	52
Stopped work	53	51	46	46	44	48
All employers left since first birth	**100**	**100**	**100**	**100**	**100**	**100**
Average number of employers left since first birth	*1.1*	*2.0*	*2.6*	*3.0*	*3.2*	*1.9*
(Number of women	*1,125*	*764*	*518*	*335*	*307*	*3,049)*

view that women leave jobs and stop work mainly for domestic reasons is a distortion of a more complex reality. At some stages of their lives, notably the family formation phase, women are more likely to stop work when they leave jobs. Throughout the rest of their working lives, however, they are more likely to change jobs than stop work and in the majority of instances to do this for the same type of job related reasons as male workers.

Occupational mobility over women's lives

Having looked at the extent to which women change employers and their reasons for doing so, we look next at whether when women change jobs they also change the type of job they do and so move from one occupational category to another. Throughout the survey women's jobs have been classified into the 12 occupational groups described in Chapter 3; in this section we examine changes of employment which resulted in movement between these twelve categories. First we examine the extent to which women worked in jobs in different occupational categories over the course of their working lives and then we examine in more detail the directions of the occupational changes they made.

We recognise throughout our analysis that the extent and nature of the occupational movement we identify is a product of our classification system. A different system with a more finely differentiated scale for example, would enable movement to be shown in greater detail and might result in greater vertical movement being shown which is currently hidden within broad categories. Similarly some of the movement between categories which we describe might not be movement in real terms as it reflects an allocation of some jobs to particular social classes which is increasingly criticised. The classic example (as we have pointed out earlier) is shop work, though as Dex argues, much of the semi-skilled work and lower level clerical work women does appear comparable in many respects, suggesting that some clerical work is also wrongly categorised (Dex, 1984b).[3]

Obviously not all changes of employment involve a change of occupation, particularly if we consider only major changes of occupation: those which involve women changing from one occupational category to another on our classification. It is generally considered quite normal for men to change jobs within an occupa-tion, for example to obtain wider experience, to move up a career ladder, or because they happen to work in particularly unstable occupations (Marsh and Heady, 1981). Employers who lose expensively trained staff in this way can only compensate by recruiting others with relevant training and experience. But if skills and experience acquired in one job are used in the next, the skills are not wasted from the individual's or society's point of view, although they may seem so to the employer. If, however, people change to a completely different occupation their skills and experience may well not be used. This is held to be a particular problem for women who have had an interrupted working life and return to a different type of job when they go back to work.

Table 10.8 shows that on average women had worked in just over two occupational groups in their working lives up to the time of the interview. Even amongst women who had worked for over twenty years the average was under three. Nevertheless, few women stayed in jobs in the same occupational category for the whole of their working lives. Almost two thirds had worked in more than one occupational group and those who had worked in only one occupation tended to be those who had spent the least time in employment so far: over half (54%) of women who had worked for 5 years or less worked in only one occupational group. However, even among women who had worked for over 20 years, a substantial minority (20%) had stayed in the same occupational category throughout their working lives.[4]

As it seems likely that women returning to the labour force after a break for children will be more likely to return to a different type of job we compare next the number of different occupational categories in which childless women had worked over their working lives in relation to those of women with children. Table 10.9 shows that childless women, on average, worked in under two occupations, whereas Table 10.10 shows that women with children have averaged well over two. Women with children were, on average, older and had worked for longer than childless women, but even where women who had worked the same number of years are compared, women with children had worked on average in more occupational categories than childless women. The differences are even bigger when

Table 10.8 Distribution and average number of different occupational categories worked in by women since leaving school by years worked since leaving school

Number of different occupational categories	Years worked since leaving school					All who have worked
	Up to 5 years	Over 5 up to 10 years	Over 10 up to 15 years	Over 15 up to 20 years	Over 20 years	
	%	%	%	%	%	%
1	54	41	30	25	20	34
2	31	31	32	30	28	30
3	12	20	24	25	26	21
4	3	6	10	14	18	10
5	0	2	4	5	6	3
6 or more	–	1	1	1	2	1
	100	**100**	**100**	**100**	**100**	**100**
Average number of different occupational categories	1.7	2.0	2.3	2.5	2.7	2.2
Base	973	1,286	1,021	729	1,228	5,237

Table 10.9 Average number of different occupational categories worked in by childless women since leaving school by years worked since leaving school

	Years worked since leaving school					All childless women who have worked
	Up to 5 years	Over 5 up to 10 years	Over 10 up to 15 years	Over 15 up to 20 years	Over 20 years	
Average number of different occupational categories	1.5	1.7	1.8	1.9	2.1	% 1.7
Base	*509*	*300*	*147*	*94*	*266*	*1,316*

Table 10.10 Average number of different occupational categories worked in by women with children since leaving school by years worked since leaving school

	Years worked since leaving school					All women with children who have worked
	Up to 5 years	Over 5 up to 10 years	Over 10 up to 15 years	Over 15 up to 20 years	Over 20 years	
Average number of different occupational categories	1.8	2.1	2.4	2.6	2.8	2.4
Base	*464*	*986*	*874*	*635*	*962*	*3,921*

allowance is made for the fact that not all the women with children in Table 10.10 have returned to work after having children. We look at these life stage differences below.

Occupational change at different life stages
In order to examine occupational mobility in greater detail we now focus on the jobs which women held at key points in their lives and the occupational categories in which they fall. By comparing jobs held at particular points in women's lives and ignoring all changes of job in between we are obviously underestimating the extent of occupational change in total, but this approach allows us to summarise the major features of occupational change for women, and to look at them in relation to movement between full and part time work. More detailed analysis of occupational mobility using these data undertaken by Dex shows that comparing jobs at two points in time does indeed underestimate total occupational mobility (Dex, 1984b). However, our approach gives a broad indication of some of the major features of occupational mobility for women, particularly that associated with childbearing, so we distinguish throughout between childless women and women who have had children.

Table 10.11 Proportion of women working in jobs in different occupational categories at different life stages

	% of women with jobs in different occupational categories	*Base*
Childless women		
First job and most recent job	40%	*1,316*
Women with children		
First job and last job before first birth	38%	*3,847**
Last job before first birth and first job since first birth	51%	*3,019†*
First job since first birth and most recent job since first birth	40%	*3,088‡*
Last job before first birth and most recent job since first birth	59%	*3,019†*

*Women who worked before first birth
†Women who worked before and since first birth
‡Women who worked since first birth

For childless women we examined net occupational change over their whole working lives to date by comparing their first with their most recent job. For women with children we took four key points. The first job, the last job before the first birth, the first job since the first birth and the most recent job since the first birth. Clearly not all women had worked before and since the first birth and so comparisons are based on women who had had both the jobs in question.

Table 10.11 shows that among childless women 40% had first jobs which were in a different occupational category from that of their most recent job. This is a similar proportion to the 38% of women with children whose first job was in a different occupational category from that of their last job before childbirth. In contrast, 51% of women with children who had worked pre- and post-childbirth were in jobs in a different occupational category when they returned to work although these women had not worked at all between the two jobs, that is these were absolutely sequential jobs separated only by a period of non-working.

When we compared the first job following the first birth with the most recent job since childbirth, we found 40% of all women who had made a return to work were in a job in a different occupational category from that of their initial post-return job. Although this is a smaller proportion than the 51% who changed occupations after a break in employment for childbearing, it must be remembered that some of this latter group had only recently returned to work following childbirth and so had had little time in which to make further occupational changes since their return. Lastly, we compared the job women were in before their first birth and their most recent job since childbirth. This showed by far the biggest difference, since for 59% of women these jobs were in different occupational categories. We shall be using this comparison in the next section to see the extent to which women who returned to different occupations following childbirth reverted to the same occupation as before childbirth later in their working lives.

This brief overview gives some idea of the extent of occupational change between key points in women's lives and demonstrates firstly that overall the extent of occupational change is quite marked and secondly that it is intensified by interruptions in work due to childbirth. We look next at the direction of these occupational changes and relate them to changes between full and part time work.

The direction of occupational change

We particularly wanted to examine the direction of occupational change over women's lifetime to see the extent of vertical mobility associated with combining employment with domestic responsibilities. It was impossible in a retrospective study covering such a timescale to ask women very many details about each job or change of job. We do not know, for example, whether changes of jobs or changes of occupations involved changes in earnings or other aspects of employment, such as promotion opportunities, information which might enable us to study in more detail the consequences of occupational change, or the full employment consequences of a break in employment. Instead we have had to take a job's position in the occupational classification used on the survey as a proxy for its quality.

Our occupational categories approximately form an ordinal scale, which enables us to study movement up and down the scale. This was based, as we described in Chapter 3, on the social class categories which themselves are normally assumed to form an ordinal scale. There are problems with this however. Even if the social class scale adequately ranks men's occupations, which is perhaps questionable, the scale has not been verified empirically for women's occupations. Results in earlier chapters indicate that it is extremely doubtful that sales occupations should be considered in any way higher than all the manual occupations. By taking social class as the basis for studying occupational mobility therefore we are working within the confines of its

limitations for women's occupations. In addition, our division and ordering of the social class categories has also not been empirically validated. As a result our analysis of occupational mobility using this scale should be viewed as giving an indication of the extent of upwards and downwards occupational change for women, but the exact proportions are a function of the scale itself and would differ somewhat if a scale known to be suitable for ordering women's jobs was available.[5]

Whatever occupational scale is used it is apparent, as Table 10.12 shows, that women were found in different occupations at different stages of their lives. This suggests that they moved occupations as they passed through different life phases. Table 10.12 shows the current occupation, using our occupational classification, of working women by their current life cycle stage. Childless women were much more likely than women with children to be found in non-manual occupations, particularly in the higher level occupations which fall in Social Classes I and II, and in the clerical occupations. Older childless women were particularly likely to be found in the higher level occupations. Women with children, in contrast, were much more likely to be in manual occupations, particularly semi-skilled domestic and unskilled occupations.

Although this cross-sectional picture is compatible with occupational movement at different life stages other possible explanations also need to be considered. For example, we know that the proportion of women currently working varies by life cycle stage. It could therefore be the case that women in manual occupations, particularly semi-skilled domestic and unskilled occupations, are more likely to be working once they have had children than women in non-manual occupations. We also need to consider generational changes. Women aged 50–59 at the time of the survey probably started in different occupations from recent school leavers and this may influence their current occupation. They were certainly less likely to have formal edu-

Table 10.12 Current occupation of working women by life cycle stage

Current occupational group	Life cycle stage							All women except full time students
	Childless women aged:		Women with youngest child aged:			Women with all children aged 16 and over, aged:		
	Under 30	30 or over	0–4	5–10	11–15	Under 50	50 or over	
	%	%	%	%	%	%	%	%
Professional	1	2	1	1	–	0	0	1
Teaching	5	14	7	6	4	4	5	6
Nursing, medical and social	6	7	9	6	7	6	7	7
Other intermediate non-manual	5	13	5	4	6	5	6	6
Clerical	48	35	19	21	29	31	22	30
Sales	9	4	8	8	11	9	10	9
Total non-manual	**74**	**75**	**49**	**46**	**57**	**55**	**50**	**59**
Skilled manual	8	6	8	5	8	7	7	7
Semi-skilled factory	10	10	9	10	10	12	13	10
Semi-skilled domestic	4	2	19	20	10	12	13	11
Other semi-skilled	3	4	4	5	3	6	3	4
Unskilled	1	3	11	14	12	8	14	9
Total manual	**26**	**25**	**51**	**54**	**43**	**45**	**50**	**41**
	100	100	100	100	100	100	100	100
Base	758	328	276	553	538	362	539	3,354

Table 10.13 First occupation in working life by age: all women who have ever worked

First occupation	Age									All women who have ever worked
	16–19	20–24	25–29	30–34	35–39	40–44	45–49	50–54	55–59	
	%	%	%	%	%	%	%	%	%	%
Professional	–	–	2	1	1	1	0	0	0	1
Teaching	0	2	6	7	5	5	3	3	2	4
Nursing, medical and social	2	4	5	4	5	5	3	2	4	4
Other intermediate non-manual	1	2	3	2	2	2	2	1	1	2
Clerical	38	39	39	37	38	36	34	25	19	33
Sales	18	17	16	16	19	15	14	17	12	16
Total non-manual	**59**	**64**	**71**	**67**	**70**	**64**	**56**	**48**	**38**	**60**
Skilled manual	9	10	9	9	8	6	10	7	10	9
Childcare	1	1	1	1	1	2	3	2	2	2
Semi-skilled factory	18	15	15	15	17	20	21	26	27	18
Semi-skilled domestic	7	4	2	3	1	3	4	7	12	5
Other semi-skilled	4	4	2	4	2	4	4	6	6	4
Unskilled	2	2	0	1	1	1	2	4	5	2
Total manual	**41**	**36**	**29**	**33**	**30**	**36**	**44**	**52**	**62**	**40**
	100	**100**	**100**	**100**	**100**	**100**	**100**	**100**	**100**	**100**
Base	*312*	*560*	*679*	*764*	*644*	*581*	*553*	*559*	*585*	*5,237*

cational qualifications which would affect the range of occupations open to them. These limitations to or difficulties of using cross-sectional data highlight the advantages of our longitudinal data. Only this sort of information allows proper measurement of change and correct interpretation of cross-sectional data.

Occupational change before childbearing

Table 10.13 does show some generational shifts or effects on occupations reflecting the shift from manufacturing to service employment over this period. Older women, for example, were more likely to have started their working lives in manual occupations, particularly semi-skilled factory work, than younger women, who were particularly likely to have started in clerical work. In addition, the youngest age group had few women in the higher occupations because most of these occupations require further education and are not started until people are in their early twenties.

We used the same key points of comparisons as in the previous section to look at the direction of net occupational mobility during the childless phase of women's lives (Tables 10.14 and 10.15). Comparing respondents' most recent job with their first job, 60% of childless women were in the same occupational category in both jobs, while for 24% the most recent job was in a higher category and for 16% it was in a lower category. A fairly similar picture is shown for women with children during the childless phase of their lives, although somewhat fewer (20%) were in a higher level occupation in the job before their first birth than in their first occupation. However, these women had worked for less time on average than the childless women and so had less time in which to move up the occupational scale. In fact, among childless women under 30 only 21% were in a higher level occupation in their most recent job, similar to the 20% of women with children, whereas 31% of childless women aged 30 and over were in a higher level job in their most recent job than in their first job. Moreover similar proportions in both groups were in lower level occupations.

Table 10.14 Occupational level of most recent job compared with first occupation in working life: childless women

	Childless women who have worked
	%
Most recent job is:	
higher	24
same	60
lower	16
level than first job in working life	**100**
Base	*1,316*

Table 10.15 Occupational level of last job before first birth compared with first job in working life: women with children

	All who worked before first birth
	%
Last job before first birth is:	
higher	20
same	62
lower	18
level than first job in working life	**100**
Base	*3,847*

Thus, there is evidence that in the absence of a break for childbearing a significant minority of women had moved up the occupational scale. Whether this is because women delay or forego childbearing in order to pursue careers or whether there is a general trend which is interrupted by childbearing is not clear. Our findings are similar to those of Greenhalgh and Stewart (1982a) who showed that single women who work full time (not necessarily childless women, though in many cases these equate) were more likely than married women to experience similar upward occupational mobility to men. Of course, we are looking only at major occupational shifts; women who move upwards in their career without changing occupation, for example, from a staff nurse to a nursing sister, cannot be detected from our data.

Occupational change after childbearing

We showed previously that 51% of women returned to

a job after childbirth in a different occupational category from that of the last job before their first birth. Table 10.16 sets out the nature of the change and shows that for 37% of women movement was downwards, while only 14% returned to a higher occupational category. This table also shows that downwards movement is strongly associated with returning to work part time: 45% of those who returned to work part time in the first instance returned to a job in a lower occupational category compared with only 19% of those who

Table 10.16 Occupational level of first job since first birth compared with last job before first birth by whether women first returned to full or part time work

	First return to work since first birth was to:		All who have worked before and since first birth
	Full time work	Part time work	
	%	%	%
First job since first birth is:			
higher	17	13	14
same	64	42	49
lower	19	45	37
level than last job before first birth	**100**	**100**	**100**
Base	957	2,062	3,019

returned full time. The majority of those returning full time stayed in the same occupational category but 17% moved to a higher category, as did 13% of those who returned part time.

However, we saw in the previous chapter that women returning to work full time do so sooner than those who return part time, and it seems likely that the longer a woman is away from work the more likely she is to return to a different occupation. This is shown in Table 10.17 which compares women returning to work full

and part time according to the length of time they were away from the labour market. Several factors have an effect on women's occupational status. It is clear, for example, that employment status does affect occupational level because among women with similar length breaks, those returning to part time jobs were much more likely to move to a lower level occupation than those returning full time. However secondly, the longer a woman was away from work altogether the less likely she was to return to the same occupation; she also became slightly more likely to move to a higher level occupation, particularly if she returned full time. We cannot tell from our results why this was so, though we suspect it may be an artefact of our classificatory system and illustrates, yet again, the dubious position of sales occupations and the heterogeneity of categories like nursing and clerical work.

As Table 10.17 shows, downward mobility does not go on increasing with length of time out of the labour market. Among women returning full time, those returning to work with a break of up to one year show the highest single proportion who moved to a lower level occupation (15%), (mostly accounted for by women returning after 6 months), no doubt because they were less likely to be returning to their old jobs. Thereafter the proportions moving down increased slowly to 25% while the proportion moving to a higher level occupation show a rather more consistent rise with length of time out of the labour market. Among women returning part time, where downward mobility was more common, the proportion moving to a lower level occupation increases to a maximum of 52% for women with over 10 years out of the labour market.

From these results we can see that both the length of time a woman spends out of the labour market and

Table 10.17 Occupational level of first job since first birth compared with last job before first birth by time between first birth and return to work and whether women first returned to full or part time work

	Time between first birth and return to work				All who worked before and since first birth
	Up to 1 year	Over 1 up to 5 years	Over 5 up to 10 years	Over 10 years	
	%	%	%	%	%
Returned to full time work following first birth					
First job since first birth is:					
higher	6	18	23	31	17
same	79	64	52	44	64
lower	15	18	25	25	19
level than last job before first birth	**100**	**100**	**100**	**100**	**100**
Base	384	246	156	171	957
Returned to part time work following first birth					
First job first birth is:					
higher	11	11	14	17	13
same	62	45	35	31	42
lower	27	44	51	52	45
level than last job before first birth	**100**	**100**	**100**	**100**	**100**
Base	371	545	603	543	2,062
All who worked before and since first birth					
First job first birth is:					
higher	8	13	16	20	14
same	70	51	39	34	49
lower	22	36	45	45	37
level than last job before first birth	**100**	**100**	**100**	**100**	**100**
Base	755	791	759	714	3,019

Table 10.18 Occupational level of most recent job compared with first job since first birth by whether most recent job was full or part time and whether first return to work since first birth was full or part time

	Most recent job was full time			Most recent job was part time			All who have worked since first birth		
	First return since first birth was to:		All	First return since first birth was to:		All	First return since first birth was to:		All
	Full time work	Part time work		Full time work	Part time work		Full time work	Part time work	
	%	%	%	%	%	%	%	%	%
Most recent job is:									
higher	19	45	30	25	17	18	21	23	23
same	69	44	58	31	67	61	56	62	60
lower	12	11	12	44	16	21	23	15	17
level than first job since first birth	**100**	**100**	**100**	**100**	**100**	**100**	**100**	**100**	**100**
Base	656	487	1,143	341	1,604	1,945	997	2,091	3,088

whether she returns to a full or part time job are associated with occupational mobility. However length of time out of the labour market following childbearing is more strongly associated with occupational mobility in general rather than either upward or downward mobility in particular. In contrast downward mobility is particularly associated with returning to work part time rather than full time.

Occupational mobility following the initial return to work

In so far as a substantial proportion of women experience downward occupational mobility on returning to work following childbirth, particularly if they return part time, the next question we attempt to answer is whether such women stay at their new occupational level or move back up again, and in particular whether

any upward movement is associated with changes between full and part time work.

We saw earlier in the chapter that 40% of women who had worked since childbirth were in a job in a different occupational group in their most recent job from that of the first job they returned to following childbirth (Table 10.11). Table 10.18 shows that 23% were in a higher level occupation and 17% in a lower level occupation in their most recent job, indicating a slight tendency to upwards rather than downward movement overall. Table 10.18 looks at these results in relation to whether the two jobs being compared were full or part time. It is clear that movements between full and part time work are very important in relation to differences in occupational level. Women who had moved to a full time job after initially returning to work part time were more

Table 10.19 Occupational level of most recent job compared with first job since first birth by whether women returned to full or part time work and length of time worked since first birth

	Length of time worked since first birth					All who worked since first birth
	Up to 5 years	Over 5 up to 10 years	Over 10 up to 15 years	Over 15 up to 20 years	Over 20 years	
	%	%	%	%	%	%
Both first job since first birth and most recent job were full time						
Most recent job is:						
higher	12	20	17	27	33	19
same	83	69	64	59	48	69
lower	5	11	19	15	19	12
level than first job since first birth	**100**	**100**	**100**	**100**	**100**	**100**
Base	227	128	112	83	96	656*
Both first job since first birth and most recent job were part time						
Most recent job is:						
higher	8	19	31	30	26	17
same	80	63	48	48	56	67
lower	12	18	21	22	18	16
level than first job since first birth	**100**	**100**	**100**	**100**	**100**	**100**
Base	744	419	220	123	89	1,604*
First job since first birth was full time, most recent job was part time						
Most recent job is:						
higher	21	22	20	24	36	24
same	30	39	30	24	29	31
lower	49	40	50	53	35	45
level than first job since first birth	**100**	**100**	**100**	**100**	**100**	**100**
Base	96	83	60	38	52	341*
First job since first birth was part time, most recent job was full time						
Most recent job is:						
higher	35	43	42	47	57	45
same	53	47	44	40	34	44
lower	11	10	14	13	9	11
level than first job since first birth	**100**	**100**	**100**	**100**	**100**	**100**
Base	62	134	126	91	70	487*

Including 35 women whose time worked since first birth is not known

148

likely to have moved up the occupational scale, while women who had moved to a part time job having initially returned full time were more likely to have moved to a lower level occupation.

Of women whose first job after childbirth was part time, but whose most recent job was full time, 45% were in a higher level occupation compared with 11% in a lower level occupation. For women whose first job following childbirth was full time, but whose most recent job was part time, the reverse was true: 25% were in a higher level job and 44% in a lower level job.

These results appear to confirm an association between downward occupational mobility and part time work; we also need to take into account however the length of time worked between the jobs in question, for, as we have shown, this affects the likelihood of occupational movement. To simplify comparisons as far as possible Table 10.19 compares the occupational level of the most recent job with that of the first job following childbirth for the four possible combinations of having a full or part time job at these two points. Looking down the columns we can see whether the difference described above and shown in the previous table holds down when the length of time worked is held constant, whereas looking along the rows enables us to see how the picture for each group changes with the length of time worked.

Looking down the columns confirms the most striking features of the results shown in the previous table: women whose first job after childbirth was full time, but whose most recent job was part time, were more likely to be in a lower level occupation in the recent job than when they first returned whereas the opposite is true for women whose first return was part time and whose most recent job was full time; they were most likely to be in a higher level occupation and least likely to be in a lower level occupation. Although women with the same work status for both jobs were generally more likely to be at the same occupational level in both jobs this becomes less true the longer they have worked, because the proportion changing occupational level increased the longer women have worked. In both groups the likelihood of being in a higher level occupation appears generally to increase with the length of time worked, although the rise is not entirely consis-

tent. These results therefore confirm the association between downward occupational mobility and part time working. They also show some evidence of a general upward movement, even among women who do not change work status, as the length of time they have of worked increases though, yet again, our caveat about the spuriousness of some movement as an artefact of the categories must be remembered.

The net result of occupational movement following childbirth

The final issue we turn to in this chapter is whether women who have experienced downward occupational mobility following childbearing revert in time to the same occupational level as they had before childbirth, or whether they remain at a lower level. Even if they move up the occupational scale on changing from part to full time work in their post-childbirth jobs they may not revert to the same occupation as before childbirth.

Table 10.20 compares women's most recent job with the last job before their first birth and shows that 21% were in a higher level occupation and 38% in a lower level occupation in their most recent job. Thus, overall there is more evidence of downward than upward movement. This table also shows that women whose most recent job was part time were very much more likely to be in lower level occupations than those whose most recent job was full time (48% compared with 20%). Similarly they were less likely to be in higher level occupations (18% compared with 27%). Among women whose most recent job was full time, there was little difference according to whether they first returned full or part time. However, among those whose most recent job was part time, those who had first returned full time (the minority) were more likely to be in a higher level occupation than those who had first returned part time. In general, therefore, whether the most recent job was full or part time seems to be the most important factor in whether women move back up the occupational structure.

But, of course, women whose most recent job was part time may have worked for shorter periods of time since childbirth than those whose most recent job was full time and therefore have had less chance to move up the occupational ladder. Table 10.21 shows, overall, some evidence of a gradual decrease over time in the propor-

Table 10.20 Occupational level of most recent job compared with last job before first birth by whether most recent job was full or part time and whether first return to work since first birth was full or part time

	Most recent job was full time			Most recent job was part time			All who have worked before and since first birth		
	First return since first birth was:		All	First return since first birth was:		All	First return since first birth was:		All
	Full time	Part time		Full time	Part time		Full time	Part time	
	%	%	%	%	%	%	%	%	%
Most recent job is:									
higher	26	28	27	26	17	18	26	19	21
same	55	50	53	27	35	34	45	39	41
lower	19	22	20	47	48	48	29	42	38
level than last job before first birth	100	100	100	100	100	100	100	100	100
Base	622	480	1,102	335	1,582	1,917	957	2,062	3,019

149

tion of women in a lower level occupation in their most recent job than in the last job before childbirth and a gradual increase in the proportion in a higher level occupation in their most recent job.

Lastly we examine occupational mobility following childbirth in relation to changes from the last job before childbirth to the first job after childbirth. Since women can be in a higher, lower or the same occupation for two sets of comparisons there are nine possible

patterns of movement. In addition, if a woman has moved to a lower level occupation immediately following childbirth and has moved up again subsequently we want to know whether she has returned to the occupational level of the job before childbirth or not.

Thus the full summary of movement between the three possible jobs under consideration involves thirteen different patterns. Table 10.22 describes the direction of movement at each phase to simplify the descriptions.

Table 10.21 Occupational level of most recent job compared with last job before first birth by length of time worked since first birth and whether most recent job was full or part time

	Length of time worked since first birth					All who have worked before and since first birth
	Up to 5 years	Over 5 up to 10 years	Over 10 up to 15 years	Over 15 up to 20 years	Over 20 years	
	%	%	%	%	%	%
Most recent job was full time						
Most recent job is:						
higher	17	23	30	30	41	27
same	62	52	49	54	40	53
lower	21	25	21	16	19	20
level than last job before first birth	**100**	**100**	**100**	**100**	**100**	**100**
Base	*276*	*251*	*229*	*173*	*161*	*1,102**
Most recent job was part time						
Most recent job is:						
higher	12	19	23	27	28	18
same	34	38	33	29	26	34
lower	54	43	44	44	46	48
level than last job before first birth	**100**	**100**	**100**	**100**	**100**	**100**
Base	*824*	*496*	*278*	*159*	*139*	*1,917**
All who have worked before and since first birth						
Most recent job is:						
higher	14	20	26	29	35	21
same	41	43	40	42	33	41
lower	45	36	34	29	31	38
level than last job before first birth	**100**	**100**	**100**	**100**	**100**	**100**
Base	*1,100*	*747*	*507*	*332*	*300*	*3,019**

*Includes 33 women whose time worked since first birth is not known

Table 10.22 Summary of occupational mobility between last job before first birth, first job since first birth and most recent job since first birth, by movement between full and part time work since first birth

Direction of occupational mobility between:		Most recent job was full time		Most recent job was part time		All who have worked before and since first birth
Last job before first birth and first job since	First job since first birth and most recent job	First return since first birth was:		First return since first birth was:		
		Full time	Part time	Full time	Part time	
		%	%	%	%	%
Down	Down	2	2	8	4	4
Down	Level	9	8	3	30	19
Down	Up to:					
	lower	2 }	8 }	3 }	4 }	4 }
	same	4 } 8	15 } 31	2 } 8	5 } 12	6 } 14
	higher	2 }	8 }	3 }	3 }	4 }
	level than before first birth					
Level	Down	6	3	27	7	8
Level	Level	49	30	23	30	33
Level	Up	9	13	15	3	8
Up	Down to:					
	lower	1 }	1 }	7 }	2 }	2 }
	same	2 } 5	4 } 6	2 } 10	1 } 4	2 } 5
	higher	2 }	1 }	1 }	1 }	1 }
	level than before first birth					
Up	Level	11	5	4	9	8
Up	Up	1	2	2	1	1
		100	**100**	**100**	**100**	**100**
Base		*622*	*480*	*335*	*1,582*	*3,019*

Results are shown both overall and according to movement between full and part time work following childbirth. The most common pattern of movement, exhibited by 33% of women who had worked before and since childbirth, was to stay at the same level at all three stages under consideration. Women working full time, both in their first job after childbirth and in their most recent job, were particularly likely to show this pattern (49%). A further 19% moved down in occupational level following the initial break in employment for childbirth and were then at the same level in their most recent job. Women who had returned to part time work and were in part time work in their recent job were particularly likely to show this pattern (30%). Altogether 14% of women had been occupationally downwardly mobile on their initial return to work but had moved up by their most recent job; 6% had returned to the level they were in before childbirth and 4% each in higher and lower levels.

Thus, 10% had recovered from the initial downward movement by returning to the same or a higher level occupation. This pattern was particularly common among women whose initial return was to part time work but whose most recent job was full time. It is clear that these dominant patterns can be explained in terms of movement between full and part time work if a move to part time work is associated with downward mobility and a move to full time work with upward mobility. However such movement does not entirely explain the pattern seen. The time dimension is not shown, but from previous tables it will be apparent that occupational mobility increases with length of time out of the labour market or time worked since returning to work, as does the likelihood of movement between full and part time work.

Summary and conclusions
In contrast to the previous chapter which looked at movement in and out of the labour market, this chapter examined movement within the labour market. It is often suggested that women are not stable employees; our evidence seriously challenges this. There was considerable variation in how many employers women had worked for; the average was just under five, but this varied according to the number of years women had worked and their phase of life. Childless women in the first five years of their working life had worked for less than two years per employer on average, while those who had worked for five to ten years had averaged 3.4 years per employer. Job changing became less frequent the longer the childless phase of life lasted. Older childless women appear to be very stable employees, averaging over 9 years per employer, which implies that they stayed considerably longer than this with later employers since they were likely to have had some shorter employment spells earlier in their working lives.

In the period of working life after the start of childbearing women appear to change employers at first and to become less likely to change employers later in working life. It is not surprising that women change jobs during

the childbearing period, moreover, changes between full and part time work generally involve changes of employer and often a complete change of occupation. Comparing women who had worked for similar lengths of time it was apparent that among those who had only worked for a short period of time women with children changed employers more frequently than childless women, while among those who had worked longest they were the more stable employees.

In the majority of cases women left employers for job-related or non-domestic reasons, particularly to go to a better job. Nevertheless, as might be expected, women with children were more likely than childless women to leave jobs for domestic reasons, mainly pregnancy, but also other domestic reasons such as problems with childcare or with sick or elderly dependants. However a significant minority of childless women also left work for domestic reasons, including reasons connected with their husband's employment. There was no evidence that, overall, domestic reasons dominated women's job behaviour. Clearly during the family formation phase women were more likely to leave jobs and stop work in connection with pregnancy and childbirth, but during the remainder of their working lives domestic reasons were subsidiary to other reasons for changing from one employer to another.

On average women had worked in just over two occupational categories. Only a third of women had only worked in one occupational category and those tended to be young childless women. Women with children were much more likely than childless women to have changed occupations. During the childless phase of their lives around 40% of women worked in a different occupation in their most recent job, or their last job before childbearing, from their first occupation. A greater degree of occupational change was associated with breaks in employment for childbearing: 51% of women returned to work initially to a different occupation from that before childbirth and only a minority of those who changed appeared to return later to their original occupation. By the time of the interview 59% of women were working in a different occupation in their most recent job compared with the last job before their first birth.

In order to study the direction of occupational change we assumed that the categories of our occupational classification could be considered hierarchical and therefore examined the extent to which women moved 'up' and 'down' this occupational scale. Clearly this procedure takes no account of vertical movement within an occupational category, and the ordering of the occupational categories is certainly open to question. However, the extent and nature of occupational change among women is such that it would be detected on almost any occupational scale even if the exact proportions moving up and down are a function of the particular scale used.

Among childless women 60% were in the same occupational category in their most recent job as in their first job. Those whose most recent job was in a different category were somewhat more likely to have moved up the occupational scale and that was particularly the case for older childless women. The majority of women with children were also to be found in the same occupational category at the beginning and end of the pre-childbearing phase of their lives, although those who were not were almost as likely to have moved down as up.

In contrast, among 51% of women who had changed occupational level on returning to work after child-birth, 37% had moved downwards; only 14% returned to a higher level occupation. Downward mobility was strongly associated with returning to part time work: 45% of those who returned part time returned to a lower level occupation compared with 19% of those who returned full time. The association between down-ward occupational mobility and part time working held even when variations in the length of time out of the labour force for childbirth were allowed for.

Indeed occupational mobility after the initial returning to work following childbirth was strongly influenced by changes between full and part time work. Women who returned initially to part time work but subsequently changed to full time work were most likely to have moved up the occupational scale. By contrast, women who returned initially to full time work, but subse-quently worked part time were most likely to have moved downwards. Women whose most recent job was full time were much more likely to have regained or exceeded the occupational level they had before their first birth than those whose most recent job was part time, regardless of whether their initial return was to full or part time work. Even among those who had worked for comparable lengths of time differences be-tween full and part time workers were still apparent.

Only 10% of women had both moved down the occupa-tional scale following childbirth and subsequently moved back up to the same or a higher scale; such a pattern was strongly associated with an initial return to part time work and a subsequent move to full time work. Women staying in part time work were likely to have moved down the scale on return and then stayed at the same level. Overall then, changes in work status explained the largest proportion of occupational mobil-ity following childbearing, but change occurred for other reasons as the increased likelihood of change with increasing time worked indicates.

Notes

[1] Our study is more detailed than the analysis of occupational mobil-ity over 1965–1975 conducted by Greenhalgh and Stewart on the National Training Survey (1982a, 1982b). However this latter study is able to compare working men and women's occupational mobility in this period – a comparison we cannot make. Dex's analysis of women's lifetime occupational movement and careers compliments ours in that she again focusses on the level of the individual in contrast to our aggregate approach. She has constructed a range of occupational profiles and looks at the labour market experience and occupational attachment of women with different occupational pro-files. In addition she analyses the movement between industrial sectors that women exhibited as they changed jobs and links this with macro-economic data to explore theories of women's margi-nality in the labour market (Dex, 1984b).

[2] Because we relied on the work history data with its attendant prob-lem of recall we could not distinguish in our data between when women stopped work and became unemployed from when they stopped work and became economically inactive. We would expect this to apply differentially to childless women and women with children as well as to younger and older women, who are affected differently by secular change in unemployment rates.

[3] Goldthorpe's important criticism of some of the recent class analy-sis of women and their husbands also refers to the problems of inadequate occupational and social class classification of some of the lower level non-manual jobs done predominantly by women (Goldthorpe, 1983).

[4] See Dex (1984b) for further details of life-long occupational attach-ment.

[5] Following on from our approach Dex has looked at occupational mobility in more detail and has re-ordered and combined some of the occupational categories on the basis of analysis of their similar-ities and differences. She has also taken the analysis further by looking at movement over the whole of particular phases of women's lives rather than focussing on jobs at key points as we have done (Dex 1984b).

Chapter 11 Looking for jobs: priorities and job search strategies

Introduction

This chapter examines how women look for jobs. In particular it looks at what aspects of jobs are important to women and whether different groups of women have different job priorities and job search strategies. In Chapter 7 we identified two groups of non-working women who were looking for work at the time of the survey. Women in the group categorised as unemployed as they said they were not working because they were looking for work were seen to be currently in the labour market. Most of them (74%) were out of work because they had been dismissed, been made redundant, or had terminated their jobs for reasons to do with the job. The other group who had given different reasons for not working but were also looking for work were seen by it as currently out of the labour market but seeking to re-enter it. Most of the women in this category (87%) could be called 'domestic returners', as their main reason for being out of the labour market at the time of the interview was domestic. In addition, as pointed out in Chapter 10, women like men also move around in the labour market changing jobs without a break, both within organisations and between organisations (Curran, 1982).

It might be supposed that women in these different labour market situations behave differently. Indeed, much of the recent interest in the process of re-entry to the labour market for domestic returners presupposes that these women are very different from other women workers in the types of jobs they want, the aspects of jobs they value and the way they find jobs (Chaney, 1981; Johnson, 1980; Yohalem, 1980). In this chapter we examine whether there are differences by comparing the three groups of women. There are limitations to how many of the finer aspects of the process of re-entry and women's doubts and ambivalences about their situation can be revealed by data obtained through structured questionnaires. We therefore also refer in the chapter to more qualitative research carried out at about the same time as our study.

The survey collected information about how women looked for work from women in two different situations. Firstly we asked women looking for a job at the time of the interview about their job search. Secondly we asked women who had recently found a new job how they looked for work and found their job. Taken together this gave us information about how women were looking for work in 1980 and how women who had successfully found a new job between 1978 and 1980 had done so. It also provided a basis for us to compare the strategies of the successful with those who were still looking for a job.

Women who had found jobs were not in fact strictly comparable with women who were still looking. Firstly, more women will be looking for a job than will subsequently start a new job, as some women will give up the search for various reasons, while others will continue to look unsuccessfully. Secondly, over a two year period, proportionately more women will look for and find jobs (sometimes more than one) than the proportion looking at the time of the interview. Moreover the labour market was changing over the period so that women looking for a job in 1980 faced more difficulties than those looking in 1978. Consequently, while we look at the process of job seeking in terms of both successful strategies and the behaviour of women looking for a job, comparing and contrasting the groups where appropriate, comparison is not possible in all cases.

We begin the chapter by describing the extent of job changing amongst the sample of women between 1978 and 1980, and then outline the main characteristics of the different groups of women looking for a job in 1980 and during the previous two years. We compare women's job priorities, establish the importance women in 1980 attached to finding a job and then examine different groups of women's job search behaviour describing both the strategies of the successful and the situation women were experiencing in 1980 as they looked for a job.

The extent of job changing

We saw in Chapter 7 that 11% of non-working women were catogorised as unemployed and looking for work and a further 6% although not catogorised as unemployed were also looking for work. These groups represent 4% and 2% respectively of the total sample of women. Among women who were working at the time of the interview 9% said they were looking for a new job; these comprise 5% of the total sample of women. Altogether, therefore, 11% of the women in the study were looking for a job at the time of their interview in 1980, as Table 11.1 shows. A third of the sample had had a change of employment during the preceeding two years: 7% had left a job without obtaining another and 26% had obtained at least one new job. The two thirds

Table 11.1 Current position of women who are looking for jobs

	% of all women
Working	
Looking for another job	5
Unemployed	
Main reason for not working is looking for work	4
Domestic returner	
Mainly domestic reasons for not working, but also looking for work	2
Total currently looking for jobs	**11**
Base	*5,588*

153

Table 11.2 Employment position of women in the past two years

	%
Not worked at all	28
Worked continuously for the same employer	39
Left a job without obtaining another	7
Obtained at least one new job	26
	100
Base	5,588

who had not changed their job or work status were made up of 28% who had not worked at all during the two years and 39% who had worked continuously for the same employer (Table 11.2).

From women's work histories we identified what they had been doing immediately before starting their new job. This showed whether they had been working in another job, or if they had not been working, whether this was for mainly domestic or non-domestic reasons.

Table 11.3 Proportion of women who found jobs in the past two years by their position before they found a job

	% of all women
Working	
Changed employers without a break in employment	11%
Unemployed	
Found a job following a period of not working for non-domestic reasons	10%
Domestic returner	
Found a job following a period of not working for domestic reasons	9%
Total who found a job in the past two years	**26%***
Comprising those who found 1 job	19%
2 jobs	5%
3 jobs	1%
4 or more jobs	1%
Base	5,588

Categories do not add to 26% as some women appear in more than one category

Table 11.3 shows that in the past two years 11% of all women had changed employers without a break in employment, 10% had started a job following a period of non-domestic absence from work and 9% had started a job following a period of domestic absence. Of course, women may have started more than one job in this two year period. We showed in Chapter 10 how young women often change jobs frequently at the start of their working lives. Similarly, as some redundancy studies show, workers without jobs may take any job to get back to work and then change quickly to something

better (MacKay, 1971; Herron, 1975). In fact, as Table 11.3 also shows, 19% of women had started only one new job in the relevant two years but 7% had started more. Some of these women had had more than one job start of the same type. This was most likely for those who changed employers and least likely following a period of domestic absence.

Multiple job starts presented us with data collection problems since we could not overburden those informants who had had more than one job by collecting full details of all their job starts in the period. We therefore asked women in detail only about the most recent instance of each type of job start; if someone had changed employer more than once, for example, we only asked about the last occasion, though if she had made a start after domestic absence and subsequently had changed jobs we asked about both. As a consequence we only collected detailed information about 80% of all the jobs women obtained in the two years. These details include a relatively higher proportion of all domestic starts and a lower proportion of employer changes because there were more of the latter per person.

The characteristics and life situation of women job seekers

We have already described in Chapter 7 the characteristics of the two groups of non-working women who were looking for a job. Here we focus more on the domestic circumstances of job seekers, comparing their position in the life cycle, whether they wanted full or part time work and whether they had to make arrangements for childcare.

When we looked at the stage in their life cycle of the women in the different groups, both among those looking for jobs and those who had found jobs in the past two years, it was clear that there were major differences between women looking for a job or starting work following domestic absence and the other groups, as Table 11.4 illustrates. The vast majority (91% and 85%) of domestic returners were mothers of children under 16, and in the case of those currently looking for work 61% had a youngest child under 5. In contrast, childless women (most of whom were under 30) were the largest group in all the other categories and were

Table 11.4 Proportion of women at different life cycle stages who are looking for work or have found a job in the past two years

Life cycle stage	Currently looking for a job			Found a job in the past two years: was previously		
	Working	Unemployed	Domestic returner	Working	Unemployed	Domestic returner
	%	%	%	%	%	%
Childless women:						
aged under 30	38 } 46	36 } 44	1 } 2	42 } 48	59 } 63	2 } 2
aged 30 or over	8	8	1	6	4	2
Women with children under 16:						
youngest child aged 0–4	6	12	61	10	8	39
5–10	19 } 19	13 } 38	20 } 91	17 } 39	8 } 25	34 } 85
11–15	15	13	10	12	9	12
Women with all children 16 or over:						
aged under 50	7 } 14	7 } 18	5 } 7	6 } 13	5 } 12	5 } 11
aged 50 or over	7	11	2	7	7	6
	100	**100**	**100**	**100**	**100**	**100**
Base	290	211	107	557	462	454

Table 11.5 Whether women currently looking for work or who had found a job in the past two years were looking for full time or part time work

Whether looking for full or part time work	Currently looking for a job			Found a job in the past two years: was previously		
	Working	Unemployed	Domestic returner	Working	Unemployed	Domestic returner
	%	%	%	%	%	%
Full time	57	53	14	64	71	16
Part time	41	43	83	36	29	84
Don't know	1	2	3	..	..	..
Other	1	2	0	..	..	..
	100	100	100	100	100	100
Base	*290*	*211*	*107*	*557*	*462*	*454*

the majority (63%) of the unemployed women who had found a job in the past two years. However, women with dependent children formed significant minorities in all the other groups, the proportions varying from 25% to 40%.

It was noticeable that the differences between either group of domestic returners and women in other labour market positions were more marked than differences between women who in 1980 were looking for work and those who had found a job in the preceding two years in any of the other categories. Some differences were apparent between the two unemployed categories, but it is not possible without further information to tell whether this was because unemployed women who were childless were more successful than those who had children at finding jobs, or whether changes in the employment situation over the period resulted in more women with children being unemployed and looking for work in 1980.

Differences between domestic returners and the other two groups of women were, as we would expect, equally marked when we looked at the hours of work women preferred. Table 11.5 shows that while the majority of women looking for or having found a job after domestic absence were looking for or had found part time work, (83% and 84% respectively), full time work predominated among the other groups, although large minorities of both unemployed women and working women were looking for part time work. However, women who had actually changed employers or found a job after being unemployed were more likely to be in full time work

than those currently trying to change employers or unemployed were to be looking for full time work. Whether this is because those looking for full time work were more successful at finding it, or whether some women looking for part time work actually took full time jobs or gave up looking altogether we cannot tell.

We asked women who were looking for or who had found part time work how many hours a week they wanted to work and what arrangement of hours they wanted. The majority wanted to work more than ten hours but under 30 hours a week. Domestic returners were more likely than other women to want to work fewer hours, but even so twice as many of them (19%) had taken a job with less than 10 hours than were looking for such a part time job (9%).

Table 11.6 shows that the arrangement of part time hours these women wanted is similar to those of all women working part time described in Chapter 4. Most women wanting to work part time had young children and therefore wanted to work in the mornings or during school hours. However, significant proportions, particularly of those returning after domestic absence, wanted evening work, (16% and 20% respectively), presumably because their husbands would be available to look after the children at that time.

Childcare arrangements were much as we would expect from Chapter 4. Almost all those women with pre-school children, most of whom were domestic returners, needed to make or had made arrangements for the care of their children while they worked. Those

Table 11.6 Times of day when work sought by women wanting to work part time who are looking for work or found a job in the past two years

Times of day when work sought	Currently looking for a job			Found a job in the past two years: was previously		
	Working, looking for part time work	Unemployed, looking for part time work	Domestic returner looking for part time work	Working, looking for part time work	Unemployed, looking for part time work	Domestic returner looking for part time work
	%	%	%	%	%	%
School hours in term time only	18	7	26	13	11	19
School hours including the holidays	14	13	13	19	14	14
Mornings only	39	33	20	26	30	22
Afternoons only	3	4	3	7	8	6
Evenings	4	10	16	8	12	20
Lunchtimes	1	0	1	1	1	1
Short days	5	1	1	2	2	2
1–4 full days	4	6	0	4	2	1
Other	1	8	7	7	2	4
Don't mind	10	14	5	15	19	12
Don't know	1	4	8	..	..	..
	100	100	100	100	100	100
Base	*119*	*91*	*88*	*199*	*133*	*372*

who did not were planning to work, or already did work, at home. Substantial proportions of women with school age children also needed to make arrangements for their care. Interestingly, more women looking for work said they intended to use non-family care arrangements like childminders or creches than in practice used them; less than 10% of women who had returned to work after domestic absence in fact used a childminder. In the main, women relied firstly on husbands and then on their mother (in-law) for help with childcare.

The decision to return to work

A considerable amount of research exists on the problems and behaviour of women returning to paid work after having children (Rothwell, 1980) and as we have shown, the family constraints on the work women do are considerable. Quite clearly a woman's decision to return to work affects her family in various ways. We asked women whether their husbands had any views about whether or not they should start work again and, if they had, whether they were generally in favour or against them starting work. About a third, 36%, of women looking for work and 42% of women who had found a job in the past two years said their husbands had no views as Table 11.7 shows. We do not know, however, whether husbands actually had no views or had not been asked for them. As Chaney shows, a quarter of the married women in her study had not discussed returning to work with their husbands prior to getting a job (Chaney, 1981). Rather, they typically found a job which fitted in with existing family life and explained the absence of any discussion by saying their job did not affect their husband.

Table 11.7   Husband's views about whether wives should start work again following domestic absence

Husband's views	Currently looking for a job: domestic returner	Found a job in the past two years: domestic returner
	%	%
Husband is/was generally:		
in favour of wife starting work	41	43
against	19	12
Husband had no views	36	42
Other/qualified answers	4	3
	100	**100**
Whether women thought of the decision to return to work as:		
their own decision	41	41
a joint decision with their husband	59	59
	100	**100**
Base	*80*	*350*

Over 40% of women in each group said that their husband was in favour of their starting work, but a small minority of women described their husbands as being generally against them starting work. Noticeably slightly more of those looking for work said this than of those who had found a job in the past two years (19% and 12% respectively). This difference might be explained by women reporting current antagonism but not remembering past difficulties as the situation faded or possibly attitudes changed. Alternatively, it may be that women with husbands who are opposed to their starting work are more likely to stop looking for a job

than women with more supportive husbands. A majority of women (59%) in both groups, however, saw their decision to return to work as a joint one with their husband.

Recent research on the process of returning to work shows that for many women returners this is rarely planned in detail well in advance. A small minority of women may make definite plans to return by a certain date and look systematically for a job at the appropriate time. Many more think in general terms of 'when the children reach school age', for example. However, as both Chaney (1981) and Johnson (1980) have shown, for many other women there appears to be an unspecified period when they may be looking around in a general sort of way, possibly beginning to discuss the process with other people and the actual search period may not be begun until some definite job possibilities appear. Yet others, as we show later in the chapter, may not look around at all, but just be offered a job.

Table 11.8   Whether wives talked to people other than husbands about whether they should start work following domestic absence

Who else wives had talked to about the decision to start work	Currently looking for a job: domestic returner	Found a job in the past two years: domestic returner
	%	%
Family	43	23
Friend	50	16
Others	3	3
No-one else (except husband)	38	66
Base	*80*	*350*

Percentages do not add to 100 because some women talked to more than one person

Table 11.9   The views of people, other than husbands, whom wives had talked to about whether they should start work following domestic absence

Other people's views	Currently looking for a job: domestic returner	Found a job in the past two years: domestic returner
	%	%
People (other than husbands) generally:		
encouraged women to start work	56	73
discouraged them	6	3
Had no views either way	16	19
Some encouraged, some discouraged	16	3
Didn't know what their views were	6	2
	100	**100**
Base	*50*	*120*

We asked women whether they had talked to people (other than their husbands) about starting work again. As Table 11.8 shows, only 38% of women who were looking for a job said they had not talked to anyone apart from their husband about starting work again compared with 66% of those who had found a job in the past two years. Possibly some women in the latter group had forgotten the discussions they had had. On the whole women in our survey found the people they talked to were generally encouraging. However, as Table 11.9 shows, rather more of the group who had found a job in the past than of those looking in 1980 described other people as being encouraging (73% compared with 56% respectively).

Why women work and their job priorities

We looked at the reasons working women gave for working and explained our rationale for asking women this question in Chapter 6. Quite clearly it was less problematic to ask women looking for work their reasons for working, particularly for those women seeking to re-enter the labour market after a domestic break. In this section we compare the reasons for working given by the three groups of women who were looking for a job in 1980 and, where appropriate, draw on the findings of Chapter 6 to contrast them with the reasons given by working women in general. Approximately 9% of working women were looking for a job at the time of the interview. It must therefore be remembered that the group of working women who were looking for a job were a small sub-group of all working women in the sample.

In describing women's reasons for working we highlight only those where particular groups of women differ markedly from the rest. Looking at all the reasons given for working in Table 11.10 it is clear that overall somewhat fewer domestic returners endorsed the view that they wanted a job because they needed money for essentials than women in the other two groups. Closer inspection, however, indicates that they were not dissimilar from those looking for part time work in the other two groups; thus the major difference was between those looking for full time work and those looking for part time work. Amongst those looking for part time work, domestic returners were less likely to say that they were looking for work in order to buy extras

than those looking for part time work in the other two groups. The unemployed were more likely than other groups to select the statement that 'work is the normal thing to do'; this reflects the preponderance of young childless women in the group.

Those already in work but looking for another job were most likely to give as reasons for working that they enjoyed working or wanted to follow their career. The differences between job changers working full time and other women was so marked on these two dimensions that it suggests that these women may be job changing for positive reasons, namely through extra commitment to working and to their career, rather than for negative reasons, a conclusion Dex also draws from her more detailed analysis (Dex, 1984b). It is also noticeable that job changers looking for full time work were more likely to endorse financial need – money for essentials – and career aspirations than women working full time in general.

Turning to the main reason women gave for working, also shown in Table 11.10, similarities and differences between the groups become easier to see. A majority of women in all groups emphasised financial reasons as their main reason for working. Those in the labour market, either in work or unemployed, emphasised financial need more than domestic returners; they also gave financial autonomy ('to earn money of my own') as a main reason more often than domestic returners. Those looking for part time work were more likely than those looking for full time work to say they wanted work to obtain money for extras, but domestic returners looking for part time work were less likely than women looking for part time work in the other two groups to say this.

Table 11.10   All reasons and main reason for working given by women who were currently looking for a full or part time job

Reasons for working	Currently looking for a job																	
	Working			Unemployed			Domestic returner			Working			Unemployed			Domestic returner		
	Full time work	Part time work	All	Full time work	Part time work	All	Full time work	Part time work	All	Full time work	Part time work	All	Full time work	Part time work	All	Full time work	Part time work	All
	All reasons for working									*Main reason for working* %	%	%	%	%	%	%	%	%
Working is the normal thing to do	19%	7%	14%	28%	12%	21%		1%	2%	4	2	3	10	6	8		–	1
Need money for essentials such as food, rent or mortgage	62%	45%	54%	55%	45%	51%		43%	46%	41	42	41	41	36	40		33	36
To earn money to buy extras	31%	53%	40%	27%	52%	37%		46%	43%	9	29	17	8	28	17		22	22
To earn money of my own	42%	34%	38%	35%	34%	34%		30%	27%	17	9	14	20	16	18		11	11
For the company of other people	37%	45%	42%	35%	42%	37%		48%	44%	4	6	5	4	7	5		18	16
Enjoy working	52%	38%	46%	32%	36%	33%		31%	32%	13	8	11	10	6	8		9	9
To follow my career	37%	10%	26%	15%	7%	11%		8%	8%	12	3	8	5	1	3		1	1
Other reasons	1%	2%	1%	6%	1%	4%		8%	7%	1	1	1	3	1	2		6	5
										100	100	100	100	100	100		100	100
Base	165	119	290*	111	91	211*	15†	88	107*	165	119	290*	111	91	211*	15†	88	107*

Percentages for 'All reasons' total more than 100 as informants mentioned several reasons
*Includes informants who did not know whether they wanted full or part time work
†Base too small to show percentages

Leaving aside the financial reasons for working, the most common non-financial reason given by those currently working was that they enjoyed working (11%); this was followed by wanting to follow a career (8%). Whilst enjoying work was also prominent amongst the non-financial reasons given by the other two groups (8% and 9%), in the case of the unemployed 'working is the normal thing to do' was mentioned equally frequently (8%), whereas for the domestic returners wanting 'the company of other people' was a more common reason (16%); work in this context was seen as an antidote to domestic isolation. The difference in their response from that of the two groups of women in the labour market suggests that 'company' may be more important in motivating women to re-enter the labour market than it continues to be once they are in it.

Having described the general reasons for working given by those women in the sample who were looking for a job we now turn to the degree of importance they attached to achieving their objective soon (shown in Table 11.11). As one would expect, among the two groups already in the labour market, the unemployed attached greater importance to getting a job soon than those already in work. Within this group those looking for full time work attached greater importance to this than those looking for part time work. Only 8% of the unemployed women looking for full time work said it was not very important to find a job soon, compared with 29% of the equivalent group amongst those in

work. Amongst the part time workers the figures were 32% and 46% respectively. The domestic returners were similar to the part time workers in the other categories in that a substantial minority did not rate it very important to find a job soon and only just over a quarter did consider it very important. It is not possible to know from this study why some women who were looking for work said it was not very important to find a job soon. Other research however, in particular the Cragg and Dawson study, shows that some women, particularly those seeking to combine domestic responsibilities with paid work by having a part time job, both have an acute appreciation of the difficulties they face in getting a part time job and feel others are rightly ahead of them in the job queue (Cragg and Dawson, 1984).

Finally in this section, having looked at the groups of respondents' general attitudes to working and at the importance they attach to getting a job, we turn to the specific aspects of a job to which they attach priority. As Tables 11.12 and 11.13 show, those women currently in work but looking for a new full time job emphasised in particular the need to have work they liked doing; being able to make use of their abilities and a friendly work environment were also emphasised; they also attached importance to good pay and a secure job. A similar picture was presented by unemployed women looking for full time work, except that a lower emphasis was given to liking a job or being able to use their abilities. In contrast those looking for part time work,

Table 11.11 The importance of finding a job soon for women currently looking for a full or part time job

Importance of finding a job soon	Currently looking for a job								
	Working			Unemployed			Domestic returner		
	Looking for:			Looking for:			Looking for:		
	Full time work	Part time work	All	Full time work	Part time work	All	Full time work	Part time work	All
	%	%	%	%	%	%	%	%	%
Very important	41	24	33	65	26	46		22	26
Fairly important	30	30	30	27	42	34		32	31
Not very important	29	46	37	8	32	19		46	43
	100	**100**	**100**	**100**	**100**	**100**		**100**	**100**
Base	165	119	290*	111	91	211*	15†	88	107*

*Includes informants who did not know whether they wanted full or part time work
†Base too small to show percentages

Table 11.12 Proportion of women currently looking for a full or part time job who rate eight different aspects of jobs as essential or very important

Aspects of jobs	Currently looking for a job								
	Working			Unemployed			Domestic returner		
	Looking for:			Looking for:			Looking for:		
	Full time work	Part time work	All	Full time work	Part time work	All	Full time work	Part time work	All
Work you like doing	96%	85%	91%	82%	86%	84%		81%	79%
Good prospects	68%	40%	56%	60%	38%	50%		31%	34%
Convenient hours	57%	85%	69%	57%	82%	68%		88%	87%
A good rate of pay	80%	67%	75%	81%	53%	68%		56%	62%
A secure job	81%	78%	79%	80%	63%	72%		57%	61%
Friendly people to work with	80%	82%	81%	85%	86%	86%		83%	81%
An easy journey to work	46%	70%	56%	54%	69%	60%		62%	63%
The opportunity to use your abilities	81%	69%	76%	72%	67%	70%		59%	58%
Base	165	119	290*	111	91	211*	15†	88	107*

*Includes informants who did not know whether they wanted full or part time work
†Base too small to show percentages

Table 11.13 Average importance ratings of eight different aspects of jobs for women currently looking for a full or part time job

Aspects of jobs	Currently looking for a job								
	Working			Unemployed			Domestic returner		
	Looking for:			Looking for:			Looking for:		
	Full time work	Part time work	All	Full time work	Part time work	All	Full time work	Part time work	All
Work you like doing	1.6	1.9	1.7	1.9	1.9	1.9		1.9	2.2
Good prospects	2.1	2.6	2.4	2.4	2.9	2.6		3.0	2.9
Convenient hours	2.4	1.9	2.2	2.5	1.8	2.2		1.6	1.7
A good rate of pay	1.9	2.1	2.0	2.0	2.4	2.1		2.3	2.2
A secure job	1.9	2.0	1.9	2.0	2.4	2.2		2.5	2.4
Friendly people to work with	1.9	1.9	2.0	2.0	2.0	2.0		2.3	2.0
An easy journey to work	2.5	2.1	2.3	2.4	2.2	2.3		2.2	2.2
The opportunity to use your abilities	1.9	2.1	2.0	2.2	2.1	2.1		2.4	2.3
Base	165	119	290*	111	91	211*	15†	88	107*

*Includes informants who did not know whether they wanted full or part time work
†Base too small to show averages

while they also wanted enjoyable work and friendly workmates, did not put the same emphasis as those looking for full time work on being able to use their abilities, earn good rates of pay or have a secure job; rather they emphasised the importance of convenient hours.

Women's job search behaviour

People use a variety of methods to find jobs and may of course use different methods concurrently. Some may look consistently while others, possibly because they become discouraged or rely on informal methods, may look 'on and off' over a period. Yet others may find jobs without actually looking if they were offered one directly by an employer. We were particularly interested in whether women returning to work after a domestic absence differed significantly from other women in how they sought and found jobs and the types of jobs they wanted.

Pilot work had suggested that a significant proportion of women, particularly domestic returners, found a job without looking for it and some returned to the same employer as they had worked for before they stopped work. We therefore asked all women who had started a new job in the two years prior to the interview firstly whether they had gone back to the same employer and secondly whether they had looked for a job or were offered one, checking, if they were offered one, whether the employer contacted them first. Table 11.14 shows that while only a small proportion of women who had been unemployed or domestic returners went back to the same employer (4% and 11% respectively), proportionately more women found a job without looking for it. Domestic returners were most likely to have been offered a job without applying for one (29%), compared with 20% of those working and looking for a job and 17% of the unemployed. Similar proportions (24%–28%) of those looking for part time work in all three groups had been offered jobs, as had 29% of domestic returners looking for full time work but among those looking for full time work in the other two groups only 15% and 13% had been offered jobs without applying.

A few women said they had not looked for work but also said they had applied for a job and been offered one. Without studying the process of return to work after a domestic absence in more detail it is difficult to know to what extent women who said they were offered

Table 11.14 Whether women who had found a job in the past two years returned to the same employer as they worked for before they stopped work and whether they looked for work or were offered a job without looking

	Found a job in the past two years: was previously								
	Working			Unemployed			Domestic returner		
	Looking for:			Looking for:			Looking for:		
	Full time work	Part time work	All	Full time work	Part time work	All	Full time work	Part time work	All
	%	%	%	%	%	%	%	%	%
Returned to:									
same employer	–	–	–	3	8	4	12	10	11
different employer	100	100	100	51	90	60	87	89	88
First job in working life	–	–	–	46	2	36	1	1	1
	100	100	100	100	100	100	100	100	100
Did not look for a job: employer offered job	15	24	20	13	26	17	29	28	29
applied and was offered job	1	3	2	1	2	1	7	4	5
Looked for job	83	73	78	86	72	81	64	67	66
	100	100	100	100	100	100	100	100	100
Base	358	199	569*	329	133	497*	72	372	454*

*Includes informants who did not know whether they wanted full or part time work

159

a job without looking were engaged in any form of job search prior to starting work again or were at least thinking about returning to work. Pilot work showed, and the Sheffield study bears this out (Johnson, 1980), that for some women the initial return to work is unplanned or temporary (often to help an old employer out at a peak period or to cover for an ill friend or relative), but that once a woman realises she can make some childcare arrangements and have a part time job her taste for work, for whatever reason now re-established, carries on.

We look next at the type of work women were looking for. A sizeable minority of women in all groups said they did not know what they wanted or did not mind what work they did; this was highest among domestic returners of whom approximately a quarter said this (Table 11.15). Women currently trying to change jobs were most likely to be looking for the higher level non-manual jobs (18%), particularly those 21% looking for full time work. This was in contrast to around 8% of women in the other groups, both those currently looking and those who had found a job in the past two years. In general, women trying to change jobs or who had changed jobs in the past two years were most likely to be looking for non-manual jobs, while domestic returners were most likely to be looking for semi-skilled or unskilled jobs. In Chapter 10 we showed that women returning to work after childbearing frequently returned to a lower level job than before, particularly if they returned to part time work. Whether women returning to work look initially for lower level jobs because they know that these are more likely to be available to them at the right times of day or in convenient locations or learn this through the experience of looking around and trying to find work, we cannot tell from our data.

Table 11.15   Type of work sought by women currently looking for a job or who had found a job in the past two years

Type of work sought	Currently looking for a job								
	Working			Unemployed			Domestic returner		
	Looking for:			Looking for:			Looking for:		
	Full time work	Part time work	All	Full time work	Part time work	All	Full time work	Part time work	All
	%	%	%	%	%	%	%	%	%
Professional	2	1	2	–	–	–			
Teachers	13	5	10	2	–	1		2	2
Nursing, medical and social	6	6	6	5	6	6		7	6
Other intermediate non-manual	7	1	4	–	–	–		2	2
Clerical	33	37	35	35	26	31		26	23
Sales	5	8	6	10	15	12		8	9
Skilled	6	2	4	4	8	5		2	5
Semi-skilled factory	4	2	3	12	9	11		5	8
Semi-skilled domestic	7	7	7	4	9	6		7	8
Other semi-skilled	2	1	2	1	3	2		5	5
Unskilled	1	7	3	2	7	4		8	6
Inadequately described	1	2	1	0	–	0		1	1
Don't mind	6	13	9	21	12	17		23	20
Don't know	7	8	7	4	5	5		4	5
	100	100	100	100	100	100		100	100
Base*	165	119	290†	111	91	211†	15‡	88	107†

Type of work sought	Found a job in the past two years: was previously								
	Working			Unemployed			Domestic returner		
	Looking for:			Looking for:			Looking for:		
	Full time work	Part time work	All	Full time work	Part time work	All	Full time work	Part time work	All
	%	%	%	%	%	%	%	%	%
Professional	1	–	0	0	–	0	–	–	–
Teachers	3	1	2	4	2	4	–	–	–
Nursing, medical and social	8	4	6	4	4	4	4	3	3
Other intermediate non-manual	3	–	3	1	1	1	–	1	1
Clerical	43	29	39	39	32	37	24	18	19
Sales	8	9	9	10	9	10	7	9	9
Skilled	4	5	4	7	2	6	7	2	3
Semi-skilled factory	7	9	8	5	3	5	15	6	8
Semi-skilled domestic	3	11	6	6	13	7	4	13	11
Other semi-skilled	1	1	1	1	2	2	2	1	1
Unskilled	1	10	4	0	5	2	4	12	11
Inadequately described	2	–	1	2	1	2	2	1	1
Don't mind	13	17	14	16	19	16	17	26	25
Don't know	2	3	3	3	5	3	2	2	2
	100	100	100	100	100	100	100	100	100
Base*	298	145	446†	282	96	409†	46	250	300†

*Excludes informants who were not looking for work but the employer offered a job
†Includes informants who did not know whether they wanted full or part time work
‡Base too small to show percentages

The steps taken to look for work

Jobs can be looked for in a variety of formal and informal ways; by looking at newspaper advertisements, asking friends or relatives, approaching employers directly, registering at private employment agencies, or using the public employment service (Jobcentres and employment offices). Table 11.16 shows the proportions of women using each of these methods. Women who were looking for work at the time of the interview on average used more methods to find a job than women who had found a job in the previous two years; it is likely that people forgot some of the steps they took when asked about them after a lapse of time. It is interesting to note, however, that women looking for full time work, on average, used more methods of finding work than women looking for part time work and not all of this difference is accounted for by their being more likely to have registered for work at a government employment office. However, whether this is because those looking for part time work are generally less intensive in their job search, have less information about what methods to use or feel some methods are less appropriate ways of finding part time work is not clear. Overall though, unemployed women used most methods of looking for work. They averaged between 3–4 methods each compared with 2–3 for women changing jobs and domestic returners. As only 54% of the women who were unemployed in 1980 were registered as unemployed, registration alone is unlikely to explain this.

Asking women which steps they took to find a job does not tell us how intensively particular methods were used; for example whether women glanced at newspaper advertisements casually from time to time or studied them carefully and frequently. However, it is apparent from Table 11.16 that the majority of women in all groups looked at newspaper advertisements, particularly those currently looking for a job. Asking friends and relatives was also a common method, and in most groups was used equally by those seeking full time and part time work, and particularly by the currently unemployed. This group was also most likely to approach employers directly, although substantial proportions of all groups used this method to look for work. The three more formal methods, registering with private agencies or employment offices and looking in Jobcentres were more likely to be used by those seeking full time rather than part time work in most groups. The unemployed were most likely to use the public employment services, which is in line with the findings of other studies (Daniel, 1974 and 1981b; White 1983).

The higher proportion of women looking for full as opposed to part time work who register with government agencies also ties in with the findings of other studies, for example the detailed examination conducted by Johnson for the Manpower Services Commission which shows the limited use women seeking part work make of official agencies, often through lack of information about their services or a preference for

Table 11.16   The steps taken to find a job by women currently looking for work or women who had found a job in the past two years

Steps taken to find a job	Currently looking for a job								
	Working			Unemployed			Domestic returner		
	Looking for:			Looking for:			Looking for:		
	Full time work	Part time work	All	Full time work	Part time work	All	Full time work	Part time work	All
Looking at newspaper advertisements	83%	89%	85%	79%	87%	82%		81%	78%
Asking friends/relatives	50%	48%	49%	68%	66%	67%		57%	55%
Approaching employers directly	36%	29%	33%	54%	40%	48%		25%	30%
Registering at private agencies	19%	15%	18%	14%	14%	14%		9%	8%
Looking in Jobcentres	52%	54%	53%	83%	74%	79%		51%	51%
Registering at government employment offices	22%	14%	19%	80%	45%	65%		20%	23%
Other steps taken	13%	6%	11%	4%	6%	5%		4%	4%
*Base**	165	119	290†	111	91	211†	15‡	88	107†

Steps taken to find a job	Found a job in the past two years: was previously								
	Working			Unemployed			Domestic returner		
	Looking for:			Looking for:			Looking for:		
	Full time work	Part time work	All	Full time work	Part time work	All	Full time work	Part time work	All
Looking at newspaper advertisements	72%	57%	67%	75%	72%	74%	50%	67%	64%
Asking friends/relatives	37%	42%	39%	52%	49%	51%	37%	44%	43%
Approaching employers directly	36%	47%	40%	43%	39%	42%	41%	44%	44%
Registering at private agencies	28%	11%	22%	23%	15%	21%	20%	6%	8%
Looking in Jobcentres	43%	32%	39%	63%	64%	63%	57%	36%	39%
Registering at government employment offices	24%	12%	20%	54%	35%	57%	33%	14%	17%
Other steps taken	2%	1%	2%	3%	1%	2%	2%	7%	6%
*Base**	298	145	446†	282	96	409†	46	250	300†

Percentages do not add to 100 because some women used more than 1 method
*Excludes informants who were not looking for work but the employer offered a job
†Includes informants who did not know whether they wanted full or part time work
‡Base too small to show percentages

Table 11.17 The reasons women currently looking for work or who had found a job in the past two years gave for not registering at a government employment office or Jobcentre

Reasons for not registering	Currently looking for a job								
	Working			Unemployed			Domestic returner		
	Looking for: Full time work	Part time work	All	Looking for: Full time work	Part time work	All	Looking for: Full time work	Part time work	All
Not really looking/not urgent	18%	31%	24%		19%	14%		36%	34%
Adverse comments/considered and rejected	31%	17%	25%		29%	24%		30%	31%
Prefer other ways	18%	16%	17%		12%	15%		8%	8%
Didn't think/know about it	18%	19%	18%		29%	35%		20%	20%
Other reasons	20%	19%	20%		15%	15%		11%	11%
Base	*130*	*103*	*237**	*22†*	*50*	*74**	*10†*	*70*	*82**

Reasons for not registering	Found a job in the past two years: was previously								
	Working			Unemployed			Domestic returner		
	Looking for: Full time work	Part time work	All	Looking for: Full time work	Part time work	All	Looking for: Full time work	Part time work	All
Not really looking/not urgent	11%	11%	11%	1%	11%	5%		21%	20%
Adverse comments/considered and rejected	22%	25%	23%	26%	35%	29%		31%	30%
Prefer other ways	49%	38%	45%	49%	33%	44%		25%	27%
Didn't think/know about it	16%	20%	18%	24%	32%	26%		23%	23%
Other reasons	10%	9%	10%	5%	2%	4%		6%	6%
Base	*229*	*129*	*360**	*105*	*64*	*199**	*31†*	*216*	*251**

Percentages total to more than 100 as informants mentioned several reasons
*Includes informants who did not know whether they wanted full or part time work
†Bases too small to show percentages

informal methods (Johnson, 1980). At the time of our survey women looking for full or part time work could register at Jobcentres for a job regardless of whether they were eligible for unemployment benefit. However, those who were eligible for benefit were obviously more likely to do so. All women who did not mention registering at a government employment office or Jobcentre were asked their reasons for not doing so. These are shown in Table 11.17. There were noticeable differences between women looking for work in 1980 and those who had found a job. The latter group were more likely to say that they preferred or had used other ways of finding a job. Whether this is a real difference between those who were successful at finding jobs and those still looking or is affected by problems of recall is not possible to determine.

What is interesting, however, is the proportion of women who said they were not registered because they were not really looking or not looking urgently for a job. Since this was an open question at our main stage interview this finding is even more surprising. It is understandable, perhaps, that a proportion of women who are trying to change jobs may not be looking with a serious commitment to change. However, a proportion of women without jobs also said this, even among the unemployed, but there were marked differences between women wanting full and part time work. The latter were much more likely to give as an explanation for not registering that they were not really looking for work. This ties in with the analysis in Chapter 7 that for some women registering for employment is equated with seriously looking for work and being unemployed.

Table 11.18 Way by which women who had found a job in the past two years heard of their job by whether they were looking for a full or part time job

Way by which first heard of job	Found a job in the past two years: was previously								
	Working			Unemployed			Domestic returner		
	Looking for: Full time work	Part time work	All	Looking for: Full time work	Part time work	All	Looking for: Full time work	Part time work	All
	%	%	%	%	%	%	%	%	%
Newspaper advertisements	34	27	32	24	33	26	20	32	30
Friend/relative	22	33	26	25	32	26	22	34	33
Direct application to employer	11	20	14	10	14	12	24	19	19
Private employment agency	13	6	11	7	4	6	9	1	2
Jobcentre/employment office	14	6	12	31	11	26	26	6	9
Other	5	7	6	3	5	3	–	7	6
	100	**100**	**100**	**100**	**100**	**100**	**100**	**100**	**100**
Base*	*298*	*145*	*446†*	*282*	*96*	*409†*	*46*	*250*	*300†*

*Excludes informants who were not looking for work but the employer offered a job
†Includes informants who did not know whether they wanted full or part time work

Job search 1978 to 1980

This section examines the way in which those women who had found jobs obtained them. We asked those women who had looked for a job how they first heard of the job they obtained. As Table 11.18 shows, the two most frequent sources of a job were newspaper advertisements and the informal network of friends and relatives. Women looking for a part time job were more likely to hear of the job they obtained through friends or relatives than women wanting full time work. They were less likely than full time workers to use the public employment service or private employment agencies.

There were some differences, however, between the groups in the extent to which women wanting full or part time work found a job in the same way. More women changing employers and looking for a full time job found it through a newspaper advertisement or private employment agencies than unemployed women or domestic returners who wanted a full time job. They were also much less likely to use the public employment services. These differences in part reflect the different types of jobs women returning to work after unemployment or a domestic absence are likely to obtain compared with women changing jobs. A higher proportion of job changers obtain white-collar, clerical and secretarial jobs in which many private employment agencies tend to specialise.

We show in Table 11.19 the length of time women who had found a job between 1978 and 1980 said they had spent looking for work. Women changing employers appeared to find a new job most quickly: 63% said they had looked for less than a month and 44% in fact, said they had looked for less than a fortnight. Unemployed women by contrast had looked the longest: 60% had looked for over a month and a higher proportion of unemployed women had been looking for work over a longer period of time: over a third (35%) had looked for three months or longer compared with 27% of domestic returners and 16% of women changing employers.

Job search is not just measured by the length of time for which people look but also the degree of commitment with which they look for work. We attempted to assess this by asking women who had looked for a job for longer than a month whether this was 'more or less continuously' or 'on and off'. Understandably perhaps, 20% of women who had changed employers said they had looked 'on and off' and there was little difference in the proportions of full and part time workers saying this. While a similar proportion of unemployed women (21%) said they had looked 'on and off' there were marked differences between women who had looked for full and part time work: 16% of women who wanted full time work said this compared with 35% of those who looked for part time work. In fact, this latter group were more akin to domestic returners, who overall both had a much higher proportion who gave this response (30%) and showed little difference between women looking for a full or part time job in this respect. This does not necessarily mean that women looking 'on and off' for work were less keen to find work; alternative explanations are possible. It is highly likely, for example, that the types of jobs these women wanted were much scarcer and harder to get and therefore that the job search was a particularly discouraging experience. However, if intensity of job search is a measure of attachment to work, it seems possible to say that these women, for whatever reason, were less attached to working than those who looked continuously.

Some hint as to the type of factors affecting women's job search can be found by looking at the difficulties recorded by successful job seekers, shown in Table 11.20. While scarcity of jobs at all or of the type wanted were mentioned by sizeable proportions of all groups, particularly the unemployed, women looking for part time work, especially the domestic returners, were also likely to say there were no jobs with the hours they wanted. The unemployed were slightly more likely than other women to feel that lack of experience or qualifications was one of the factors causing them difficulty in getting a job: 9% of those wanting full time work said this.

Table 11.19 Length of time spent looking for a job by women who had found a job in the past two years

How long women had looked for work	Found a job in the past two years: was previously								
	Working			Unemployed			Domestic returner		
	Looking for:		All	Looking for:		All	Looking for:		All
	Full time work	Part time work		Full time work	Part time work		Full time work	Part time work	
	%	%	%	%	%	%	%	%	%
Less than 2 weeks	42	50	44	20	28	22	29	33	32
2 weeks but less than 1 month	20	16	19	19	14	18	16	19	19
1 month but less than 3 months	22	20	21	27	21	26	29	20	22
3 months but less than 6 months	8	8	8	18	10	16	13	16	15
6 months or more	8	6	8	16	27	19	13	12	12
	100	**100**	**100**	**100**	**100**	**100**	**100**	**100**	**100**
Looked for under 1 month	62	66	63	40	43	40	44	52	51
Looked continuously over 1 month	17	16	17	44	22	39	29	16	18
Looked on and off over 1 month	21	18	20	16	35	21	27	31	30
	100	**100**	**100**	**100**	**100**	**100**	**100**	**100**	**100**
Base*	298	145	446†	282	96	409†	46	250	300†

*Excludes informants who were not looking for work but the employer offered a job
†Includes informants who did not know whether they wanted full or part time work

Table 11.20 Reasons for difficulty in finding jobs given by women who had found a job in the past two years and who had experienced difficulties

Reasons for difficulty in finding jobs	Found a job in the past two years: was previously								
	Working			Unemployed			Domestic returner		
	Looking for:			Looking for:			Looking for:		
	Full time work	Part time work	All	Full time work	Part time work	All	Full time work	Part time work	All
	%	%	%	%	%	%		%	%
Few jobs at all around here	60	66	61	74	63	71		67	69
No jobs of the type wanted	64	64	64	72	73	72		60	60
No jobs with hours wanted	19	69	38	18	65	30		84	75
Too old/young	6	2	4	4	2	4		2	4
Lack of experience/qualifications	6	2	4	9	2	7		1	1
Other difficulties	7	14	10	10	10	10		7	10
Base	*89*	*55*	*145**	*142*	*51*	*196**	*22†*	*102*	*124**

Percentages total more than 100 as informants mentioned several reasons
*Includes informants who did not know whether they wanted full or part time work
†Base too small to show percentages

Job search in 1980

The situation was, of course, rather different in several ways for those looking for work in 1980 compared with 1978. Comparatively the economic situation had worsened and general unemployment was higher. Moreover, these women were still looking for a job at the time of the interview. It is therefore only possible to talk about how long they had looked up to that point and the difficulties already encountered. We turn to these next. Table 11.21 shows that only a small proportion of women, between 13% and 21%, said they had been looking for a job for less than a month. Amongst those trying to change jobs and the unemployed, the majority had been looking for a job for over three months (63% and 55% respectively). Domestic returners had on average been looking for slightly less time: 48% had looked for three months or longer.

Interestingly, there was not much difference between women wanting full and part time work in the length of time they had looked. Women wanting part time work, however, were more likely to say they had looked 'on and off' rather than continuously, though amongst these, those who were unemployed were least likely to say this: 45%, compared with 65% of job changers and

63% of domestic returners. Brief comparison of Tables 11.19 and 11.21 shows that women looking for a job in 1980 reported markedly longer periods of job search. Undoubtedly this is largely accounted for by the change in the economic climate.

However, it is also probable that people looking back on an incident may telescope time. For example, other studies show that women, particularly those returning to work, date their period of looking from when something likely came up rather than the more ill defined period of 'beginning to look' which the women who were looking at the time of our survey may well include. The difficulties reported in 1980 (Table 11.22) were much the same as those reported by women who had been successful job seekers in 1978–80, with the interesting exception that job changers who wanted full time work were more likely than those wanting part time work to say there were no jobs of the type wanted: 74% compared with 68%. Unemployed women who wanted full time work were markedly less likely to say this: 48% did compared with 72% who wanted part time work. In addition more of the unemployed in 1980 gave their age as a reason for difficulty; usually these were older women experiencing similar problems to

Table 11.21 Length of time spent looking for a job by women currently looking for a job

How long women had looked for work	Currently looking for a job								
	Working			Unemployed			Domestic returner		
	Looking for:			Looking for:			Looking for:		
	Full time work	Part time work	All	Full time work	Part time work	All	Full time work	Part time work	All
	%	%	%	%	%	%		%	%
Less than 2 weeks	6	5	6	9	13	11		1	4
2 weeks but less than 1 month	13	8	11	11	7	10		18	17
1 month but less than 3 months	20	20	20	25	23	24		31	31
3 months but less than 6 months	21	24	22	21	22	21		22	21
6 months or more	40	43	41	34	35	34		28	27
	100	**100**	**100**	**100**	**100**	**100**		**100**	**100**
Looked for under 1 month	20	13	17	21	20	21		20	21
Looked continuously over 1 month	23	21	22	44	35	40		17	19
Looked on and off over 1 month	57	65	61	35	45	39		63	60
	100	**100**	**100**	**100**	**100**	**100**		**100**	**100**
Base*	*165*	*119*	*290**	*111*	*91*	*211**	*15†*	*88*	*107**

*Includes informants who did not know whether they wanted full or part time work
†Base too small to show percentages

Table 11.22 Reasons for difficulties in finding jobs given by women currently looking for a job who have experienced difficulties

Reasons for difficulty in finding jobs	Currently looking for a job								
	Working			Unemployed			Domestic returner		
	Looking for: Full time work	Part time work	All	Looking for: Full time work	Part time work	All	Looking for: Full time work	Part time work	All
	%	%	%	%	%	%		%	%
Few jobs at all around here	56	60	58	77	76	76		72	68
No jobs of the type wanted	74	68	71	48	72	59		63	62
No jobs with hours wanted	17	72	40	19	59	36		89	80
Too old/young	5	5	5	10	10	10		–	–
Lack of experience/qualifications	6	3	4	7	6	8		–	–
Other difficulties	22	9	17	21	10	16		8	10
Base	126	97	229*	99	81	187*	14†	73	90*

Percentages total to more than 100 as informants mentioned several reasons
*Includes informants who did not know whether they wanted full or part time work
†Base too small to show percentages

Table 11.23 Proportion of women currently looking for a job who rated different methods of job seeking as very or fairly useful

Different methods of job seeking	Currently looking for a job								
	Working			Unemployed			Domestic returner		
	Looking for: Full time work	Part time work	All	Looking for: Full time work	Part time work	All	Looking for: Full time work	Part time work	All
Looking at advertisements	91%	93%	92%	82%	88%	85%		87%	87%
Approaching employers directly	72%	67%	70%	65%	65%	65%		63%	66%
Using the government employment office/jobcentres	57%	60%	58%	72%	53%	65%		54%	57%
Asking around people you know	56%	56%	55%	67%	60%	64%		60%	60%
Using private employment agencies	51%	37%	46%	28%	25%	27%		38%	37%
Base	165	119	290*	111	91	211*	15†	88	107*

*Includes informants who did not know whether they wanted full or part time work
†Base too small to show percentages

those unemployed men nearing retirement age have when looking for a job.

We asked women who were looking for work to say how useful they thought different methods of looking for work were and their answers are shown in Table 11.23. 'Looking at advertisements' was rated as very or fairly useful by high proportions of women in all groups. 'Approaching employers directly' was seen as useful by about two thirds of women in all groups though more unemployed women looking for a full time job rated the public employment services as useful than a direct approach to employers. Generally more women looking for a change of employer rated the government agencies useful than rated either 'asking around people you know' or private employment agencies. Fewest people in all groups held private employment agencies to be very or fairly useful methods, reflecting no doubt the more specialised parts of the labour market they cover. What is of interest, however, is that more people rated methods as very or fairly useful than might be expected from the usefulness of the method to those who had found jobs. For example, a direct approach to an employer was seen as a useful method by large numbers of women. However, as we saw from Table 11.17, only a small proportion of women found a job in that way, fewer, in fact, than got a job via a friend or relative yet this latter method was rated as useful by fewer women. A similar phenom-

enon is also noted in Martin and Wallace's more detailed and longitudinal study of effective job search methods in their research on redundant women (Martin and Wallace, 1984).

It is very difficult to make any assessment of the labour market situation women are facing without some measure of the tightness of the local labour market. Our study could not collect these data, though in their analyses at an aggregate level both Joshi and Dex use standard unemployment and/or vacancy measures. Thus, while we asked women who were looking for work whether they had actually applied for any jobs, lack of an application cannot necessarily be taken to be a sign of less interest in getting a job; it could equally well reflect a greater local scarcity of possible jobs. With that proviso we show in Table 11.24 the proportion of women in each group who had applied for a job and the proportion who had found out about these jobs from a government agency, either an employment office or a Jobcentre, in Table 11.25.

A majority of the women who were trying to change jobs or who were unemployed had applied for at least one job (57% and 68% respectively). In both groups higher proportions of women looking for full time work had applied than women looking for part time work. In contrast only 44% of the domestic returners had applied for a job. Since domestic returners would be applying in the main for part time jobs it was noticeable that fewer of them had applied than those women wanting part time work in the other groups who were already in the labour market. Whether this reflects a lesser confidence about their abilities as workers, a greater tentativeness about returning to work or fewer suitable jobs is not possible to determine. What is striking, however, is that women who were most likely to be in urgent need of a job, namely those who were unemployed and wanted full time work, were most likely to have made at least one job application: 75% had. Unemployed women were also more likely to say they had found out about the job(s) they applied for through a government employment office or Jobcentre,

Table 11.24 Proportion of women currently looking for a job who had applied for jobs

	Currently looking for a job								
	Working			Unemployed			Domestic returner		
	Looking for:			Looking for:			Looking for:		
	Full time work	Part time work	All	Full time work	Part time work	All	Full time work	Part time work	All
Proportion of women who had applied for jobs	61%	52%	57%	75%	60%	68%		42%	44%
Base	165	119	290*	111	91	211*	15†	88	107*

*Includes informants who did not know whether they wanted full or part time work
†Base too small to show averages

Table 11.25 Proportions of women currently working and who had applied for jobs who had found out about the jobs from a government employment office or Jobcentre

	Currently looking for a job								
	Working			Unemployed			Domestic returner		
	Looking for:			Looking for:			Looking for:		
	Full time work	Part time work	All	Full time work	Part time work	All	Full time work	Part time work	All
Proportion of women who had found out about jobs from a government employment office or Jobcentre	22%	14%	20%	57%	31%	46%		14%	22%
Base	97	59	160*	81	55	142*	9†	35	45*

*Includes informants who did not know whether they wanted full or part time work
†Base too small to show percentages

Table 11.26 Proportions of women currently looking for a job who would be willing to go on a course

	Currently looking for a job								
	Working			Unemployed			Domestic returner		
	Looking for:			Looking for:			Looking for:		
	Full time work	Part time work	All	Full time work	Part time work	All	Full time work	Part time work	All
Willing to go on a course	82%	81%	82%	80%	70%	75%		60%	62%
Base	165	119	290*	111	91	211*	15†	88	107*

*Includes informants who did not know whether they wanted full or part time work
†Base too small to show percentages

Table 11.27 Whether women who were willing to go on a course wanted to attend full or part time

Would prefer to attend:	Currently looking for a job								
	Working			Unemployed			Domestic returner		
	Looking for:			Looking for:			Looking for:		
	Full time work	Part time work	All	Full time work	Part time work	All	Full time work	Part time work	All
	%	%	%	%	%	%		%	%
Full time course	57	17	40	67	21	48		4	9
Part time course	26	69	44	16	73	40		92	85
Don't mind	17	15	16	16	6	12		4	6
	100	**100**	**100**	**100**	**100**	**100**		**100**	**100**
Base	136	96	237*	89	64	157*	10†	53	66*

*Includes informants who did not know whether they wanted full or part time work
†Base too small to show percentages

particularly those women looking for a full time job (57%). In all groups women looking for part time work were less likely to hear about the job(s) they applied for through government agencies than women looking for full time work, which following the findings shown in Table 11.18 is not surprising.

Finally, we asked all women looking for a job whether they would be willing to go on a course beforehand if it would help them find a job and if so whether they preferred a full or part time course. In a sense this is not so much a question about willingness to train as a measure of how keen women are to get a job; other research shows people looking for work generally have an instrumental approach to training as one possible way to improve their chances in the labour market. In addition, we know from Chapter 5 that a taste for further training is associated with previous experience of training. Thus women already in the labour market, particularly those in jobs, may have had more recent experience of training. Our results therefore have to be treated with care.

Table 11.26 shows that women who were working were most likely to be willing to go on a course: 82% said they would be willing to do this, with no significant difference between women wanting full or part time work. Unemployed women wanting full time work were equally willing to go on a course. The difference between these three groups and the others was rather more marked however. Unemployed women looking for a part time job and domestic returners, most of whom also wanted part time work, were less willing to go on a course, though in all cases at least 60% were willing to do this. However, there was a significant difference in all groups between women preferring a full or part time training course as Table 11.27 shows. There was, as might be expected, a marked preference for part time courses amongst women looking for part time work, particularly amongst women returning to work after a period of domestic absence. Quite clearly the same factors which operate to constrain a woman's willingness to work full time operate to affect the amount of time she can spend on a training course.

Summary and conclusions
This chapter has looked at how women look for and find jobs and has focussed on two groups of respondents; the 11% of women who were looking for a job at the time of the interview and the 26% of women who had found a job in the two years prior to the survey. Women were either seen as in the labour market whilst looking for a job, that is either working or unemployed, or alternatively they were seen as attempting to re-enter the labour market after a period of domestic absence. Throughout the chapter we compared the responses of women in these three different labour market positions, distinguishing also between women looking for full or part time work.

Women in the labour market were markedly different from women attempting to re-enter it. The latter group were overwhelmingly mothers of children under 16, whilst childless women were the largest single group of women amongst both working and unemployed women. Domestic returners were much more likely to be looking for part time work (over 80% were), although part time work was also wanted by a minority, albeit a fairly sizeable minority, of working or unemployed women. Domestic returners were also much more likely to be concerned with the issue of childcare either in terms of getting working hours to fit in with domestic responsibilities or in terms of making alternative childcare arrangements.

Domestic returners' reasons for working differed from those of the other groups. This was largely because the differences between women wanting full or part time work were pronounced. Overall, financial reasons for working were paramount in all groups, but women in the labour market emphasised financial need or financial autonomy more than women returning to work. Even when we compared women wanting part time work, domestic returners were less likely to mention financial reasons and more likely to mention the sociability work afforded them. This difference was so marked that it is clear that the 'company' dimension of working is more powerful as a motivator bringing women back into the labour market than it continues to be once they are back in the labour market. No doubt it is partly for these reasons that domestic returners and women looking for part time work in general were less likely to stress the importance of finding a job soon, while it was particularly important for unemployed women looking for full time work to find a job quickly. Domestic returners were likely too to be less concerned than working women with the 'quality' of a job. They were not choosing to look for a better job as most of the working women were, but were looking for a job. Women wanting part time work, in contrast, tended to trade off aspects of a job such as good pay, security and the opportunity to use one's abilities in favour of convenient hours.

Not all women who get a job look for it; some are offered a job without looking. This is more likely to happen to women wanting part time work and is quite an important way in which women re-enter the labour market, often when previous employers ask them back. For other women the type of job they look for and the way they look for work depends on their labour market position. Women without a job are rather different from women looking for a change of job. The latter group are more likely to be looking for higher non-manual jobs and using private employment agencies and are less likely to be using the public employment services. Unemployed women used all methods of job search, including the public employment services, more frequently than other women looking for a change of job or those re-entering the labour market. Women wanting part time work were both less likely to look for all types of non-manual jobs and used all methods of job search less.

By looking at how successful job searchers found jobs the survey throws some interesting light on the strategies job searchers use. In all groups a high proportion of jobs were found through newspaper advertisements or the informal network of friends and relatives, the latter method being particularly useful for finding a part time job. Amongst women without a job, those looking for full time work found a sizeable proportion of jobs through the public employment services. There was, however, an interesting discrepancy between the methods women looking in 1980 rated as useful and the methods which produced a job for successful job searchers. The former, for example, rated a direct approach to an employer more highly than asking friends and relatives. Yet fewer jobs were obtained through the direct approach method.

Women experienced a range of difficulties in finding a job. Some difficulties were common to all groups, reflecting a general shortage of jobs; others were experienced by women in particular situations facing more specific difficulties. Women wanting part time work, for example, cited the lack of jobs with the hours they wanted; unemployed women were more likely to cite their lack of qualifications or experience, while unemployed women looking in 1980 also gave their age as a cause of difficulty; these were usually older women. Even though they were experiencing difficulty in finding a job, about half the women looking in 1980 had applied for jobs, though the unemployed, particularly those looking for full time jobs, had applied for more jobs than working women and domestic returners wanting part time work. It is not possible to say, however, whether this was evidence of greater work attachment on the part of the unemployed or women wanting full time work, or whether there were in fact fewer jobs for which domestic returners could apply. If willingness to go on a training course is evidence of interest in getting a job then women in the labour market, particularly those looking for a full time job, were more attached to having a job than domestic returners.

In conclusion, in this chapter we have looked at women's job search behaviour not only to illuminate this in itself, but more particularly to continue our examination of whether unemployed women and domestic returners are markedly different in their labour market priorities and behaviour. What is clear from our findings is that a woman's labour market position cannot be looked at in isolation from whether she wants full or part time employment, as both labour market position and employment status are related to attitudes and behaviour, though as we have shown their relative strength varies according to the issue. Our findings suggest, however, that it is not helpful in terms of understanding the needs of women wanting a job to assign all women without paid work who are looking for a job to one category. As well as distinguishing between women in the labour market and women attempting to re-enter it, it is also necessary to know whether women are looking for full or part time work.

Chapter 12 Attitudes to women's role at work and home

Introduction

In our society (and, indeed, generally in industrial society) women and men are seen as having different expectations with respect to paid work arising out of their different roles in both the market economy and the domestic economy. Earlier chapters have presented evidence to show that women are spending increasingly more of their working lives in paid employment, but continue to combine this with a major share of domestic and childcare work. In the recent past married women have been seen as having a choice about whether they work or not and, insofar as the vast majority of women marry at some time, this notion of choice affects both how women view their actual or potential work and home roles and, perhaps more importantly, how women are viewed and treated both at home and in paid work. However, dominant assumptions of this kind vary with time and it is clear that the whole issue of the extent and nature of choice for women is currently changing. Nowadays it would sound odd, for example, to ask young women whether they would go on working after marriage; currently the choice of whether to work or not is essentially associated with the event of childbearing. The concept of choice therefore exists chiefly for married women who have children, although in practice not all such women will be in circumstances that enable them to exercise a choice about whether to work or not.

In this chapter we examine data on the general attitudes of the women and the husbands in the survey towards the position of women at home and at work. Clearly attitudes to the balance between work and home will be an important part of the context in which women chose to enter or re-enter employment. The relationship between attitudes and behaviour is not necessarily straightforward. Initial attitudes may determine whether women work or not in particular circumstances or the type of work commitment or ambitions they have (Dex, 1982; Spitze and Waite, 1980). However, once a choice is made attitudes may be modified by the subsequent experience resulting from that choice.[1]

Another difficulty when collecting attitudes at one point in time is in assessing changes in attitudes between different generations of women. We know there have been generational changes in women's employment behaviour; far more women with young children are working currently than was the case when the oldest women in the sample had young children. We would therefore expect to find differences in the attitudes of the older and younger women to whether women with young children should work. However, again we cannot determine the dynamics of the relationship between generational differences in behaviour and attitudes when the information about attitudes is confined to one particular point in time. We are able, however, in this chapter to relate some of the survey data to those collected by Hunt in 1965 and this gives us a check on the internal validity of our data as well as being of interest in its own right.

With the above caveats in mind the chapter shows how women's attitudes to women's roles at home and at work relate to the choices that they have made about working and how they differ for women at different life stages. We also look at the attitudes expressed by the husbands of the married women who were interviewed. It is of particular interest to look at the views of young childless women who expect to have children, since these women have not yet had to face the issue of whether to work when they have children, though their attitudes to work will be influenced by their expectations about marriage and motherhood (Maizels, 1970; Brown, 1976; Sharpe, 1976).

It is clear from what we have said up to this point that we would expect the increasing participation of women in the labour force to have the potential to affect general attitudes towards labour market and domestic work (Huber and Spitze, 1981). However, as we pointed out in the introductory chapter, legislation can also be seen as part of a process of changing attitudes as well as an outcome of wider changes in social values and behaviour. Our survey was conducted five years after major legislation on equal pay and opportunities for women was introduced and implemented. We cannot measure directly how the Equal Pay Act, Sex Discrimination Act and the maternity provisions of the Employment Protection Act have affected women, but we did ask women how important they felt the main provisions of the legislation were. We discuss their attitudes as responses to the values underlying these provisions at the end of the chapter.

Women's general attitudes to home and work

In order to identify and measure general attitudes to the relationship between work and domestic commitments and the importance of work to women, we showed women twelve statements about women and work and asked them to indicate the extent to which they agreed or disagreed with each one. These statements were taken from a longer list used in pilot work and generated from a variety of sources including previous studies and versions of or modifications to popular statements (Hunt, 1968; Marsh, 1979). The relationships between women's opinions on each statement were analysed to discover whether opinions on particular statements tended to cluster together and therefore could be said to be explained by the existence of an underlying attitude.[2]

Our analysis showed that women's answers to seven of the statements were interrelated and that these statements appeared to be tapping traditional attitudes to women's role at home and work. Answers to a further three statements were also interrelated and these appeared to reflect women's attitudes to whether work is advantageous for women, particularly to women with families. Answers to the remaining two statements were not closely related to each other or to any of the other two groups of statements. Table 12.1 lists the statements in the order of the strength of their contribution to the underlying attitudes (factors) which they appear to be measuring. Table 12.1 also shows the extent of agreement or disagreement with each of the twelve statements for all the women in the sample.

Although the statements were designed to identify and measure underlying attitudes it is interesting to look at women's opinions on each in its own right. Only 25% of women agreed with the view that 'a woman's place is in

the home', but almost half the women (46%) agreed with a less extreme statement: 'a husband's job is to earn the money; a wife's job is to look after the home and family'. Agreement with the latter, however, is not incompatible with thinking that women should have paid jobs as well. Interestingly, in view of the unemployment situation at the time of the survey, 49% of women disagreed with the statement 'in times of high unemployment married women should stay at home' compared with 35% who agreed Although 41% of women agreed that 'a job is alright, but what most women really want is a home and children', 55% disagreed with the statement 'women can't combine a career and children'. However, about half agreed that 'most working women with families want jobs with no worries or responsibilities'. The statement associated with traditional attitudes with which the highest proportion of women disagreed, 66%, was 'most married women only work for pin money – they don't need a job'; 20% agreed with this, only 6% strongly.

Turning to the second group of statements it is clear that most women do not think that work and children are incompatible: 71% agreed with 'if her children are well looked after it's good for a woman to work' and only 12% disagreed. The majority of women (67%) also agreed that 'having a job is the best way for a

Table 12.1 Extent of agreement with statements expressing general opinions about women and work: all women

Attitude statements		Agree strongly	Agree slightly	Neither agree nor disagree	Disagree slightly	Disagree strongly	
Traditional attitudes to home and work							
A woman's place is in the home	%	11	14	18	16	41	100
			25			57	
A husband's job is to earn the money; a wife's job is to look after the home and family	%	20	26	21	16	17	100
			46			33	
In times of high unemployment married women should stay at home	%	15	20	16	20	29	100
			35			49	
A job is alright, but what most women really want is a home and children	%	18	23	25	17	17	100
			41			34	
Women can't combine a career and children	%	12	17	16	28	27	100
			29			55	
Most working women with families want jobs with no worries or responsibilities	%	19	30	17	20	14	100
			49			34	
Most married women only work for pin money – they don't need a job	%	6	14	14	25	41	100
			20			66	
Attitudes to the benefits of work to women and family							
If her children are well looked after it's good for a woman to work	%	40	31	17	7	5	100
			71			12	
Having a job is the best way for a woman to be an independent person	%	36	31	17	9	7	100
			67			16	
A woman and her family will all be happier if she goes out to work	%	8	21	32	22	17	100
			29			39	
Other statements							
If a woman takes several years off to look after her children she should expect her career to suffer	%	11	33	30	20	16	100
			44			36	
Married women have a right to work if they want to, whatever their family situation	%	47	24	12	10	7	100
			71			17	

Base (=100%)   5,588

woman to be an independent person'. However, opinion was more divided over the last statement, 'a woman and her family will all be happier if she goes out to work', with 29% agreeing and 39% disagreeing and a high proportion of women (32%) taking a middle view or not having an opinion. Women were also more divided as to whether a woman should expect her career to suffer if she took several years off to care for children; 44% felt she should, whilst 36% disagreed with this view. But the statement dealing with the basic issue that 'married women have a right to work if they want to, whatever their family situation' attracted much more support; 71% of women agreed with this, 47% strongly.

The overall picture conveyed by these results is that only a minority of women nowadays hold to the traditional view that 'a woman's place is in the home'; although most endorse the right and need of married women with families to work, work is considered by many women to be secondary to home and family and something to be accommodated to domestic demands. However, these overall results conceal big differences between the views of working and non-working women. We therefore show their views separately in Table 12.2.

Differences between the answers of working and non-working women are most apparent for the first three statements shown. Working women were much less likely than non-working women to agree that 'a woman's place is in the home', 'a husband's job is to earn the money; a wife's job is to look after the home and family', or 'in times of high unemployment married women should stay at home'. Nevertheless, substantial minorities of non-working women also disagreed with these statements. The remaining four statements expressing traditional attitudes to women and work all imply that, although work has a subsidiary role in women's lives compared with the home and family, it nevertheless has a role. The working and non-working women's answers differed less on these statements, although non-working women tended to express more traditional views.

It is perhaps not surprising that working women were more likely than non-working women to endorse statements about the benefits of work to women; however over half the non-working women also agreed that 'if her children are well looked after it's good for a woman to work' and 'having a job is the best way for a woman to be an independent person'. Neither group was so convinced that 'a woman and her family will all be happier if she goes out to work', although the working women were more likely to agree with this. Working women were slightly more likely to disagree with the statement that 'if a woman takes several years off to look after her children she should expect her career to

Table 12.2 Extent of agreement with statements expressing general opinions about women and work: working and non-working women

Attitudes statements	Working/non-working	Agree strongly	Agree slightly	Neither agree nor disagree	Disagree slightly	Disagree strongly	
Traditional attitudes to home and work A woman's place is in the home	Working % Non-working %	7 19	13 18	17 21	18 13	45 29	100 100
A husband's job is to earn the money; a wife's job is to look after the home and family	Working % Non-working %	16 30	26 26	22 21	17 13	19 10	100 100
In times of high unemployment married women should stay at home	Working % Non-working %	10 25	19 22	15 17	22 16	34 19	100 100
A job is alright, but what most women really want is a home and children	Working % Non-working %	15 24	24 23	25 24	18 15	18 13	100 100
Women can't combine a career and children	Working % Non-working %	10 16	16 19	14 21	30 24	30 20	100 100
Most working women with families want jobs with no worries or responsibilities	Working % Non-working %	18 20	31 29	16 19	21 18	14 14	100 100
Most married women only work for pin money – they don't need a job	Working % Non-working %	5 9	13 15	11 17	25 26	46 32	100 100
Attitudes to the benefits of work to women and family If her children are well looked after it's good for a woman to work	Working % Non-working %	45 32	31 31	15 21	6 9	3 7	100 100
Having a job is the best way for a woman to be an independent person	Working % Non-working %	41 29	31 29	16 19	8 12	4 11	100 100
A woman and her family will all be happier if she goes out to work	Working % Non-working %	9 6	24 16	34 28	21 24	12 26	100 100
Other statements If a woman takes several years off to look after her children she should expect her career to suffer	Working % Non-working %	10 13	33 33	19 21	21 19	17 14	100 100
Married women have a right to work if they want to, whatever their family situation	Working % Non-working %	49 43	24 25	11 13	10 11	6 8	100 100

Base (=100%) Working women 3,354
Non-working women 1,941

suffer' and to agree with the view that 'married women have a right to work if they want to, whatever their family situation'.

We now return to the grouping of the individual statements to give overall measures on the two main attitudes identified. The measures used (factor scores) were standardised to allow comparisons to be made between them. Standardisation takes account of the different contribution of each statement to the overall measures and the different numbers and distribution of statements. This means that the measures used are relative rather than absolute; we can say that one group of women has a higher measure on traditional attitudes than another group but we cannot say whether women in the sample as a whole are high or low on this measure. To facilitate comparisons between sub-groups on each attitude measure women were divided into three groups: high scorers, medium scorers and low scorers. (High and low scorers were defined as more than 0.5 standard deviations from the mean and medium scorers were within 0.5 standard deviations of the mean.) This enabled us to compare the proportion of women in particular subgroups falling in each of the three groups on each attitude measure.

Looking first at traditional attitudes to home and work

we compare in Table 12.3 women in the different working status categories. Non-working women were more likely than working women to have high scores on traditional views and less likely to have non-traditional views. Among the working women those working full time were less likely to have high scores on traditional views than those working part time. Full time students, however, were least likely to hold traditional views and over half were in the lowest scoring category, with non-traditional views. This suggests that women's views on this dimension may be a function of age or life stage as well as working status.

Table 12.4 shows how the proportions of women in the three categories varies for women at different life stages, with working and non-working women shown separately. Looking first at the bottom set of figures, for all women, it seems there is a relationship with age rather than life stage; older childless women were more likely to have traditional views than childless women under 30 while, among women who had children, those aged 50 or over with grown-up children were more likely to hold traditional views than those under 50 or women with younger children, the majority of whom were under 50.

It may seem surprising that the results for women with

Table 12.3 Level of traditional attitudes to home and work by work status

Level of traditional attitudes to women and work	Working full time	Working part time	All working	Not working	Full time student	All women
	%	%	%	%	%	%
1 (Traditional)	21	29	24	41	12	30
2	39	43	41	38	33	39
3 (Non-traditional)	40	28	35	21	55	31
	100	100	100	100	100	100
Base	1,877	1,477	3,354	1,941	293	5,588

Table 12.4 Level of traditional attitudes to home and work by life cycle stage for working and non-working women

Level of traditional attitudes to home and work	Life cycle stage							All women
	Childless women aged:		Women with youngest child aged:			Women with all children aged 16 and over, aged:		
	under 30	30 and over	0–4	5–10	11–15	Under 50	50 or over	
Working women	%	%	%	%	%	%	%	%
1 (Traditional)	20	28	17	21	26	23	36	24
2	39	38	41	39	40	43	45	41
3 (Non-traditional)	41	34	42	40	34	34	19	35
	100	100	100	100	100	100	100	100
Base	758	328	276	553	538	362	539	3,354
Non-working women								
1 (Traditional)	38	61	29	43	43	57	56	42
2	38	26	42	36	39	31	33	37
3 (Non-traditional)	24	13	28	21	18	12	11	21
	100	100	100	100	100	100	100	100
Base	129	86	762	315	172	106	371	1,941
*All women**								
1 (Traditional)	20	35	26	29	30	30	45	30
2	38	36	42	38	40	41	40	39
3 (Non-traditional)	43	29	32	33	30	29	16	31
	100	100	100	100	100	100	100	100
Base	1,161	416	1,041	877	714	468	911	5,588

*Including full time students

youngest children of different ages were very similar. However, the explanation is apparent when the results for working and non-working women are compared. At each life cycle stage non-working women were more likely to hold traditional views than working women, but traditional views were also most common among the older women. For women with children the proportion working was greater when the age of the youngest child was greater and so the two relationships are working in opposite directions, largely cancelling one another out. It is interesting to note also that even among childless women under 30, the non-working women were more likely to hold traditional views than the working women, despite the fact that the majority were unemployed rather than not working from choice.

A possible explanation for this finding may lie in the fact that women without qualifications tended to hold more traditional views than better qualified women, and unqualified women were more vulnerable to unemployment. Table 12.5 shows that amongst both working and non-working women those with the highest qualifications were most likely to hold non-traditional attitudes whilst those with no qualifications were likely to hold traditional views. Similarly, among working women those in the highest level occupations were least likely to hold traditional views. A number of other factors may also be important, but insofar as they are also related to working status and life stage, it is difficult to show the relationship in simple tables. Further analysis of these data using regression techniques has been carried out by Dex, which confirms that having 'more educational qualifications reduces women's expression of traditional views about the sexual divisions of labour' (Dex, 1984b).

Differences in women's attitudes to the benefits of work for women were examined in a similar manner. Table 12.6 shows how these vary between women according to their working status. This shows, as we would expect, a significant difference in the attitudes of working and non-working women. The students, who would expect to work soon, were similar to the working women. What is interesting about these results for working women is that there is no difference between full and part time workers in the proportions judging work to be beneficial or not, unlike the response on the traditional factor where part time workers were less likely to be non-traditional than full timers. This is quite understandable in that the attitude statements are about the general benefits or not of working at all, rather than the amount of work being done.

Table 12.7 shows the relationship between attitudes to the benefits of work to women and life cycle. Given the very strong relationship of these views to work status it

Table 12.5 Level of traditional attitudes to home and work for working and non-working women by their highest qualification

Level of traditional attitudes to home and work	Highest qualification				All women
	'A' level or above	'O' level or equivalent	CSE or equivalent	No qualifications	
	%	%	%	%	%
Working women					
1 (Traditional)	12	19	27	31	24
2	33	42	43	43	41
3 (Non-traditional)	55	39	30	26	35
	100	**100**	**100**	**100**	**100**
Base	617	665	538	1,534	3,354
Non-working women					
1 (Traditional)	25	33	37	49	41
2	39	41	37	37	38
3 (Non-traditional)	37	27	26	14	21
	100	**100**	**100**	**100**	**100**
Base	248	320	266	1,107	1,941
*All women**					
1 (Traditional)	15	22	30	38	30
2	35	40	41	40	39
3 (Non-traditional)	50	38	29	22	31
	100	**100**	**100**	**100**	**100**
Base	925	1,112	825	2,726	5,588

*Including full time students

Table 12.6 Level of attitudes to the benefits of work to women and family by work status

Level of attitudes to the benefits of work to women and family	Working full time	Working part time	All working	Not working	Full time student	All women
	%	%	%	%	%	%
1 (Work beneficial)	35	35	35	21	33	30
2	47	46	47	40	45	44
3 (Work not beneficial)	18	19	18	39	22	26
	100	**100**	**100**	**100**	**100**	**100**
Base	1,877	1,477	3,354	1,941	293	5,588

Table 12.7 Level of attitudes to the benefits of work to women and family by life cycle stage for working and non-working women

Level of attitudes to the benefits of work to women and family	Life cycle stage							All women
	Childless women aged:		Women with youngest child aged:			All children aged 16 and over, women aged:		
	Under 30	30 to 59	0–4	5–10	11–15	Under 50	50 or over	
	%	%	%	%	%	%	%	%
Working women								
1 (Work beneficial)	28	30	35	37	37	41	37	35
2	51	48	48	46	46	42	44	47
3 (Work not beneficial)	21	22	16	16	16	17	19	18
	100	100	100	100	100	100	100	100
Base	758	328	276	553	538	362	539	3,354
Non-working women								
1 (Work beneficial)	32	26	19	19	20	18	23	21
2	42	41	40	39	40	51	39	40
3 (Work not beneficial)	26	33	41	42	40	31	39	39
	100	100	100	100	100	100	100	100
Base	129	86	762	315	172	106	371	1,941
*All women**								
1 (Work beneficial)	30	29	23	31	33	36	31	30
2	49	47	43	44	45	44	42	44
3 (Work not beneficial)	21	24	34	26	22	20	27	26
	100	100	100	100	100	100	100	100
Base	1,161	416	1,041	877	714	468	911	5,588

*Including full time students

is more interesting to look first at working and non-working women separately than to compare the overall results. Among the working women there was very little difference among women with children; the main distinction is that childless women were less likely than women with children to think work is beneficial to women. Among the non-working women the reverse was true: childless women were more likely to think work is beneficial than women with children, and there was again not very much difference among the various categories of women with children. Thus among women with children there were big differences between the views of working and non-working women, whereas among the childless women under 30 the dif-

ferences were not very great. Among the older childless women those who were not working were more likely than those who were working to doubt that work is beneficial to women.

These results probably reflect both the choices about working or not which women have actually had to make and the experiences they have had. Women with children have inevitably made choices, and their views can be expected to reflect the choice they have made. Thus, we would expect more mothers of young children who were working to feel working was beneficial than non-working mothers. It is likely too, that some of the older childless women have chosen not to work and their

Table 12.8 Level of attitudes to the benefits of work to women and family by highest qualification for working and non-working women

Level of attitudes to the benefits of work to women and family	Highest qualification				All women
	'A' level or above	'O' level or equivalent	CSE or equivalent	No qualifications	
	%	%	%	%	%
Working women					
(Work beneficial)	29	31	33	39	35
2	50	50	48	44	47
3 (Work not beneficial)	21	29	19	17	18
	100	100	100	100	100
Base	617	665	538	1,534	3,354
Non-working women					
1 (Work beneficial)	13	14	18	25	21
2	37	40	40	42	40
3 (Work not beneficial)	50	46	42	33	39
	100	100	100	100	100
Base	248	320	266	1,107	1,941
*All women**					
1 (Work beneficial)	26	25	28	34	30
2	45	48	45	43	45
3 (Work not beneficial)	29	27	27	23	25
	100	100	100	100	100
Base	925	1,112	825	2,726	5,588

*Including full time students

attitudes reflect this choice. However, for most younger childless women the situation is more complex. Firstly, for those who were working, the choice they will make about working when they have children lies in the future, if and when they experience having children and a period of not working. Since we showed in Chapter 6 that young childless women were less likely to be attached to working than women with children who had chosen to work, it is perhaps doubly understandable that they are less likely than women working with children to think this is beneficial. Secondly many of the young childless women were in fact looking for work and therefore likely to be more akin in their attitudes and situation to their working contemporaries than older childless women.

Looking at other factors which might relate to women's attitudes to the benefits of work to women, Table 12.8 shows that women with qualifications were more likely than those with no qualifications to think work beneficial; this was true of both working and non-working women. However there was little difference in the views of women with different level qualifications.

Wives' and husbands' general attitudes to women's home and work roles
Although we cannot compare women's attitudes to home and work to those of men in general we thought

husband's attitudes were likely to be particularly interesting and we therefore compared the attitudes of the sample of husbands we interviewed with the attitudes of their wives. Table 12.9 compares their opinions on each of the individual statements which contributed to the two overall measures. It is clear that on each of the statements relating to traditional views about home and work the husbands had more traditional views than the wives and were more likely to 'agree strongly' than wives who, if they agreed, were more likely to 'agree slightly'. On one item there was considerable unanimity: 65% of husbands and wives rejected the view that 'most married women only work for pin money – they don't need a job' though there was less unanimity over whether 'in times of high unemployment married women should stay at home': 50% of wives disagreed compared with 43% of husbands.

Husbands and wives differed most on the view that 'a job is alright but what most women really want is a home and children': 35% of wives disagreed with this compared with 20% of husbands. Although about half the wives and husbands (48% and 52% respectively) agreed that 'most working women with families want jobs with no worries or responsibilities', wives were more likely to reject this view than husbands: 37% did compared with 28%. Opinions on the three statements of attitudes to the benefits of work to women showed less difference between wives and husbands. We would

Table 12.9   Extent of agreement with statements expressing general opinions about women and work: wives and husbands

Attitudes statements	Wives/ husbands	Agree strongly	Agree slightly	Neither agree nor disagree	Disagree slightly	Disagree strongly	
Traditional attitudes to home and work							
A woman's place is in the home	Wives %	11	16	18	16	39	100
	Husbands %	17	15	22	17	29	100
A husband's job is to earn the money; a wife's job is to look after the home and family	Wives %	21	27	21	16	15	100
	Husbands %	26	24	24	16	10	100
In times of high unemployment married women should stay at home	Wives %	16	19	15	20	30	100
	Husbands %	22	19	16	18	25	100
A job is alright, but what most women really want is a home and children	Wives %	19	20	26	17	18	100
	Husbands %	27	25	28	12	8	100
Women can't combine a career and children	Wives %	12	18	17	26	27	100
	Husbands %	22	16	16	24	22	100
Most working women with families want jobs with no worries or responsibilities	Wives %	18	30	15	20	17	100
	Husbands %	25	27	20	19	9	100
Most married women only work for pin money – they don't need a job	Wives %	7	15	13	24	41	100
	Husbands %	9	13	13	26	39	100
Attitudes to the benefits of work to women and family							
If her children are well looked after it's good for a woman to work	Wives %	39	31	18	7	5	100
	Husbands %	35	29	21	8	7	100
Having a job is the best way for a woman to be an independent person	Wives %	35	31	16	12	6	100
	Husbands %	29	35	17	9	10	100
A woman and her family will all be happier if she goes out to work	Wives %	10	21	30	21	18	100
	Husbands %	9	20	29	22	20	100
Other statements							
If a woman takes several years off to look after her children she should expect her career to suffer	Wives %	11	33	19	18	20	100
	Husbands %	21	31	17	17	13	100
Married women have a right to work if they want to, whatever their family situation	Wives %	47	24	12	9	8	100
	Husbands %	44	22	10	12	11	100

Base (= 100%)   Wives   724
Husbands 724

Table 12.10 Comparison of levels of husbands' and wives' traditional attitudes to home and work and attitudes to the benefit of work to women and family by wife's working status

| | Working status of wives | | | | | | | | | |
| | Working full time | | Working part time | | All working | | Not working | | All wives* | |
	Wives	Husbands	Wives	Husbands	Wives	Husbands	Wives	Husbands	Wives	Husbands
Level of traditional attitudes to home and work	%	%	%	%	%	%	%	%	%	%
1 (Traditional)	17	31	29	38	23	35	44	51	31	41
2	40	38	41	39	41	39	31	35	37	37
3 (Non-traditional)	43	30	30	23	36	26	25	14	32	22
	100	100	100	100	100	100	100	100	100	100
Level of attitudes to the benefits of work to women and family										
1 (Work beneficial)	34	34	32	31	33	32	19	15	27	26
2	49	43	48	45	48	44	42	43	46	43
3 (Work not beneficial)	17	23	20	24	19	24	39	42	27	31
	100	100	100	100	100	100	100	100	100	100
Base	192	192	251	251	443	443	278	278	724	724

*Including full time students

expect this, as the concepts expressed in the attitudes are broader and allow more latitude within themselves. Even so, the wives tended to be more convinced than the husbands of the benefits of work to women; 70% of wives, for example, agreed that 'if her children are well looked after it's good for a woman to work', compared with 64% of husbands.

The opinions on the individual statements were reflected in the overall measures shown in Table 12.10. Husbands, as we have said, were more likely than wives to hold traditional views; however their views were associated with the working status of their wives in the same way as women's views were associated with their own working status (that is, the husbands of working wives were more likely to hold non-traditional views). Compared with the big difference between husbands and wives on traditional attitudes however, differences in attitudes to the benefits of work to women were small; but it was noticeable that the husbands of working wives were less likely to view work as beneficial to women than the working wives were, whereas there were no significant differences between husbands of non-working women and their wives.

Views about whether women in different situations should work

When we were designing the survey we were aware that there was continuing public debate over the circumst-

ances in which women should or should not work. As women's changing labour market behaviour in the intervening years since Hunt's survey (Hunt, 1968) might indicate a change of views about when women should work, we decided to explore this. We expected that the women we interviewed would have views about the circumstances under which women should or should not work, and that to a certain extent their general views would reflect the particular choices they had made or expected to make. We therefore asked all women to consider whether women in five different situations should work or not. The situations were chosen to represent a typical gradation of family responsibilities: a single woman with no family responsibilities, a married woman with no children, a married woman whose children have all left school, a married woman whose children are all at school and a married woman with children under school age. The categories from which women were asked to choose answers were: 'she ought to go out to work if she's fit', 'it's up to her whether to go out to work or not', 'she should only go out to work if she really needs the money' and 'she ought to stay at home'. These questions are based on those used in the 1965 survey of women's employment (Hunt, 1968) so for some of the situations we can compare the views of women in 1980 with those of women in 1965.

Table 12.11 shows the distribution of answers women chose for the five situations presented. Three of these

Table 12.11 Women's views about whether or not women with different family responsibilities should work

| Views about whether women ought to work | A single woman with no family responsibilities | A married woman | | | | | | |
| | | With no children | | Whose children have all left school | Whose children are all at school | | With children under school age | |
	1980	1980	1965	1980	1980	1965	1980	1965
	%	%	%	%	%	%	%	%
She ought to go out to work if she's fit	78	33	13	11	3	3	0	0
It's up to her whether to go out to work or not*	21	62	75	80	50	35	15	5
She should only go out to work if she really needs the money	1	4	9	8	36	39	25	15
She ought to stay at home	0	1	1	1	11	20	60	78
Don't know	0	0	1	0	0	3	0	2
	100	100	100	100	100	100	100	100
Base	5,588	5,588	7,391	5,588	5,588	7,391	5,588	7,391

*Wording on 1965 survey: 'she has the right to work if she wants'

were covered by the 1965 survey, and so the 1965 results are shown alongside for comparison. In two of the five situations the majority of women had clear views about what a woman ought to do, whereas in the remaining three situations the majority of women felt the choice was up to individual women. The majority of women (78%) felt a single woman with no family responsibilities ought to go out to work and 21% had no strong overriding view and felt it was up to the woman herself to decide. Full time students were slightly less likely than other women to think that single women ought to work, possibly because they could envisage studying as a valid alternative. Women were more prescriptive however about married women with pre-school children. A majority (60%) felt a woman in this situation ought to stay at home and 25% said she should only go out to work if she needed the money. No one felt a woman with pre-school children ought automatically to go out to work (this was the only group where this was so), but 15% of women had no overriding view and felt it was up to the individual woman whether she worked or not.

The views expressed about the situation of married women with no children or with children of school age or older were more open. The majority of women said it was up to the woman concerned whether 'to go out to work or not', though there were quite marked differences in the proportion having no overriding view of their own in the three situations. Women were much more likely to say a married woman with no children or with children who had all left school should go out to work or that she should decide herself whether to work or not than they were for married women with school age children. Although 50% of women said a woman with school age children should decide herself whether to work or not, 36% of women felt she ought not to work unless she needed the money and 11% felt she should not work at all. By contrast, 33% of women said a married woman with no children 'ought to go out to work if she's fit' and 62% said it was up to her to decide.

Looking at the 1965 results tells us how women's views have changed with time. The change in attitudes has been slightly more marked for childless women. In 1965

only 13% of women thought a married woman with no children ought to go out to work compared with 33% in 1980; in 1965 9% thought a married woman with no children should only go out to work if she needed the money compared with 4% in 1980. For women with children of school age or younger, fewer women in 1980 were prepared to express a definite view; more felt it was up to the individual woman. In 1965, 35% of women compared with 50% in 1980 said this in situations where a woman's children were all at school, and 5% compared with 15% of women said mothers with pre-school children should decide whether to work or not.

Whereas a majority of women in 1965 said a woman with pre-school or school age children either ought to stay at home or only work if she needed the money, by 1980 only 47% said this of women with school age children, and 85% said it of women with pre-school children, compared with 59% and 93% in 1965. We can see therefore, that between 1965 and 1980 there have been some interesting changes of attitudes. Women in 1980 are more prescriptive about married women with no children working; more felt 'they ought to work if they were fit', and less prescriptive than they were in 1965 about married women with children not working. Though marked, the changes are not revolutionary; 60% of women felt mothers of pre-school children should stay at home.

We also analysed women's views in 1980 by their current work status. Overall the results did not differ very much. The most significant differences between working and non-working women were their views about women with school age and pre-school children, shown in Table 12.12: 16% of non-working women thought women with school age children ought to stay at home compared with 9% of working women, whilst 65% of non-working women thought women with pre-school children should stay at home compared with 57% of working women. But as we shall show in more detail below, women's views were related to their own situation. Thus of women with pre-school children, 56% of those who were not working thought married women with pre-school children ought to stay at home compared with half of those who were working. Full time

Table 12.12   Women's views about whether married women with school age and pre-school children should work by work status

Views about whether women ought to work	Working full time	Working part time	All working	Not working	Full time student	All women
	%	%	%	%	%	%
A married woman whose children are all at school						
She ought to go out to work if she's fit	3	2	3	3	7	3
It's up to her whether to go out to work or not	49	55	51	45	59	50
She should only go out to work if she really needs the money	37	35	36	36	31	36
She ought to stay at home	10	8	9	16	3	11
	100	**100**	**100**	**100**	**100**	**100**
A married women with children under school age	%	%	%	%	%	%
She ought to go out to work if she's fit	0	0	0	1	1	1
It's up to her whether to go out to work or not	16	17	16	13	14	15
She should only go out to work if she really needs the money	25	28	26	21	30	25
She ought to stay at home	59	55	57	65	55	60
	100	**100**	**100**	**100**	**100**	**100**
Base	*1,877*	*1,477*	*3,354*	*1,941*	*293*	*5,588*

students were less likely than other women to think that a married woman with school age children should stay at home, but had similar views to the working women about women with pre-school children. However, amongst working women slightly fewer women working part time thought women with children under school age should stay at home than women working full time. This is likely to be explained by differences in the views of women who have and have not had children, and so we examined the views of women at different life stages, taking into account whether or not they were currently working.

What is interesting though not unexpected is that the views of women at different life stages do not vary with respect to three of the situations presented. Views about whether single women or married women with no children ought to work were not significantly different for women at different life stages, and their views about married women whose children had all left school were mainly related to work status rather than life stages. In fact, at all life stages, non-working women were more likely than working women to think either that such women 'should either only work if they needed the money' or 'should stay at home'. However, when we looked at women's attitudes to whether women with school age or younger children should work it was clear that both life stage and work status were important variables, as is shown in Table 12.13.

The pattern of results is very similar to that shown in the previous section on traditional attitudes to home and work with which Dex shows these results are correlated. The views of women with children vary significantly according to their work status, whereas the views of young childless women do not, as they have yet to make a decision about whether to work or not when they have children. In addition there appears to

Table 12.13 Women's views about whether married women with school age and pre-school children should work by life cycle stage and work status

Views about whether women ought to work	Childless women aged:				Woman with youngest child aged:						Woman with all children 16 and over aged:				All women	
	Under 30		30 or over		0–4		5–10		11–15		Under 50		50 or over			
	Work-ing	Not work-ing	Work-ing	Not work-ing	Work-ing	Not work-ing	Work-ing	Not work-ing	Work-ing	Not work-ing	Work-ing	Not work-ing	Work-ing	Not work-ing	Work-ing	Not work-ing
	%	%	%	%	%	%	%	%	%	%	%	%	%	%	%	%
A married woman whose children are all at school																
She ought to go out to work if she's fit	4	8	2	1	5	4	2	2	2	2	1	–	1	3	3	3
It's up to her whether to go out to work or not	48	41	37	29	70	55	66	46	54	36	49	32	41	33	52	44
She should only go out to work if she really needs the money	38	39	42	38	24	32	28	36	37	40	41	41	42	39	36	36
She ought to stay at home	9	11	19	30	1	8	4	15	6	20	9	27	15	25	9	15
	100	**100**	**100**	**100**	**100**	**100**	**100**	**100**	**100**	**100**	**100**	**100**	**100**	**100**	**100**	**100**
A married woman with children under school age																
She ought to go out to work if she's fit	0	1	–	1	1	1	0	–	–	1	–	–	–	0	0	1
It's up to her whether to go out to work or not	14	11	10	6	43	19	22	10	12	12	11	5	9	8	16	13
She should only go out to work if she really needs the money	22	24	19	16	33	24	35	24	29	19	28	12	20	16	26	21
She ought to stay at home	63	62	70	77	23	56	42	66	59	68	60	83	70	76	57	65
	100	**100**	**100**	**100**	**100**	**100**	**100**	**100**	**100**	**100**	**100**	**100**	**100**	**100**	**100**	**100**
Base	758	129	328	86	276	762	553	315	538	172	362	106	539	371	3,354	1,941

Table 12.14 Extent of agreement with statements about whether or not women with different family responsibilities should work: wives and husbands

Views about whether women ought to work	A single woman with no family responsibilities		A married woman with no children		A married woman whose children have all left school		A married woman whose children are all at school		A married woman with children under school age	
	Wives	Husbands	Wives	Husbands	Wives	Husbands	Wives	Husbands	Wives	Husbands
	%	%	%	%	%	%	%	%	%	%
She ought to go out to work if she's fit	78	76	31	30	10	10	2	2	0	0
It's up to her whether to go out to work or not	21	21	64	63	82	77	51	44	15	12
She should only go out to work if she really needs the money	1	2	4	5	8	10	36	35	27	17
She ought to stay at home	0	0	1	1	0	2	10	18	58	70
Don't know/can't say	0	0	0	1	0	0	1	1	0	1
	100	**100**	**100**	**100**	**100**	**100**	**100**	**100**	**100**	**100**

Base (=100%) Wives = 724
Husbands = 724

be an age trend: older women regardless of whether they have had children or not are more likely to think women with children should stay at home.

We were particularly interested to compare women's general attitudes with their own situation and it is interesting to see from Table 12.13 that women's views were not always consistent with their actual behaviour: 23% of women with a child under 5 who were working thought women with children under school age should stay at home. This was a much larger discrepancy than amongst mothers working with school age children where 4% thought mothers of school age children should not work. It ties in, however, with our earlier findings (in Chapter 6) that working mothers of pre-school children comprise those working under financial duress as well as those working because they want to. Finally, young childless women again seemed more traditional in their views than women with young children, which suggests that views may change once they actually have children and are faced with the experience of children and the reality of choice.

As in the previous section, we also examined the views of the sample of husbands. Table 12.14 compares their views with those of their wives. There were no appreciable differences in their views about childless women, regardless of marital status; however their views did differ about whether women with children should work. The husbands, as previously, held more traditional views, particularly with regard to women with pre-school children, 70% thinking that such women should stay at home, whereas 58% of wives held that view. Further analysis showed, as in the previous section, that husbands' views were associated with the choices their wives had made about work in relation to children, and also tended amongst the older men to be less tolerant about women working.

Young childless women's views of their future
Research on the life and career expectations and aspirations of young women has increased considerably over the last few years. Some studies are concerned to establish young women's attitudes towards their future (Rauta and Hunt, 1975), while others examine the structure of educational and work opportunities young

women face and their sex-role socialisation (Sharpe, 1976; Weinriech, 1978; Wolpe, 1978; Deem, 1980). Yet other studies in discussing women's experience of and attitudes to particular work situations explore the variations between young, unmarried women's reactions to and expectations about lifetime paid work and older women's experiences of it (McNally, 1979; Pollert, 1981; Wood, 1981; Cavendish, 1982). We have already shown in Chapter 6 that young women seemed less attached to working than women at later life cycle stages who had faced the choice of whether to combine paid work with childcare and other domestic demands or not. In this section we examined the attitudes of women before such choices have actually been faced and relate them to their future plans. Whilst their decisions are yet to be made, young women, however, are fully aware of their expected roles as wives and mothers. As much research shows, their attitudes towards working and aspirations about jobs are accordingly heavily influenced by this alternative to working (Sharpe, 1976). In addition the initial work experience of many young women may only serve to confirm them in a view that marriage and motherhood offers a better alternative to physically demanding, boring or routine 'dead-end' jobs (Pollert, 1981).[3]

We asked young women about their expectations about having children and their consequent employment plans. The majority of childless women under 30 expected to have children in the future, and a few of the older childless women also expected to have children. We asked all childless women who expected to have children whether they thought they would want to continue working, apart from a period of maternity leave, or whether they would give up work. Altogether 27% thought they would continue working, 68% said they would give up work at least for some time and 5% were undecided about whether they would continue or not. The majority of those who said they would stop work when they had children expected to go back later. Altogether only 4% said they did not think they would go back to work again and 5% were unsure. Thus 91% expected either to continue working or to return later, a figure substantially the same as the proportions of women with children who do eventually return to work quoted in Chapter 9. Comparison with women's views

Table 12.15 Employment intentions of childless women who expect to have children in future by current work status

Employment intentions if has children	Working	Unemployed	Full time student	All childless women who expect to have children
	%	%	%	%
Would continue working, apart from a period of maternity leave	22	28	42	27
Would give up work, but return:	69	55	53	64
before youngest child starts primary school	8	6	5	7
when youngest child is at primary school	43	29	26	38
when youngest child is at secondary school	16	14	16	16
when youngest child leaves school	1	3	4	2
at a later time	1	3	2	1
Undecided about whether would return	5	12	3	5
Does not expect to return	4	5	2	4
	100	**100**	**100**	**100**
Base	587	79	215	881

in 1965 is made slightly difficult because our questions were necessarily different from Hunt's questions which were premised on marriage as the (potential) disruption to working life. Even so she found that about a fifth of the single women under 40 who expected to stop work after marriage, chiefly to have children, did not expect to work again (Hunt, 1968). This suggests quite a marked shift in attitudes.

Women who planned to return to work were asked when they expected to do so. Table 12.15 summarises the employment intentions of all childless women who expect to have children, and shows how their intentions vary by their current employment status. The 27% who planned to continue working, apart from a period of maternity leave, is significantly higher than the 17% of women who had first births in the past five years who returned to work within six months, shown in Chapter 9. Of course we do not know whether all these women will actually carry out their intentions when they have a child and therefore whether there will be in fact a substantial increase in the proportion of women continuing work fairly immediately after childbearing.

Only 7% of women thought they would stop work for a time but start again before their youngest child started primary school; the most popular time for planning to start work again was when the youngest child started school. At this time women are, of course, available to work part time during school hours without having to make special childcare arrangements, and, as we have seen, many women seek this kind of working arrangement. A smaller proportion, 16%, did not plan to start work until all their children were at secondary school and a tiny minority (3%) expected to wait longer than this. These intended timings of returns are, however, different from those of recent women returners shown in Chapter 9. Young women anticipate spending more time out of the labour market than young mothers have been spending recently.

Table 12.15 also shows that these women's plans varied by their current working status: 42% of those still in full time education thought they would continue working compared with 28% of the unemployed and 22% of those in work. We have seen elsewhere that the better qualified women were more likely to return to work quickly after having children and so we might expect the students to be more likely to plan to continue working. It remains to be seen, however, whether actual experience of work or being at home with children results in a change of intention for many of them. It is noticeable that 12% of the unemployed were undecided about whether they would return, but this is scarcely surprising in view of their inevitable uncertainties about future employment. Irrespective of work status, those planning to return to work were most likely to say they would do so when their youngest child was at primary school and there was little variation in the proportions of all groups who expected to wait until their youngest child was at secondary school.

We already have some idea of the likely attitudes of those young childless women who expected to have children to working generally, since we have looked at the attitudes of students and of young childless women who were working or unemployed. In summary, young childless women who expected to have children were less likely than other women to hold traditional views about home and work; within this group students held the least traditional views whereas the unemployed held more traditional views. These women tended not to take extreme views about the benefits of work to women and their views in this respect varied little according to their current working status.

Table 12.16   Level of traditional attitudes to home and work and attitudes to the benefits of working for women and family of childless women who expect to have children, by their employment intentions

	Employment intentions if has children							All childless women who expect to have children
	Continue working	Return before youngest starts primary school	Return when youngest is at primary school	Return when youngest is at secondary school	Return when youngest leaves school or later	Don't know whether would return	Would not return	
	%	%	%	%	%	%	%	%
Level of traditional attitudes to home and work								
1 (Traditional)	12	18	19	22	47	37	56	21
2	34	40	39	44	40	46	27	39
3 (Non-traditional)	54	42	42	34	13	17	17	41
	100	**100**	**100**	**100**	**100**	**100**	**100**	**100**
Level of attitudes to the benefits of work to women and family								
1 (Work beneficial)	47	39	27	12	20	15	–	29
2	41	43	56	56	33	51	23	49
3 (Work not beneficial)	12	18	17	32	47	34	77	22
	100	**100**	**100**	**100**	**100**	**100**	**100**	**100**
Base	238	61	333	138	30	45	30	881*

Includes 6 cases with no information about employment intentions

Table 12.17 The views of childless women who intend to have children about whether married women with school age and pre-school children should work by their employment intentions

Views about whether women ought to work	Employment intentions if has children							All childless women who expect to have children
	Continue working	Return before youngest starts primary school	Return when youngest is at primary school	Return when youngest is at secondary school	Return when youngest leaves school or later	Don't know whether would return	Would not return	
	%	%	%	%	%	%	%	%
A married women whose children are all at school								
She ought to go out to work if she's fit	9	5	4	2	3	–	–	5
It's up to her whether to go out to work or not	55	61	53	46	30	32	23	50
She should only go out to work if she really needs the money	33	29	37	41	53	49	50	38
She ought to stay at home	3	5	5	11	13	19	27	7
	100	**100**	**100**	**100**	**100**	**100**	**100**	**100**
A married woman with children under school age								
She ought to go out to work if she's fit	1	–	0	–	–	–	–	0
It's up to her whether to go out to work or not	23	20	7	3	3	7	7	12
She should only go out to work if she really needs the money	30	37	28	15	20	7	7	25
She ought to stay at home	46	42	65	82	77	86	86	63
	100	**100**	**100**	**100**	**100**	**100**	**100**	**100**
Base	238	61	333	138	30	45	30	881*

Includes 6 cases with no information about employment intentions

We went on to look at the relationship between these women's attitudes to home and work and their expectations about employment if they have children. Table 12.16 shows a strong relationship between the measure of traditional views and plans about returning to work in the expected direction: the highest proportion of women with high scores on traditional views was found among women who planned to return to work latest or not at all; women who planned to continue working were most likely to hold non-traditional views. Attitudes to the benefits of work to women and families showed in general a similar relationship, with women who planned to return soonest being most likely to hold views that work is beneficial, whereas none of the women who did not plan to return to work were in the high scoring category.

We also looked at how the views of young childless women about whether women in different circumstances should work related to their own employment plans. The divergence of views according to their own plans was most apparent with respect to married women with school age and pre-school children, and so we show these in Table 12.17. Although we would expect the women who plan to continue working to hold much more permissive views than those who do not expect to return to work, which Table 12.17 shows, the most interesting feature of the results is the significant proportions of women whose views about what women ought to do do not correspond with their own expectations. Among women who planned to start work when their youngest child was at primary school 5% did not think women with children at school ought to work; a

further 37% thought a woman should only do so if she really needed the money. Even among women who planned to continue working or to return before their youngest child was at primary school 3% and 5% respectively thought women with school age children should stay at home.

The discrepancy between attitude and intention is even more apparent with respect to women with pre-school children: 46% of women who planned to continue working and 42% of those who expected to return before their youngest child started primary school thought women with pre-school children ought to stay at home, (even if they really needed the money which working would provide), and only 23% and 20% of these two groups thought it was up to such women themselves whether to work or not. It is possible that these young women with apparently discrepant attitudes knew or expected that financially they would have to work when they had young children and are comparable to the group of young mothers identified both above and in Chapter 6 who appeared to be working under financial duress.

Attitudes towards equal opportunity legislation
Major legislation was passed in the seventies which was aimed specifically at giving women greater equality with men, particularly in the field of employment. We could not examine in detail women's knowledge of or reaction to the Equal Pay and Sex Discrimination Acts or the maternity provisions of the Employment Protection Act, though some other studies have attempted to do this (Daniel, 1980 and 1981a; Commission of the

Table 12.18 Proportions of women rating as 'very important' six different legislative provisions by work status

Legislative provisions	Proportion rating as 'very important'				
	Working full time	Working part time	All working	Not working	All women*
The opportunity for boys and girls to study the same subjects at school	80%	81%	80%	77%	79%
Equal credit and mortgage facilities for men and women	82%	77%	80%	74%	78%
Laws giving men and women equal pay for equal work	76%	70%	74%	70%	73%
The right to 6 weeks maternity pay if a woman has been in her job for two years	69%	71%	70%	68%	69%
Laws making it illegal to treat men and women differently at work	69%	65%	67%	62%	66%
The right for a woman to return to her job within 6 months of having a baby	50%	48%	49%	44%	47%
Base	*1,877*	*1,477*	*3,354*	*1,941*	*5,588*

*Including full time students

European Communities, 1980; Snell *et al,* 1981). Nor did we attempt to measure the impact of this legislation; a survey of this kind could not cover all aspects of the impact or effectiveness of the legislation and it might well be argued that the lapse of four and a half years was still too short a time for the impact of the equal opportunity legislation to be felt. However, we were interested in knowing how important our sample of women felt some of the main provisions of the legislation were for women. Asking women how important provisions were is not so much evaluating the effectiveness of the legislation as investigating their attitudes towards the value propositions underlying the legislative provisions.

We selected six particular aspects of the legislation and asked women to rate their importance on a three point scale: very important, fairly important and not very important. Table 12.18 lists the provisions women were asked to consider and shows the importance they attached to each. The two rated highest in importance were not directly work related: 79% rated as very important the opportunity for boys and girls to study the same subjects at school and 78% thought that equal

credit and mortgage facilities for men and women were very important. Whether they were rated as very important by the largest proportions of women because they were the most general of the provisions, reflecting broad principles of equality or opportunity in educational and financial matters, likely to be equally applicable and of interest to women in a range of diverse circumstances, is not possible to say, though this seems likely.

Of the four legislative provisions relating to work, the provisions about discrimination on grounds of sex was the most general; the two statements dealing with aspects of the maternity provisions, namely maternity pay and reinstatement, were very specific, embodying no explicit comparisons with men or reference to principles of equality and the statement about equal pay was in between. Three of the work related provisions were valued markedly more highly than the fourth which dealt with reinstatement after maternity leave which was the only provision that the majority of women (53%) did not rate as very important. The most important of the work related provisions was equal pay: 73% of women rated laws giving men and women equal

Table 12.19 Proportions of women rating as 'very important' six different legislative provisions by life cycle stage

Legislative provisions	Childless women aged:				Women with youngest child aged:								Women with all children 16 or over aged:			
	Under 30		30 or over		0–4		5–10		11–15				Under 50		50 or over	
	Work-ing	Not work-ing	Work-ing	Not work-ing	Work-ing	Not work-ing	Work-ing	Not work-ing	Work-ing	Not work-ing	Work-ing	Not work-ing	Work-ing	Not work-ing	Work-ing	Not work-ing
The opportunity for boys and girls to study the same subject at school	78%	63%	79%	68%	82%	78%	82%	79%	80%	83%			83%	86%	80%	76%
Equal credit and mortgage facilities for men and women	79%	64%	84%	76%	76%	74%	82%	73%	77%	75%			83%	81%	80%	73%
Laws giving men and women equal pay for equal work	79%	66%	77%	69%	80%	77%	74%	69%	71%	69%			69%	72%	66%	58%
The right to six weeks maternity pay if a woman has been in her job for two years	73%	66%	56%	51%	77%	76%	73%	63%	68%	62%			66%	67%	70%	64%
Laws making it illegal to treat men and women differently at work	70%	56%	70%	57%	76%	65%	68%	58%	65%	68%			65%	62%	61%	58%
The right for a woman to return to her job within six months of having a baby	53%	51%	43%	39%	63%	49%	49%	37%	46%	38%			44%	39%	42%	39%
Base	*758*	*129*	*328*	*86*	*276*	*762*	*553*	*315*	*538*	*172*			*362*	*106*	*539*	*371*

pay for equal work as very important. Maternity pay, as the second most valued of the work provisions, was rated very important by 69% of women, while 66% thought laws making it unlawful to treat men and women differently at work were very important. Women's reactions to the fourth work provision (reinstatement after maternity leave) were interesting. It is impossible to know whether this reflected a lesser likelihood of being interested in or having experienced a return after maternity leave, or a greater reluctance to condone women with very young children returning to work, an attitude discussed earlier in the chapter, or a realisation that reinstatement rights on their own were of limited significance, as Daniel's respondents argued (Daniel, 1980). It is likely that all these aspects underlie the response.

It might be thought that a woman's employment status would affect her attitudes, particularly to work related provisions. Table 12.18 shows that working women were slightly more likely than non-working women to give ratings of very important to each of the six provisions; the differences between the two groups being greatest for equal credit and mortgage facilities, the right to return to work within 6 months of having a baby and laws making it illegal to treat men and women differently at work. But the difference is not very great and does not apply to work related provisions. There were also some differences between full and part time working women, with the former being more likely to rate as very important equal pay laws, equal credit and mortgage facilities and laws making it illegal to treat men and women differently at work.

We also looked at whether there was a life cycle effect and found a tendency for the younger women to be more likely to value each provision. However, this was less apparent when working and non-working women were considered separately, which is done in Table 12.19. In general working women at each life stage attached more importance to each provision than the non-working women, but there were a few interesting exceptions among women with a youngest child aged 11–15 and the younger women whose children were all over 16. Non-working women here, in rating the statements of very general principles of equality, may have been thinking as much in terms of their own children's chances as reflecting their own experiences.

Finally we compared the views of the husbands in our sample with those of their wives (Table 12.20). As before, husband's responses were more traditional than those of their wives in that they were less likely to rate the provisions as very important, although they rated them in the same order of importance as their wives had done. It made no appreciable difference to husband's views whether their wives worked or not.

Summary and conclusions
This chapter has focussed on women's general attitudes to working and has looked more broadly at their views about the position of women in society and the roles of

Table 12.20 Proportions of wives and their husbands rating as 'very important' six different legislative provisions

Legislative provisions	Proportion rating as 'very important'	
	Wives	Husbands
The opportunity for boys and girls to study the same subjects at school	81%	75%
Equal credit and mortgage facilities for men and women	80%	75%
Laws giving men and women equal pay for equal work	73%	70%
The right to 6 weeks maternity pay if a woman has been in her job for two years	72%	64%
Laws making it illegal to treat men and women differently at work	67%	65%
The right for a woman to return to her job within 6 months of having a baby	50%	44%
Base	799	799

men and women. Findings have been presented on specific issues, covering women's reactions to popular statements about women, paid work and domestic responsibilities; situations in which women should or should not work; young women's views about their future labour market behaviour and the main provisions of the equal opportunity legislation.

From responses to a series of propositions about women's home and work roles we identified the extent to which respondents held traditional or non-traditional views and thought paid work beneficial for women or not. Only a minority of women supported the traditional view that 'a woman's place is in the home'; rather, a large proportion agreed that 'married women have the right to work if they want to' and do not just work for 'pin money'. Most women, in fact, accepted that working is beneficial for a woman. Even so it is clear that paid employment was rarely seen as a central life interest; it is accommodated to and balanced with domestic demands and for most women takes a secondary role in their lives to their family. The fact that we do not know accurately how this compares with men's attitudes is a reflection of the fact we rarely if ever ask men these questions; it might be very illuminating to do so.

There was variation in women's responses dependent on their employment status, age and educational qualifications. Students were most likely to hold non-traditional views about women's home and work roles followed by young working women, especially those working full time. The most traditional views were held by older non-working women, particularly amongst those who had no children. In all instances, women with higher educational qualifications were less likely than other women in comparable life circumstances to hold traditional views.

Women's reactions to whether work was beneficial or not for women followed a somewhat similar pattern, but were more closely associated with their current work status. Working women were more likely to regard working as beneficial, and full and part time workers did not differ significantly in this though women with children were more likely to think work was beneficial than childless women. Amongst non-working women the opposite was the case; childless women, who tended to be young, were more likely to think work was beneficial. What we cannot know very easily from these data is whether these attitudes were the result of women's experiences and choices about children and working or whether the choices reflect prior values. Dex's findings show that the more work experience a woman has the more likely she is to have work committed attitudes, though current employment has more overall effect on her attitudes (Dex, 1984b). Husbands in general had more traditional views than wives.

Women in 1980 were more likely than women in Hunt's 1965 survey to feel that whether a married woman with children worked or not was her decision, but they were still prescriptive in certain instances. For example, 60% thought a married woman with pre-school children should stay at home; they were also increasingly likely in 1980 to think married women with no children should work: 33% did so compared with 13% in 1965. Working women and younger women were less likely to think women with young children should stay at home than were non-working women. There were also some interesting discrepancies between women's attitudes and their own behaviour, particularly amongst those mothers of children under 5 who were working; 23% of these women thought women with pre-school children should not work. It is likely either that these mothers were working only from financial necessity, or that they were able to make adequate provision for their children's care but did not believe that women in general would be so fortunate.

Young women's views about their future working lives reflected the changes in women's labour force participation we have documented throughout this study. The vast majority expected to return to work after having children, more than expected to in 1965 when Hunt asked a similar question. A surprisingly large minority (27%) expected to continue working throughout their childbearing period, taking maternity leave; this is rather higher than current levels of continuous working and may be overly optimistic. In contrast most other young women showed a tendency to anticipate staying out of paid work for longer than women have been doing recently. They may well be underestimating the financial and social attractions of paid work which a period at home may highlight. Whilst young women overall were more likely than older women to have non-traditional views and think working was beneficial, young women who intended to continue working or return quickly after having children had the least traditional attitudes about a woman's role. The only exception was the sizeable minority of young women

amongst those who expected to work when they had pre-school children who felt mothers should not do this.

Finally women's attitudes to the main provisions of the equal opportunity legislation showed that, whether they knew much about the legislation or not, (our questions were not designed to test this), most women agreed that most of the provisions were important for women. The legislation therefore accorded with dominant social values amongst women, and indeed husbands, though they were slightly less likely than wives to endorse them. The broad general principles of 'equality of opportunity in education between boys and girls' and 'equal credit and mortgage facilities for men and women' were most highly valued, whilst the right to reinstatement after maternity leave was valued least, even amongst women working full time. A woman's age, work status and position in the life cycle were all likely to affect her response to the legislation in a similar way as with all our other attitude measures; with the exception that higher than expected proportions of non-working mothers of school age children endorsed the general non-discriminatory values embodied in the educational and general discrimination at work provisions, possibly reflecting wider concern about their children's opportunities.

This chapter has shown that there has been a shift in the views both women of working age and their husbands hold about women's role in combining paid and unpaid work. This change is commensurate with women's greater participation in paid work in direction and degree. For, though marked, the change in attitudes is not dramatic; women's views by and large still reflect their need to combine paid work with the major share of domestic responsibilities and the greater priority they therefore accord to their family than to paid work. In this sense then the attitude changes can be seen to mirror the substantial increase in part time rather than full time employment that has characterised the last twenty years.

Notes
[1] This is not to say it is not possible nor interesting, using multivariate analysis, to look at the variations in attitudes of women with different labour market experiences and status (Dex, 1984b; Huber and Spitze, 1981).

[2] An account of the factor analysis is given in the technical report (Martin and Roberts, 1984). In adopting this approach our analysis differs from that undertaken simultaneously on the data by Dex who combined all the attitudinal data collected in the survey prior to factor analysis (Dex, 1984b).

[3] As Feldberg and Glenn (1984) argue it is critically important to go beyond pure gender models in attempting to explain women's orientations to work and incorporate dimensions of the job and work experience as explanatory variables as well.

Chapter 13 Overview: The place of employment in women's lives

Introduction

In the earlier chapters of this report we have provided a description and analysis of the data from the survey under a number of headings and have summarised our findings at the end of each chapter. This final chapter draws together the main findings and takes an overview of the main issues arising out of the study. Figures are rarely presented in this chapter as the data have already been described and the main findings are discussed in a different order from that in which they were presented chapter by chapter.

As the study was based on a nationally representative sample of women of working age in Great Britain in 1980, it is possible to use our findings to discuss the position of women of this age in general terms. It is helpful to remember though that of the 5,588 women in our sample 60% were working in a paid job, 5% were unemployed, 5% were students and 30% were out of the labour market at the time of the survey. By contrast, most of the sub-sample of 799 husbands were working.

The survey was undertaken after a period of economic and social change during which women's participation in employment rose. There had been an increasing public debate about women's roles in society and important legislation about women's rights and opportunities at work had been introduced. There had been a period of sustained growth in women's labour force participation over the post-war period, such that by 1980 women constituted about 40% of the total labour force and about 10 million women were economically active. The most dramatic aspect of this was the marked increase in the proportion of married women who were working, very largely in newly emerging part time jobs, many of which were in the service industries. By the end of the 1970s the rate of growth of women's labour market participation had slowed down, married women's economic activity had levelled off and the rate of unemployment amongst women was increasing. Hunt had examined women's attitudes to employment and their work and home roles in the sixties when women's employment rate was steadily increasing prior to the dramatic change in the 1970s; fifteen years on, in 1980, it was time to map out afresh the effect of these changes for both work and home (Hunt, 1968).

The principal aim of the survey was to establish the place of employment in women's lives. It was intended to examine when and why women take paid employment; the nature of this employment; the meaning paid work has for women and the consequences to them of not working in paid employment. The survey aimed to explore the extent to which the nature of women's involvement in and attachment to paid work was influenced by the different roles men and women play in our society largely in relation to family and domestic organisation.

To examine the influence of the division of labour in the family and household on women and men's different labour market position is not, however, to imply that all women are affected equally by domestic factors or that this division of labour is immutable. As we have shown in earlier chapters, women in similar domestic situations may make different employment decisions, and as we can see from the evidence of our survey, as well as from the many anthropological, historical and comparative accounts of women's economic and social roles, there have been different attitudes to and practices in organising domestic work, and women's ability to take employment has varied accordingly (Oakley, 1972; Rowbotham, 1973; Sullerot, 1977; United Nations, 1977). An exposition of what factors shape and maintain this allocation of roles between the sexes is clearly beyond the scope of this survey, but other studies reveal that a range of explanations are currently available (Barratt, 1980; Beechey, 1977 and 1978; Cooper, 1982; Gardiner, 1975; Kuhn and Wolpe, 1978; Mitchell and Oakley, 1976; Oakley, 1981; Radcliffe Richards, 1982; Reid and Wormald, 1982).

We confine ourselves here to examining the evidence from the survey on the sexual division of labour and its relevance for women's position in the labour market. First we review the data from the survey on the domestic circumstances of our women respondents and the effect of their unpaid domestic work and responsibilities on the nature of their participation in the labour market. We then go on to examine the extent of women's participation in paid work, taking a lifetime perspective and looking at the degree to which younger cohorts in the sample differ from the older, both in the extent to which they work and the changing pattern of this. Thirdly, we consider women as workers, describing the nature of their employment, their behaviour in the labour market and their attitudes to working and their jobs. Non-working women are discussed next as we look at some aspects of their position, identify the proportion of non-working women who were unemployed or looking for work and describe women's diverse reactions to not working. Finally, women's general attitudes to home and work are described and the implications of these for the place of employment in women's lives are explored. While the recession became deeper over the three years since the survey we do not judge this has materially affected our findings on women's participation in the labour market or on the domestic organisation of labour.[1]

The sexual division of labour and domestic demands on women

A distinctive lifetime pattern of domestic work for women is clear from our survey. Young women living at home with their parents have little domestic responsibility, but this increases dramatically as women set up their own households, usually on marriage. The main peak in domestic responsibility comes with young children; for some families there may be a second peak if they take on the regular care of an elderly or sick relative, whilst the small minority of people who care, for example, for a permanently handicapped child have a considerably increased amount of domestic work.

It is impossible to discuss the impact of domestic work on women's employment without discussing the effect of marital status, how wives and husbands divide paid employment and unpaid domestic work between them and, more importantly, whether the woman has children or not. Marital status alone does not affect whether or not women work. The presence of children and particularly the age of the youngest child is a more crucial determinant of both whether or not women work and whether this is full or part time (though marital status affects the latter). Women who have had children are more likely to work part time than women who have not, and married women are more likely to do this than non-married women. So it is not marital status *per se* so much as the family roles men and women play within marriage which are important in their consequences for women's employment.

In most couples the wife is the primary houseworker, doing all or most of the housework. Even when they worked full time, only a minority of wives said they shared housework equally with their husbands. Some part of the explanation lies in the fact that the husband was almost always the primary breadwinner, working longer hours, with both higher gross and hourly earnings. When both husband and wife worked full time, only 20% of wives had the same or a higher rate of pay. Another part of the explanation lies in the different socialisation men and women have and their correspondingly different expectations about their lifetime employment.

The division between husbands' and wives' responsibilities is significantly and usually permanently reinforced by children. Almost all husbands in our sample were economicaly active, but only 65% of wives were; most of the economically inactive women were mothers of young children who expected to work again once their children were older. They were therefore in a temporary phase in their lives when the separation of employment and domestic responsibilities between them and their husbands was most marked. The majority of wives returning to work tended to work part time, at least

initially, so that while almost all husbands in our sample worked full time, more working wives worked part time than full time. The very different nature of men and women's employment is also exemplified by the variation in the hours women work, both in terms of the number of hours women work a week, and the daily or weekly pattern of hours worked. A five day week is the norm; part timers tended to reduce their hours rather than work fewer days. Women with young children worked fewer hours than women whose children are older.

There is also a close association between the times of day women work and the ages of their children, reflecting women's childcare needs. Caring for a family involves a considerable amount of time, effort and work. It is clear that women, because of their role as wives and mothers, do more of this both at any point in time and in total over their lifetime than their husbands, whose main economic role is that of primary wage earner. If we discount full time schooling as a form of childcare, very few women used institutional care. Wives therefore are chiefly responsible for the care of children, although husbands are the most frequent providers of childcare when mothers work, followed by the child's grandmother.

Many fewer women care for an elderly or sick relative or friend than look after children, a husband and a home and this tends to be done by older women. Married women are equally as likely as single women of the same age to be looking after an adult dependant. However, only a small minority of women with this responsibility, mainly non-working women, felt it had either prevented them from working or restricted the hours they worked. Caring for a family does, however, have important consequences for women's lifetime involvement in employment, the type of employment opportunities they have, and the importance they attach to having paid work.

The extent of women's lifetime employment

Most studies of women's employment discuss the extent of women's employment in terms of the post-war rise in women's labour market participation and in particular show the sharp increase in the proportions of mothers of young children who are working, chiefly part time. The survey documents this comprehensively, showing how employment status varies with a woman's position in the life cycle and how the proportion of women working has risen with successive birth cohorts of women. But, more interestingly perhaps, because longitudinal data was collected through retrospective work histories, it is possible to see the proportion of their lives women spend working in paid jobs, their pattern of movement in and out of employment and between full and part time jobs. This adds considerably to our knowledge about the extent of women's lifetime employment.

It is now normal practice for women to work full time until the birth of their first child. Marriage, unless it is associated with an early birth, is now rarely a reason for stopping work, though it was for a proportion of the oldest women in our survey. Almost all women who have a child have a break from employment; only 4% of the women with children we interviewed had been in the labour market continuously throughout their working lives and some of these are likely to leave subsequently to have a further child. What is striking, is that very high proportions of women return to work after having a child and that contrary to popular assumptions this is not a new phenomenon. For example, over 90% of women who had a first birth in the late fifties and early sixties had returned to work at some stage and among older women the proportions were not much lower: 87% of women who had a first birth in the early forties had subsequently returned to employment.

However, women are returning to work more quickly after having a baby; for example, half the women who had a first baby between 1975–79 had returned to work within 4 years, while it was considerably longer (9.6 years) before half of the women who had a first baby between 1950–54 had returned. Similarly, the median time of return to work after the latest birth has fallen from around 7½ years for latest births in 1950–54 to just over 3½ years for latest births in 1975–79. These increasingly early returns to work are related to a developing pattern of returning between births. As nearly half the women (47%) whose latest birth had been between 1975–1979 had been employed for some time between their first and latest birth, it is clear that the two-phase model of women's employment is increasingly a less accurate description of how a large group of women behave in the labour market. Broadly, women with children may be divided into two groups: mothers who work between births and return to work soon after their latest birth and mothers who more closely approximate to the two-phase or bimodal pattern and do not return to work at all until their last child is of school age.

One likely consequence of women returning to work sooner is that they spend more of their working life in the labour market. While the oldest women had spent about 60% of their total working life in employment, younger women had spent proportionately more. For example, women in their early thirties, whom we would expect to have spent proportionately less of their working life in employment because they were likely to be out of the labour market looking after young children or only recently returned to work, had worked on average 66% of their working lives. It is apparent then that the well documented increase in women's levels of employment which characterized the sixties and seventies can very largely be attributed to women spending more time at work over their lifetime.

The importance of part time working in facilitating this increase by enabling women to combine caring for young children with paid work is clear. Cross-sectional data, for example, show that few working women with a young child work full time. Though the proportion of women working full time increases amongst older

women, it never regains the high level characteristic of childless women under 30. Women's work histories, however, show that the movement between full and part time employment is more varied than a cross-sectional picture suggests. For while the dominant pattern may be for women to be increasingly likely to work full time the longer they have been back at work, some women, particularly those returning early after a first birth, initially go back full time and change subsequently to part time work; some work part time throughout their post-children work phase and a few return later after having children but go back full time.

Overall, women are spending an increasing proportion of their lives in employment, though very few adopt the typical male pattern of continuous lifetime employment as a full time worker. Most interruptions to employment are caused for domestic reasons. Though women with children tend to have more breaks in their employment than childless women, childless women are also liable to spend some of their working life out of employment for both domestic and non-domestic reasons. While there is considerable diversity in women's patterns of lifetime employment, trend evidence suggests that more and more women will be attached to the labour market for most of their working lives, even if for some of them this will be in a part time capacity. It is likely that this will have implications for women's position in the labour market and the importance they attach to working.

Women workers' relationship to work

Most women's relationship to the labour market in our society, as in industrial societies more generally, is potentially different from most men's. Firstly, men and women are likely to regard employment differently and correspondingly boys and girls are likely to be socialised into a different set of expectations. Thus girls tend to make educational, training and job choices predicated on the assumption that they will be wives and mothers. They will have a working life interrupted for childbirth and childrearing, usually characterised by partial employment so as to enable them to do the domestic work involved in looking after a husband, children and a home. Boys, by contrast, expect that they will be the primary wage earner and that employment is or should be the main lifetime occupation necessary to support a wife and children.

Women, unlike men, are assumed to have, and indeed may feel, an element of choice in whether they work or not at certain stages of their lives. Of course not all women have a choice either in principle or in practice. In principle only women with access both to an alternative means of economic support and usually a socially acceptable alternative role such as being a married woman with children, have a choice and in practice some of these feel they have to work. Wives' earnings, even if they are only a subsidiary wage, are often very important for a family's basic income. Nevertheless the possibility of choice does have consequences for women's orientations towards work.

The data from this survey show that in one sense women, like men, work mainly for the money. The majority of women had a high financial dependence on working. Non-married women, particularly lone parents working full time, were more financially dependent and more likely to say they worked 'for essentials' but even so, over a quarter (28%) of women working part time said 'working for essentials' was their main reason for working. The importance of financial motivation is also underlined by the greater emphasis placed on this by women looking for a job; more said they needed a job 'for essentials' than amongst working women generally.

The vast majority of women were committed in varying degrees to working; indeed only 6% of working women definitely wished they did not go out to work. While full and part time workers show no difference in this respect there are some interesting life cycle variations. The fact that young childless women are less attracted to working than women who have returned to work is very interesting and suggests that the pull of anticipated domesticity and motherhood reduces young women's interest in working while the experience of being at home makes some women more interested in working. In addition, childless women over 30 were the most likely of all groups to show high intrinsic attachment to work. The complexities of women's work attachment are highlighted most clearly in the responses of the group of mothers of pre-school children who work full time. Some, chiefly those in higher level and well paid jobs, showed a high intrinsic attachment to work, while others in lower level, less well paid jobs were clearly only working because of financial necessity.

Money however is not the aspect of a job most women rate as most important. Women working either full time or part time rated 'work you like doing' the most important aspect of a job, though part timers held 'convenient hours' to be equally important. Indeed these are an absolutely crucial requirement for part time workers, for, if the hours are not right, women wanting to combine employment and their domestic responsibilities cannot work at all. The consequence of this is that part time workers often make certain trade-offs, attaching less importance to a 'good rate of pay' than to 'convenient hours', even when they work mainly for money. Thus they are less likely than full time workers to stress the importance of pay and a secure job and are more likely to emphasise the importance of having friendly people to work with. Job priorities, of course, reflect what people want within the implicit framework of what they feel or know is possible. Both full and part time workers accorded relatively low priority to the career aspects of a job or the opportunity to use their abilities, though these were of more importance to both younger women and women working full time.

It is not unexpected that the majority of women were generally satisfied with their jobs as most workers say this in response to job satisfaction questions. However, women who had to work for basic essentials, who tended to be in lower level jobs, appeared to have a general sense of dissatisfaction with their job, whereas women who said they worked because they enjoyed working and were often found in higher level jobs reported much higher levels of satisfaction. Often this was attributable to their satisfaction with intrinsic aspects of their jobs such as the opportunity it afforded them to use their abilities or to do work they liked doing.

Most working women have to combine paid work with domestic responsibilities too and for some women coping with both sets of demands was difficult. It was particularly difficult for women with dependent children, especially if they worked full time, and most of all for non-married working mothers running a household single handed. It is clear that while the social and domestic circumstances of women influence the way they think about work, the type of job they do and their employment situation also have an effect on women's reactions to working.

The nature of women's employment

Adult workers face a structure of opportunities in the world of paid work which reflects men and women's different roles and labour market positions. This survey has not collected data from employers on the characteristics of women's employment or on the demand side influences on the nature and structure of women's jobs.[2] We can, however, provide some information on the nature of women's employment through data from the women respondents themselves on their occupation, pay and conditions of employment.

Women work in a much more restricted number of occupations than men, with markedly fewer women in the very top jobs. Part time workers are even more likely to be in lower level occupations than full time workers. Women are also more likely to be in service industry jobs, particularly if they work part time. At the workplace level, 63% of women in our study worked only with other women doing the same kind of work as them and part timers were much more likely to work only with other women: 70% did compared with 58% of full time workers. Women working full time in the service industries, particularly in higher non-manual jobs, were much more likely to be working with men.

An employee based study cannot establish the causes of this marked occupational segregation; it is also difficult to establish precisely the magnitude of its effects, though we examined the factors with which it is associated. It is striking, for example, that women who work with men were more likely than women who work in 'women only' jobs to have higher levels of pay and access to good conditions of employment and opportunities for further training and promotion in their jobs. It is not therefore surprising that women working in 'women only' jobs were much more likely than women working with men to think of their jobs as 'women's work' which men would not be prepared to do chiefly because the jobs are low paid, boring or only suitable for women. Thus many women in our survey experienced the labour market as highly segregated on the basis of sex, with men doing both different jobs and more of the supervisory and managerial jobs. Their husbands' experience of occupational segregation is even more marked as most (81%) worked only with other men and almost none (2%) had a female supervisor. Husbands were much more likely than wives to think of their work as gender specific.

While it is clear that in broad terms, men and women's experience of the labour market is markedly different, it is also important to note that there were differences between women, associated in particular with their employment status as full or part time workers. Women working part time are more likely to be in lower level occupations: over half of part timers are in Social Classes IV and V occupations for example, compared with just under a quarter of women working full time. It is these differences in occupational level which largely account for the different hourly rates of pay of full and part time workers since we found few significant differences in the hourly pay of full and part time workers within the same occupational group.

Overall, part time workers are less likely to have access to or to have good provision of conditions of employment like paid holidays, sick pay or an occupational pension scheme. They are also less likely to have promotion and training opportunities in their jobs and less likely either to be a member of, or to have the opportunity to belong to, a union. In general a woman's employment status as a full or part time worker had a stronger effect on her access to good pay and job benefits than her occupational level and whether she worked with men as well as only with women. While part time workers clearly have less good pay and job benefits than full time workers the differences in coverage by statutory provision are much less marked: 67% of full time workers were covered by employment protection legislation compared with 60% of part time workers.

Occupational segregation and employment status are clearly interconnected and have an important effect on women's pay and general employment conditions. The most 'privileged' group of women are those who work with men in full time higher non-manual jobs. They are more likely to have better pay and conditions and job opportunities than all other women, and can be seen as forming a primary sector of the female workforce. All other groups of women in varying degrees have the pay and employment conditions and labour market position associated with secondary sector workers. A further characteristic associated with secondary workers is job instability, both as a cause and consequence of their labour market position; we therefore examined when women leave jobs and the frequency and nature of this.

Job changing and occupational mobility
The common charge often levied against women employees, that they leave jobs to have babies or to fit in with their husband's job changes, implies that women leave jobs chiefly for domestic reasons and are therefore very different as employees from men. This view distorts a more complex reality however. Women obviously do leave jobs and leave the labour market for domestic reasons, but they also leave jobs without leaving the labour market either by changing directly to a new employer or by being unemployed. Their reasons for leaving an employer also may be domestic or job-related in that women, like men, may move voluntarily to a better job, or involuntarily if they are dismissed or made redundant.

On average women work for between 4–5 employers during their working life though the range is wide. Amongst women who have worked for more than 20 years, for example, a third had worked for less than 5 employers and a quarter for 8 or more. Younger women leave jobs at a more frequent rate than older women. Indeed, the highest rate of change of employer is amongst women in their first five years at work, when it is also high for young men.

More women leave an employer to change straight to another job than leave to stop work and women are more likely to leave an employer for a job-related rather than a domestic reason. For example, women left jobs for domestic reasons about 40% of the time and were more likely to do this earlier in their working lives. Even though women with children are more likely to leave an employer for a domestic reason, childless women leave jobs for domestic reasons in about a quarter of cases. Domestic responsibilities impinge on women's working lives and job changing behaviour most in the first ten years after having a first child though even here they do not predominate.

While occupational change may occur whenever a change of job involves a change of level or type of work, occupational change is particularly associated with absence from the labour market for childrearing and so women with children tend to have had both more occupations and more experience of vertical mobility than women without children. Childless women do change occupations also though and are more likely over their lifetime to rise to higher level occupations than to go down the occupational scale.

A substantial minority of women, however, experience downward occupational mobility on re-entering the labour market when they return to work after childbearing. Women are much more likely to return to a lower level job if they go back part time; 45% of women going back to a part time job experienced downward occupational mobility. The length of time a woman spends out of the labour market also has an effect on her mobility; the longer a woman delays her first return the more likely she is to return to a lower level occupation. The small minority who returned within 6 months mostly returned to the same level of occupation, usually with the same employer they had before childbirth.

However, while length of service is important, it is clear that employment status has the stronger association with downward mobility. Women returning full time are less likely than women returning part time after the same length of absence to move to a lower level occupation. The strong association of part time employment status with downward occupational mobility is also shown very strikingly by the fact that women who first return to work full time after childbearing and subsequently change to work part time are particularly likely to experience downward mobility. A return to full time working may lead to upward occupational mobility. Women therefore can, and a small minority do, recover the occupational standing they had prior to childbearing and some move higher than this.

Unemployment and economic inactivity amongst non-working women

At the time of the interview about a third of women of working age (35%) were neither in a paid job nor full time students, but as we have shown, this is a temporary phase in most women's lives. Non-working women are a very heterogeneous group exhibiting various degrees of current attachment to the labour market. Some want jobs and may broadly be defined as economically active, while others have withdrawn either temporarily or permanently from the labour market to look after their families or have retired early from paid work through illness or injury. Deciding which non-working women are unemployed is difficult, for as we anticipated, the usual registered or unregistered measures are not straightforwardly applicable to women.

Instead we constructed a scale of attachment to the labour market (on the basis of women's answers to a series of questions) and separated all non-working women into five groups along an unemployed – permanently economically inactive continuum. Three groups comprised 80% of non-working women who in varying degrees were economically inactive as they did not have a job and did not want one at all, at least at that stage of their lives. The other 20% were divided into the unemployed (14%), so called because they had no paid job but said that they were looking for one, and the remainder (6%) who gave a domestic explanation as to why they did not have a job but subsequently told us they were looking for work; most of these women were domestic returners. The rather blunt nature of registration as a guide to unemployment status can be seen in that while 79% of the women who were registered were in the two economically active groups, only 54% of the unemployed and 31% of the domestic returner group were registered. Moreover some women registered as unemployed were also found in the groups of economically inactive women.

Because non-working women are so heterogeneous summary measures of their financial position and attitudes to their situation are not very meaningful, though in broad terms it is possible to say that women were less likely to be financially stressed and much more likely to

have positive attitudes towards not working the more economically inactive they were. However, given concern to establish the extent and nature of unemployment amongst women, interest must focus on the extent to which the two groups of women who were looking for work share similar situations or reactions.

Unemployed women were younger and were more likely to be single and childless than other women looking for work most of whom were domestic returners. They were also more likely to have worked within the last year and very much more likely to have both left their last job and not worked since for non-domestic reasons. In addition unemployed women were more likely to define themselves as 'unemployed' and as we have seen more of them than in any other group of non-working women (54%) were likely to be registered as unemployed. They were also more likely to be looking for full time jobs (53%) while the vast majority of domestic returners (83%) wanted part time jobs. These differences very largely reflected their different domestic situations; only 37% of unemployed women had dependent children compared with 91% of domestic returners.

Marital status differences, and by implication the presence or absence of an economic partner, may also partly account for the difference between these two groups in the importance they attached to finding a job soon. Unemployed women were much more likely than domestic returners to say it was important to get a job soon; of the unemployed, 81% said it was important compared with 57% of domestic returners. Unemployed women were more similar to women working full time in that more of them felt the loss of not working. A higher proportion of domestic returners on the other hand had positive views about not having a job. Among both groups of women in the labour market, however, fewer expressed positive views about not working than was the case among economically inactive women.

Yet despite differences in personal characteristics and work involvement between unemployed women and domestic returners, there was much greater similarity than difference between the two groups about the financial aspects of not working. About a third of both groups said they found it very difficult to manage financially. Over 40% worried about money quite often or almost all the time. Although a higher proportion of domestic returners said they and their husband could manage to save than was the case among the unemployed women, their general financial stress scores were very similar; more than two thirds in each group had a medium or high level of financial stress. While both groups had a higher financial need to work than the other groups of non-working women, the unemployed women's attitudes revealed they had a slightly higher financial need than domestic returners. They were more comparable to full time workers while domestic returners were more akin to part timers, though they had a lower financial need to work than part time workers in fact showed.

Women like men do not just react to the financial aspects of not working; they also have views about the other dimensions of not working including the loss or gain of a social role and identity. Non-working women were generally positive about not having a job and being at home in marked contrast to how working women in general reacted to the hypothetical prospect of not working. Unemployed women, alone amongst non-working women, expressed a negative attitude to not working; their dissatisfaction at being at home and eagerness to start work was particularly apparent. By contrast, domestic returners had both a lower commitment to working and were less likely to feel useless, bored or depressed by being at home. However, though they were less dissatisfied at not working than unemployed women, they were markedly less enthusiastic about being at home than other non-working women.

Women who were least likely to work again, those who had retired permanently or had not worked for a long time, were most likely to feel happiest about not having a job since, as might be expected, there was considerable congruence between their employment status and their attitudes. However, when we looked at women's levels of psychological stress, non-working women scored higher than working women even after allowing for the greater likelihood of non-working women having dependent children which tended to be associated with high stress scores. Amongst non-working women, the unemployed and other women looking for work had higher stress scores than the economically inactive women.

Women's attitudes to home and work: the place of employment in their lives

In one sense this study bears witness to a general change in social values, particularly among women, in relation to a woman's position in society and the role of paid work in her life. While behaviour is no simple guide to attitudes, nor attitudes straightforward determinants of behaviour, the fact that more women now work for more of their lives than women did in the recent past and that they do this by combining paid work and domestic work has meant that expectations about women's roles have changed. This can be seen very clearly when young childless women discuss their work intentions. Almost all expect to have children and intend to work again after childrearing; indeed more than a quarter say they do not intend to take a break at all, which is higher than the proportion who currently work continuously over the family formation phase.

The change must not be overstated however; most women are still primary domestic workers and secondary wage earners in a family. They do the major part of the domestic and childrearing work throughout their lives and as a consequence contribute both less hours of paid work and less gross income; indeed at some stages

they do no paid work as they take on the primary responsibility for the care of young children. To a large extent women's general attitudes about the importance of paid work for women reflects this sexual division of labour.

Most women agree that work is financially important for women; few think wives only work for 'pin money' or should leave the labour market when unemployment is high. However, work is held to be less central to women's lives than to men's, even though the benefit of working is recognised either in general terms or as the best way to be independent. While only a minority of women think women cannot combine a career and children, it is clear that these are rarely considered equally important, since a majority of women feel a home and children is a woman's prime aim and main job and endorse the view that family responsibilities may conflict with having a demanding paid job. As might be expected, working women tend to have less traditional views while non-working women tend to be more traditional in outlook. Older women and those who are less well qualified also tend to support a more traditional view of women's position. Husbands are likely to be more traditional than their wives, though their views are slightly less traditional about a woman's place if their wives are working.

To a certain extent, women's views about the relative place of work and home in women's lives is illustrated by their views about when women should or should not work. Our sample tended to feel a single woman should work to support herself whilst a mother of pre-school children should stay at home; in other instances they generally felt the choice was for the woman herself. Comparison with the views expressed in the 1965 survey, conducted by Audrey Hunt, showed that women in 1980 were both more likely to emphasise a woman's right to choose and to stress employment rather than staying at home when they had strong views about what women should do. Working women were less prescriptive than non-working women about when women should work. Interestingly however, women sometimes held views which differed from what they actually did; nearly a quarter of the women who were working with a child under 5 felt women with pre-school children should stay at home, for example.

This study provides comprehensive findings on a range of issues of central concern for an understanding of both women's position in the labour market and the place employment has in women's lives. It is clear that while women's relationship to paid work is different from men's it has also been changing as economic and social changes have increasingly brought women into the labour market. That there are limits to this change is clear too. We have shown that the way in which men and women share paid and domestic work in industrial societies has important implications for the priority they accord family life and employment, and that broadly the sexes take different roles on this. So because most married women have the primary responsibility for childrearing and domestic work their husbands are the primary wage earners. In one sense then women do not participate in the labour market on the same terms as men over their lifetime and the conditions under which they offer themselves, for example as part time workers, may go some way to explaining the segregated and secondary nature of much of the work they do.

At the same time most women spend the greater part of their potential working life in the labour market and our data show that this is increasing. For women, like men, money is an important motivator but they also have a broader commitment to work. While both behaviour and attitudes towards work are changing the change is, however, gradual. Our data suggest that most women accept or accommodate to the sexual division of labour we have described. Only small minorities were either very traditional or very radical in their attitudes towards women's roles or position in society. Insofar as older women were more traditional, and younger and more highly qualified women more non-traditional, this may be evidence of a continuing shift in women's attitudes. There is certainly general endorsement of the social values underlying the equal opportunity legislation of the 1970s, but little evidence that women see themselves becoming in the near future equal or joint wage earners on the same terms as their husbands. The current arrangement of family life simply precludes this for most married women.

Our study has shown the choices women in the 1980s are making about combining work and home and the factors which influence these choices. Most women are happy about their balance of home and work, and often part time employment has been a crucial way in which they have achieved this. For the minority of women who choose or need to effect a different balance the position is less clear cut. Some, like lone parents, as we have shown, may be particularly disadvantaged by having to combine domestic and paid work without a partner. Other women may make a different choice, emphasising paid work; if they are highly qualified and work full time in higher level jobs they are most likely of all women to work on comparable terms with men. What is clear is that most women, unlike most men, both have the choice and often still have to choose.

Notes

[1] Women and girls in employment did not appear to suffer disproportionately between June 1979 and June 1983. Using the supplementary series, which includes an allowance for undercounting, the number of men working in June 1983 was 87% of the figure for 1979 as compared with 90% for women working full time, whilst women working part time have actually increased by 2%. Women and girls are concentrated in the service industries where fewer jobs have been lost overall than in manufacturing. See also Labour Market Quarterly Report (1984).

[2] Employers' behaviour and attitudes have been studied by others who have examined the extent to which employers' strategies to organise work and their manpower policies reflect this view (Hunt, 1975; Berg, 1981; McIntosh, 1980; EOC, 1981; Barron and Norris, 1976; Craig *et al*, 1982b, 1984; Parcel and Mueller, 1983; Snell *et al*, 1981; Wilkinson, 1981).

Printed in the UK for Her Majesty's Stationery Office
Dd. 737125   PS 3250409   C45   5/84   E&S 37078

References

AGASSI J B (1979), *Women on the Job*, Lexington Books, Lexington.

ARNOLD E, HUGGETT C, SENKER P, SWORDS ISHERWOOD N and SHANNON C Z (1982), *Microelectronics and Women's Employment in Britain*, Science Policy Research Unit Occasional Paper Series No 17, University of Sussex.

BARKER D L and ALLEN S (eds) (1976a), *Sexual Divisions and Society: Process and Change*, Tavistock Publications, London.

BARKER D L and ALLEN S (eds) (1976b), *Dependence and Exploitation in Work and Marriage*, Longman, London.

BALAN J, BROWNING H L and JELIN E (1973), *Men in a Developing Society*, University of Texas Press, Austin and London.

BARRATT M (1980), *Women's Oppression Today: Problems in Marxist Feminist Analysis*, Verso, London.

BARRETT M and McINTOSH M (1982), *The Anti-social Family*, Verso/NLB, London.

BARRON R D and NORRIS G M (1976), 'Sexual Divisions and the dual labour market', in BARKER D L and ALLEN S (1976b).

BEECHEY V (1977), 'Female Wage Labour, Capitalist Production', *Capital and Class 3*, pp 45–66.

BEECHEY V (1978), 'Women and Production: Critical analysis of some sociological theories of women's work', in KUHN A and WOLPE A M (eds) (1978).

BERG I (ed) (1981), *Sociological Perspectives on Labour Markets*, Academic Press, London.

BERTAUX D (ed) (1981), *Biography and Society: the life history approach in the social sciences*, Sage Publications, London.

BEYNON H and BLACKBURN R M (1972), *Perceptions of Work, Variations within a Factory*, Cambridge University Press, Cambridge.

BLACKBURN R M and MANN M (1979), *The Working Class in the Labour Market*, Macmillan, London.

BONE M (1977), *Pre-school children and the need for day care*, HMSO.

BOSANQUET N and DOERINGER P D (1973), 'Is there a dual labour market in Great Britain?' *The Economic Journal* vol 83 June.

BRANNEN P (ed) (1975), *Entering the world of work: some sociological perspectives*, HMSO.

BROWN C, LEVIN E J, ROSA P J, RUFFELL R J and ULPH D T (1982), *Preliminary Family Labour Supply Estimates*, H M Treasury Project, Direct Taxation and Short Run Labour Supply, Working Paper No.10, Department of Economics, University of Stirling.

BROWN G W and HARRIS T (1978), *Social Origins of Depression: A Study of Psychiatric Disorder in Women*, Tavistock, London.

BROWN R (1976), 'Women as Employees: Some Comments on Research in Industrial Sociology', in BARKER D L and ALLEN S (1976b).

BROWN R, CURRAN M and COUSINS J (1983), *Changing Attitudes to Employment?* Department of Employment Research Paper No 40, London.

BUXTON N K and MacKAY D I (1977), *British Employment Statistics*, Basil Blackwell, Oxford.

CARROLL P (1981), *The Social and Psychological Effects of Unemployment Upon Young People*, Department of Employment (unpublished paper), London.

CAVENDISH R (1982), *Women on the Line*, Routledge and Kegan Paul, London.

CENTRAL STATISTICAL OFFICE (1968), *Standard Industrial Classification*, HMSO.

CHANEY J (1981), *Social Networks and Job Information: the situation of women who return to work*. Equal Opportunities Commission/Social Science Research Council, Manchester.

CHERRY N (1976), 'Persistent job changing — is it a problem?', *Journal of Occupational Psychology*, 49.

CHETWYND J and HARTNETT O (eds) (1978), *The Sex Role System*, Routledge and Kegan Paul, London.

CLAYDON S (1980), 'Counting our skills: the National Training Survey', *Employment Gazette*, November, pp 1150–1154.

COMER L (1972), *Wedlocked Women*, Feminist Books, London.

COMMISSION OF THE EUROPEAN COMMUNITIES (1979), *European Men and Women in 1978*, Brussels.

COMMISSION OF THE EUROPEAN COMMUNITIES (1980), *Women of Europe: Supplement No 5*, Brussels.

COOPER A (1982), 'Sex, Gender and Society' in REID I and WORMALD E 1982.

COOTE A and KELLNER P (1980), *Women Workers and Union Power*, New Statesman Report No 1.

COUSINS J, CURRAN M and BROWN R (1983), *Employment in the Inner City: an extended report*, University of Durham. Department of Sociology Working Paper.

CRAGG A and DAWSON T (1984), *Unemployed Women: a study of attitudes and experiences*, Department of Employment Research Paper No. 47.

CRAIG C, GARNSEY E and RUBERY J (1982a), 'The Determinants of Non Job Evaluated Payment Systems: Employees' Survey', *Report to the Department of Employment*.

CRAIG C, GARNSEY E and RUBERY J (1984), *Pay in Small Firms: Women and Informal Pay Structures*, Department of Employment Research Paper No 48.

CRAIG C, RUBERY J, TARLING R and WILKINSON F (1982b), *Labour Market Structure, Industrial Organisation and Low Pay*, Cambridge University Press, Cambridge.

CURRAN M M (1981), 'The Relationship between Attitudes and Work Histories', Paper to British Sociology Association, Industrial Sociology Group, June 1981 (unpublished).

CURRAN M M (1982), *Processes of Change in Work Histories: Finding, Leaving and Losing Jobs*, Urban Employment Study Working Paper, Department of Sociology and Social Policy, University of Durham.

DANIEL W W (1972), *Whatever Happened to the Workers at Woolwich?* PEP, London.

DANIEL W W (1974), *A National Survey of the Unemployed*, PEP Broadsheet No 546, London.

DANIEL W W (1980), *Maternity Rights: the experience of women*, PSI No 588, Policy Studies Institute, London.

DANIEL W W (1981a), *Maternity Rights: the experience of Employers*, PSI No 596, Policy Studies Institute, London.

DANIEL W W (1981b), *The Unemployed Flow: Stage 1 Interim Report*, Policy Studies Institute, London.

DANIEL W W and MILLWARD N (1983), *Workplace Industrial Relations in Britain*, Heinemann Educational Books, London.

DAVIES R, HAMILL L, MOYLAN S and SMEE C H (1982), 'Incomes in and out of Work', *Employment Gazette*, June, pp 237–243, 334, 340.

DEEM R (ed) (1980), *Schooling for Women's Work*, Routledge and Kegan Paul, London.

DEPARTMENT OF EMPLOYMENT (1974), *Women and Work: a Statistical Survey*, Manpower Paper No 9, HMSO.

DEPARTMENT OF EMPLOYMENT (1974), *Women and Work: Sex Differences and Society*, Manpower Paper No 10 HMSO.

DEPARTMENT OF EMPLOYMENT (1975), *Women and Work: A Review*, Manpower Paper No 11, HMSO.

DEPARTMENT OF EMPLOYMENT (1975), *Women and Work: Overseas Practice*, Manpower Paper No 12, HMSO.

DEPARTMENT OF EMPLOYMENT (1980), *New Earnings Survey, Part A*, HMSO.

DEPARTMENT OF EMPLOYMENT (1983), 'A changing labour force: constants and variables', *Employment Gazette*, February.

DEPARTMENT OF EMPLOYMENT (1984), *Employment Gazette*, January, HMSO.

DEPARTMENT OF TRANSPORT (1983), *National Travel Survey: 1978/79*, HMSO.

DEX S (1978), 'Measuring Women's Unemployment', *Social and Economic Administration*, volume 12, No 2.

DEX S (1982), *Black and White school-leavers: the first five years of work*, Department of Employment Research Paper No 33.

DEX S (1984a), *Women's work histories: an analysis of the Women and Employment Survey'*, Department of Employment Research paper No 46, HMSO.

DEX S (1984b), *Women's Work Histories – Part II: an analysis of Women and Employment Survey*: Part II of a report submitted to the Department of Employment (unpublished).

ELIAS P (1981), 'The MRG/EOC Occupational Classification', *Data Paper (3),* Institute for Employment Research, University of Warwick.

ELIAS P and MAIN B (1982), *Women's Working Lives,* National Training Survey Research Report, Institute of Employment Research, University of Warwick.

EQUAL OPPORTUNITIES COMMISSION (1978), *I want to work . . . but what about the kids?,* Manchester.

EQUAL OPPORTUNITIES COMMISSION (1980), *Women and Government Statistics,* Research Bulletin No 4, Manchester.

EQUAL OPPORTUNITIES COMMISSION (1981), *Women and Underachievement at Work,* Research Bulletin No 5, Manchester.

FELDBERG R and GLENN E N (1984), 'Male and female: job versus gender models in the sociology of work' in SILTANEN J and STANWORTH M (eds) (1984).

FOGARTY M P, ALLEN A J, ALLEN I and WALTERS P (1981), *Women in Top Jobs 1968–79,* Heineman, London.

FONDA N and MOSS P (eds) (1975), *Mothers in Employment,* Brunel University.

GAMARNAKOW E, MORGAN D, PURVIS J and TAYLORSEN D (1983), *The Public and the Private: Social Patterns of Gender Relationships,* Heinemann Educational Books, London.

GARDINER (1975), *'Women's Domestic Labour'* in New Left Review, 89.

GOLDTHORPE J H with LLEWELLYN C and PAYNE C (1980), *Social Mobility and Class Structure in Modern Britain,* Clarendon Press, Oxford.

GOLDTHORPE J H (1983), 'Women and Class Analysis; in Defence of the Conventional View', *Sociology* Vol 17, No 4.

GRAHAM H (1983), 'Do her answers fit his questions? women and the survey method', in GAMARNAKOW *et al* (1983).

GREENHALGH C (1980), 'Male and female differentials in Great Britain: is marriage an equal opportunity?' *Economic Journal* 90, No. 360, pp 751–775.

GREENHALGH C A and STEWART M B (1982a), *Occupational Status and Mobility of Men and Women,* Warwick Economic Research Paper No 211, University of Warwick.

GREENHALGH C A and STEWART M B, (1982b) *Work History Patterns and the Occupational Attainment of Women* Warwick Economic Research Paper No 212, University of Warwick.

GREENHALGH C A and STEWART M B, (1982c) 'The Effects and Determinants of Training', Warwick Economic Research Paper No 213, University of Warwick.

GREENHALGH C A and STEWART M B (1982d), 'The Training and Experience Dividend' *Employment Gazette,* August.

GREER G (1971), *The Female Eunuch,* McGraw-Hill.

HAKIM C (1979), *Occupational Segregation* Department of Employment Research Paper No 9.

HAKIM C (1981), 'Job Segregation trends in the 1970s', *Employment Gazette,* December.

HAKIM C (1982), *Secondary Analysis in Social Research,* George Allen and Unwin, London.

HAMILL L (1979), *Wives as sole and joint breadwinners,* Government Economic Service Working Paper No 15.

HARRISON R (1976), 'The Demoralising Experience of Prolonged Unemployment', *Employment Gazette,* April, pp 339–348.

HERRON F (1975) *The Labour Market in Crisis,* Macmillan, London.

HOME OFFICE (1974), *Equality for Women,* Cmnd 5724 HMSO.

HUBER J and SPITZE G (1981), 'Wives' Employment, Household Behaviours and Sex–Role Attitudes' in *Social Forces,* Vol 60: 1 September.

HUNT A (1968), *A Survey of Women's Employment,* HMSO.

HUNT A (1975), *Management Attitudes and Practices towards Women at Work,* HMSO.

HUNT A (1980), 'Some gaps and problems arising from Government Statistics on Women at Work', in EOC, (1980).

HUNT J (1982), 'A Woman's Place is in her Union', in WEST (1982).

HUNT P (1980), *Gender and Class Consciousness,* Macmillan, London.

IPM/MSC (1981), *Employee Potential: Issues in the development of Women,* Institute of Personnel Management, London.

IRVINE J, MILES I and EVANS J (eds) (1979) *Demystifying Social Statistics,* Pluto Press, London.

JOHNSON R (1980), *A study of Re-entrants to Employment after Domesticity and the role of the Manpower Services Commission in the Re-entry Process* Final Report (unpublished) Manpower Services Commission, Sheffield.

JOSHI H (1981), 'Secondary workers in the employment cycle': Great Britain, 1961–1974, *Economica,* 48 pp 29–44.

JOSHI H (1984), *Women's Participation in Paid Work: Further Analysis of the Women and Employment Survey,* Department of Employment Research Paper No 45.

JOSHI H, LAYARD R and OWENS S (1981), *Female Labour Supply in Post-War Britain: A Cohort Approach* Centre for Labour Economics Discussion Paper No 79, London School of Economics.

JUSENIUS C L and SHORTLIDGE R L (1975), *Dual Careers: a longitudinal study of labor market experience of women* Vol 3, Centre for Human Resource, The Ohio State University, Columbus, Ohio.

KUHN A and WOLPE A M (eds) (1978) *Feminism and Materialism,* Routledge and Kegan Paul, London.

LAND H (1976), 'Women: Supporters or Supported', in BARKER D L and ALLEN S, (1976a).

LAND H (1978), 'Sex-role stereotyping in the social security and income tax systems' in CHETWYND J and HARNETT O (eds) (1978).

LAYARD R *et al* (1978), *The Causes of Poverty: Background Paper 5,* Royal Commission on the Distribution of Income and Wealth, HMSO.

McINTOSH A (1980), 'Women at Work: A Survey of Employers' *Employment Gazette,* November pp 1142–1149.

MACKAY D I (1971), 'After the Shake-Out' *Oxford Economic Papers,* 24, (1) March.

McNALLY F (1979), *Women for Hire: a study of the Female Office Worker,* Macmillan, London.

MAIZELS J (1970), *Adolescent needs and the transition from School to Work,* Athlone Press, London.

MANPOWER SERVICES COMMISSION (1981), *No Barriers Here?* Manpower Services Commission, Sheffield.

MANPOWER SERVICES COMMISSION (1984), *Labour Market Quarterly Report,* February, MSC, Sheffield.

MARSH A (1979), *Women and Shiftwork,* HMSO.

MARSH A and HEADY P with MATHESON J (1981), *Labour Mobility in the Construction Industry,* HMSO, London.

MARSH C (1982), *The Survey Method,* George Allen and Unwin, London.

MARTIN J (1978) *The Changing Role of Work in Married Women's Lives,* MSc thesis, University of London (unpublished).

MARTIN J and ROBERTS C (1984), *Women and Employment: technical report,* OPCS, London.

MARTIN R and WALLACE J G (1984), *Working Women in Recession: Employment, Redundancy and Unemployment,* Oxford University Press, Oxford.

MITCHELL J and OAKLEY A (eds) (1976), *The Rights and Wrongs of Women,* Penguin, Harmondsworth.

MOSS P (1980), 'Parents at Work', in MOSS P and FONDA N (eds).

MOSS P and FONDA N (eds) (1980) *Work and the Family,* Temple South, London.

MOYLAN S, MILLAR J and DAVIES R (1984), *For Richer for Poorer? DHSS Cohort Study of the Unemployed,* Department of Health and Social Security, Social Research Branch Research Report No. 11, HMSO.

NATIONAL UNION OF TEACHERS/EQUAL OPPORTUNITIES COMMISSION (1980), *Promotion and the Woman Teacher* NUT, London.

Ni BHROLCHAIN M (1983) *Women's work during family formation in Britain 1956–76,* Centre for Population Studies Research Paper 83–4, London School of Hygiene.

194

NISSEL M, 'Women in Government Statistics: Basic Concepts and Assumptions', EOC (1980).

NISSEL M and BONNERJEA L (1982), *Family Care of the Handicapped Elderly: Who Pays?*, PSI No 602, London.

NIXON J (1979), *Fatherless families on FIS*, HMSO.

OAKLEY A (1972), *Sex, Gender and Society*, Temple Smith, London.

OAKLEY A (1974), *The Sociology of Housework*, Martin Robertson, Oxford.

OAKLEY A (1981), *Subject Women*, Martin Robertson, 1981, Oxford.

OAKLEY A and R (1979), 'Sexism in Official Statistics' in IRVINE J, MILES I and EVANS J (eds) (1979).

OECD (1979) *Equal Opportunities for Women*, Organisation for Economic Development and Co-operation, Paris.

OECD (1980) *Women and Employment: Policies for Equal Opportunities*, Organisation for Economic Development and Co-operation, Paris.

OECD (1982), *The Challenge of Unemployment*, Organisation for Economic Development and Co-operation, Paris.

OPCS (1970), *Classification of Occupations*, HMSO.

OPCS (1982a), *General Household Survey 1980*, HMSO.

OPCS (1982b), *Labour Force Survey 1979*, HMSO.

PAHL J (1980), 'Patterns of money management within marriage', *Journal of Social Policy* Vol 9 (3), pp 315–335.

PARCEL T L and MUELLER C W (1983), *Ascription and Labour Market: Race and Sex Differences in Earnings*. Academic Press, London.

PARNES H A (1975), 'The National Longitudinal Surveys: New Vistas for Labour Market Research', in *American Economic Review, Papers and Proceedings*, Vol LXV, No 2, May pp 244–249.

PARKER S (1978), *Older Workers and Retirement*, HMSO.

PILGRIM TRUST (1938), *Men Without Work* Cambridge University Press, Cambridge.

PLUMMER K (1983), *Documents of Life: An introduction to the problems and literature of a humanistic method*, Allen and Unwin, London.

POLLERT A (1981) *Girls, Wives, Factory Lives*, Macmillan, London.

POPAY J, RIMMER L and ROSSITER C (1983), *One parent families: parents, children and public policy*, Study Commission on the Family, Occasional paper No 12.

PORTER M (1983), *Home, Work and Class Consciousness*, Manchester University Press, Manchester.

PRANDY K, STEWARD A and BLACKBURN R M (1982), *White-collar Work*, Cambridge University Press, Cambridge.

RADCLIFFE RICHARDS J (1982), *The Sceptical Feminist*, Penguin, Harmondsworth.

RAUTA I and HUNT A (1975), *Fifth form Girls: their hopes for the future*, HMSO.

REID I and WORMALD E (eds) (1982), *Sex Differences in Britain*, Grant MacIntyre, London.

RESEARCH SERVICES (1976), *People and their Work 1975*, Technical Report Vol I, Research Services Ltd, London (mimeo).

RIMMER L and POPAY J (1982), 'The Family at Work', *Employment Gazette*, June pp 255–260.

ROBARTS S with COOTE A and BALL E (1981), *Positive Action for Women: the next step in Education Training and Employment*, NCCL, London.

ROBERTS K *et al* (1981), *Unregistered Youth Unemployment and Outreach Careers Work, Part I: Non-registration*, Department of Employment Research Paper No 31.

ROBERTSON J A S and BRIGGS J M (1979), 'Part-time Working in Great Britain', *Employment Gazette* July, pp 671–675.

ROBINSON O and WALLACE (1984), *Part-time Employment and Sex Discrimination Legislation in Great Britain*. Department of Employment Research Paper No. 43.

ROSSITER C and WICKS M (1982), *Crisis or Challenge? Family Care, Elderly People and Social Policy*, Study Commission on the Family, Occasional Paper No 8, London.

ROTHWELL S (1980), 'United Kingdom' in YOHALEM A M (ed) (1980).

ROWBOTHAM S (1973), *Hidden from History*, Pluto Press, London.

SCHLACKMAN (1979), *Women and Unemployment. A Qualitative Preliminary Research Report*. Q Search, Schlackman Research Organisation, London.

SHARPE S (1976), *Just like a Girl: How girls learn to be women*, Harmondsworth: Penguin.

SHAW L B (ed) (1983), *Unplanned Careers: The working lives of middle-aged women*, Lexington Books, D.C. Heath and Co.

SHIMMIN S, McNALLY J and LIFF S (1981), 'Pressures on Women Engaged in Factory Work', *Employment Gazette*, August, pp 344–349.

SHOWLER B and SINFIELD A (eds) (1980), *The Workless State* Martin Robinson, Oxford.

SIEBERT W S and SLOANE P J (1980), 'The measurement of sex, and marital status discrimination at the work place', *Economica* Vol 48 (190), pp 125–141.

SILTANEN J and STANWORTH M (1984), *Women and the Public Sphere*, Hutchinson, London.

SINFIELD A (1981), *What Unemployment Means*, Martin Robertson, Oxford.

SNELL M W, GLUCKLICH P and POVALL M (1981), *Equal Pay and Opportunities*, Department of Employment Research Paper No 20.

SPITZE G D and WAITE L J (1980), 'Labor Force and Work Attitudes, Young Women's early experiences', *Sociology of Work and Occupations*, Vol 7, (1), February p 3–32.

STAGEMAN J (1980, *Women in Trade Unions*, Adult Educational Department Paper No 6, University of Hull.

SULLEROT E (1977), 'The Changing Roles of Men and Women in Europe' in United Nations (1977).

THOMAS G (1944), *Women at Work, 1944*, Wartime Social Survey.

TURNER S and DICKINSON F (1978), *In and Out of Work: a Study of Unemployment, Low Pay, and Maintenance Services*, North Tyneside CDP, Home Office, London.

UNITED NATIONS (1977), *The Changing Roles of Men and Women in Modern Society: Functions Rights and Responsibilities*, Vol 2. New York.

WAJCMAN J (1983), *Women in Control* Open University Press, Milton Keynes.

WANDOR M (ed) (1973), *The Body Politic: Writings from the Women's Liberation Movement in Britain 1969–1972*, Stage 1, London.

WARR P, BANK M and ULLAH P (1985), 'The Experience of Unemployment amongst Black and White Urban teenagers' (forthcoming).

WEBB M (1982), 'The Labour Market' in REID I and WORMALD E (eds) (1982).

WEINREICH H (1978), 'Sex-role socialisation' in CHETWYND J and HARTNETT O (1978).

WEST J (ed) (1982), *Work, Women and the Labour Market*. Routledge and Kegan Paul, London.

WHITE M (1983), *Long Term Unemployment and Labour Markets*, PSI No 622, Policy Studies Institute, London.

WHITE M and GOBEDIAN A (forthcoming), *Job Evaluation and the Equal Pay Act*, Policy Studies Institute, London.

WILKINSON F (ed) (1981), *The Dynamics of Labour Market Segmentation*, Academic Press, London.

WOLPE A M (1978), 'Education and the sexual division of labour' in KUHN A and WOLPE A M (1978).

WOOD D (1982), *Men Registering as Unemployed in 1978 – A Longitudinal Study*, Working Paper No 1, DHSS.

WOOD S (1981) 'Redundancy and Female Employment', *Sociological Review* Vol 29, No 4, November pp 649–683.

WOOD S and DEY I (1983), *Redundancy: Case Studies in Co-operation and Conflict*, Gower, Aldershot.

YOHALEM A M (ed) (1980), *Women Returning to Work: Policies and Progress in Five Countries*, Frances Pinter, London.

ZABALZA A and ARRUFAT J (1983), *Wage Differentials between Married Men and Women in Great Britain: The Depreciation Effect of Non-Participation*, Discussion Paper No. 151, Centre for Labour Economics, London School of Economics.

Printed in the UK for HMSO
Dd. 737125 C.45 5/84